PROGRESSIVE INDUSTRIAL POLICY IN EUROPE

Amid accelerating global warming, the digital revolution and rising geopolitical tensions, industrial policy has taken centre-stage in EU policymaking. Consequently, initiatives such as the Green Deal Industrial Plan, the CHIPS & Science Act, the Important Projects of Common European Interest (IPCEIs) and the InvestAI initiative have been developed or proposed recently. Meanwhile, by reintroducing competitiveness and security as primary objectives for industrial policy, European policymakers appear to backtrack on the social and environmental agenda, while not effectively addressing critical governance deficits and financing gaps. European industrial policy is thus at a critical juncture, and its strategic trajectory is currently under discussion. The volume intervenes into current industrial policy debates from a critical perspective. Achieving sustainable, inclusive and effective industrial policy depends on embracing a progressive approach that prioritises broad stakeholder engagement, effective governance and accelerated implementation, instead of a push for rearmament and geopolitical competition.

Progressive Industrial Policy in Europe serves as a key reference for scholars and students in a diverse range of academic disciplines. The volume is also intended for researchers active at trade unions, think tanks and NGOs, along with policymakers and specialised civil servants at supranational, national and local levels.

Werner Raza is Director of Research at the Austrian Foundation for Development Research (ÖFSE). His research focuses on development economics and policy, international trade, global value chain analysis, and industrial upgrading, with a regional focus on Europe, Latin America, and Northern and Eastern Africa.

Christa Schlager is Head of the Economic Policy Department at the Chamber of Labour, Vienna. She has written extensively on European industrial policies, fiscal issues, climate policies, and gender issues.

Viktor Skyrman is a political economist and postdoctoral researcher based at the Department of Business Studies, Uppsala University, and the European University Institute, Florence. He researches issues related to industrial policy, finance and economic development in various contexts.

Michael Soder is an economist at the Economic Policy Department of the Chamber of Labour, Vienna. He is also a lecturer at the Vienna University of Economics and Business and the University of Applied Sciences Campus Vienna.

"As this volume shows, Europe faces a crossroads. One path is a narrow, defensive industrial policy centred on competitiveness and security, with the risk of entrenching incumbents and exacerbating inequalities. The other is a progressive industrial policy, mission-oriented and inclusive, designed to accelerate the green and digital transitions while spreading their benefits fairly."

Mariana Mazzucato, *Institute for Innovation and Public Purpose (IIPP), University College London*

"Industrial policy is back on the EU agenda, but with much confusion on goals and tools. This book offers a clear map of how industrial policy could reshape production systems in Europe making them greener, more advanced and employment-friendly."

Mario Pianta, *Scuola Normale Superiore, Florence*

"Far-reaching and rapid technological, demographic and geopolitical changes, against the background of the need to decarbonise our economies, require a paradigm shift in Europe. No longer can it rely solely on fragmented and market-driven solutions. This book contributes important building blocks towards constructing a genuine European industrial policy capable of enabling Europe to face these challenges."

Andrew Watt, *European Trade Union Institute, Brussels*

"This is a timely and thought-provoking book that helps us not only to think about what should be the focus and ambition of future-looking industrial policy, but also how we can deliver such an ambitious agenda. An inspiration but also a practical guidebook for the ones who think we need to think and act big to create a better future."

Erkki Karo, *Tallinn University of Technology*

"To date, the EU's industrial policy strategy has been largely ineffective in increasing environmental, social and economic resilience. This book convincingly explains why this is the case and what needs to change."

Hans-Jürgen Bieling, *University of Tübingen*

PROGRESSIVE INDUSTRIAL POLICY IN EUROPE

Edited by Werner Raza, Christa Schlager, Viktor Skyrman, and Michael Soder

Routledge
Taylor & Francis Group
LONDON AND NEW YORK

Designed cover image: Andriy Onufriyenko: Getty Images

First published 2026
by Routledge
4 Park Square, Milton Park, Abingdon, Oxon OX14 4RN

and by Routledge
605 Third Avenue, New York, NY 10158

Routledge is an imprint of the Taylor & Francis Group, an informa business

Funding Body: *ÖFSE – Austrian Foundation for Development Research*

For Product Safety Concerns and Information please contact our EU representative GPSR@taylorandfrancis.com. Taylor & Francis Verlag GmbH, Kaufingerstraße 24, 80331 München, Germany.

British Library Cataloguing-in-Publication Data
A catalogue record for this book is available from the British Library

ISBN: 978-1-041-25197-2 (hbk)
ISBN: 978-1-041-25196-5 (pbk)
ISBN: 978-1-003-74556-3 (ebk)

DOI: 10.4324/9781003745563

Typeset in Times New Roman
by KnowledgeWorks Global Ltd.

CONTENTS

FIGURES AND TABLES

Figures

Tables

ACRONYMS AND ABBREVIATIONS

$	Dollar
€	Euro
APP	Asset Purchase Program
BITs	Bilateral Investment Treaties
BN	Billion
BNDES	Banco Nacional de Desenvolvimento Econômico e Social; National Bank for Economic and Social Development (Brazil)
BRICS	Brazil, Russia, India, China, and South Africa
CBAM	Carbon Border Adjustment Mechanism
CCS	Carbon Capture and Storage
CCU	Carbon Capture and Utilisation
CHIPS Act	(The US) Creating Helpful Incentives to Produce Semiconductors Act
CINEA	European Climate, Infrastructure and Environment Agency
CRM	Critical Raw Materials
CRMA	Critical Raw Materials Act
CSDDD	Corporate Sustainability Due Diligence Directive
CSPP	Corporate Securities Purchasing Program
CSRD	Corporate Sustainability Reporting Directive
CTIP	Clean Trade and Investment Partnership
DARPA	Defense Advanced Research Projects Agency
DB	Development Bank
DRC	Democratic Republic of Congo
EC	European Commission
ECA	European Chips Act
ECB	European Central Bank

ECLAC	Economic Commission for Latin America and the Caribbean
EDG	European Green Deal
EDR	Energy Dependency Rate
EEA	European Environmental Agency
EFSD+	European Fund for Sustainable Development Plus
EFSI	European Fund for Strategic Investments
EGF	European Globalisation Adjustment Fund for Displaced Workers
EIB	European Investment Bank
EIC	European Innovation Council
EIF	European Investment Fund
ERC	European Research Council
ESF+	European Social Fund+
ESG	Environmental, Social and Corporate Governance
ESIF	European Structural and Investment Funds
ESM	European Stability Mechanism
ETS	Emission Trading Scheme
EU	European Union
EU-ETS	EU Emission Trading System
EV	Electric Vehicle
FTA	Free Trade Agreement
FTT	Financial Transaction Tax
GBER	General Block Exemption Regulation
GDIP	Green Deal Industrial Plan
GDP	Gross Domestic Product
GFC	Global Financial Crisis (2007–2009)
GHG	Greenhouse Gas Emissions
ICM	Informal Coordination Mechanism
ICT	Information and Communication Technologies
IEA	International Energy Agency
IMF	International Monetary Fund
IP	Industrial Policy
IPCEI	Important Projects of Common European Interest
IPR	Intellectual Property Right
IRA	Inflation Reduction Act
ISDSs	Investor-State Dispute Settlements
JTM	Just Transition Mechanism
KET	Key Enabling Technologies
LNG	Liquified Natural Gas
MEP	Member of Parliament
MERCOSUR	Southern Common Market (Mercado Común del Sur)
MFF	Multiannual Financial Framework
MoU/MoUs	Memorandum of Understanding/Memoranda of Understanding
MS	Member States

NECP	National Energy and Climate Plans
NGEU	NextGenerationEU
NGO	Non-Governmental Organisation
NRRP	National Recovery and Resilience Plans
NZIA	Net Zero Industry Act
ÖFSE	Austrian Foundation for Development Research
PDA	Project Development Assistance
PDR	Progressive Derisking
PEPP	Pandemic Emergency Purchase Programme
PoE	Pockets of Efficiency
RJTP	Regional Just Transition Plans
RRF	Recovery and Resilience Facility/Fund
SCF	Social Climate Fund
SGP	Stability and Growth Pact
SIFA	Sustainable Investment Facilitation Agreements
SRM	Strategic Raw Materials
STEM	Science, Technology, Engineering, and Mathematics
STEP	Strategic Technologies for Europe Platform
STI	Science, Technology, and Innovation
TCF	Temporary Crisis Framework
TFEU	Treaty on the Functioning of the European Union
TJTP	Territorial Just Transition Plans
TLTRO	Targeted Longer-Term Refinancing Operation
TRIPS	Trade-Related Aspects of Intellectual Property Rights
TTCs	Twin Transformation Councils
UNCTAD	United Nations Conference on Trade and Development
UNIDO	United Nations Industrial Development Organization
WTO	World Trade Organization

CONTRIBUTORS

José Miguel Ahumada is an Assistant Professor at the Institute of International Studies, University of Chile. He has a PhD in Development Studies from the University of Cambridge and an MSc in Development Studies from the London School of Economics.

David Barmes is a Policy Fellow at the LSE Grantham Research Institute, where he focuses on sustainable central banking, financial supervision, and macroeconomic coordination.

Gaston Bronstering researches the role and influence of index providers for economic decision-making at the International Relations Department, London School of Economics. He has worked as a researcher at the academic think tank Sustainable Finance Lab associated with the Utrecht School of Economics and conducted research for the United Nations Environment Programme.

Valeria Cirillo is Associate Professor of Economics at the University of Bari Aldo Moro. She is affiliated to the Institute of Economics at the Sant'Anna School of Advanced Studies, Pisa. She is Associate Editor of the *Italian Economic Journal* (Springer) and Associate Editor for *Structural Change and Economic Dynamics* (Elsevier).

Marialuisa Divella is Assistant Professor of Economics at the Department of Political Sciences, University of Bari Aldo Moro. Her research explores the economics of innovation, science and technology policy, industrial organisation, and regional development, with a focus on the interplay between technological change and labour market dynamics.

Eustachio Ferrulli is a Postdoctoral Researcher at the University of Bari, specialising in labour market inequalities, education policy, and equality of opportunity. His work examines the intersection of economic disparities, skills development, and labour market outcomes, with a focus on European contexts.

Béla Galgóczi is Senior Researcher at the European Trade Union Institute (ETUI) in Brussels. He has published in the *European Journal of Industrial Relations* and writes extensively on employment, social policies, and sustainable development.

Lidia Greco is a Full Professor of Economic and Labour Sociology at the University of Bari, Italy. Her main fields of interest are economic and industrial development, labour market and policies, gender and the third sector. She has worked at various European universities and research centres and at Duke University, USA.

Dario Guarascio is an Associate Professor at the Department of Economics and Law at Sapienza University of Rome. He holds a PhD in Economics. His working areas are economic policy, economics of innovation, development and labour economics, growth theory, evolutionary economics, econometrics, and European studies.

Philipp Heimberger (PhD) is an Economist at the Vienna Institute for International Economic Studies, where he leads the macro research group. His main research interests span macroeconomics, public finance, political economy, meta-analysis, and meta-science.

Rainer Kattel is Deputy Director and Professor of Innovation and Public Governance at the Institute for Innovation and Public Purpose (IIPP), University College London. He has published extensively on innovation policy, its governance and specific management issues. His book *How to Make an Entrepreneurial State: Why Innovation Needs Bureaucracy* (with W. Drechsler and E. Karo) won the Academy of Management's George R. Terry Book Award in 2023.

Karin Küblböck is an Economist and Senior Researcher at the Austrian Foundation for Development Research, with a focus on natural resource policies, private sector development, international trade and investment policies. She is also a lecturer at the University of Vienna and other universities. She is also a mediator and professional facilitator.

Mariana Mazzucato is Professor in the Economics of Innovation and Public Value and Founding Director of the Institute for Innovation & Public Purpose (IIPP), University College London. She is, amongst others, the author of *The Entrepreneurial State: Debunking Public vs. Private Sector Myths* (2013), and *Mission Economy: A Moonshot Guide to Changing Capitalism* (2021).

Simela Papatheophilou is a legal scholar and Junior Researcher at the Austrian Foundation for Development Research. She investigates how international law influences development and how development policy is reflected and implemented in legal instruments.

Werner Raza is Director of Research at the Austrian Foundation for Development Research (ÖFSE). His research focuses on development economics and policy, international trade, global value chain analysis, and industrial upgrading, with a regional focus on Europe, Latin America, and Northern and Eastern Africa.

Christian Reiner has a doctoral degree in economic geography (University of Salzburg) and is a Senior Lecturer at the Department of Geography and Regional Research, University of Vienna. His research interests include structural change, growth policy, innovation, human capital mobility, industrial policy, green growth, and policy evaluation.

Jelena Reljic is an Assistant Professor in the Department of Economics and Law at Sapienza University of Rome. She holds a PhD in Economics. Her research primarily focuses on the economics of innovation, labour economics, and economic policy, and has been published in various international peer-reviewed journals.

Christa Schlager is Head of the Economic Policy Department at the Chamber of Labour, Vienna. She has written extensively on European industrial policies, fiscal issues, climate policies, and gender issues.

Viktor Skyrman is a political economist and postdoctoral researcher based at the Department of Business Studies, Uppsala University, and the European University Institute, Florence. He researches issues related to industrial policy, finance, and economic development in various contexts.

Agnieszka Smoleńska is Senior Policy Fellow at the LSE Centre for Economic Transition Expertise (CETEx) leading the work on transition planning in the financial sector. She joined the Grantham Research Institute on Climate Change and the Environment as a Visiting Fellow in 2023.

Michael Soder is an Economist at the Economic Policy Department of the Chamber of Labour, Vienna. He is also a Lecturer at the Vienna University of Economics and Business and the University of Applied Sciences Campus Vienna.

Fernando Sossdorf is an Assistant Professor at the Institute of International Studies, University of Chile, focusing on international political economy and industrial policy. He also serves as Editor-in-Chief of the *Latin American Journal of Trade Policy*. Previously, he worked at the Economic Commission for Latin America and the Caribbean (ECLAC).

Roman Stöllinger is Assistant Professor at the Economics of Technology and Innovation (ETI) section of Delft University of Technology (TU Delft), and a Senior Research Associate at the Vienna Institute for International Economic Studies (wiiw). He also works regularly as an expert for industrial development for the United Nations Industrial Development Organization (UNIDO).

Bernhard Tröster is an Economist (PhD) with a specialisation in international development and financial markets. He is a Senior Researcher at the Austrian Foundation for Development Research with a focus on international trade, commodities and development. In addition, he is an external lecturer at several universities in Austria.

Francesco Zezza is a Postdoctoral Researcher in the Department of Economics and Law of Sapienza University of Rome. He holds a PhD in Economics from the University of Siena. His research interests include theoretical and applied stock-flow consistent macroeconomic modelling, economic policy, monetary economics, and regional economics.

ACKNOWLEDGEMENTS

This book is the result of a two-year joint research project by the Austrian Foundation for Development Research (ÖFSE) and the Chamber of Labour Vienna (AK Wien). The publication was made possible with the support of the Vienna Chamber of Labour's Science Network (Netzwerk Wissenschaft der AK Wien).

Werner Raza (ÖFSE) wishes to gratefully acknowledge the critical support extended by Christa Schlager and Michael Soder (both AK Wien), as well as the commitment shown by Viktor Skyrman during and after his research visit to ÖFSE to make this project a success.

First important inputs to the project were provided by five commissioned background papers. Our thanks go to all authors, that is, Dario Guarascio, Jelena Reljic, Francesco Zezza, Valeria Cirillo, Marialuisa Divella, Eustachio Ferrulli, Lidia Greco, Viktor Skyrman, Rainer Kattel, and Dragana Damjanovic, for their excellent work and high commitment under severe time pressure.

The editors would also like to thank all participants of the three workshops that provided important venues for the critical discussion of our ideas, analyses and proposals. The first workshop on "Labour-oriented approaches to the Twin Transformation in the European Union" took place on 6th and 7th June 2024 in Vienna. Inspiring inputs were, amongst others, provided by Claudio Cozza (University of Naples "Parthenope"), Andrea Egger (ABIF Vienna), Gabriele Schmid (AK Wien), Yannis Dafermos (SOAS London), Wolfgang Polt (formerly Joanneum Research), Peter Kaufmann (KMU Forschung Austria), Dragana Damjanovic (Technical University, Vienna), Julia Eder (AK Wien) and Martin Reiter (Austrian Trade Union Confederation). The second workshop presented a report on the state of EU industrial policies and was held on 10th February 2025 in Brussels. Valuable insights on innovation policy were provided by Erkki Karo (Tallinn University of Technology). The third workshop was held on 16th September 2025 in Brussels. For extensive comments on the draft chapters of this book, we are grateful to Cornel Ban (Copenhagen Business School), Sotiria Theodoropoulou (ETUI), Mario Pianta (SNS Florence), and Andrew Watt (ETUI).

Judith Vorbach, Florian Wukovitsch, and their team at AK Europa provided excellent organisational support for the two workshops in Brussels, as well as for the presentation event on the Digital Book on Progressive Industrial Policy published in cooperation with Social Europe, which was held on 15th September 2025 in Brussels. Special thanks go to our distinguished panellists Sara Matthieu (MEP, Group of the Greens/European Free Alliance), Outi Slotboom (DG GROW), Isabelle Barthès (industriAll Europe), and Rainer Kattel (IIPP/UCL) for their appreciative inputs and critical comments.

Last, but not least, we gratefully acknowledge the reports of two anonymous referees, and would like to extend our warm thanks to Ingrid Pumpler (ÖFSE) for, as always, very careful organisational and editorial assistance throughout the entire project.

It goes without saying that any errors and omissions are the sole responsibility of the editors.

FOREWORD

Mariana Mazzucato

Industrial policy has returned to the European Union's agenda with remarkable force. For decades, economic governance in Europe was dominated by the belief that the role of the state was simply to fix market failures while leaving the direction of growth to market forces. Today, that view is no longer tenable. The climate emergency, the digital revolution, geo-economic rivalries, and the war in Ukraine have made clear that markets do not automatically produce socially desirable outcomes. They must be shaped – by design, with purpose, and through capable public institutions.

This is the essence of the entrepreneurial state (Mazzucato, 2018a): not a passive fixer of problems, but an active shaper and co-creator of markets. From the internet to renewable energy, history shows that transformative innovations did not emerge spontaneously from the private sector alone. They were catalysed by bold public investments, risk-taking, and coordination across different sectors. Recognising this role does not diminish the importance of business or civil society; it elevates the need for genuine partnerships in which the public sector sets direction and crowds in innovation (Mazzucato, 2024).

The EU has already taken steps in this direction. The European Green Deal, the Green Deal Industrial Plan, and the Missions framework in Horizon Europe all signal an ambition to use industrial policy as a tool for transformation (Mazzucato, 2018b). But these ambitions risk being diluted if they are reduced to competitiveness slogans or captured by vested interests. As the Draghi Report on European competitiveness starkly underlines (Draghi, 2024), Europe has fallen behind the US and China in critical technologies. Yet the response cannot be a race to the bottom in subsidies or deregulation. Industrial policy must be rooted in a distinctly European vision of public value: innovation that advances sustainability, inclusion, and resilience, not just short-term profits (Mazzucato and Ryan-Collins, 2022).

This is why missions matter (Mazzucato, 2021). Missions are not abstract aspirations; they are practical instruments for transforming our economies. A mission like achieving 100 carbon-neutral cities by 2030 forces us to think across silos, mobilising innovation in energy, transport, housing, and digital infrastructures (Mazzucato, 2018c). It also requires mobilising finance, regulation, and citizen engagement in ways that open new pathways for inclusive, sustainable growth. Missions orient both public and private investment around a shared purpose, ensuring that resources are directed where they can have the greatest systemic impact.

But missions cannot succeed without the right public sector capacities (Mazzucato and Kattel, 2020). Too often, governments are tasked with delivering transformative strategies without the skills, structures, or resources to do so. Fragmented agencies, rigid procurement rules, and short-term funding cycles undermine the state's ability to experiment, learn, and adapt. What is needed is investment in the dynamic capabilities of the public sector: the ability to anticipate and shape technological change, to coordinate across levels of government, to partner effectively with citizens and trade unions, and to govern ambitious programmes over the long term (Kattel and Mazzucato, 2018). Without such capacities, missions risk becoming declarations without delivery.

The debate on industrial policy in Europe increasingly emphasises strategic autonomy. This is understandable in a world where dependencies in energy, raw materials, and digital technologies have been weaponised. Yet autonomy should not be mistaken for isolationism. The question is not whether Europe can decouple from the world, but whether it can shape globalisation around values of sustainability, equity, and democracy. That means building resilient domestic capacities while forging fair partnerships with the Global South and ensuring that industrial policy serves people and planet rather than narrow corporate interests.

As this volume shows, Europe now faces a crossroads. One path is a narrow, defensive industrial policy-centred on competitiveness and security, with the risk of entrenching incumbents and exacerbating inequalities. The other is a progressive industrial policy, mission-oriented and inclusive, designed to accelerate the green and digital transitions while spreading their benefits fairly (Mazzucato *et al.*, 2024).

Three priorities stand out:

First, Europe must double down on missions. Ambitious, measurable goals provide the compass for industrial policy. They galvanise innovation and direct investment towards solving our biggest challenges, rather than scattering resources or reacting piecemeal to crises.

Second, Europe must strengthen its public sector capabilities. Missions cannot be outsourced. They require public institutions that are empowered, skilled, and confident in their role as co-creators of markets. This means changing how we design and fund agencies, how we govern procurement, and how we evaluate success – not by cost savings alone, but by the public value created.

Third, finance must be aligned with purpose. Europe's fiscal and monetary frameworks should enable long-term, mission-oriented investment rather than constrain it. Institutions like the European Investment Bank and the European Central

Bank must be mobilised to support patient capital, crowd in private finance, and ensure that funding flows where it matters most.

The renaissance of industrial policy is an opportunity for the EU to lead – not by copying the US or China, but by forging a model that is distinctly European: democratic, sustainable, and inclusive (Mazzucato, 2025). This requires courage to set direction, capacity to deliver, and commitment to ensuring that industrial policy works for all.

The contributors to this book rightly remind us that industrial policy is not an end in itself. It is a tool for shaping our economies towards outcomes that matter for society. Europe must resist the temptation to reduce industrial policy to a competitiveness race or a security shield. Instead, it should seize this moment to embrace a mission-oriented approach, underpinned by capable public institutions and guided by the values of justice and sustainability.

If Europe can do this, it will show the world that markets are not forces of nature to be obeyed, but human institutions to be designed – for resilience, prosperity, and shared progress. This is the true promise of a progressive industrial policy: not only to confront today's crises, but to shape a better future.

References

Draghi, M. (2024) *The future of European competitiveness: A competitiveness strategy for Europe*. European Commission. Brussels.

Kattel, R. and Mazzucato, M. (2018) Mission-oriented innovation policy and dynamic capabilities in the public sector. *Industrial and Corporate Change*, 27(5), 787–801.

Mazzucato, M. (2018a) *The entrepreneurial state: Debunking public vs. private sector myths*. 10th Anniversary Edition, Penguin Books. London.

Mazzucato, M. (2018b) *Mission-oriented research & innovation in the European Union: A problem-solving approach to fuel innovation-led growth*. Publications Office of the European Union. Brussels.

Mazzucato, M. (2018c) Mission-oriented innovation policies: challenges and opportunities. *Industrial and Corporate Change*, 27(5), 803–815.

Mazzucato, M. (2021) *Mission economy: A moonshot guide to changing capitalism*. Penguin. UK.

Mazzucato, M. (2024) Good growth requires getting public-private partnerships right. *Project Syndicate*, 23 December 2024, https://www.project-syndicate.org/commentary/uk-labour-industrial-strategy-should-be-mission-not-sector-oriented-by-mariana-mazzucato-2024-12.

Mazzucato, M. (2025) *The broken economic order: How to rewire the international system in the age of Trump. Foreign Affairs*, Februar 25, 2025. https://www.foreignaffairs.com/south-africa/broken-economic-order-mariana-mazzucato..

Mazzucato, M., Doyle, S., and Kuehn Von Burgsdorff, L. (2024) *Mission-oriented industrial strategy: global insights*. UCL Institute for Innovation and Public Purpose's (UCL IIPP) Publication Series. London.

Mazzucato, M. and Kattel, R. (2020) COVID-19 and public-sector capacity. *Oxford Review of Economic Policy*, 36(Issue Supplement_1), S256–S269.

Mazzucato, M. and Ryan-Collins, J. (2022) Putting value creation back into "public value": From market-fixing to market-shaping. *Journal of Economic Policy Reform*, 25(4), 345–360.

INTRODUCTION

The Why, How, and for Whom of Industrial Policy for the Twin Transformation?

Werner Raza, Christa Schlager, Viktor Skyrman, and Michael Soder

After decades of marginalisation, industrial policy is back on the European Union's (EU) political agenda. While this shift in economic policy discourse is to be welcomed in principle, from a progressive economic and political point of view, it is very important to carefully think about the why, how and for whom of industrial policy. What are the motivations for industrial policy, which objectives shall be achieved, who should be the beneficiaries of industrial policy, who shall sit at the table when it comes to taking decisions, and finally, who will be responsible for implementation? These are the questions that are inquired about in the contributions to this volume. Although contributors come from different institutional and disciplinary backgrounds, our common motivation is to present an industrial policy agenda that is effective in promoting a green and digital transformation, while being socially balanced and democratically legitimated.

The original motivations underlying the EU's contemporary industrial policy measures were connected to the existential challenge of the climate crisis as well as with the exigencies of the digital revolution. More recently, however, the crisis of the liberal international order and the rivalries between the US and China, as well as the war in Ukraine, have led European policymakers to increasingly embrace a geopolitical approach to economic policymaking, thereby prioritising security considerations over the green and social agendas.

As a consequence, initiatives such as the European Green Deal (EGD), the Important Projects of Common European Interest (IPCEIs), as well as a plethora of Member State policies developed during the last five years, have become reconfigured. The concern with the lack of dynamism of the EU economy and its technological backlog vis-à-vis the US and China (as e.g. analysed by the Draghi Report) has led the new European Commission to refocus the debate on promoting the EU's global competitiveness. As a general principle, while all of these programmes have

DOI: 10.4324/9781003745563-1

typically been designed and implemented in close cooperation with the corporate sector, the interests of other stakeholders, including trade unions and civil society more generally, have not been taken onboard to the same degree.

What is particularly worrying from our point of view is that by re-introducing competitiveness as a primary objective, the new Commission intends to backtrack on the EU's social and environmental standards. Instead, security objectives are becoming the central motivation for doing industrial policy in the future. By overlooking that alone in 2024, 63,000 people in the EU are estimated to have died from heat stress (Janoš *et al.*, 2025), the concept of security as used by the Commission is ignorant of already existing threats to the life and well-being of EU citizens. By cutting spending for the green and – to a lesser extent – digital transformation, while redirecting funds to military rearmament, for instance, via the ReArm Europe Plan/Readiness 2030 initiative, EU policymakers are in the process of adopting a one-sided approach trading off human security for military security. Industrial policymaking in the EU thus seems to be at a critical juncture, and its strategic trajectory for the coming years is currently undergoing a problematic shift.

Against this evolving background, this edited volume aims at intervening into this debate from a critical perspective. Our basic premise is that for industrial policy to be sustainable and successful, an inclusive approach based on democratic deliberation and participation is central. A progressive industrial policy is thus defined by integrating the interests of all affected stakeholders, including workers and civil society.

The objectives of the edited volume are thus (i) to assess existing industrial policy initiatives and programmes and identify weaknesses and deficits, both with respect to their design and implementation; (ii) to introduce additional elements critical for the inclusiveness and thus long-term success of industrial policy, both on the company-, sector-, governance and macroeconomic level; and (iii) to propose a programme for action for progressive industrial policy for the Twin Transformation, both in the EU, and on the global level.

Before presenting the outline of the book, the next sections shortly address a number of basic conceptual issues that give a background to the understanding of industrial policy applied in this collected volume. We address the following questions in particular: (i) What precisely is industrial policy? (ii) How should it be motivated?, and (iii) What are the necessary requirements for successful industrial policy?

Defining industrial policy

Following Juhász *et al.* (2023: 4), we define "industrial policies as those government policies that explicitly target the transformation of the structure of economic activity in pursuit of some public goal". The goals of industrial policy can vary greatly, from promoting innovation, productivity, economic growth, to promoting the climate transition, increasing the security of supply with critical medicines, promoting regional development, support organic agriculture, etc. (Breznitz and Gingrich, 2025). Though traditionally focused on manufacturing, it is important to note that in this definition industrial policy could also entail the promotion of other economic sectors, including services and agriculture.

Motivating industrial policy

Throughout history, different arguments have been advanced to support industrial policy, both from an economic and political perspective. In the following, we will first consider conventional economic arguments before discussing a number of rationales often neglected by mainstream economics.

The more recent mainstream economics discussion has focused attention on market failures as the principal rationale for industrial policy. Juhász *et al.* (2023), for instance, refer to different kinds of market failures. Externalities refer to situations in which economic activities might lead to social costs and benefits, respectively, which are unaccounted for in private business decisions. Thus, private productive activities may harm society in the case of, e.g. generating environmental pollution, or alternatively confer a benefit to society, e.g. in the case that a (mining) company diversifies its supply chain, which in turn generates security of supply benefits for society at large. Another form of market failure is coordination (or agglomeration) failures, i.e. situations in which the profitability of a firm depends on the activities of other firms, either because certain goods and services are complements, or because they are upstream or downstream activities in a value chain. Without government intervention, private opportunity costs might prevent investment in such activities, notwithstanding their social value. A third rationale discussed by Juhász *et al.* (2023) refers to activity-specific public goods, i.e. situations in which a certain economic activity depends on specific types of public goods (e.g. investment in a port or road infrastructure) and governments have to decide which public good to provide.

To be sure, all types of market failure are pervasive in economic life. As such, the concept of market failure provides a general justification for government intervention, which a fortiori can be applied to industrial policy interventions more specifically. There are, however, other economic rationales for industrial policy that go beyond the scope of market failures, but are pertinent to legitimise the types of industrial policy required for our current circumstances. These relate to two issues in particular: the nature of production and of structural transformation, and the role of the state (Andreoni and Chang, 2019; Chang and Andreoni, 2020).

A critical feature of production in capitalist economies is that it entails commitments under uncertainty. Such commitments, particularly as they relate to investment into new production technologies for the green or digital transformation, are specific and irreversible, and happen in the uncertain expectation of future profits by selling future products in the market. High uncertainty and high profitability benchmarks under the profound financialisation of our economies, with shareholders in the driver's seat, thus act as constraints on private sector investments into productive capabilities. Consequently, the private sector will likely underinvest, and the pace of the desired structural transformation of the economy will remain below expectations. To unlock productive investment, this requires state intervention via different forms of industrial policy, e.g. by generating demand via public procurement, by constraining foreign competition via tariff protection, by providing subsidised public loans or investment guarantees, or by extending affordable financing via public development banks.

Even if private investment takes place at the required scale, the ensuing structural transformation would lead to side effects that require government action. In contrast to the neoclassical idea that structural change will be a rather smooth process driven by comparative advantage, this is rarely the case in complex modern economies. In the process of structural transformation, the interdependencies between sectors tend to unfold in a disproportionate way across the sectors and production activities. As Andreoni and Chang (2019: 13) emphasise, "this means that not everything changes at the same speed or at the same time. Different sectors (and their constituting activities) will expand at different growth rates, each of them following different structural cycles". For instance, the shift to electric vehicle production in the EU entails not only the build-up of an entire production system including the sourcing and processing of the required raw materials, battery production, car parts assembly, and final assembly, but is also dependent on investment into a public charging infrastructure and in renewable energy production, as well as the re- and upskilling of the workforce.

Moreover, structural interdependencies tend to trigger circular and cumulative processes of development and underdevelopment, as already highlighted by Gunnar Myrdal in the 1950s (Myrdal, 1958). Thus, structural dynamics are not only disproportionate across sectors of the same economy but also tend to be non-linear across countries. Some countries may be more successful in promoting structural change than others, with the result being increased structural heterogeneity in a macro-region and marked growth differentials between countries. In the case of the EU, this necessarily implies the extension of regional and cohesion policies.

Early movers will not only develop a number of sectors first, but in doing so, they are also engaged in a gradual process of domestic technological development. In many cases, this process also means that these early industrialisers are the first to acquire dominant positions in the manufacturing of production technologies. Given that structural change and technological development are thus intertwined, and time is of the essence in acquiring a dominant position not only in the production of the respective goods and services, but also in the development of the respective production technology, it is unsurprising that latecomers will typically use the existing technology supplied by the early movers, in particular by way of import and emulation (Reinert, 2009). By improving productive capabilities and pursuing (late) industrialisation by way of state-led industrial policy strategies, countries at the periphery of the capitalist world economy could achieve an autonomous position, where they would not depend on the arbitrary will of foreign powers and their companies (as argued by 19th century figures such as Hamilton, List, and Carey as well as 20th century structuralist economists including Prebisch, Furtado, and Sunkel). The fact that, for instance, China, as a latecomer (relative to the EU), has arrived at dominating the global solar panel industry, follows this logic, and would not have been possible without massive industrial policy support (Raza *et al.*, 2021b). These structural interdependencies and the tensions that might appear in the process within and between all involved economic sectors, as well as across countries, particularly in the EU, thus need to be actively managed.

Lastly, both in the context of a changing international political environment with increased inter-state competition, and with respect to security of supply in the context of heightened crisis dynamics due to climate change or pandemics, security considerations have become important rationales for industrial policy.

Some institutional and macroeconomic requirements for successful industrial policy

Based on a critical reading of the literature on the Developmental State (Fine *et al.*, 2013; Woo-Cumings, 1999), the fundamental political requirement for successful industrial policy is the existence of a societal coalition supporting industrial policy. The corporate sector, but particularly in a democratic political system, also significant segments of civil society, including trade unions, the media, as well as academia, need to agree on the basic need and strategic trajectory of industrial policy. Given often widely divergent ideological beliefs and substantive interests in modern societies, such an agreement cannot be taken for granted, but needs to be actively constructed and sustained. The more recent discussion in the EU and other industrialised countries has been motivated by specific economic challenges, including security of supply for essential products (e.g. pharmaceuticals), the build-up of technological capacities in strategic sectors (e.g. semiconductors), or industrial policy for the green transition (e.g. in the case of e-mobility and battery technologies). In contrast to a market-driven approach to industrial policy, respectively, with the role of the state confined to a regulatory as well as incentivising role, the influential work of Marianna Mazzucato has emphasised that industrial policy initiatives of this type should be pioneered by a state that performs an entrepreneurial function (Mazzucato, 2015, 2021). Specific societal challenges should be concretised into "missions", with well-defined objectives, responsibilities, performance criteria and applicable instruments (Mazzucato *et al.*, 2024). It is, however, important to emphasise that the entrepreneurial state will only be able to define and sustainably implement its missions if it is supported by a coalition of social forces.

Such support will, moreover, have to be maintained over the longer term. For this, industrial policy needs an institutional structure, both for the purposes of an ongoing process of change, as well as for the eventual mediation of any conflicts emerging along the way. The requisite institutional setup will critically involve the government, both in its role as a political leader of industrial policy and mediator of any potential conflicts, but also in terms of implementing industrial policy via its administrative apparatus. Political leadership should be instituted at the highest level of government, preferably in the office of the prime minister (or in the case of the EU, the President of the Commission). Given the silo structure of existing political-institutional systems (e.g. ministries, or DGs in the Commission), strong horizontal coordination of the diverse entities competent for specific industrial policies is of the essence. The latter is meant to include both coordination at the political level, e.g. via a standing council, composed of ministers and led by the prime minister (or EC Commissioners and EC President, respectively), and coordination among the different ministries and agencies tasked with implementation of specific policies. The coordination of administrative implementation should typically reside with an industrial policy agency, i.e. a separate entity outside the standard ministerial bureaucracy, that reports directly to the prime minister and/or the minister competent for industrial policy. Clearly, institutional setups might differ in detail, given states' specific bureaucratic cultures. The important lesson from the industrial policy literature is that for any industrial policy strategy to be successful, strong political leadership, close coordination and implementation by a competent administrative apparatus is of critical importance.

State capacities and their build-up are thus essential for implementing industrial policies and for maintaining directionality. Again, this cannot be taken for granted, but it will need time and effort. After some three decades of neoliberalism and public austerity, state capacities in many industrialised countries, including in the EU, have been systematically eroded, with technical capacities and capabilities having been outsourced to the private consultancy industry in particular (Mazzucato and Collington, 2023). It is thus important to systematically include the dimension of institutional capacity-building into any industrial policy strategy at the EU as well as Member State level.

At the international level, sovereign wealth or development funds have acquired a prominent role in recent decades as a conduit to promote investment into strategic industries (Raza *et al.*, 2021a). While existing at the Member State level (e.g. Solidium in Finland, ÖBAG in Austria), the EU has so far not followed through on the idea of establishing a European Sovereignty Fund. Public ownership in this context is either motivated by the desire to develop a strategic sector by strengthening the capital base of a company (via equity participation), or by the desire to safeguard national (security) interests (e.g. to prevent hostile takeovers). In the latter case, it might suffice for the government to hold a minority stake (e.g. 25% + 1 share) or a golden share, i.e. a share that gives special rights to governments with respect to certain strategic decisions of a company.

Finally, industrial policy needs to be supported by accommodative macroeconomic policies. Historical precedent, indeed, suggests that macroeconomic mismanagement bears responsibility for many failed cases of late industrialisation. By promoting structural change industrial policy typically focuses on the supply-side of the economy, thus often overlooking relevant demand-side constraints. These can take the form of overvalued exchange rates, unsustainable trade deficits, external debts, foreign currency shortages, increased inequalities, and resultingly, domestic underconsumption (Storm, 2020).

Relevant policy areas thus relate in particular to fiscal and monetary policies, including exchange rate policy. The latter should provide for stable exchange rates vis-à-vis major trade partners and prevent the national currency from being overvalued (Bresser-Pereira and Rugitsky, 2018). Capital controls might be used to regulate potentially destabilising short-term capital flows, or to manage foreign currency reserves (particularly in the case of low-income countries). Fiscal policy should support industrial policy by providing various financial incentives (e.g. guarantees, grants, subsidised loans), by designing an investment-friendly tax system, by using government procurement for stimulating domestic production, or by actively managing public ownership in state-owned enterprises (Ocampo, 2020). Interest rates should remain low and ideally not exceed the average growth rate of GDP, which entails to resort to alternative means (e.g. price caps, coordinated wage policy) to fight surges of inflation, if necessary. Monetary policy might also indirectly support industrial policy via various means, e.g. by purchases of government bonds or those of public development banks.

***

This short overview of the literature on industrial policy wanted to highlight two important lessons: firstly, as no clear blueprint exists, industrial policy is technically challenging, involving a highly variegated set of horizontal, sectoral, but also macroeconomic processes involving multiple stakeholders. Success is not guaranteed, and failures are inevitable. As a consequence, secondly, industrial policy is essentially a political project. For its success, it depends not only on good technical planning and implementation, but on sustained political support, not only from political elites, but also from a coalition of social forces. Such support must be proactively forged and sustained over time. Though this is indeed challenging, we can hardly imagine a time when the need for industrial policy has been higher than now.

Outline of the volume

The book is divided into five parts. Part I starts with an assessment of EU economic dependencies, in the fields of energy (*Dario Guarascio, Jelena Relic, and Francesco Zezza*), critical raw materials (*Bernhard Tröster, Simela Papatheophilou and*

Karin Küblböck), and technology (*Christian Reiner and Roman Stöllinger*). A shared conclusion of the contributions is that while the EU has started to confront these external dependencies, progress is markedly slow, and more effective and determined action will be necessary to achieve the EU's respective targets of strategic autonomy, including through industrial policy. A reduction of dependencies, e.g. with respect to energy imports or of critical raw materials, will most importantly require a more rapid transition to a renewable energy system and a fully fletched circular economy in the EU, while at the international level, just and sustainable global cooperation with partners particularly in the Global South will be crucial.

Part II addresses the employment impacts of the Twin Transformation. The text by *Marialuisa Divella, Valeria Cirillo, Lydia Greco, and Eustachio Ferrulli* provide a preliminary assessment of the Just Transition Initiative and its implementation in Italy, Spain and Germany. Hailed by the Commission as proof that "it is leaving no one behind", according to the authors, its scope is however too limited, implementation has been rather slow, is marked by institutional capacity constraints, and a lack of comprehensive and forward-looking regional planning. Instead, the authors emphasise the need for a longer-term programme horizon, strengthened administrative capacities and a more inclusive territorial planning process, including trade unions and civil society. According to *Béla Galgóczi's* analysis, the challenges of the employment transition have not only to do with managing the employment losses in carbon-intensive old industrial sectors, but with the slow pace of building up green industries and economic activities providing new jobs. Thus, EU industrial policy has an important role to play in accelerating the green transformation by promoting green sectors and jobs. The competitiveness of the EU economy, so dear to the EU policymakers, will critically depend upon the ability to create new competitive advantages in a shifting global economy, where other powers, such as the US and in particular China already enjoy technological leads in green and digital technologies.

In Part III, the contributions discuss deficits and challenges in the governance of industrial policy in the EU. On the basis of a critical review of EU industrial policies to date, the contribution by *Werner Raza* identifies the lack of strategic outlook, legitimacy and directionality as major deficits of the prevailing industrial policy approach. With respect to legitimacy, he argues that long-term societal support for industrial policy for the Twin Transformation will critically depend on both input and output legitimacy. On both accounts, the current institutional policy setup needs major reform. Conditionalities, including social conditionalities, are suggested as an instrument with the potential to improve not only on the legitimacy issue, but also on the directionality of the EU EP. With respect to strategic outlook, Raza calls for a strategy based on Defensive Regionalism, that is, a refoundation of EU industrial policy based on a socially inclusive and participatory approach that promotes economic resilience and autonomy, accelerates the green transformation and guides the digital transformation to the benefit of workers and citizens in the EU. The contribution by *Rainer Kattel* looks at the deficits of the EU innovation system, characterised by institutional fragmentation, bureaucratic processes and limited innovation generation. The paper argues that on all levels of European governance, policymakers should pay closer attention to designing and developing organisational ecosystems for innovation, focusing on fostering dynamic capabilities and allowing for experimentation.

The contributions to Part IV address the macro-financial framework for effective industrial policy in the EU, and in particular, the existing investment funding gap. The article by *Viktor Skyrman* discusses various options to increase EU-level funding capacities for the twin transformation. Observing that the success of the prevailing de-risking approach has been limited, Skyrman (i) calls for conditionalities linking subsidies extended to companies to re-investment of profits, (ii) suggests to expand the scope for EU-level taxation, particularly on financial transactions, wealth and capital gains, and (iii) proposes to leverage Europe's Development Banks for scaled-up credit allocation and equity funding. Upon the basis of a critical assessment of the new EU fiscal rules, *Phillip Heimberger* discusses options to expand the fiscal space for additional public expenditure for the Twin Transformation. Besides advocating for modifications to key technical assumptions underpinning the new rules, and an expansion of national co-financing for EU programmes, he proposes to establish a permanent EU Investment Fund financed by issuing bonds on EU capital markets. In a similar vein, Last, but not least, the role of monetary policy and the ECB is explored by *Gaston Bronstering, Agnieszka Smoleńska and David Barmes*. According to their analysis, the ECB's measures to support the green transition remain fragmented and insufficiently connected to the broader EU sustainability agenda. To this end, the authors identify practical pathways for aligning monetary policy to the EU's sustainability agenda, such as the ECB using EU sustainability definitions (Taxonomy, Green Bond Standard), greening its collateral frameworks, and implementing Green Targeted Longer-Term Refinancing Operations (Green TLTROs).

In the final Part, proposals for a progressive industrial policy agenda promoting the Twin Transformation are presented. In a Global North-South context, the paper by *José Miguel Ahumada and Fernando Sossdorf* identifies critical elements for promoting green industrial policy in the Global South. These include, inter alia, (i) putting foreign direct investment to the use of productive diversification, (ii) building up regional production networks and stronger regional funding structures, (iii) ensuring digital sovereignty, and (iv) strengthening the institutional capacities for industrial policy. With respect to the EU and by way of synthesising all contributions to the edited volume, the concluding chapter by *Werner Raza, Christa Schlager, Viktor Skyrman and Michael Soder* proposes a progressive agenda for industrial policy based on six pillars: (1) Enhancing spaces of participation; (2) Ensuring a fair distribution of benefits and costs; (3) Accelerating the twin transformation agenda; (4) Promoting a governance framework with capacities and capabilities; (5) Closing the funding gap, and (6) Cooperating with partners on the Global Twin Transformation.

Clearly, democratic politics in the EU stands at crossroads. Using public money and industrial policy for military rearmament, while cutting spending on the green transformation and the welfare state, will not deliver on economic growth and employment, but instead deepen the ecological crisis and social inequities, while likely exacerbating geopolitical conflicts. Instead of ultimately playing into the hands of authoritarian populists, industrial policy in the EU should promote a new economic model in the interest of both the planet and the people. Our hope is that this collection will make a small contribution to this project.

References

Andreoni, A. and Chang, H.-J. (2019) 'The Political Economy of Industrial Policy: Structural Interdependencies, Policy Alignment and Conflict Management'. *Structural Change and Economic Dynamics*, 48, 136–150. doi:10.1016/j.strueco.2018.10.007.

Bresser-Pereira, L. C. and Rugitskyn, F. (2018) 'Industrial Policy and Exchange Rate Scepticism'. *Cambridge Journal of Economics*, 42(3), 617–632. doi:10.1093/cje/bex004.

Breznitz, D. and Gingrich, J. (2025) 'Industrial Policy Revisited'. *Annual Review of Political Science*, 28(1), 329–350. doi:10.1146/annurev-polisci-033123-020253.

Chang, H.-J. and Andreoni, A. (2020) 'Industrial Policy in the 21st Century'. *Development and Change*, 51(2), 324–351. doi:10.1111/dech.12570.

Fine, B., Saraswati, J., Pirie, I., Tavasci, D., al-Jazaeri, H., and Lee, K.-H. (eds.) (2013) *Beyond the Developmental State: Industrial Policy into the Twenty-First Century*. London, UK: Pluto Press.

Janoš, T., Quijal-Zamorano, M., Shartova, N., Gallo, E., Fernando Méndez Turrubiates, R., Beltrán Barrón, N. D., Peyrusse, F., and Ballester, J. (2025) 'Heat-Related Mortality in Europe during 2024 and Health Emergency Forecasting to Reduce Preventable Deaths'. *Nature Medicine*. doi:10.1038/s41591-025-03954-7.

Juhász, R., Lane, N., and Rodrik, D. (2023) 'The New Economics of Industrial Policy'. https://drodrik.scholar.harvard.edu/publications/new-economics-industrial-policy (accessed 25 October 2025).

Mazzucato, M. (2015) *The Entrepreneurial State: Debunking Public vs. Private Sector Myths*. New York, NY: PublicAffairs.

Mazzucato, M. (2021) *Mission Economy: A Moonshot Guide to Changing Capitalism*. New York, NY: Harper Business.

Mazzucato, M. and Collington, R. (2023) *The Big Con: How the Consulting Industry Weakens Our Businesses, Infantilizes Our Governments and Warps Our Economies*. London, UK: Allen Lane.

Mazzucato, M., Doyle, S., and Kuehn von Burgsdorff, L. (2024) *Mission-Oriented Industrial Strategy: Global Insights*. London, UK: Institute for Innovation and Public Purpose. www.ucl.ac.uk/bartlett/public-purpose/sites/bartlett_public_purpose/files/mission-oriented_industrial_strategy._global_insights_2024.pdf (accessed 25 October 2025).

Myrdal, G. (1958) *Economic Theory and Underdeveloped Regions*. London, UK: Methuen and Company.

Ocampo, J. A. (2020) 'Industrial Policy, Macroeconomics and Structural Change'. In *The Oxford Handbook of Industrial Policy, Oxford Handbooks Ser*, eds C. Cramer, H.-j. Chang, and R. Kozul-Wright. Oxford, UK: Oxford University Press USA – OSO, 63–92.

Raza, W., Grumiller, J., Grohs, H., Madner, V., Mayr, S., and Sauca, I. (2021a) *215 Assessing the Opportunities and Limits of a Regionalization of Economic Activity*. Wien: Arbeiterkammer Wien. https://emedien.arbeiterkammer.at/viewer/image/AC16166392/1/LOG_0003/ (accessed 25 October 2025).

Raza, W., Grumiller, J., Grohs, H., Essletzbichler, J., and Pintar, N. (2021b) *Post Covid-19 Value Chains: Options for Reshoring Production Back to Europe in a Globalised Economy*. Brussels: Study for the European Parliament's Committee on International Trade.
Reinert, E. S. (2009) 'Emulation versus Comparative Advantage: Competing and Complementary Principles in the History of Economic Policy'. In *Industrial Policy and Development: The Political Economy of Capabilities Accumulation, The Initiative for Policy Dialogue Series*, eds Mario Cimoli, Giovanni Dosi, and Joseph E. Stiglitz. Oxford, UK; New York, NY: Oxford University Press, 79–106.
Storm, S. (2020) 'Macro-Policy, Labour Markets, and Industrial Policy'. In *The Oxford Handbook of Industrial Policy, Oxford Handbooks Series*, eds Arkebe Oqubay, Christopher Cramer, Ha-joon Chang, and Richard Kozul-Wright. Oxford, UK: Oxford University Press USA – OSO, 451–484.
Woo-Cumings, M. (ed.) (1999) *The Developmental State*. Ithaca, NY: Cornell University Press.

PART I

External Dependencies of the European Union and How to Tackle Them

1

STRUCTURAL ASYMMETRIES AND THE LIMITS OF CONTEMPORARY INDUSTRIAL POLICY

The Risk of Green Divergence in the EU

Dario Guarascio, Jelena Reljic, and Francesco Zezza

1.1 Introduction

The Russia-Ukraine war – followed by escalating tensions in the Middle East, including the conflict in Gaza, attacks on the shipping in the Red Sea, and growing frictions between Israel, the US, and Iran – has brought energy security back to the forefront of European policy concerns. These shocks risk to drive up oil and gas prices and destabilize global supply routes, exposing once again the EU's structural dependence on energy imports.

Energy is no longer just an environmental issue – it is a central driver of inflation, monetary policy, and macroeconomic stability (Ferreira *et al.*, 2024). To manage this instability, the European Union (EU) has begun retooling its economic strategies. Alongside climate goals, policymakers now emphasize resilience: reducing exposure to external shocks while strengthening domestic capacities.

This shift has spurred a reorientation of EU industrial and energy policy. The European Commission has moved beyond market incentives, actively supporting domestic production in critical clean technologies such as solar PV, batteries, and wind turbines (Kleimann *et al.*, 2023; Veugelers *et al.*, 2024). Flagship initiatives like REPowerEU aim to decarbonize the EU by 2050 while ending dependence on Russian fossil fuels by 2027.

Still, the EU remains structurally vulnerable. Although renewable generation is growing, it remains insufficient, while fossil fuel imports – and green technology suppliers – remain concentrated in a few non-EU countries. As energy interdependence becomes a geopolitical tool, Europe's exposure is not just economic, but also strategic (Crespi *et al.*, 2025).

These vulnerabilities are unevenly distributed. Member states vary widely in their energy mix, industrial structure, innovation capacity, and fiscal space. Some,

DOI: 10.4324/9781003745563-3

like Sweden and Germany, are leaders in renewable deployment and green R&D. Others, particularly in Southern and Eastern Europe, rely heavily on fossil fuels and lack the fiscal and technological resources to accelerate the transition. Those most exposed often have the weakest capacity to respond – a dynamic that echoes the EU's experience during past crises (Celi *et al.*, 2020).

The implications are significant. Energy shocks may raise production costs, squeeze households, and disrupt industrial competitiveness. These effects are amplified when structural weaknesses – like high dependency and limited diversification – coincide with limited policy space. As during the global financial and COVID-19 crises, there is a risk that asymmetric resilience deepens internal divergence (Gräbner *et al.*, 2020).

Understanding these asymmetries is therefore vital. This chapter contributes to this by mapping the key structural dimensions of EU energy vulnerability and resilience. Section 1.2 reviews the main theoretical and empirical approaches to measuring vulnerability and resilience, and outlines our theoretical approach. Section 1.3 presents a comparative analysis of EU member states, highlighting persistent divides and relevant shifts over time. Based on the mapping provided, Section 1.4 discusses how core-periphery dynamics may affect, exacerbate, or alleviate Member States vulnerability and resilience to energy shocks. We conclude by proposing some policy responses. Our goal is to support more effective, coordinated policymaking grounded in a nuanced understanding of structural exposure.

1.2 Energy vulnerability and resilience: concepts and indicators

The concepts of *energy vulnerability* and *resilience* are increasingly prominent in energy policy debates, yet they are often misrepresented or used interchangeably. While closely related, they refer to distinct dimensions of a country's position vis-à-vis energy shocks (Stirling, 2014). *Energy vulnerability* captures the degree to which an economy is exposed to adverse energy events – such as supply disruptions, price volatility, or overdependence on specific fuels or suppliers – and the likelihood that such shocks will generate serious economic or social costs (Gnansounou, 2008; Gupta, 2008). *Energy resilience*, in contrast, concerns the ability to absorb, adapt to, and recover from such shocks, often reflecting structural strengths such as domestic energy capacity, diversified supply networks, or technological capabilities (Aldieri *et al.*, 2021; Gatto and Drago, 2020, 2023).

In practice, two countries may face similar levels of vulnerability yet differ substantially in their resilience. For example, while both may rely on imported gas, only one may possess the infrastructure, fiscal space, or green technology base needed to manage a disruption. The EU's recent experience following the outbreak of war in Ukraine illustrates this asymmetry: although all Member States were exposed to supply constraints and price shocks, their capacity to adapt – through supplier diversification, household protection, or renewable scaling – was highly uneven (Guarascio *et al.*, 2025b).

Given the multifaceted nature of these concepts, no single metric can adequately capture them. Instead, a multidimensional approach is required, drawing on a combination of structural, technological, and institutional factors (Nardo *et al.*, 2005; Sovacool and Mukherjee, 2011). Literature has long acknowledged the need to go beyond narrowly defined indicators such as import dependency or energy prices (OECD, 2008; Percebois, 2007), and adopt a broader set of variables that reflect both exposure and adaptive capacity. The challenge lies in identifying indicators that are both conceptually relevant and empirically tractable across countries and overtime.

This chapter adopts a framework comprising five interrelated dimensions, widely recognized in the literature and supported by data availability for EU countries: *energy availability*, *energy affordability*, *technological efficiency*, *energy intensity*, and *environmental sustainability*. Each of these dimensions encompasses both sources of vulnerability and potential levers of resilience.

- *Energy availability* reflects the degree to which an economy depends on external energy sources and the extent to which it can meet demand through domestic production. Key indicators include the import dependency rate (by fuel type), supplier concentration (often measured using a Herfindahl-Hirschman Index), and renewables deployment (Cohen *et al.*, 2011; Le Coq and Paltseva, 2009).
- *Energy affordability* relates to the capacity of households and firms to access energy services at stable, predictable prices. Measures of electricity price volatility and household vulnerability – such as the share of households in arrears or unable to adequately heat their homes – capture the distributional and social dimensions of energy shocks (Fan *et al.*, 2022; Willand *et al.*, 2023).
- *Technological efficiency* captures a country's ability to innovate and upgrade. Investment in R&D and green patenting activity reflects the potential for longer-term structural adjustment (Aldieri *et al.*, 2021). The extent and quality of employment in clean energy sectors, as well as research intensity, further enhance resilience through spill-overs and absorptive capacity.
- *Energy intensity* refers to the structure of the production system. Economies heavily reliant on energy-intensive manufacturing are typically more vulnerable, particularly when substitution towards alternative energy sources is difficult (He *et al.*, 2017). This is captured by total primary energy supply (TPES) per unit of GDP and by the weight of energy-intensive sectors in output.
- Finally, *environmental sustainability* is increasingly central to the assessment of energy systems. Countries with high levels of greenhouse gas (GHG) emissions, land degradation, or unsustainable water usage face additional vulnerabilities, particularly as they come under increasing regulatory and environmental stress (Chen and Lei, 2018; Zhang *et al.*, 2024).

These dimensions interact in complex and sometimes contradictory ways. For example, diversification typically improves resilience by reducing exposure to single sources or suppliers – but if diversification involves higher reliance on carbon-intensive fuels or unstable regions, it may introduce new forms of vulnerability. Similarly, greater installed capacity can enhance flexibility, but underutilized infrastructure can lead to inefficiencies and rising costs. A robust assessment must therefore consider the trade-offs and synergies across indicators and country contexts.

Table 1.1 summarizes the key components and indicators selected for the empirical mapping in the following section. The choice of indicators balances conceptual relevance with data availability across EU countries and time comparability.

TABLE 1.1 Measuring vulnerability and resilience to energy shocks: dimensions and indicators

Dimension	*Component*	*Selected indicator*	*Higher level leads to:*	
			Vulnerability	*Resilience*
Energy availability	Renewables	Share of renewables in energy mix	↓	↑
	External dependency	Import dependency	↑	↓
	Supplier concentration	Import concentration	↑	↓
Energy affordability	Energy poverty	Households in arrears with energy bills	↑	↓
	Price level	Electricity prices for household consumers	↑	↓
	Price stability	Electricity price volatility	↑	↓
Technological efficiency	Investment	Investment in green technologies (% 2022 GDP)	↓	↑
	Innovation capacity	Cumulative private R&D expenditure in clean tech 2010–2022 (% 2022 GDP)	↓	↑
	Green patenting	Relative advantages in green technologies	↑	↓
Energy intensity	Industrial structure	Employment share of energy-intensive industries	↓	↑
	Resource productivity	GDP per kg of resources	↓	↑
	Energy use	TPES per unit of GDP	↑	↓
Sustainability	Land use	Land use with heavy env. impact	↑	↓
	Emission intensity of GDP	GHG emissions per unit of GDP	↑	↓
	Carbon intensity of electricity production	GHG emissions per kWh	↑	↓

Source: Own elaboration.

1.3 Mapping energy vulnerability and resilience in the EU

This section presents a comparative analysis of EU Member States' structural vulnerability and resilience to energy shocks, drawing on the conceptual framework and indicators discussed earlier. The mapping is based on a combination of time-series and cross-sectional data, enabling us to capture both persistent national characteristics and the effects of recent shocks. By focusing on five main dimensions – energy availability, energy affordability, technological capacity, energy intensity, and sustainability – we explore how structural conditions shape countries' exposure and response potential. Our findings reveal strong polarization in Europe, with sharp differences not only across but also within core and peripheral country groups.

1.3.1 Availability, affordability, and sustainability

The structure of the European energy system remains fundamentally shaped by long-standing dependencies on fossil fuels and external suppliers. Despite recent progress, the EU's aggregate energy mix still reveals a considerable reliance on oil, natural gas, and solid fuels. As shown in Figure 1.1, renewables have grown steadily since the early 2000s, from 6.2% to nearly 18%, supported by climate commitments and public investment. However, in 2022 fossil fuels still accounted for more than 60% of total gross available energy in the EU. This persistent dependence reflects both path dependency and the inertia embedded in energy-intensive infrastructures – especially in transport, heating, and heavy industry.

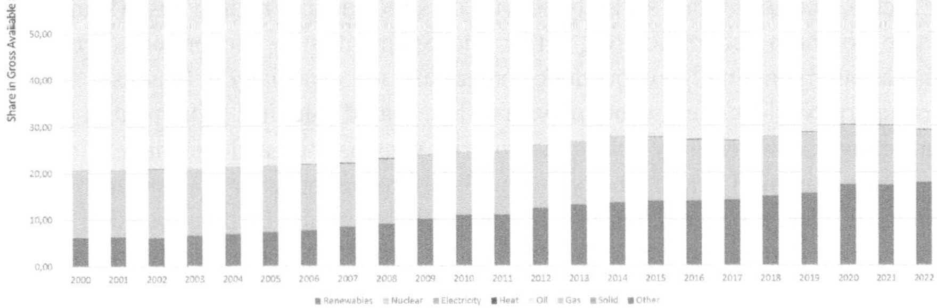

FIGURE 1.1 Energy mix of the EU 27, 2000–2022 (%)

Notes: Figures refer to the share of various energy sources in Gross Available Energy.

Source: Eurostat, own elaboration.

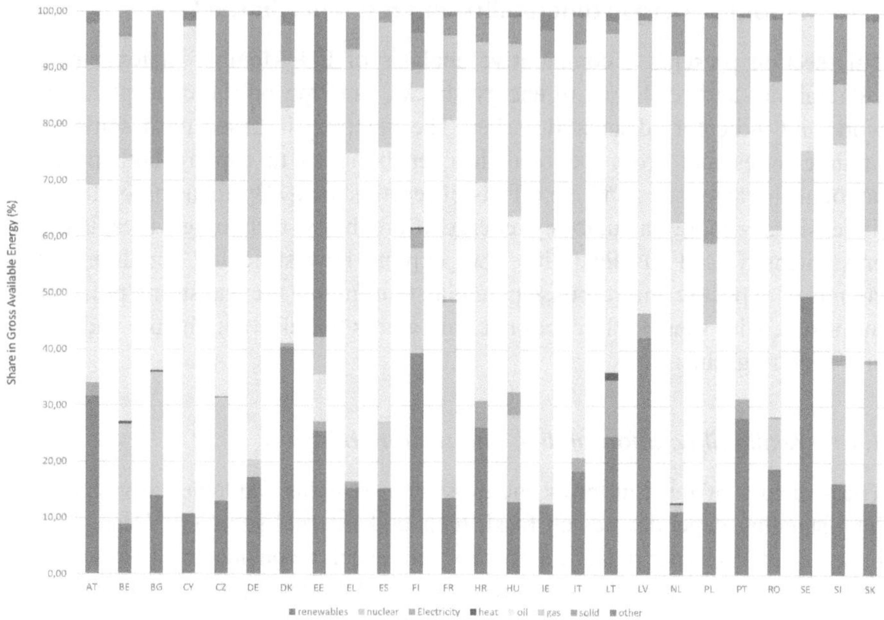

FIGURE 1.2 Energy mix of EU Member States, 2022 (%)

Notes: Figures refer to the share of various energy sources in Gross Available Energy. Countries are sorted by the share of renewables.

Source: Eurostat, own elaboration.

Zooming in at the national level, Figure 1.2 highlights sharp divergences across EU Member States in the composition of their energy mix. Northern countries, such as Sweden (nearly 50% renewables), Latvia, and Finland, lead in renewable penetration, often thanks to early investments in hydropower and, more recently, wind. In contrast, several countries in Central and Eastern Europe – such as Poland, Czechia, and Bulgaria – still rely heavily on solid fuels or natural gas. Meanwhile, large Southern economies (e.g., Italy and Spain) display moderately diversified mixes but maintain high dependence on gas and oil, especially in final uses such as transport. Nuclear energy, too, plays a differentiated role: it is prominent in France and Slovakia but entirely absent in countries such as Italy and Denmark.

Such structural heterogeneity has implications not only for the sustainability of national energy systems but also for their efficiency and carbon intensity. Figure 1.3 reports data on energy and carbon intensity of GDP. The two metrics tend to correlate: countries with high levels of energy use per unit of output also tend to exhibit high GHG emissions per euro of GDP. Notably, Poland, Bulgaria, and the Czech Republic emerge as particularly carbon- and energy-intensive economies, reflecting both an industrial structure still reliant on energy-heavy production and the limited diffusion of clean technologies. Conversely, countries such as Ireland, Sweden, and the Netherlands show higher levels of resource efficiency and lower

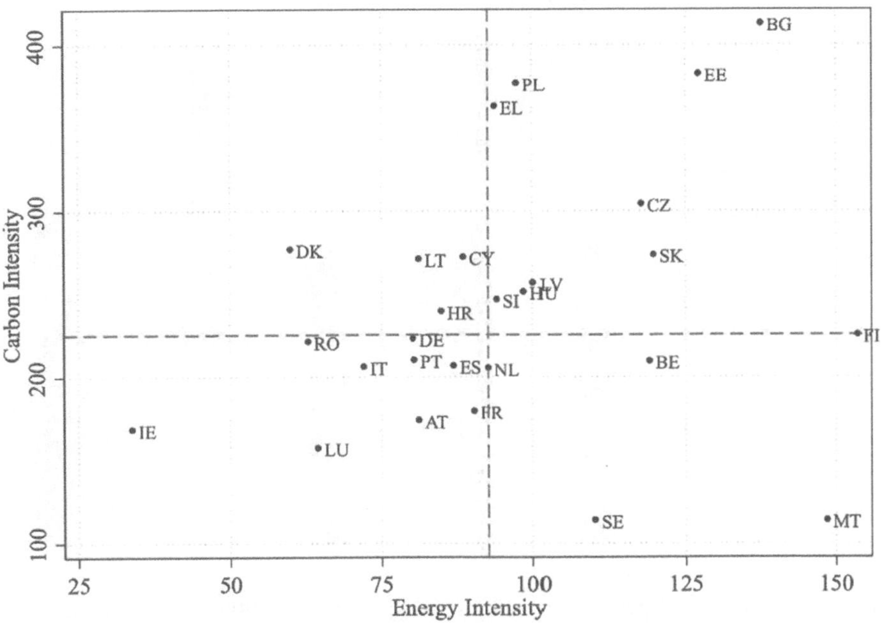

FIGURE 1.3 Energy and carbon intensity of GDP, 2022

Notes: Dashed lines denote median values. Energy intensity is defined as Gross Available Energy, expressed in thousand tonnes of oil equivalent, per million euro of GDP. Carbon intensity is defined as Greenhouse Gas emissions, expressed in thousand tonnes, per million euro of GDP. GDP is expressed at current prices, in purchasing power standards.

Source: Guarascio *et al.* (2025b).

emissions intensity, albeit for different reasons – including a strong service orientation (as in Ireland's case) or high nuclear reliance (i.e., France).

Crucially, the vulnerability of EU Member States is shaped not only by what kind of energy they use, but also by where it comes from. The European energy system is deeply integrated into global supply chains, many of which have come under pressure in recent years due to geopolitical instability. As shown in Figure 1.4, overall import dependency for oil and gas remains high at the EU level, with minimal reduction since the early 2000s. The composition of imports has shifted slightly – reflecting efforts to diversify away from Russian energy – but dependency remains elevated across all major fossil fuels. This is confirmed by Figure 1.5, which maps total import dependency by Member State. Small open economies such as Cyprus, Malta, and Luxembourg depend almost entirely on external sources. Larger economies like Italy, Germany, and the Netherlands also exhibit high import ratios, despite greater diversification.

The implications are clear: the structure of European energy systems embeds multiple forms of vulnerability – technological, social, and geopolitical. These are magnified when fossil-based and import-intensive mixes combine with high carbon intensity and low efficiency. In such configurations, even temporary shocks – such

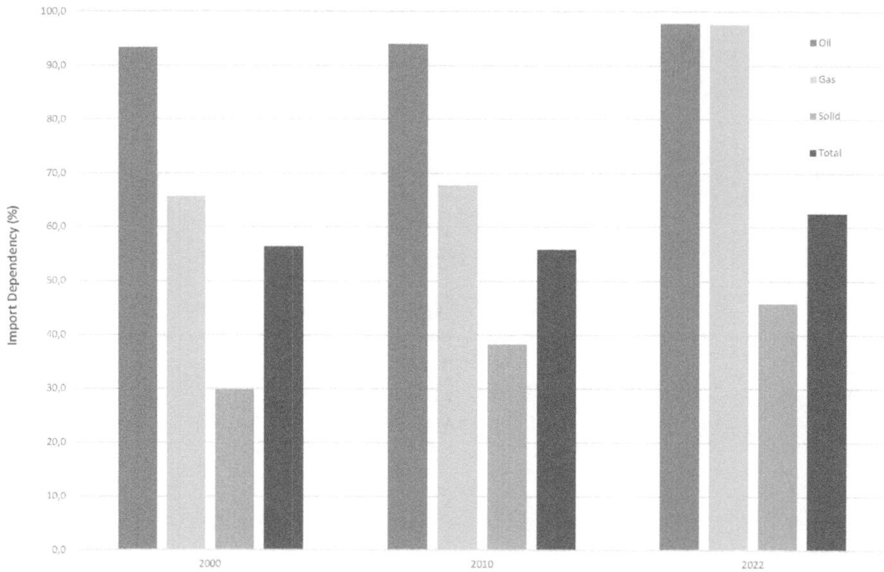

FIGURE 1.4 Import dependency rate by source (%), EU27, 2000, 2010, and 2022

Source: Eurostat, own elaboration.

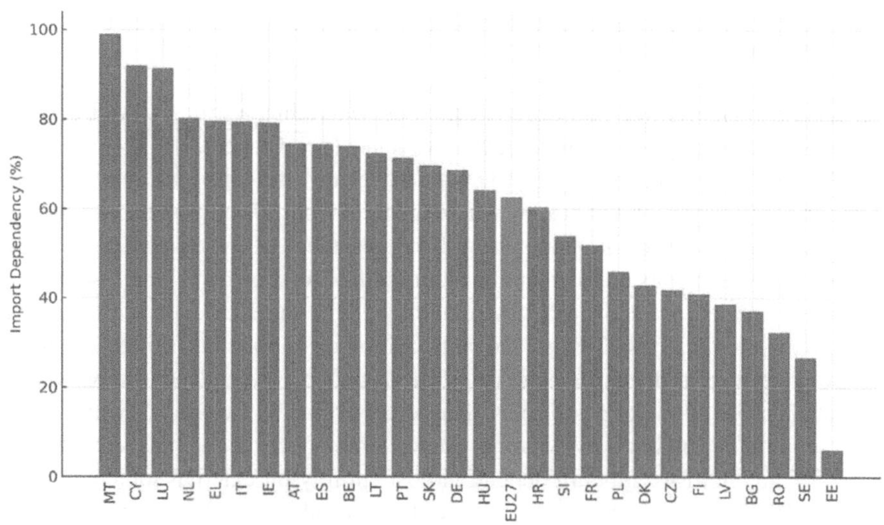

FIGURE 1.5 Import dependency, total (%), EU Member States, 2022

Notes: Countries are sorted by the degree of import dependency.

Source: Eurostat, own elaboration.

as a supply disruption or a price spike – can generate substantial macroeconomic and distributional consequences, particularly in those countries with limited fiscal or institutional capacity to absorb them. This structural exposure is a key feature of the European energy landscape and a critical obstacle to achieving a smooth and equitable green transition.

Figures 1.6 and 1.7 further deepen the analysis by focusing on the geopolitical dimension of energy dependency, a key axis of vulnerability. Figure 1.6 introduces the Energy Import Vulnerability (EIV) index, a composite measure capturing both the share of energy imported from non-EU countries and the concentration of these imports among suppliers. Countries positioned in the upper-right quadrant of the diagram exhibit both high dependency on external suppliers and a narrow base of energy partners – a configuration that sharply increases their exposure to geopolitical

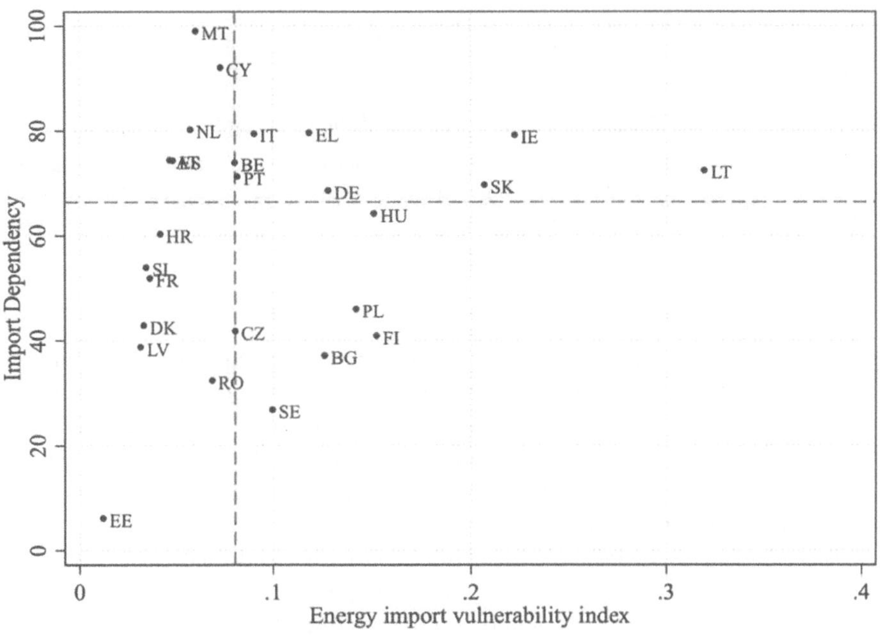

FIGURE 1.6 Import dependency and Import Vulnerability, 2022

Notes: Dashed lines denote median values. The Energy Import Vulnerability (EIV) measures a country's reliance on non-EU energy imports and the concentration of import origins. A higher EIV value means greater vulnerability, while a lower value indicates a more secure and diversified energy import structure. It is a composite indicator calculated as follows: $EIV = ImpDep^{non\text{-}EU} * Imp^{HHI}$. Where, $ImpDep^{non\text{-}EU}$ is the share of energy imported from outside the EU, reflecting a country's dependency on non-EU energy sources Imp^{HHI} is the Energy Import Origin Concentration Index, based on the Herfindahl-Hirschman Index (HHI). It measures the diversification of a country's energy import sources and ranges between 0 and 1, where lower values indicate more diversified energy import origins and *vice versa* (i.e., higher values indicate more concentrated import origins).

Source: Guarascio *et al.* (2025b).

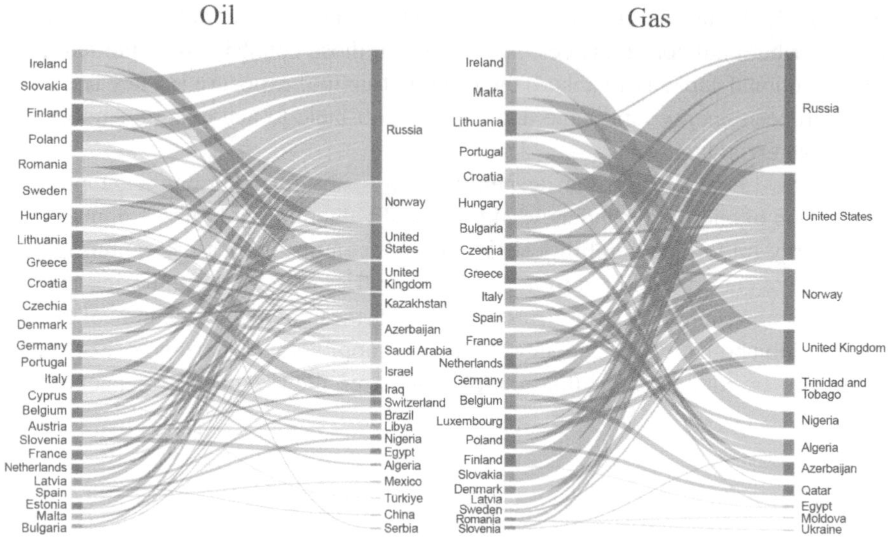

FIGURE 1.7 Sankey Diagram of import shares and top three suppliers

Notes: Countries on the left are sorted by the share in total import of their top three suppliers. Suppliers (right-hand side) are sorted by the sum of import shares of EU partners. The larger the flow, the higher the share of partner j in country i imports.

Source: Eurostat, own elaboration.

shocks and supply disruptions. Examples include Cyprus, Slovakia, and Hungary. These countries rely heavily on a few suppliers – often geographically or politically unstable – leaving them vulnerable to price volatility and strategic manipulation. Conversely, economies like France, Sweden, or the Netherlands combine greater diversification with lower dependency, positioning themselves more securely along this dimension.

The EIV index encapsulates both the quantitative and qualitative aspects of energy dependence, going beyond aggregate import shares to assess the strategic fragility of supply chains. This approach reflects a broader rethinking in the energy vulnerability literature, which has increasingly incorporated geopolitical risk and market concentration into assessments of resilience (Cohen *et al.*, 2011; Le Coq and Paltseva, 2009). As underscored by recent disruptions in Red Sea shipping and the weaponization of energy flows in the context of the Russia-Ukraine war, this dimension of vulnerability is no longer hypothetical but politically salient and economically consequential.

Figure 1.7 complements this picture by mapping the distribution of top suppliers of oil and natural gas for EU Member States in 2022. It visualizes not just dependency but supplier concentration, by illustrating the dominant role that a handful of third countries – most notably Russia, the US, Norway, Kazakhstan, and the UK – still play in the European energy matrix. Countries are sorted on the left according to the share of their top three suppliers in total energy imports. When the bulk of imports comes from just one or two providers, resilience is significantly impaired, as substitutability is limited and reconfiguration costly. This has been evident since the outbreak of the Russia-Ukraine war: once Europe stopped importing cheap Russian energy resources, it had to abruptly turn to far more costly short-term options – such as LNG from the US[1] – or find new suppliers and routes, which however need large infrastructure investment, that will take years to implement before being able to significantly reduce the degree of vulnerability.

From a policy standpoint, this evidence strengthens the argument that diversification alone is insufficient if not accompanied by parallel investments in renewables, storage, and infrastructure. Otherwise, new bottlenecks and vulnerabilities may simply replace the old ones.

Finally, Figure 1.8 turns to a different, but equally critical, form of vulnerability. Combining indicators of price volatility and social hardship (such as arrears on energy bills or the inability to heat one's home), this figure reveals stark differences in the distributional exposure of households to energy shocks. Southern and Eastern European countries are characterized by high price volatility and large shares of households in energy poverty. Italy stands out with Greece, Portugal, and Spain for the highest price volatility recorded, while Bulgaria, Hungary, Lithuania, and Romania have the highest share of households suffering from energy poverty. These are not just outcomes of market dynamics but reflect deeper structural weaknesses: poor housing insulation, inefficient appliances, regressive pricing regimes, and weak income support systems.

By contrast, Northern countries such as Sweden and Denmark maintain low household vulnerability despite comparable energy prices, suggesting the effectiveness

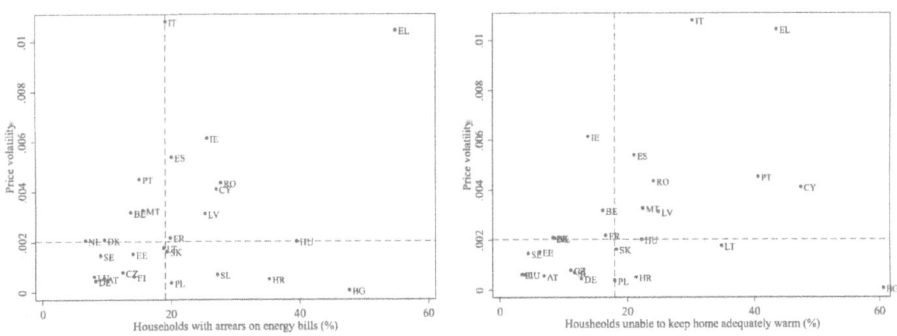

FIGURE 1.8 Household vulnerability to energy price shocks

Notes: Dashed lines denote median values. Variance in electricity prices in computed for the period 2010–2022, Vulnerable households are defined as the % of households, below 60% of median equivalized income, with arrears on energy bills or who are unable to keep their home adequately warm.

Source: Guarascio *et al.* (2025b).

of social protection mechanisms and energy efficiency policies. Social and technological dimensions of vulnerability often correlate – countries with high import dependence and low efficiency tend to also underperform on affordability and distribution. This highlights the need for integrated strategies that address supply security, decarbonization, and inequality as interlocking challenges, rather than isolated policy areas.

Overall, the combined analysis of import structure, supplier concentration, and social vulnerability reveals a multi-scalar map of exposure that is at once geopolitical, infrastructural, and distributional. These forms of vulnerability reinforce each other, particularly in Member States with limited fiscal space and institutional capacity. While technical solutions such as diversification and grid interconnection are essential, our findings reiterate the need for structural and redistributive interventions, including targeted support for vulnerable households, investment in domestic renewable supply chains, and the rebalancing of EU fiscal rules to enable national-level resilience building.

1.3.2 Technology, efficiency, and intensity

Structural resilience to energy shocks does not depend solely on low exposure to fossil fuels or reduced import dependency. It is shaped by a more complex configuration of economic structure, technological capabilities, and policy levers. Figure 1.9 maps EU Member States along four critical dimensions of resilience, each plotted against import dependency. This visualization highlights the nexus between energy structure and strategic autonomy, identifying country-specific configurations that may support or hinder their transition.

In the top-left panel, we observe the relationship between energy intensity (measured as gross available energy in kilograms of oil equivalent per thousand euros of GDP in purchasing power standards, PPS) and import dependency. Countries in the upper-right quadrant – including Belgium, Slovakia, and Malta – combine high import dependency with inefficient energy systems, pointing to structural fragility. These economies are doubly vulnerable: they consume large amounts of energy relative to output and rely heavily on foreign supply. By contrast, Denmark and Romania exhibit both low energy intensity and lower import ratios, signalling, in the case of Denmark, a stronger resilience capacity grounded in more efficient, less fossil-intensive productive structures. Several countries – such as Germany, Italy, and Spain – lie in an intermediate position: while their energy intensity is relatively contained, high dependency on imports remains a key risk factor.

The top-right panel plots the share of employment in energy-intensive industries (i.e., with above-median final energy consumption) against import dependency. Here again, the top-right quadrant is particularly relevant for identifying vulnerable configurations: countries such as Slovakia, Germany, Italy, Austria, and Hungary emerge as heavily reliant on energy-intensive manufacturing while also being

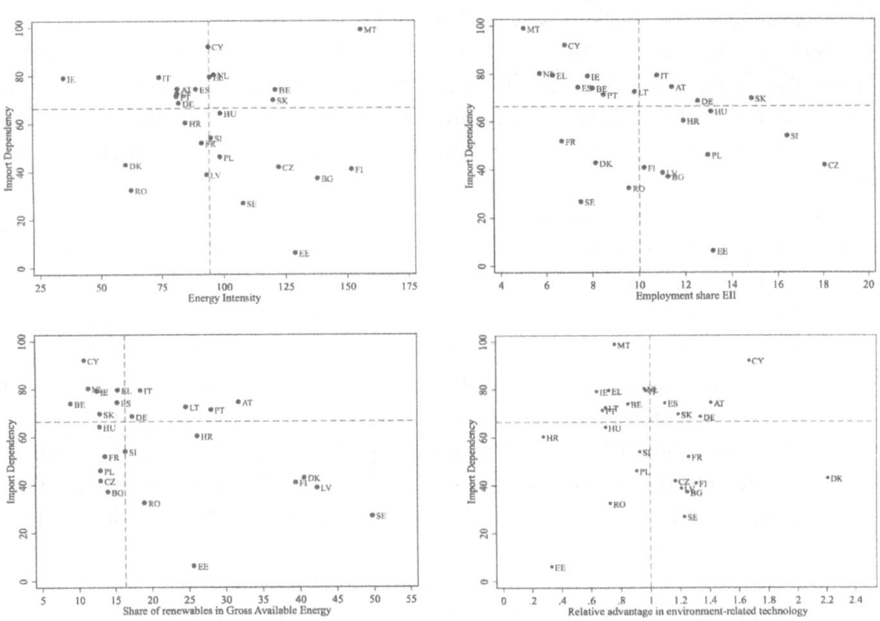

FIGURE 1.9 Different dimensions of resilience and vulnerability

Notes: Dashed lines denote median values. Energy intensity is defined as Gross Available Energy (GAE), expressed in kilograms of oil equivalent (KGOE), per thousand euro of GDP, expressed in purchasing power standards (PPS). Employment in energy intensive industries (EII) is the share of those aged 15–64 employed in manufacturing sectors with above the median share of final energy consumption in total manufacturing final energy consumption. The share of renewables in GAE is computed from energy balances. Relative advantage in environment-related technology is computed using patents in environment-related technologies. Countries positioned above the horizontal line – representing a relative specialization index greater than 1 – exhibit specialization in these technologies. This indicates that their share of environment-related patents in total patents (across all technologies) exceeds the world average, reflecting a relative advantage in green innovation.

Source: Guarascio *et al.* (2025b).

highly dependent on energy imports. These economies face compounded risks from price shocks, given the exposure of key tradable sectors to volatile fossil fuel costs. At the opposite end, France, Denmark, and Sweden appear structurally more resilient, reflecting more service-oriented labour markets and a relatively diversified energy base.

The bottom-left panel compares the share of renewables in gross available energy to import dependency. This is particularly illustrative of strategic asymmetries in the composition of national energy systems. Nordic countries – Sweden, Finland, Denmark, and Latvia – show high renewable penetration alongside low import dependency, underscoring their capacity to meet energy demand through domestic, low-carbon sources. Meanwhile, countries like Belgium, the Netherlands, and

Ireland display low deployment of renewables and remain almost entirely dependent on imported fossil fuels. Notably, several large economies – such as Germany, France, Italy, and Spain – combine high import dependency with only moderate renewable shares. This highlights the uneven pace of the energy transition across the EU and the urgent need for accelerated deployment in high-demand countries.

Finally, the bottom-right panel shifts the focus to technological capacity. Countries above the horizontal line specialize in environment-related technologies – meaning that their share of environment-related patents in total patents exceeds the global average. This metric captures not just innovation effort but also technological direction, signalling a strategic orientation towards green technologies. Nordic countries all occupy favourable positions, with high specialization and relatively lower dependency. By contrast, many countries in the South and East show low green patenting and remain heavily reliant on imports. This reflects the strong technological asymmetries that underpin energy vulnerability in the EU: innovation capacity is spatially concentrated, and path dependency limits convergence.

Taken together, this evidence reveals that structural drivers of vulnerability and resilience are both multi-dimensional and unevenly distributed. A small group of countries – mostly in the North – manage to combine energy efficiency, low dependency, technological specialization, and a declining role for energy-intensive manufacturing. Other countries, particularly in Eastern and Southern Europe, face complex trade-offs: they are still locked into carbon-intensive productive systems, lack green technological capabilities, and remain highly exposed to external supply shocks. In between, several large economies – including France, Germany, Italy, and Spain – show moderate positioning on most dimensions, suggesting that policy choices will be decisive in determining their future trajectory.

Investments in green technologies and R&D are crucial for vulnerable countries to reduce the technological gap. Unsurprisingly, countries with higher public investment into green R&D from 2011 to 2020 are those that, by 2022, had a relative advantage in environment-related technologies, with green technologies forming a substantial part of this. Notably, Scandinavian countries and Austria are leaders in this area, illustrating the positive impact of sustained public investment in green R&D.

Beyond these internal asymmetries, however, an additional critical question arises: does the EU risk replacing its over-reliance on Russian energy resources with an over-reliance on Chinese-manufactured green technologies? To address this question, Figure 1.10 presents two industrial indicators of resilience: the number of green manufacturing plants and employment in renewable energy technologies. The former is broken down by technology – batteries, heat pumps, solar PV, and wind – and provides a proxy for domestic manufacturing capacity in clean tech. Germany stands out as the leader, particularly in wind and solar equipment, followed by Italy and Spain. Some smaller countries also show notable specialization,

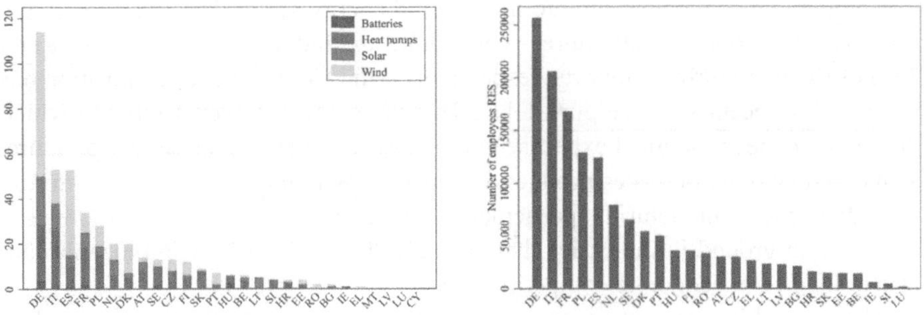

FIGURE 1.10 Green manufacturing plants and employment in renewable energy sectors (RES), 2022

Notes: Direct employment includes RES equipment manufacturing, RES plant construction, engineering and management, operation and maintenance, biomass supply and exploitation. Indirect employment refers to secondary activities, such as transport and other services (source: EurObserv'ER Employment and Turnover Report).

Source: Guarascio *et al.* (2025b).

such as Hungary in battery production and Denmark in wind turbines. While these figures offer a useful snapshot, it is important to note that the number of facilities does not necessarily correlate with production capacity. Nevertheless, employment data broadly confirms the same patterns. Germany, France, and Spain concentrate a significant share of renewable energy jobs, suggesting stronger industrial ecosystems and greater potential to benefit from the ongoing transition. Eastern European countries – with the partial exception of Hungary – remain under-industrialized in these sectors.

European resilience is also undermined by persistent structural gaps in domestic production and increasing strategic dependencies in clean-tech value chains. In the solar industry, most of the EU employment is concentrated in downstream deployment activities, whereas manufacturing of photovoltaic panels employs only around 8% of the workforce, less than 50,000 persons across the EU (Tagliapietra *et al.*, 2023). This sharply contrasts with China, which accounts for more than 2.7 million jobs in the sector, largely in manufacturing, underscoring Europe's production lag and dependence on foreign supply (Caravella *et al.*, 2024). While solar panel deployment in the EU has surged in response to falling prices, ambitious decarbonization targets and government incentives, this expansion has coincided with a steep rise in imports, further consolidating the Union's role as a net importer. The fact that 96% of solar panel imports originate from China highlights a critical vulnerability – a highly concentrated and non-diversifiable dependence – which exposes the EU to supply chain disruptions and geopolitical risks (Crespi *et al.*, 2021). These developments underscore the urgency of investing in domestic solar manufacturing capacity to reduce dependence and foster industrial resilience.

Comparable challenges emerge in the wind energy sector. Despite a relatively less concentrated import structure – with China and India accounting for 61% and 32% of EU wind turbine imports, respectively – the Union's net trade position has worsened in recent years (Figure 1.11). This indicates that even sectors in which the EU holds technological expertise and historical leadership are under pressure, as internal demand outpaces production capacity. Without targeted policies to expand domestic manufacturing, particularly in emerging green technologies, the EU risks ceding ground in industries that are central not only to decarbonization but also to long-term economic competitiveness.

The EU's ability to scale up green industrial capacity is further constrained by asymmetric fiscal capabilities and fragmented policy frameworks. Current state aid rules – designed primarily to limit distortions to competition – require that Member States justify their green subsidies by demonstrating that they address specific market failures (European Commission, 2023). In practice, this system

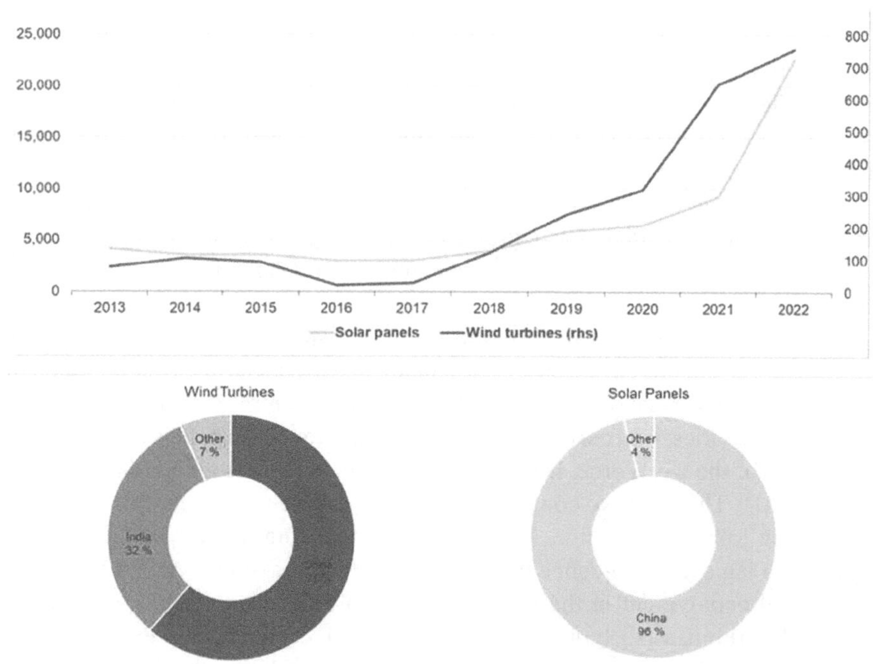

FIGURE 1.11 Extra-EU imports of green energy products, 2012–2020 (million €)

Notes: The upper panel of the figure shows the extra-EU imports of green energy products, in million euros. Solar panels are reported on the left-hand side, wind turbines on the right-hand side. The lower panel shows instead the import origin as of 2022.

Source: Guarascio *et al.* (2025b).

favours wealthier Member States with greater fiscal space and administrative capacity to navigate complex regulatory processes. This leads to a situation where core countries with proactive industrial policy and ample fiscal space end up investing more than high energy-importing and structurally more vulnerable peripheral Member States in Southern Europe (Darvas *et al.*, 2024; Heimberger *et al.*, 2024). Similarly, while some Eastern Member States have mobilized relatively higher levels of environmental state aid, often supported by cohesion funds, these efforts remain insufficient to compensate for broader structural gaps and technological disadvantages.

This uneven geography of green investment not only exacerbates existing industrial asymmetries but also threatens to fragment the transition itself. Without a cohesive EU-wide framework that integrates fiscal and competition policy with climate and industrial strategy, the green transition may reinforce the structural divides that have long characterized the European economy. The contrast with more interventionist approaches adopted in the US (through the Inflation Reduction Act) and China (via long-standing industrial planning) is striking and increasingly consequential for the EU's global competitiveness (Barbieri *et al.*, 2019; Guarascio *et al.*, 2025a).

Lastly, the challenge is not merely economic, but also geographical. Many Southern and Eastern European countries benefit from abundant solar irradiation and favourable wind conditions – comparative advantages that in principle should allow them to play a leading role in the clean energy transition. Nonetheless, these potential strengths are often underutilized due to weak public investment, limited domestic manufacturing, and fragmented policy support. Recent evidence shows that these countries are significantly underperforming relative to their resource endowments (Kakoulaki *et al.*, 2021), raising questions about the effectiveness of current cohesion mechanisms in the context of the European Green Deal. Without stronger coordination and targeted support from the EU level, these structural disparities are likely to persist or to even widen, thus undermining the promise of a just and inclusive transition.

In sum, the configuration of resilience factors across EU Member States reveals persistent and structurally embedded asymmetries. Technological capacity, industrial specialization, and the composition of employment vary widely and overlap with historical patterns of core – periphery divergence. These gaps not only condition the ability of countries to adapt to shocks, but also shape their capacity to actively participate in and benefit from the green transition. A European strategy for resilience must therefore address both current vulnerabilities and the structural drivers that inhibit convergence in resilience-building assets. Table 1.2 summarizes our analysis of energy vulnerability and resilience across the five dimensions of energy availability, energy affordability technological efficiency, energy intensity and environmental sustainability for the EU-27, providing a Heat Map for all indicators as of 2022.

TABLE 1.2 Heat map for vulnerability and resilience indicators in EU Member Countries, 2022 (DATA in Excel Sheet)

Dimension	Availability			Affordability			Efficiency			Intensity			Sustainability		
Component	Renewables	External dependency	Supplier concentration	Energy poverty	Price level	Price stability	Investment	Innovation capacity	Green patening	Industrial structure	Resource productivity	Energy use	Land use	Emission intensity of GDP	Carbon intensity of electricity production
Selected Indicator	Share of renewables in energy mix	Import dependency	Import concentration	Households in arrears with energy bills	Electricity prices for household consumers	Electricity price volatility	Investment in green technologies (% 2022 GDP)	Cumulative private R&D expenditure in clean tech 2010-2022 (% 2022 GDP)	Relative advantages in green technologies	Employment share of energy-intensive industries	GDP per kg of resources	TPES per unit of GDP	Land use with heavy env. impact	GHG emissions per unit of GDP	GHG emissions per kWh
EU 27	21.3	62.5	21.0	19.3	0.4	0.3	1.4	0.4		10.1	2.5	87.8	3.9	262.5	291.9
Austria	31.7	74.5	11.4	9.6	0.3	0.1	0.6	0.4	1.41	11.5	3.3	81.4	7.4	182.4	141.8
Belgium	8.8	74.0	13.4	13.8	0.5	0.3	1.6	0.2	0.85	8.0	0.9	121.1	2.5	226.6	139.8
Bulgaria	14.0	37.1	29.5	47.7	0.2	0.0	2.0	0.1	1.25	11.2	2.1	137.9	3.5	1059.3	476.9
Cyprus	10.7	92.0	18.4	26.9	0.5	0.4	0.6	0.2	1.67	6.8	1.9	93.8	5.3	349.4	555.1
Czechia	13.0	41.8	25.7	12.6	0.2	0.1	0.1	0.1	1.17	18.2	3.0	122.2	6.7	555.8	488.3
Germany	17.3	68.6	21.0	8.3	0.4	0.0	1.8	0.9	1.34	12.5	1.1	81.9	2.8	240.9	420.1
Denmark	40.5	42.9	9.4	9.7	0.4	0.2	2.0	1.6	2.21	8.1	3.6	60.2	4.8	247.2	201.8
Estonia	25.6	6.2	24.0	14.1	0.3	0.2	1.1	0.1	0.33	13.7	2.2	128.6	3.5	604.6	489.9
Greece	15.4	79.6	14.4	54.8	0.4	1.0	2.0	0.0	0.72	6.2	3.4	94.4	3.6	482.6	376.7
Spain	15.3	74.3	6.9	20.1	0.6	0.5	1.3	0.2	1.10	7.4	3.2	88.7	4.2	255.2	217.8
Finland	39.4	40.9	37.7	14.3	0.3	0.1	2.4	0.6	1.31	10.3	2.2	151.7	2.6	206.2	130.2
France	13.6	51.9	7.5	19.9	0.4	0.2	1.1	0.2	1.26	6.7	4.0	91.0	4.7	184.5	78.8
Croatia	26.1	60.3	8.7	35.3	0.4	0.1	0.6	0.0	0.28	12.1	1.8	84.5	4.7	421.0	242.3
Hungary	12.9	64.2	30.8	39.5	0.1	0.2	0.6	0.1	0.70	13.1	1.6	98.7	2.4	463.2	228.7
Ireland	12.5	79.2	29.8	25.5	0.2	0.6	0.9	0.1	0.64	8.2	1.6	34.7	2.5	164.3	333.2
Italy	18.5	79.4	11.9	19.1	0.6	1.1	0.6	0.2	0.97	10.8	4.0	74.0	7.1	242.0	378.4
Lithuania	24.6	72.4	42.3	18.8	0.3	0.2	0.6	0.0	0.70	9.8	2.0	81.3	4.3	513.6	177.2
Latvia	42.3	38.7	23.9	25.2	0.4	0.3	0.0	0.1	1.21	11.0	4.8	92.9	13.9	401.7	136.3
Netherlands	11.3	80.2	10.0	6.7	0.0	0.2	2.6	0.5	0.96	5.8	1.6	96.1	3.5	216.2	325.0
Poland	13.0	46.0	34.6	20.0	0.4	0.0	1.5	0.1	0.91	13.0	1.8	98.5	5.2	714.5	733.2
Portugal	28.0	71.3	13.6	15.1	0.5	0.5	1.5	0.1	0.68	8.5	0.9	81.0	2.7	293.0	225.2
Romania	19.0	32.4	22.5	27.6	0.5	0.4	1.2	0.1	0.73	9.6	2.2	62.4	3.4	536.1	297.9
Sweden	49.7	26.8	26.6	9.1	0.4	0.1	2.5	0.3	1.23	7.5	2.3	107.8	3.4	93.7	41.1
Slovenia	16.4	54.0	14.7	19.4	0.3	0.2	0.2	0.1	0.93	16.4	0.8	94.7	2.9	345.7	257.5
Slovakia	12.9	69.6	38.0	27.1	0.3	0.1	0.2	0.0	1.19	14.9	1.7	120.2	2.5	410.8	142.0

Note: The heat map uses colouring from light grey to dark grey. Light grey indicates favourable values (e.g., high energy availability, low import dependency, low import concentration, etc.) for a country, dark grey indicates unfavourable values (e.g., low energy availability, high import dependency, high import concentration, etc.).

Source: Eurostat, IEA, World Bank – WDI, own elaboration.

1.4 Conclusions

The energy crisis triggered by the Russia-Ukraine war exposed the structural vulnerabilities of Europe's energy system. Despite recent advancements in renewable deployment and a shift towards resilience-oriented policy, fossil fuels still dominate the EU's energy mix, and external supply chains – particularly for oil, gas, and clean tech inputs – remain highly concentrated. Our analysis shows that vulnerability to energy shocks is not merely a function of current price volatility or temporary supply disruptions. Rather, it reflects deeper structural asymmetries embedded in production systems, institutional capacities, and technological capabilities.

The mapping exercise conducted in this chapter reveals a fragmented and unevenly equipped European energy landscape. A core group of countries, notably in the North, displays high levels of energy efficiency, environmental performance, and innovation capacity. Others – particularly in the East and South – remain locked into carbon-intensive trajectories, with limited fiscal space and technological readiness to manage the transition. This divide is not just environmental or economic – it is geopolitical and social, cutting across multiple axes of inequality and capacity.

Critically, the green transition cannot be reduced to a uniform technological shift. It is a political and economic transformation that demands differentiated strategies tailored to national conditions. Countries with high exposure and low resilience require coordinated investment – both public and private – in renewable infrastructure, housing retrofits, and innovation ecosystems. Without such efforts, they risk falling further behind, deepening regional divergence and undermining the cohesion of the Union.

This calls for a strategic realignment of EU policy. Instruments like REPowerEU, the Green Deal Industrial Plan, and the Strategic Technologies for Europe Platform (STEP) must go beyond market incentives to actively support capacity-building in structurally disadvantaged regions. Moreover, fiscal rules and state aid regulations need reform to enable the scale and scope of public investment required to address long-standing asymmetries. Without stronger coordination and solidarity, the EU's ambition to lead the global green transition may falter – not due to lack of technology or targets, but because of its fragmented political economy and uncoordinated industrial policies.

Ultimately, building a resilient and equitable energy union requires more than climate ambition. It requires confronting the uneven geography of vulnerability and resilience that defines the EU today. Only by addressing these foundational disparities can Europe move towards a transition that is not only green, but also just and inclusive.

Note

1 Updated figures concerning the EU's imports of LNG gas are available at: https://www.consilium.europa.eu/en/infographics/where-does-the-eu-s-gas-come-from/

References

Aldieri, L., Gatto, A., and Vinci, C. P. (2021) Evaluation of energy resilience and adaptation policies: An energy efficiency analysis, *Energy Policy*, 157, 112505.

Barbieri, E., Di Tommaso, M. R., Tassinari, M., and Marozzi, M. (2019) Selective industrial policies in China: Investigating the choice of pillar industries, *International Journal of Emerging Markets*, 16(2), 264–282.

Caravella, S., Crespi, F., Cucignatto, G., and Guarascio, D. (2024) Technological sovereignty and strategic dependencies: The case of the photovoltaic supply chain, *Journal of Cleaner Production*, 434, 140222.

Celi, G., Guarascio, D., and Simonazzi, A. (2020) A fragile and divided European Union meets Covid-19: Further disintegration or 'Hamiltonian moment'? *Journal of Industrial and Business Economics*, 47(3), 411–424.

Chen, W., and Lei, Y. (2018) The impacts of renewable energy and technological innovation on environment-energy-growth nexus: New evidence from a panel quantile regression, *Renewable Energy*, 123, 1–14.

Cohen, G., Joutz, F., and Loungani, P. (2011) Measuring energy security: Trends in the diversification of oil and natural gas supplies, *Energy Policy*, 39(9), 4860–4869.

Crespi, F., Caravella, S., Menghini, M., and Salvatori, C. (2021) European technological sovereignty: An emerging framework for policy strategy, *Intereconomics*, 56(6), 348–354.

Crespi, F., Cerra, R., and Zezza, F. (2025) Coopetitive Technological sovereignty: A strategy to reconcile international collaboration with knowledge and economic security. *Intereconomics*, 60(2), 73–80.

Darvas, Z., Welslau, L., and Zettelmeyer, J. (2024) The implications of the European Union's new fiscal rules, *Bruegel Policy Brief*. https://www.bruegel.org/policy-brief/implications-european-unions-new-fiscal-rules

European Commission (2023) State Aid Scoreboard 2023, Advance Access published 2023.

Fan, S., Zha, S., Zhao, C., Sizheng, F., and Li, M. (2022) Using energy vulnerability to measure distributive injustice in rural heating energy reform: A case study of natural gas replacing bulk coal for heating in Gaocheng District, Hebei Province, China, *Ecological Economics*, 197, 107456.

Ferreira, V., Ferreira, J. P., Guarascio, D., and Zezza, F. (2024) Shockflation in the EU: Sectoral shocks, cost-push inflation and structural asymmetries in core and periphery countries, *Public Economics – Working Paper* No. 254, Advance Access published 2024.

Gatto, A. and Drago, C. (2020) A taxonomy of energy resilience, *Energy Policy*, 136, 111007.

Gatto, A. and Drago, C. (2023) *On Energy Resilience and Energy Vulnerability Measurement, Environment, Development and Sustainability*, Advance Access published September 19, 2023. https://doi.org/10.1007/s10668-023-03222-z

Gnansounou, E. (2008) Assessing the energy vulnerability: Case of industrialised countries, *Energy Policy*, 36(10), 3734–3744.

Gräbner, C., Heimberger, P., Kapeller, J., and Schütz, B. (2020) Is the Eurozone disintegrating? Macroeconomic divergence, structural polarisation, trade and fragility, *Cambridge Journal of Economics*, 44(3), 647–669.

Guarascio, D., Reljic, J., Cucignatto, G., Simonazzi, A., and Celi, G. (2025a) Between Scylla and Charybdis: Long-term drivers of EU structural vulnerability, *Review of Keynesian Economics*, 13(1), 112–140.

Guarascio, D., Reljic, J., and Zezza, F. (2025b) Energy vulnerability and resilience in the EU: Concepts, empirics and policy, *Journal of Industrial and Business Economics*, 52, 683–726. https://doi.org/10.1007/s40812-025-00340-9

Gupta, E. (2008) Oil vulnerability index of oil-importing countries, *Energy Policy*, 36(3), 1195–1211.

He, P., Ng, T. S., and Su, B. (2017) Energy-economic recovery resilience with input-output linear programming models, *Energy Economics*, 68, 177–191.

Heimberger, P., Welslau, L., Schütz, B., Gechert, S., Guarascio, D., and Zezza, F. (2024) Debt sustainability analysis in reformed EU fiscal rules: The effect of fiscal consolidation on growth and public debt ratios, *Intereconomics*, 59(5), 276–283.

Kakoulaki, G., Kougias, I., Taylor, N., Dolci, F., Moya, J., and Jäger-Waldau, A. (2021) Green hydrogen in Europe – A regional assessment: Substituting existing production with electrolysis powered by renewables, *Energy Conversion and Management*, 228, 113649.

Kleimann, D., Poitiers, N., Sapir, A., Tagliapietra, S., Véron, N., Veugelers, R., and Zettelmeyer, J. (2023) Green tech race? The US Inflation Reduction Act and the EU Net Zero Industry Act, *World Economy*, 46(12).

Le Coq, C. and Paltseva, E. (2009) Measuring the security of external energy supply in the European Union, *Energy Policy*, 37(11), 4474–4481.

Nardo, M., Saisana, M., Saltelli, A., Tarantola, S., Hoffman, A., and Giovannini, E. (2005) *Handbook on Constructing Composite Indicators: Methodology and User Guide*, OECD Statistics Working Papers: date last accessed at Handbook on Constructing Composite Indicators: Methodology and User Guide.

OECD (2008) *Handbook on Constructing Composite Indicators: Methodology and User Guide*, OECD.

Percebois, J. (2007) Energy vulnerability and its management, *International Journal of Energy Sector Management*, 1(1), 51–62.

Sovacool, B. K. and Mukherjee, I. (2011) Conceptualizing and measuring energy security: A synthesized approach, *Energy*, 36(8), 5343–5355.

Stirling, A. (2014) From Sustainability to Transformation: Dynamics and Diversity in Reflexive Governance of Vulnerability. In: Hommels, A. Mesman, J. and Bijker, W. (eds.) *Vulnerability in Technological Cultures* (pp. 305–332,), The MIT Press.

Tagliapietra, S., Veugelers, R., and Zettelmeyer, J. (2023) Rebooting the European Union's Net Zero Industry Act, *Policy Brief*, 15(23), 1–12.

Veugelers, R., Tagliapietra, S., and Trasi, C. (2024) Green industrial policy in Europe: Past, present, and prospects, *Journal of Industry, Competition and Trade*, 24(1), 4.

Willand, N., Torabi, N., and Horne, R. (2023) Recognition justice in Australia: Hidden energy vulnerability through the experiences of intermediaries, *Energy Research & Social Science*, 98, 103013.

Zhang, H., Song, Y., Zhang, M., and Duan, Y. (2024) Land use efficiency and energy transition in Chinese cities: A cluster-frontier super-efficiency SBM-based analytical approach, *Energy*, 304, 132049.

2

TACKLING EU CRITICAL RAW MATERIALS DEPENDENCIES

Bernhard Tröster, Simela Papatheophilou, and Karin Küblböck

2.1 Introduction

The properties of many mineral raw materials are indispensable for a wide range of products. They are key inputs for industrial goods and high-tech applications, and some are irreplaceable for climate-friendly and digital technologies for the twin transformation as well as in the aerospace and defence industries (European Commission and Joint Research Centre, 2023). Consequently, the build-up of new industrial capacities in these areas depends not only on the access to but also on the capabilities to process these raw materials. Ensuring the availability of ferrous, base, and minor metals has become a core priority for modern high-tech societies and a prerequisite for strategic autonomy in production.

The European Union (EU) is one of the major global users of metals, but is heavily dependent on the import of most minerals and metals. This dependence is not a new phenomenon. For decades, concerns about security of supply and risks to the manufacturing industry in Europe have repeatedly arisen – especially in times of crisis. The European Commission, for instance, identified potential risks for the industrial sectors of the European Community already in 1975 after the first oil shock, with many similarities with current communications (Commission of the European Communities, 1975; Risch, 1978). The discussions back then resemble those of today in many respects.

However, securing access to mineral resources has not become a major strategic priority for the EU until recently, as the resources needed for EU industrial production were readily available in sufficient quantities (Montanuniversität Leoben, 2004). Until 2008, the domestic extraction of metal ores in the EU has not expanded in line with rising consumption compared to 1970. Material flow accounts show that overall domestic extraction of metal ores in the EU has declined

DOI: 10.4324/9781003745563-4

by one-third between 1970 and 2008, while the domestic material input of mineral ores – the sum of domestic extraction and imports – has almost doubled over the same period (UNEP International Resource Panel (IRP), 2025).

China's rapid economic growth since the early 2000s and its fast emergence as a dominant actor in raw material extraction and processing triggered the first EU policies to secure access to raw materials in the late 2000s. Even though the EU gap between domestic extraction and material consumption has declined thereafter, the overall level of import dependency remains high.

This imbalance has become even more pressing as the twin transformation drives up demand for specific raw materials. If Europe is to expand production of clean-tech and digital goods domestically in pursuit of strategic autonomy, it faces a dual challenge: first, to expand extraction and processing where mineral resources are available within the EU; and second, to secure reliable and sustainable supplies from abroad for those resources that are not available within the EU. The extractive sector and the metals industry are therefore no longer peripheral but central to Europe's industrial policy agenda.

This chapter examines these dynamics in three steps: first, by analysing how minerals demand is changing in the context of the green and digital transition and rising defence spending; second, by tracing the evolution of EU policies to address supply risks and industrialisation plans; and third, by assessing opportunities and deficits of these raw material policies and strategies.

2.2 Material requirements of the twin transition

The shift to clean energy technologies and digitalisation is expected to drive an unprecedented surge in demand for many minerals. The technologies at the heart of this transformation like solar photovoltaic, wind turbines, electro vehicles, and energy storage are significantly more resource-intensive than their fossil-based predecessors. IEA (2021) estimates that a typical electric vehicle (EV) requires six times the mineral input of a standard car, and wind plants demand nine times more minerals than gas-fired generators. With higher shares of renewables in the energy production, the mineral intensity per unit of power capacity increases significantly (IEA, 2021). The digital transformation further intensifies demand for metals, e.g., for data transmission networks, data storage and centres, and electronic devices for private applications and industrial uses such as robotics or drones.

Spurred by the increasing use of artificial intelligence, data centres, 5G networks, and cloud computing, the electrification of data infrastructure could, for instance, significantly worsen copper deficits until 2030 (Hoppe and Laursen, 2024). At the same time, clean energy and mobility technologies are increasingly using digitalisation and automation, indicating the interconnections between these demand factors (Soubeyran and Nae, 2025). Similarly, many raw materials can be used for dual-use, i.e., both civil and military purposes. Consequently, the demand for many minerals is expected to surge significantly. In the IEA's energy transition scenarios to meet climate goals, clean energy applications are becoming dominant in mineral demand, accounting for over 40% of total copper and rare earths demand, 70% of nickel and cobalt, and almost 90% of lithium consumption (IEA, 2021). Global mineral demand could nearly triple by 2030 and quadruple by 2040 under such scenarios.

The growth in material demand for selected minerals would be even higher. For the EU, a forecast study by the Joint Research Centre (JRC) expects that demand in the EU for lithium, graphite, and nickel could increase more than 10 times by 2030 compared to 2020 and even by around 20 times by 2050 in a high-demand scenario for 15 energy and digital technologies (Carrara *et al.*, 2023). EVs will be the main driver for these demands (Table 2.1).

The forecasts of raw material demand by the JRC rely on three main parameters: the pace of technology deployment (e.g., annual sales or installed capacity), the shares of sub-technologies with differing material requirements, and the material intensity and efficiency of each technology (the amount of material needed per unit and potential reductions through innovation) (Carrara *et al.*, 2023). In essence, the forecasts capture the material requirements for the expected uptake of green and digital technologies within the EU, irrespective of where these technologies are manufactured.

With the Net-Zero Industry Act (NZIA) and other policies of the European Green Deal, however, the EU aims to establish strong domestic production capacities for the key technologies driving the twin transition, aiming to produce 40% of strategic net-zero technologies in the EU by 2030 (European Commission, 2023b). Yet, the status of the Union's supply chains reveals a critical weakness: a profound dependence on China, not only for processed raw materials but also for the components and goods needed to scale these industries. The JRC study underscored the extent of this exposure, finding that 53 out of 70 supply chain steps for the

TABLE 2.1 Projected changes in EU demand for selected minerals

Material	*EU demand change by 2030*	*EU demand change by 2050*	*Main drivers*
Lithium	12×	20×	EV and stationary batteries
Graphite	14×	26×	Anodes in lithium-ion batteries
Cobalt	6×	5×	Cathodes in lithium-ion batteries
Nickel	10×	16×	Batteries, stainless steel, hydrogen tech
REEs*	5×	6×	Permanent magnets in wind turbines, EV motors, defence tech
Copper	6×	10×	Grid expansion, renewables, EVs

* Average change in rare earth elements (Dy, Tb, Nd, Pr).
Source: Carrara *et al.* (2023).

15 technologies vital to the green and digital transition show a very low share of production in Europe – most notably every processing step for raw materials (Carrara *et al.*, 2023).

Against this backdrop, ensuring secure access to raw materials has evolved into a fundamental prerequisite for the EU's industrial policy and its pursuit of strategic autonomy. This recognition has already prompted a notable policy shift compared to previous changes in raw material policies in the late 2000s, with raw material security increasingly framed not merely as a trade or environmental issue but as a central pillar of Europe's broader economic and geopolitical strategy.

2.3 Two stages of EU raw material policy shifts

Despite the dependence on raw material imports, for a long time related policies were not a policy priority in the EU. However, China's rapid economic growth in the early 2000s fundamentally altered global resource markets. Its soaring demand for raw materials, coupled with an interventionist industrial policy, positioned China as the dominant actor in extraction, refining, and processing of critical raw materials (CRMs) (Barteková and Kemp, 2016; Küblböck *et al.*, 2019). The increasing competition for mineral resources has become a growing cause for concern in the EU and its member states, driven also by business interests (Curtis, 2010: 9). Consequently, resource supply has become an increasingly important goal of EU foreign and trade policy, for instance, in the EU trade policy strategy "Global Europe" of 2006 (European Commission, 2006).

The EU's first coordinated response came in 2008 with the Raw Materials Initiative (RMI), launched during the German EU presidency. The RMI rested on three pillars: (1) securing raw materials from global markets, (2) fostering supply from European sources, and (3) boosting resource efficiency and recycling (European Commission, 2008). This initiative remained rooted within the liberal agenda of the EU, focusing on the market creation function of policies, with the state's role primarily understood as enabling markets to operate (Di Carlo and Schmitz, 2023).

The main focus of the RMI was to secure access to external supply mainly through trade policies such as bilateral free trade agreements, WTO procedures, but partially also via development cooperation, and resource diplomacy (Küblböck, 2013). The initiative also acknowledged the need for internal supply through domestic extraction and recycling. These internal pillars of the RMI faced obstacles because resource policy cuts across multiple governance levels. While trade and environmental policy lie largely within the EU's competence, areas such as infrastructure, spatial planning, and permitting remain under national or regional control. As a result, effective strategies required coordination among many actors. In the 2010s, the EU therefore launched and financed collaborative programmes – most notably the Horizon 2020 programme, and initiatives such as the European

Innovation Partnership on Raw Materials (European Commission, 2025c), and the EIT RawMaterials (EIT, 2025) – to foster cooperation and promote exploration, extraction, recycling, research and data management.

In 2020, the Critical Raw Materials Action Plan released by the European Commission was the starting point of a second policy shift. The plan states four goals, namely developing resilient value chains in the EU, reducing dependence on primary raw materials through a circular economy, expanding raw material supply within EU member states, and diversifying raw material sourcing from third countries. Compared to the initial RMI, the Action Plan places a stronger emphasis on resilient value chains and the circular economy (European Commission, 2023a; Rietveld *et al.*, 2022), which was also influenced by the onset of the COVID-19 pandemic. Aligned with the European Green Deal and the Industrial Strategy for Europe, it aimed to increase the EU's strategic autonomy in key manufacturing sectors. In addition, the Action Plan and an EU foresight study (Bobba *et al.*, 2020) connected access to raw materials with defence and space already before this issue became more urgent with the war in Ukraine.

The new approach towards raw material policies is therefore part of the EU's turn towards a more active industrial policy aimed at strengthening its "strategic autonomy" (Raza, 2025). Raw materials policies have become a cornerstone of industrial policies, incorporating market direction elements that reflect the strategic and long-term involvement of the state in guiding capital accumulation, rather than leaving the investment decisions solely to market forces and private companies (Van Apeldoorn and De Graaff, 2022).

To increase the domestic supply of raw materials, in 2024 the European Commission introduced the Critical Raw Materials Act (CRMA) as a binding legal act on CRMs (Regulation (EU) 2024/1252 of the European Parliament and of the Council of 11 April 2024 establishing a framework for ensuring a secure and sustainable supply of critical raw materials, 2024). It was, therefore, acknowledged that "non-regulatory actions have not been enough to ensure the EU's access to a secure and sustainable supply of critical raw materials" (Proposal for a REGULATION OF THE EUROPEAN PARLIAMENT AND OF THE COUNCIL Establishing a Framework for Ensuring a Secure and Sustainable Supply of Critical Raw Materials and Amending Regulations (EU) 168/2013, (EU) 2018/858, 2018/1724, and (EU) 2019/1020, 2023). The CRMA creates a regulatory framework introducing changes in the national laws of the member states (e.g., concerning permit procedures) and derogating several EU legislations. The CRMA focuses on fostering domestic extraction, processing, and recycling of minerals that are essential for the twin transformation. It introduces several, albeit non-binding, benchmarks, namely, to extract 10%, process 40%, and recycle 25% of the minerals consumed in the EU by 2030. Additionally, not more than 65% of imports of a single raw material should come from one country only (Tröster *et al.*, 2024).

For securing supply from external sources, the EU introduced new soft law instruments and redesigned existing policies to gain enhanced access to raw materials from third countries. The external instruments include Strategic Partnerships on Raw Materials, Sustainable Investment Facilitation Agreements (SIFAs), and Energy and Raw Material Chapters in Free Trade Agreements (FTAs) (Tröster *et al.*, 2025). Even if all benchmarks for domestic supply growth of important minerals were met, the high dependence on raw material supply from non-EU countries would remain, with 90% of mining and 60% of processing for European consumption still happening in third countries. Therefore, imports will remain the primary source of raw materials for Europe, regardless of its efforts to increase domestic extraction and processing.

2.4 Defining critical raw materials

A key element of the raw material policies in the EU is the focus on specific raw materials that were defined as critical – recognising that the key issue was not simply the share of imports, but the vulnerability of supply. The criteria for criticality in the EU are focussed since 2011 on the degree of economic importance for EU industry and the risk of supply shortages compared to most of the other assessed raw materials (European Commission, 2025a). However, the definition of these criteria as well as the metrics are subject to levels of judgment. In 2011, 14 raw materials such as gallium, cobalt, magnesium, rare earth elements, and tantalum were assessed as CRMs in the EU. By 2023, this number has more than doubled to 34 (European Commission, 2023c).

The reasons for this increase are that the number of materials assessed has grown from 41 in 2011 to 87 in 2023. Moreover, the threshold values for defining the higher economic importance and supply risk of CRMs are not set relative to the economic importance and risk metrics of all materials in the respective assessment (for instance, above the average). Instead, the threshold values are maintained consistently across all CRM lists since 2011 as defined by the European Commission (Zhang *et al.*, 2023). As formulated by the European Commission (2010: 32) "[a]ssessing criticality of raw materials is not an absolute science". It relies on available data and involves some level of judgment on the part of the authors.

The latest CRM list of 2023 introduces the new category of "strategic raw materials" (SRMs). This new category is a core element of the CRMA as several provisions only apply to SRMs, such as changes to permitting processes for strategic extractive and processing projects, benchmarks, strategic stock monitoring, stress tests, and joint purchasing. A material is assessed as "strategic" based on its significance for so-called relevant strategic technologies for the green and digital transition, or for the defence and aerospace sectors. In addition, the assessment takes into account the projected global demand growth for these materials and potential production constraints (Regulation (EU) 2024/1252 of the European Parliament and of the Council of 11 April 2024 establishing a framework for ensuring a secure and sustainable supply of CRMs, 2024 Annex I, Section 2). Thus, the SRM criteria incorporate forward-looking elements, which are absent in the CRM assessment metrics so far (Blengini *et al.*, 2017).

The CRMA lists 17 raw materials that fulfil these criteria of SRMs, including metals such as, copper, lithium, natural graphite, tungsten as well as a group of rare earth elements (see Figure 2.1). For selected CRMs, only specific grades are designated as strategic. This distinction is potentially based on their utilisation in critical technologies and defence. For example, while all types of lithium qualify as critical, only the high-purity battery grade is defined as strategic. However, also copper is part of the SRM list, despite its wide variety of uses beyond strategic technologies. Moreover, copper would not be classified as a CRM due to its low supply risk. According to the study on the CRM list 2023 (European Commission, 2023c), the expected demand growth of copper justifies, however, the classification of copper as strategic. Furthermore, SRMs are CRMs by definition (European Commission, 2023c).

Given the high importance of the SRM list in the CRMA, it is important to note that it is the Commission's task to designate SRMs. This remains an inherently political task, given that it is primarily a political decision to classify certain

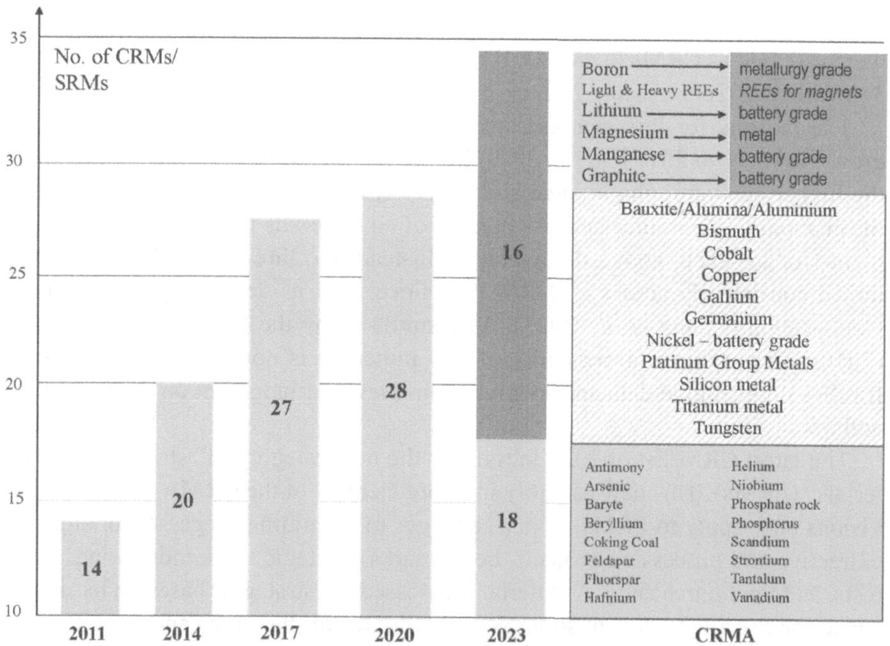

FIGURE 2.1 Critical and strategic raw materials over time

Notes: Light grey indicate CRMs and dark grey bars indicate SRMs. To enhance the figure's readability, the y-axis showing the number of CRMs/SRMs starts at 10.

Source: Own elaboration based on European Commission (2023c, 2025a).

technologies as strategic (Zhang *et al.*, 2023). There is some discretion for the Commission in defining and calculating the assessment metrics of the SRMs, as relates in particular to the needs for strategic technologies and the expected global demand. However, details about the underlying data and calculations of the SRM metrics are not published in the CRMA. Overall, this may potentially open doors to industry lobbying in the composition of the SRM list, which is updated every three years (Petitjean and Verheecke, 2023; Tansey, 2023).

2.5 Obstacles to domestic supply

With the CRMA, the EU sets a legislative measure designed to ensure more diverse supplies of critical and SRMs through domestic extraction and processing. For this purpose, the CRMA introduces measures across four main areas: facilitating Strategic Projects of minerals extraction and processing, promoting recycling and circularity, enhancing data collection and risk monitoring, and increasing transparency.

The most direct effects are expected through "Strategic Projects". The regulation aims to streamline approval procedures, arguing that Strategic Projects within the EU will have "overriding public interest". As a result, they should benefit from a simplified permitting process and less bureaucracy. At the same time, this also leads to shortened public consultation periods when projects require Environmental Impact Assessments, limiting opportunities for participation by NGOs, citizen initiatives, and neighbours (González, 2023). In March 2025, the European Commission approved 47 strategic projects in the EU (European Commission, 2025b).

Whether the public interest status of Strategic Projects will result in faster permitting depends on the capacities of public authorities and the decisions made by administrative courts. Most importantly, the permitting process represents only a fraction of the overall lead-time required to establish mines and different forms of extraction (typically up to 15 years) and will probably not significantly reduce the total time required for full implementation (Ancygier *et al.*, 2023; Manalo, 2023).

Furthermore, recycling and circularity are central to the CRMA's objectives, with member states tasked with developing national recycling programmes, implementing circularity measures, and introducing labelling systems for certain materials. However, the effectiveness of these initiatives depends heavily on national commitment and discretion, while technical, economic, and logistical challenges remain substantial. The other elements of the CRMA regarding transparency and public reporting requirements are designed to foster trust and signal the importance of raw material extraction for resilient European supply chains and job creation. Yet, reduced opportunities for community engagement and ambiguous consultation requirements for indigenous populations raise concerns about inclusivity, public acceptance, and potential political influence in project selection (Tröster *et al.*, 2024).

Despite these measures, the CRMA faces structural and economic challenges that limit its capacity to achieve better EU self-sufficiency in CRMs. High energy and labour costs, administrative burdens, and vague national recycling obligations constrain the CRMA's impact. One key shortfall of the CRMA is the lack of emphasis on reducing resource consumption – a critical point, given the known social and ecological toll of extraction and processing of minerals (Bolger *et al.*, 2021). Even with its ambitious targets, the CRMA underscores the EU's continued reliance on external sources.

2.6 Strategic partnerships as a new approach with third countries

In order to improve access to raw materials from countries outside the EU, its strategic approach has shifted – at least on paper – from the "access to raw materials on world markets at undistorted conditions" (Küblböck, 2013) to fair and sustainable access to raw materials on global markets based on "raw materials diplomacy focused on reaching out to third countries through strategic partnerships and policy dialogues" (European Commission, 2024). New and adapted external policy instruments include Raw Materials Clubs, Strategic Partnerships and Energy and Raw Material Chapters in free trade agreements (Tröster *et al.*, 2025).

Among those policies, especially the Strategic Partnerships on raw materials are closely related to EU industrial policies. These partnerships are non-binding agreements between the EU and resource-rich countries aiming to link EU production capacities with raw material supply chains in these partner countries. In doing so, the EU presents itself as a reliable partner for resource-rich countries and raw material companies and provides incentives such as support for more sustainable mining, higher investments, and mutual economic benefits. At the same time, the partnerships should signal to the industries within the EU that they can rely on long-term raw material supply from partner countries (Tröster *et al.*, 2025).

Since 2021, the EU concluded 14 Strategic Partnerships on raw materials with very different partners, ranging from the Democratic Republic of Congo (DRC), Rwanda, and Zambia, to Norway, Australia, and Serbia (European Commission, 2024). The different Memorandums of Understanding (MoUs) show that the overall structures of the partnerships are very similar. Typically, the four pillars of the agreements are (i) the development and integration of raw material value chains, (ii) cooperation in the fields of research and development, (iii) promotion of environmental, social, and governance criteria and standards, and (iv) financial and investment instruments for raw material projects.

However, the scope and targeted raw materials of the agreements vary (as shown in Table 2.2). The MoUs differ substantially in their extent, and therefore in the level of detail across these thematic pillars. Some include issues such as infrastructure or regulatory alignment, while others do not. Certain partnerships contain specific steps with respect to, e.g., research and innovation cooperation, while others merely state general goals in this area.

The aim to generate mutual benefits for both partners is prominently stated in all MoUs, but is subject to substantial differences in detail. Several MoUs

TABLE 2.2 Scope of the strategic raw material partnerships

Partner country	*Concluded in*	*Scope of the MoU*
Canada	2021	"Minerals and metals critical to the transition to a climate-neutral and digitalised economy"
Ukraine	2021	Raw materials, focus on CRMs and batteries
Namibia	2022	Raw materials, focus on CRMs and renewable hydrogen
Kazakhstan	2022	Raw materials, focus on CRMs, batteries, and renewable hydrogen
Argentina	2023	CRMs
Chile	2023	CRMs
DRC	2023	CRMs
Zambia	2023	CRMs
Greenland	2023	Raw materials, focus on CRMs
Rwanda	2024	"non-energy and non-agriculture raw materials for the green and digital transition as well as other minerals of strategic relevance to the twin transition"
Norway	2024	Raw materials, focus CRMs and batteries
Uzbekistan	2024	non-energy and non-agriculture raw materials, focus on CRMs
Australia	2024	CRMs
Serbia	2024	Raw materials, focus on CRMs for EV supply chains, EVs, and batteries

Source: Own elaboration based on MoUs.

state concretely the aim to promote local added-value (Argentina, Kazakhstan, Chile), industrialisation (Argentina), and upgrading (Kazakhstan), while others speak only of commitments to the policy goal of more local value-added and local transformation capacities (Zambia). In the case of Serbia, the goal of value chain integration is specified to include off-take agreements and has materialised into commitments by public and private sector actors to invest in a lithium battery factory linked to the planned and still controversial Jadar lithium mine (DW, 2024). In other cases, the term "value chain integration" remains vague and ambiguous.

Thus, it remains unclear what, and how, mutual benefits should be specifically achieved. This is problematic, given that the development of extractive projects potentially increases commodity-dependence of resource-rich countries, which often goes hand in hand with depressed economic and human development (Tröster *et al.*, 2020). Furthermore, upgrading in global mining value chains remains highly challenging (Pietrobelli *et al.*, 2024).

Funding for the development of raw materials projects and related infrastructure remains crucial. All MoUs include at least some elements on the deployment of financial and investment de-risking instruments for raw material projects. The Partnerships with the DRC, Zambia, Greenland, and Rwanda also cover the facilitation of financing for infrastructure projects.

European raw materials policy employs a web of different financial actors and instruments, such as the European Fund for Sustainable Development Plus (EFSD+), the Global Gateway Strategy, as well as export credit agencies and development banks of EU Member States. The EU consequently uses the well-known de-risking approach which relies on providing public money to mobilise private capital, i.e., blended finance (Küblböck and Grohs, 2019). Political economists, however, have pointed out that the success of de-risking instruments depends on the alignment with the goals of private investors (Gabor, 2023; Kampourakis, 2024). So far, there is only minor expertise to finance raw material projects in third countries via these European financial instruments.

Critics point to further issues in these partnerships: They generally fail to address illegal and irresponsible mining practices, neglect anti-corruption measures, and offer minimal transparency obligations (Fern *et al.*, 2023). MoUs with countries like Zambia, the DRC, and Rwanda include traceability and transparency standards due to concerns over smuggling and artisanal mining, whereas other partnerships remain unclear about this issue.

Further, roadmaps containing the details of the agreements and ideally also concrete projects, were envisioned to be finalised within a maximum of six months after the conclusion of the MoUs. Yet, in most cases, they have not been published, which is adding to the frustration of civil society actors, who claim that the MoUs' promises of "transparency" and "cooperation with civil society" have not been adhered to (Lobacheva and Sedova, 2024).

With the Strategic Partnerships, the EU extends its active, market-directing approach towards the twin transformation to the external sphere of raw materials supply from third countries. The development of new production capacities in the EU is actively supported by arrangements with resource-rich countries that foster the integration of EU buyer relations with extraction projects in those countries. However, the challenges of mobilising the necessary investments and the creation of mutual benefits beyond the extractive stage of the value chain remain unresolved, as the incentives offered by the EU – such as more sustainable mining, increased investment, and mutual economic gains – remain non-binding and challenging to implement in practice. This is largely due to the lack of enforceable sustainability provisions and the absence of a coherent strategy to support investment and value-added processing in the raw materials sector.

Moreover, a longstanding policy tension remains: as commodity dependence is a major reason for persistently low levels of human and economic development, resource-rich countries seek to upgrade their position in mineral value chains as a basis for their own industrialisation to benefit from the demand surge of CRMs (Jütten, 2024). These ambitions often clash with the EU's pursuit of "strategic autonomy" and the "relocation" of manufacturing back to Europe as part of its transition plans (Hool *et al.*, 2023; Höra, 2024; Leali, 2020; Wolf, 2023).

Despite the new approach via the Strategic Partnerships, the EU still applies tools rooted in a market-creating approach – such as free trade agreements and regulatory cooperation. These instruments might even gain more importance in the EU raw materials policies with third countries. In early 2025, the European Commission introduced a new instrument for cooperation – the Clean Trade and Investment Partnerships (CTIPs) – which reflect the general turn of priorities away from the Green Deal towards enhancing competitiveness (European Commission, 2025d). These new partnerships are intended to complement or enable free trade agreements and include improved access to raw materials through trade and investment regulations and regulatory cooperation. This indicates that traditional instruments like free trade agreements and regulatory cooperation remain a priority for the EU.

2.7 Conclusions

Europe's pursuit of strategic autonomy and climate goals makes the securing of SRMs a decisive challenge for its green and digital transformation. The intersection of ambitious industrial strategies, rising mineral demand, and persistent supply dependencies underscores that solutions to the EU's raw material vulnerabilities must be both immediate and forward-looking.

The time dimension is crucial. In the short to medium term, rising demand for copper, cobalt, lithium, nickel, and rare earths will be met primarily by imports, sustaining and even aggravating geopolitical and market vulnerabilities. These dependencies are expected to peak around 2030, when projected market deficits risk disrupting the deployment of clean energy and digital technologies (European Commission and Joint Research Centre, 2023; Gregoir and van Acker, 2022). In the longer run, however, demand is expected to stabilise and eventually decline as renewable infrastructures mature and circular economy measures expand secondary supply. Research from the European Commission's JRC suggests that by mid-century, recycling could cover 45–65% of base metals, 77% of battery metals, and even generate a surplus of rare earth elements for the EU.

This temporal dynamic calls for a dual strategy: securing reliable imports under fair and sustainable conditions in the short term, while simultaneously building the foundations of a circular economy that reduces external dependencies in the long term. Recycling, eco-design, and digital innovation are indispensable, but they must be complemented by strategies to reduce overall energy and material consumption. Efficiency improvements, sufficiency-oriented policies, and new consumption patterns are therefore essential. Such measures require not only technological advances but also political commitment and broad societal buy-in to ensure fair and socially accepted transitions.

Europe's resilience will ultimately depend on forging responsible international partnerships that acknowledge these time dynamics. Embedding environmental and social responsibility, local value creation, technology transfer, and civil society participation into resource cooperation will be crucial to avoid reproducing old dependencies and to align partnerships with broader development goals in resource-rich countries.

References

Ancygier, A., Waterton, O., Most, S., Quill, E., Rabiee, S., Myer, D., and Ramalope, D. (2023) *Critical and Strategic Materials: Potential Bottlenecks and the EU Perspective*. Climate Analytics.

Barteková, E. and Kemp, R. (2016) *Critical Raw Material Strategies in Different World Regions*. UNU-MERIT Working Papers, 5.

Blengini, G. A., Nuss, P., Dewulf, J., Nita, V., Peirò, L. T., Vidal-Legaz, B., Latunussa, C., Mancini, L., Blagoeva, D., Pennington, D., Pellegrini, M., Van Maercke, A., Solar, S., Grohol, M., and Ciupagea, C. (2017) EU methodology for critical raw materials assessment: Policy needs and proposed solutions for incremental improvements. *Resources Policy*, 53, 12–19. https://doi.org/10.1016/j.resourpol.2017.05.008

Bobba, S., Carrara, S., Huisman, J., Mathieux, F., and Pavel, C. C. (2020) *Critical Raw Materials for Strategic Technologies and Sectors in the EU – A Foresight Study*. European Commission.

Bolger, M., Marin, D., Tofighi-Niaki, A., and Seelmann, L. (2021) *'Green Mining' Is a Myth: The Case for Cutting EU Resource Consumption*. European Environmental Bureau & Friends of the Earth Europe.

Carrara, S., Bobba, S., Blagoeva, D., Alves Dias, P., et al. (2023) *Supply Chain Analysis and Material Demand Forecast in Strategic Technologies and Sectors in the EU – A Foresight Study*. Publications Office of the European Union, Luxembourg, https://doi.org/10.2760/386650, JRC132889.

Commission of the European Communities (1975) *The Community's Supplies of Raw Materials (COM (75) 50 No. CELEX 51975DC0050 EN TXT)*. https://eur-lex.europa.eu/legal-content/EN/TXT/?uri=CELEX:51975DC0050 (accessed 17 October 2025).

Curtis, M. (2010) The New Resource Grab: How EU Trade Policy on Raw Materials is Undermining Development. Report on behalf of Traidcraft Exchange, Oxfam Germany, WEED, AITEC, and Comhlámh.

Di Carlo, D. and Schmitz, L. (2023) Europe first? The rise of EU industrial policy promoting and protecting the single market. *Journal of European Public Policy*, 30(10), 2063–2096. https://doi.org/10.1080/13501763.2023.2202684

DW (2024, July 19) *EU und Serbien schließen Abkommen zur Lithium-Förderung*. DW. https://www.dw.com/de/eu-und-serbien-schlie%C3%9Fen-abkommen-zur-lithium-f%C3%B6rderung/a-69713261 (accessed 17 October 2025).

EIT (2025) *European Innovation Partnership on Raw Materials*. https://eitrawmaterials.eu/

European Commission (2006) *Enlargement, Two Years After: An Economic Evaluation. (No. 24; Occasional Papers)*. European Commission.

European Commission (2008) *The Raw Materials Initiative-Meeting Our Critical Needs for Growth and Jobs in Europe (No. COM(2008) 699 final)*. Koninklijke Brill NV. https://primarysources.brillonline.com/browse/human-rights-documents-online/communication-from-the-commission-to-the-european-parliament-and-the-council;hrdhrd46790058 (accessed 17 October 2025).

European Commission (2010) *Critical Raw Materials for the EU – Report of the Ad-hoc Working Group on Defining Critical Raw Materials.*

European Commission (2023a) *A Green Deal Industrial Plan for the Net-Zero Age (No. COM(2023) 62 final)*. European Commission. https://eur-lex.europa.eu/legal-content/EN/TXT/?uri=CELEX%3A52023DC0062 (accessed 17 October 2025).

European Commission (2023b) *Net-Zero Industry Act*. https://commission.europa.eu/strategy-and-policy/priorities-2019-2024/european-green-deal/green-deal-industrial-plan/net-zero-industry-act_en (accessed 17 October 2025).

European Commission (2023c) *Study on the Critical Raw Materials for the EU 2023 – Final Report*.

European Commission (2024) *Raw Materials Diplomacy*. European Commission. https://single-market-economy.ec.europa.eu/sectors/raw-materials/areas-specific-interest/raw-materials-diplomacy_en (accessed 17 October 2025).

European Commission (2025a) *Critical Raw Materials Act*. https://single-market-economy.ec.europa.eu/sectors/raw-materials/areas-specific-interest/critical-raw-materials/critical-raw-materials-act_en (accessed 17 October 2025).
European Commission (2025b) *Strategic Projects Under the CRMA*. https://single-market-economy.ec.europa.eu/sectors/raw-materials/areas-specific-interest/critical-raw-materials/strategic-projects-under-crma_en (accessed 17 October 2025).
European Commission (2025c) *The European Innovation Partnership (EIP) on Raw Materials*. https://single-market-economy.ec.europa.eu/sectors/raw-materials/eip_en (accessed 17 October 2025).
European Commission (2025d, January 29) *A Competitiveness Compass for the EU*.
European Commission and Joint Research Centre (2023) *Supply Chain Analysis and Material Demand Forecast in Strategic Technologies and Sectors in the EU: A Foresight Study*. Publications Office. https://data.europa.eu/doi/10.2760/386650
fern, SOMO, EU Raw Materials Coalition, Publish What You Pay, et al. (2023) *A Partnership of Equals? How to strengthen the EU's Critical Raw Materials Strategic Partnerships*. https://eeb.org/wp-content/uploads/2023/11/A_Partnership_of_Equals_01.pdf (accessed 14 December 2025).
Gabor, D. (2023, 17 May). The (European) Derisking State. *SocArXiv*. https://doi.org/10.31235/osf.io/hpbj2
González, A. (2023) *Ten reasons why the European Commission's proposed Critical Raw Materials Regulation is not sustainable and how to fix it*. SOMO position paper. SOMO (Centre for Research on Multinational Corporations).
Gregoir, L. and van Acker, K. (2022). *Metals for Clean Energy: Pathways to solving Europe's raw materials challenge*. KU Leuven. https://european-metals.eu/metals-for-clean-energy-ku-leuven-study/ (30 January 2025).
Hool, A., Helbig, C., and Wierink, G. (2023) Challenges and opportunities of the European Critical Raw Materials Act. *Mineral Economics*. https://doi.org/10.1007/s13563-023-00394-y
Hoppe, J. and Laursen, C. M. (2024, June 6) AI siphons copper supplies needed for green transition. *Wall Street Journal*. https://www.wsj.com/articles/ai-siphons-copper-supplies-needed-for-green-transition-8fef79e6 (accessed 17 October 2025).
Höra, E. (2024, März 19) *Building on the EU Critical Raw Materials Act: Looking for Economic Security, Offering Industrialisation?* Bertelsmann Stiftung. https://globaleurope.eu/europes-future/building-on-the-eu-critical-raw-materials-act-looking-for-economic-security-offering-industrialisation/ (accessed 17 October 2025).
IEA (2021) *The Role of Critical Minerals in Clean Energy Transitions*. International Energy Agency. https://www.iea.org/reports/the-role-of-critical-minerals-in-clean-energy-transitions (accessed 17 October 2025).
Jütten, M. (2024) *EU Latin America: Enhancing Cooperation on Critical Raw Materials*. European Parliamentary Research Service. https://www.europarl.europa.eu/RegData/etudes/BRIE/2024/767163/EPRS_BRI(2024)767163_EN.pdf (accessed 17 October 2025).
Kampourakis, I. (2024, January 18). *Unpacking the Critical Raw Materials Act*. Verfassungsblog. https://verfassungsblog.de/unpacking-the-critical-raw-materials-act/ (accessed 16 May 2024).
Küblböck, K. (2013) *The EU Raw Materials Initiative: Scope and Critical Assessment*. Vienna: ÖFSE Briefing Paper. https://doi.org/10.13140/RG.2.1.4826.4805
Küblböck, K. and Grohs, H. (2019). *Blended Finance and Its Potential for Development Cooperation*. Vienna: ÖFSE Briefing Paper No. 21. https://www.oefse.at/fileadmin/content/Downloads/Publikationen/Briefingpaper/BP21-Blending.pdf (accessed 17 October 2025).
Küblböck, K., Tröster, B., and Ambach, C. (2019) *Going Global: Chinese Natural Resource Policies and Their Impacts on Latin America*. ÖFSE Briefing Paper No. 24. https://

www.oefse.at/fileadmin/content/Downloads/Publikationen/Briefingpaper/BP24-Going-Global.pdf (accessed 17 October 2025).

Leali, G. (2020, Dezember 7) *Europe's Hunger for Lithium Sparks Tensions with Chile*. Politico. https://www.politico.eu/article/europes-hunger-for-lithium-sparks-tensions-with-chile/ (accessed 17 October 2025).

Lobacheva, M. and Sedova, T. (2024). *The Kazakhstan–EU Partnership on Critical Raw Materials*. Germanwatch. https://www.germanwatch.org/sites/default/files/20240612_Opinion%20paper_EU-Kazakhstan%20CRM%20Partnership.pdf (accessed 29 January 2025).

Manalo, P. (2023) *Discovery to Production Averages 15.7 Years for 127 Mines*. S&P Global Market Intelligence. https://www.spglobal.com/marketintelligence/en/news-insights/research/discovery-to-production-averages-15-7-years-for-127-mines (accessed 17 October 2025).

Montanuniversität Leoben (2004) *Minerals Planning Policies and Supply Practices in Europe [Executive Summary – Commissioned by the European Commission Enterprise Directorate General under Contract n° ETD/FIF 2003 0781]*. https://ec.europa.eu/docsroom/documents/1811/attachments/1/translations/en/renditions/native (accessed 17 October 2025).

Petitjean, O. and Verheecke, L. (2023) *Blood on the Green Deal*. Corporate Europe Observatory and Observatoire des Multinationales.

Pietrobelli, C., Calzada Olvera, B., Iizuka, M., and Mazzi, C. T. (2024) Suppliers' entry, upgrading, and innovation in mining GVCs: Lessons from Argentina, Brazil, and Peru. *Industrial and Corporate Change*, 33(4), 922–939. https://doi.org/10.1093/icc/dtad079

Proposal for a REGULATION OF THE EUROPEAN PARLIAMENT AND OF THE COUNCIL Establishing a Framework for Ensuring a Secure and Sustainable Supply of Critical Raw Materials and Amending Regulations (EU) 168/2013, (EU) 2018/858, 2018/1724, and (EU) 2019/1020, No. 2023/0079 (COD) (2023).

Raza, W. (2025) *Towards a Progressive Industrial Policy for the Twin Transformation in the European Union*. Vienna: ÖFSE Research Report No, 21. https://doi.org/10.60637/2025-RR21

Regulation (EU) 2024/1252 of the European Parliament and of the Council of 11 April 2024 establishing a framework for ensuring a secure and sustainable supply of critical raw materials, (EU) 2024/1252 (2024).

Rietveld, E., Bastein, T., van Leeuwen, T., Wieclaswska, S., Bonenkamp, N., Klebba, M., Le Mouel, M., and Poitiers, N. (2022) *Strengthening the Security of Supply of Products Containing Critical Raw Materials for the Green Transition and Decarbonisation*. European Parliament. https://www.europarl.europa.eu/RegData/etudes/STUD/2022/740058/IPOL_STU(2022)740058_EN.pdf (accessed 17 October 2025).

Risch, B. W. K. (1978) The raw material supply of the European Community. *Resources Policy*, 4(3), 181–188. https://doi.org/10.1016/0301-4207(78)90045-4

Soubeyran, S. and Nae, A. (2025) *The Digital Economy – Critical Minerals and Equity Markets*. FTSE RUSSELL. https://www.lseg.com/content/dam/ftse-russell/en_us/documents/research/the-digital-economy-critical-minerals-and-equity-markets.pdf (accessed 17 October 2025).

Tansey, R. (2023) *Mining the Depth of Influence: How Industry Is Forging the EU Critical Raw Materials Act*. Friends of the Earth Europe.

Tröster, B., Arnim, R., Staritz, C., Raza, W., Grumiller, J., and Grohs, H. (2020) Delivering on promises? The expected impacts and implementation challenges of the economic partnership agreements between the European Union and Africa. *Journal of Common Market Studies*, 58(2), 365–383. https://doi.org/10.1111/jcms.12923

Tröster, B., Papatheophilou, S., and Küblböck, K. (2024) *In Search of Critical Raw Materials: What Will the EU Critical Raw Materials Act Achieve? An Analysis of Legal and Factual Implications of the CRMA*. ÖFSE Research Report No. 18. https://doi.org/10.60637/2024-RR18

Tröster, B., Papatheophilou, S., and Küblböck, K. (2025) *Strategic Autonomy meets Global Dependency: Instruments and Implications of the EU's Raw Materials Policy with Third Countries*. ÖFSE Briefing Paper No. 36. https://doi.org/10.60637/2025-BP36

UNEP International Resource Panel (IRP) (2025) *Global Material Flows Database (1970–2023)* [Dataset]. https://www.materialflows.net

Van Apeldoorn, B. and De Graaff, N. (2022) The state in global capitalism before and after the Covid-19 crisis. *Contemporary Politics*, 28(3), 306–327. https://doi.org/10.1080/13569775.2021.2022337

Wolf, A. (2023) Versorgung mit kritischen Rohstoffen: Für eine nachhaltige europäische Strategie. *Zeitschrift für Wirtschaftspolitik*, 72(1), 84–108. https://doi.org/10.1515/zfwp-2023-2002

Zhang, S. E., Bourdeau, J. E., Nwaila, G. T., and Ghorbani, Y. (2023) Emerging criticality: Unraveling shifting dynamics of the EU's critical raw materials and their implications on Canada and South Africa. *Resources Policy*, 86, 104247. https://doi.org/10.1016/j.resourpol.2023.104247

3

TECHNOLOGICAL DEPENDENCIES OF THE EUROPEAN UNION

Implications for Industrial Policy

Christian Reiner and Roman Stöllinger

3.1 Introduction

Falling behind the technological frontier is one of the long-standing concerns in the EU and its member states (Cohen, 1992; Landesmann and Stöllinger, 2020; Stöllinger *et al.*, 2013). Given the dominance of the US and increasingly Chinese firms in digital technologies, there is good reason to be concerned. The EU's gap in newly emerging digital technologies and – to a lesser extent – in selected green technologies may well be reflected in lower (future) GDP growth and a failure to achieve societal and climate policy objectives (Guarascio *et al.*, 2025; Veugelers, 2024).

Falling further behind the technological frontier would be disastrous for the EU economy because it simply cannot compete on price alone. International competitiveness is both a function of technological leadership and of relative factor prices (Cantner, 2023), implying that a high-income region such as the EU economy is bound to compete on quality and technology. In a highly integrated world economy, 'gaps' in technological and/or production capabilities may not matter much, as long as the complex web of international production networks is reasonably resilient to shocks, trading partners feel bound by an international rules-based order and dependencies run both ways. Interdependencies, however, which are inevitably created in global value chains (GVCs), can be exploited both by governments (e.g., via export bans for high-tech chips) and by individual firms (e.g., via takeovers of newly emerging competitors).

Supply chain disruptions during COVID-19, the marked change in US policies towards protectionism and aggressive geopolitics, the increasing assertiveness of China, the Russian war on Ukraine and the general increase in geopolitical and geoeconomic frictions have made the EU's technological

DOI: 10.4324/9781003745563-5

dependency more worrisome in the last decade. In this new geopolitical environment, however, the EU's liberal trade and investment policy approach has much higher opportunity costs. This is because the emerging technological dependency undermines the ability to conduct autonomous policies, that is economic policies fostering the EU's interests and reflecting its values. One suggested solution is a shift in economic policy towards more technological sovereignty, even though this may involve significant opportunity costs (Edler *et al.*, 2023; Guarascio *et al.*, 2025).

The EU's technology gap feeds into the different structural vulnerabilities identified in Guarascio *et al.* (2025), of which technological dependence is one. Technological dependence is the Archilles' heel of modern economies. Not only can it result in significant profit losses and missed growth opportunities in related sectors stemming from Schumpeterian rents (Kaplinsky, 2019; Landesmann, 2015), but it exposes firms and critical infrastructure to supply disruptions and the negative consequences of strategic (or even 'punitive') trade policy of technology leaders, notably the US, and increasingly also China.

Technological dependence is therefore not compatible with open strategic autonomy, defined as '*the EU's ability to make its own choices and shape the world around it through leadership and engagement, reflecting its strategic interests and values*' (European Commission, 2021: 4).[1] The strategic interests comprise both economic and security aspects, which are tightly intertwined in essentially all technological and infrastructure domains, as evidenced, for example, by the discussions about the security of 5G networks (Voelsen, 2019), cloud solutions or telecommunication systems (see Coveri *et al.*, 2025). Similar arguments apply to green technologies: EU dependence on fossil fuels from Russia has turned into a liability. Expanding the production from renewables as well as energy efficiency gains are not only important for climate protection but also a first-order issue for security and political autonomy. In addition, weak positions in battery development and production are a threat to the competitiveness of the European car industry, a traditional stronghold of the central European manufacturing core.

Against this background, this chapter asks three questions: What is technological dependency, how dependent is the EU on foreign digital and green technologies and what industrial policies could the EU support in achieving the goal of technological sovereignty?

The remainder of this chapter is structured as follows. Section 3.2 explains what is meant by technological dependence and why it has become a problem in the new geopolitical environment. The empirics of the EU's technological dependence in digital and green technologies are analysed by quantitative and qualitative approaches in Section 3.3. Section 3.4 provides a summary and discusses the policy challenges and responses with reference to the concept of a mission-oriented industrial policy.

3.2 What is technological dependency?

If international economic exchange is free from coercion, interdependencies between economies are in principle mutual. However, given the hierarchical structure of the world-economy, highlighted by adherents of both World System theory (Wallerstein, 1974) and dependency theory (Kvangraven, 2021), these interdependencies are asymmetrical because 'core' countries are in a more powerful position than semi-peripheries and peripheral countries. These interdependencies turn into dependencies when the asymmetry is so great that one side can dictate the rules of the game.[2] This is a perception long held in the Global South. For the EU, which perceives itself as a core country, a (perceived) state of dependency is a relatively new situation, which arose in the aftermath of the ICT revolution and became apparent with the arrival of the 'Digital Age'. Further shocks such as the almost complete import dependence regarding certain medical supplies during COVID-19 or the recent weaponising of gas exports by Russia have intensified the perception of adverse dependencies in the EU.

A state of dependency is thus differentiated from interdependence because of the high degree of asymmetry in the power positions of the partners involved. In addition, and as the case of Russia shows, a neglect of a government for the welfare of its own citizens can transform economic interdependencies into risky dependencies, because the trading partner may be willing to accept damages to its own economy. Therefore, we would argue that interdependencies can become problematic for international economic relations if either (i) the asymmetries between economic partners become so large that interdependence is turned into a dependency and/or (ii) the economic partner government's objective function does not include economic welfare of its citizens as its most important argument. In both cases, deep economic integration becomes a risky strategy, because interdependencies turn into structural vulnerabilities (Guarascio *et al.*, 2025). The economic relationship between the EU and the US would be an example of significant asymmetries in power positions, the confrontation between the EU and Russia a situation in which the ruling elite of the trading partner does not consider the well-being of the citizens a priority.

Technological dependence is part of the broader concept of economic dependence. The asymmetries associated with technological dependence are manifested in unequal technological capabilities and/or positions in the global trading system. Thus, technological dependence means the absence of control over advanced technologies and/or the lack of sufficient supply of high-tech products needed to ensure the proper functioning of critical infrastructures. This follows Cantner (2023), who establishes two criteria for technological dependence, which are (i) lack of mastery and (ii) lack of access to key technologies. To which we would add a third criterion which is (iii) the availability of an alternative technology. Due to the foundational character of key technologies and international standardisation, developing domestic substitute technologies is likely to be quite challenging if a key technology has already been adopted by a critical user base.

In an EU context, technological dependence is tightly related to the strive for achieving 'open strategic autonomy'. Strategic autonomy was first mentioned in the European Council conclusions in 2013 with a view to develop European defence, technological and industrial capacities (Fabry and Veskoukis, 2021). The concept of 'open strategic autonomy' was then taken up by EU Trade Policy but never filled with life. This failure is explained, among other things, by the lack of agreement among member states of what the term is supposed to mean in concrete terms. As a result, the term remains vague and may be even counterproductive in improving the EU's economic position (Van Veen and Langenberg, 2022).

The flip side of a higher level of autonomy is that the efficiency gains from global economic integration, even if parts of these gains only resulted from distortions such as the neglect of systemic and environmental risks, cannot be exploited to their fullest extent. For this reason, a shift towards more strategic autonomy entails economic costs (Van Veen and Langenberg, 2022). Moreover, the shift does not, per se, ensure greater resilience of value chains (Fabry and Veskoukis, 2021). Thus, there is considerable scepticism against the notion of a strategic autonomy that risks leading to the politicisation of GVCs (Fabry and Veskoukis, 2021) and protectionism.

Despite these concerns, the concept of 'open strategic autonomy' may well have its merits if properly defined and applied to a specific set of technological dependencies. Van Veen and Langenberg (2022: 3–4) suggest that an 'open strategic autonomy' ought to manage specific dependencies, namely those '*that can be exploited by external actors to exercise a degree of coercive influence on the realisation of strategic EU objectives*'.

This links directly to the notion of technological sovereignty, which according to Edler *et al.* (2023) is a means to strengthen an economy's competitiveness and its capacity to conduct appropriate economic policies. The emphasis on the likelihood that trading partners exploit their positions parallels the 'special availability concerns', which according to Cantner (2023) arise in situations where dependency situations and trade wars coincide. Hence, technological sovereignty is to be seen as one of the core elements of the EU's open strategic autonomy

Making use of the above criteria for technological dependence, we can deduct that the level of technological sovereignty depends on the degree to which an economy disposes of the necessary technological knowledge and resources to use and operate vital technologies. This can be achieved either via the ability to produce the technology 'in-house'; or via the procurement from partners; or via a shift to an alternative technology which serve the same function. While less demanding than in-house production, the sourcing of technology also entails costs, including the cost of building-up and maintaining the competences and skills needed to use the purchased technology – the well-known absorptive capacity (Cohen and Levinthal, 1989). Hence, at the firm-level there is a 'make or buy' decision, which depends on a comparison of the advantages and costs from in-house production with the advantages and costs from foreign sourcing.

3.3 How technologically dependent is the EU?

The concept of technological sovereignty is complex and cannot be measured by a single indicator. As a result, a synopsis of different indicators is required to get a valid picture of potential structural problems. Generally, technological dependence is likely to be high if a technology is a critical input and domestic mastery and/or availability is lacking. Capturing the dimension of mastery of a technology, the following indicators of technological capabilities are considered: research and development (R&D) investments, scientific publications, patents, as well as production and trade in technology-intensive products.

In order to contextualise the analysis, it is useful to briefly contrast our approach with empirical studies on technological sovereignty which aim to analyse the entire portfolio of key enabling technologies (KET). A study for the European Parliament (2021), for instance, distinguishes between the following six technologies: advanced manufacturing, advanced materials, life-science technologies, micro/nano-electronics and photonics, artificial intelligence, security and connectivity technologies. The overall conclusion of that study is that the EU's technological sovereignty lags behind China and the US. The German Commission of Experts for Research and Development (2022) differentiates between 13 KETs and finds that the EU commands a revealed comparative advantage in only two of them, namely advanced manufacturing and life sciences. In comparison, China (USA) has a comparative advantage in 11 (7) out of 13 technologies. While these results are important, they are still at a very high level of aggregation. In fact, a KET can be thought of as a bundle of related technologies which are developed in the context of an international division of labour (Cantner, 2023). Determining actual technological dependencies requires a more fine-grained analysis at the level of individual products and value chains.

3.3.1 Quantitative dependence indicators

A lack of technological capabilities and associated technological dependencies can occur at different stages of the innovation chain: basic research, applied research and experimental development, production and trade. These stages are connected in complex ways, including feedback loops. However, as a useful heuristic, we follow the stages of the linear innovation model step by step.

3.3.1.1 Basic research

Basic research is the backbone of modern innovation systems. Basic research expenditure as a percentage of GDP is a broad measure for the resources devoted to basic research. The most recent available data from the OECD for 2022 indicate that the US spends about 0.5% of its GDP on basic research, EU countries spend roughly the same or less than this (France: 0.45%, Italy: 0.33%, Netherlands: 0.54%);[3] while China lags behind with 0.16%. Regarding scientific publications in science and engineering, the US accounted for 27% of global academic output in 2003, while the respective shares for the EU and China were 26% and 7%. In 2022, the picture is very different: about 27% of global publications in science and engineering are now from China and the shares of the US and the EU have dropped to 14% and 18% respectively (US National Center for Science and Engineering Statistics, 2025).

We next focus on basic research related to digital and green technologies. Table 3.1 shows the publication output in computer science and technologies

TABLE 3.1 Number of publications (fractional counts) among the world's 10% top-cited scientific publications by scientific discipline, 2009–2023

Scientific discipline	*Bibliometric indicator*	*Country*	*2009*	*2015*	*2023*	*Growth rate 2009–2023 (%)*
Computer science	Number of all publications	*USA*	29,449	30,746	36,721	25
		EU27	42,581	49,075	58,032	36
		CHN	47,880	35,487	105,406	120
	Number of top 10% publications	*USA*	6,023	5,847	6,905	15
		EU27	4,783	4,727	5,110	7
		CHN	1,535	2,375	10,863	607
	Specialisation index	*USA*	0.73	0.82	0.80	10
		EU27	0.95	1.06	0.92	−3
		CHN	1.80	1.06	1.11	−38
Renewable energy, sustainability and the environment	Number of all publications	*USA*	929	1,624	1,874	102
		EU27	1,211	2,843	4,056	235
		CHN	912	2,626	10,599	1,063
	Number of top 10% publications	*USA*	96	186	241	151
		EU27	148	261	302	104
		CHN	91	330	1,198	1,215
	Specialisation index	*USA*	0.75	0.69	0.49	−35
		EU27	0.88	0.98	0.76	−14
		CHN	1.12	1.25	1.33	19

Note: The specialisation index measures specialisation by comparing national and world scientific publications; values greater than 1 indicate specialisation.

Source: OECD, Scientometric and bibliometric indicators.

related to fighting climate change. In computer science, the EU published the second-highest number of articles in 2009 after China. In 2023, the EU is still in front of the US but the gap to China has widened substantially as China's publication growth rate was more than three times higher (120% vs. 36%). Focusing on highly cited papers, the performance of the EU appears less impressive. This development suggests that China has increasingly concentrated on publishing high quality papers: while publications in computer science have grown since 2009 by 120%, top publications have expanded by more than 600%. For the EU, high impact publications grew only by 7%, while total publications in this field expanded by 36%. Regarding renewables, the EU consistently outperforms the US but was overtaken by China between 2009 and 2023. Once again, the shortfall of the EU compared to China is higher for high-impact publications than for publications in general. These results clearly indicate the high quality of the Chinese science system, while the EU is losing ground in the segment of high-impact publications, particularly in computer science and renewable energy.

In terms of academic specialisation, the specialisation index in Table 3.1 suggests that China is the most specialised country, while the EU and the US are less specialised in the two disciplines. However, the EU is more focused on digital and green technologies than the US, with a more pronounced advantage in renewable energy. What is more, the US has experienced a rapid decline in its specialisation in renewable energy.

A more detailed analysis by the German Commission of Experts for Research and Development (2022) differentiates between six digital technologies: big data, internet of things, artificial intelligence, digital security technologies, microelectronics and digital mobility technologies. China publishes the largest number of publications in all fields except for digital security technologies, which is dominated by the EU.[4] Perhaps somewhat surprisingly, the EU performs better than the US in all six digital technologies, suggesting that the EU's scientific base is still strong (Veugelers, 2024). Focusing on AI-related journal articles, China accounts for about 36% of global output in 2022, which is more than the EU and the US combined (14.5% and 11.6% respectively) (German Commission of Experts for Research and Development, 2024). Once again, however, this picture changes if we restrict the analysis of AI publications to the 10% most frequently cited papers: The EU falls back to the third position, clearly behind the US which is itself increasingly outperformed by China.[5]

For renewable energy technologies, analyses by the European Commission suggest that in 2010 the EU was leading in the following four out of five technologies in terms of number of publications: solar, li-ion batteries, heat pumps and carbon capture and storage. China, on the other hand, produces the highest output of wind-energy related papers. Eleven years later, China holds the pole position in all five technologies, while the EU is at the second place and the US in third position (García-Herrero *et al.*, 2023).

3.3.1.2 Applied research

Turning to applied research, the focus shifts from the university sector to the business sector and from publications to corporate R&D efforts (an input measure) and patents (an output measure). Figure 3.1 shows total R&D expenditures to GDP (i.e., basic and applied research, providing a broad metric of technological capabilities and absorptive capacities) and business expenditure on R&D as a percentage of GDP. The EU's R&D expenditure grew at the slowest rate in comparison to the US and China. In the last years, total R&D spending of the EU has grown slowly, almost stagnating at about 2%, i.e., far below the 3% goal which should have been achieved by 2010 according to the Lisbon strategy. The R&D gap is, however, much wider in business R&D, where EU companies spend just about half as much as US firms and 70% of Chinese firms. Analysis of R&D in clean energy technologies reveals that the EU spends more public money as a % of GDP on R&I than China, Japan and South Korea and the US, but lags behind in private R&I expenditures. Most recent data for 2022 suggest that EU firms invest about 0.2% of GDP, while Japan, South Korea or China spend between 0.6% and 0.8%; US clean energy tech firms, however, invest even less than EU firms (European Commission, 2025).

As can be seen from Table 3.2, the share of EU firms among the global top 1,000 firms in terms of R&D investment declined from 20% (2005) to about 19% (2023) and from 24% (2005) to approximately 22% (2023) for the group of top 250 firms. A deeper drop can be observed for the US and Japan, but the US still holds a much higher share of leading R&D firms than the EU (35% vs. 19%). Contrary to that, China was able to raise its proportion among the globally leading firms from 0.5% to about 20%, almost on a par with Europe. Even more telling might be the percentage of R&D investment: In 2005 (2023), about 26% (22%) of global investment

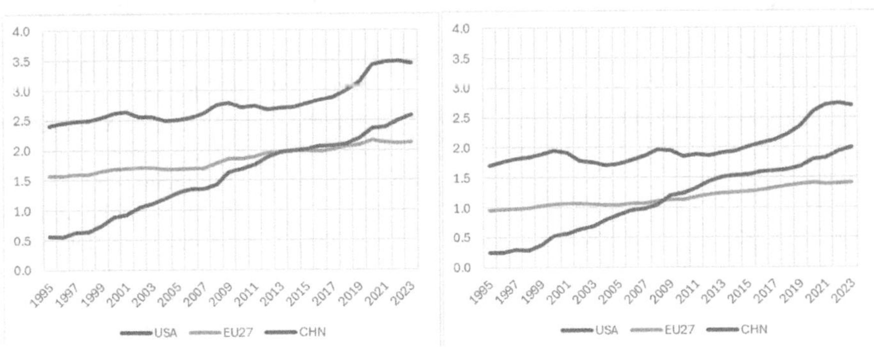

FIGURE 3.1 Gross domestic expenditure on R&D as a % of GDP (left panel) and business expenditure on R&D as a % of GDP (right panel), 1995–2023

Source: OECD, MSTI.

TABLE 3.2 Performance of top 1,000 world-leading firms in R&D, 2005–2023

2005

	% no. of firms among top 1,000 firms	*% no. of firms among top 250 firms*	*% of R&D among top 1,000*	*% R&D to sales*	*Top 3 sectors**
EU27	20.0%	24.0%	25.5%	3.6%	Automobiles & parts, Pharmaceuticals, Industrial machinery
CHN	0.5%	0.4%	0.8%	0.6%	Oil & gas producers, Telecommunications equipment, Semiconductors
JPN	19.5%	19.6%	21.0%	3.8%	Chemicals, Automobiles & Parts, Electronic equipment
USA	41.8%	42.4%	41.2%	4.4%	Semiconductors, Software, Biotechnology

2015

	% no. of firms in top 1,000 firms	*% no. of firms in top 250 firms*	*% in R&D top 1,000*	*% R&D to sales*	*Top 3 sectors**
EU27	21.7%	24.0%	23.7%	4.2%	Pharmaceuticals & Biotechnology, Industrial Engineering, Automobiles & Parts
CHN	8.9%	6.8%	7.3%	2.5%	Automobiles & Parts Construction & Materials, Industrial Engineering
JPN	15.9%	17.6%	17.0%	4.2%	Electronic & Electrical equipment, Chemicals, Automobiles & Parts
USA	35.1%	37.2%	40.8%	6.2%	Technology Hardware & Equipment, Software & Computer Services, Pharmaceuticals & Biotechnology

(Continued)

TABLE 3.2 (Continued)

2023					
	% no. of firms in top 1,000 firms	*% no. of firms in top 250 firms*	*% in R&D top 1,000*	*% R&D to sales*	*Top 3 sectors**
EU27	19.2%	21.2%	21.7%	4.9%	Pharmaceuticals & Biotechnology, Automobiles & Parts, Industrial Engineering
CHN	21.6%	18.8%	18.3%	4.0%	Electronic & Electrical Equipment, Software & Computer Services, Automobiles & Parts
JPN	10.4%	10.4%	12.3%	4.5%	Automobiles & Parts, Electronic & Electrical Equipment, Chemicals
USA	34.9%	36.8%	43.1%	9.1%	Software & Computer Services, Pharmaceuticals & Biotechnology, Technology Hardware & Equipment

* Defined as the three sectors with the largest numbers of companies. Sectors are ordered in descending order of importance.

Source: Author's own calculations based on EU Industrial R&D Investment Scoreboard data.

of the top 1,000 firms came from EU companies. Contrary to this decline, the US firms were able to defend their share of about 42%. This was possible because US firms more than doubled their R&D intensity (measured as R&D over sales) from 4.4% to over 9%. The EU firms, meanwhile, could raise their R&D intensity by merely 34%, significantly less than Chinese firms, which were able to boost their R&D intensity by 60% between 2015 and 2023. This discrepancy between the EU companies on the one hand and US and Chinese companies on the other hand can largely be explained by diverging structural change patterns: while the dominant R&D-intensive EU firms continue to be active in broadly the same economic sectors, Chinese firms quickly moved from more traditional sectors in 2005 to ICT-related activities in 2023, which have higher R&D intensities than traditional medium-tech sectors like automotive or industrials. As a result, some scholars see the EU caught in a 'middle-innovation trap' (Fuest *et al.*, 2024).

ICT hardware and software represent the two sectors with the largest R&D investment outlays among the global top 1,000 firms in terms of R&D investment (European Commission, 2024a). Health, automotive and industrials are the next three sectors in descending order of total R&D investment. As was already pointed out above, the EU is trailing behind the US and China in ICT: in 2023, the number of ICT hardware firms among the top 1,000 firms were as follows: 34 (EU), 109 (US) and 123 (China). In ICT software, the respective numbers indicate a more pronounced concentration in the US: 24 (EU), 163 (US) and 68 (China). But even the few top European ICT companies underperform relative to the US companies. While US ICT hardware companies have about the same R&D intensity as EU firms, their profitability is much higher (20% vs. 13%) and their R&D expenditures per employee are more than two times larger. The Chinese companies are less profitable and have lower but quickly rising R&D intensity and R&D expenditures per employee, a clear sign that they shift from production capabilities towards innovation competencies. Regarding ICT software, the EU hosts just 24 firms, 9 firms less than in 2013. The US, on the other hand, increased its number of firms in this sector from 123 (2013) to 163 (2023). China is catching up, expanding its number of ICT software firms among the top 1,000 firms from 24 to 68. In 2023, the discrepancy between the EU and US firms is staggering: The profitability of US firms is 60% higher, the R&D intensity almost three times higher and the R&D expenditures per employee 4.6 times larger. Chinese software companies outperform the EU companies in both R&D intensity and R&D investments per employee. As a result, the shortfall of EU's ICT companies is even more pronounced in the field of ICT software, which is the fastest growing sector in terms of R&D investment globally.

Patents are a key indicator for applied research, and substantial performance differences in patenting between countries is one possible metric for revealing technological dependencies (Guarascio *et al.*, 2025). Figure 3.2 illustrates the development of patents in the broad fields of ICT and climate-change mitigation technologies. The right panels in Figure 3.2 display the share of patents in the respective technology among all patents of the country. These shares can be interpreted as an indicator for the specialisation of the innovation system. The results for ICT and climate change mitigation technologies are quite different, indicating technological strengths and weaknesses of the EU. For ICT, the EU patent output has stagnated since about 2003 at about 10,000 patents, while the US and China have continuously increased their patent output. In 2013, China outperformed the EU and in 2017 the US. This catching-up and overtaking by China is mirrored by the high degree of specialisation in ICT. The EU displays not only the lowest patent output in absolute numbers, but also the lowest degree of technological specialisation in ICT.

In climate change mitigation technologies, however, the EU has become more specialised over time, with approximately 15% of all patents in 2020 being in the realm of climate change mitigation technologies. The EU files more patents than the US and China, although China is catching up rapidly, and if current trends continue it might be a question of a few years until China closes the gap with the EU.

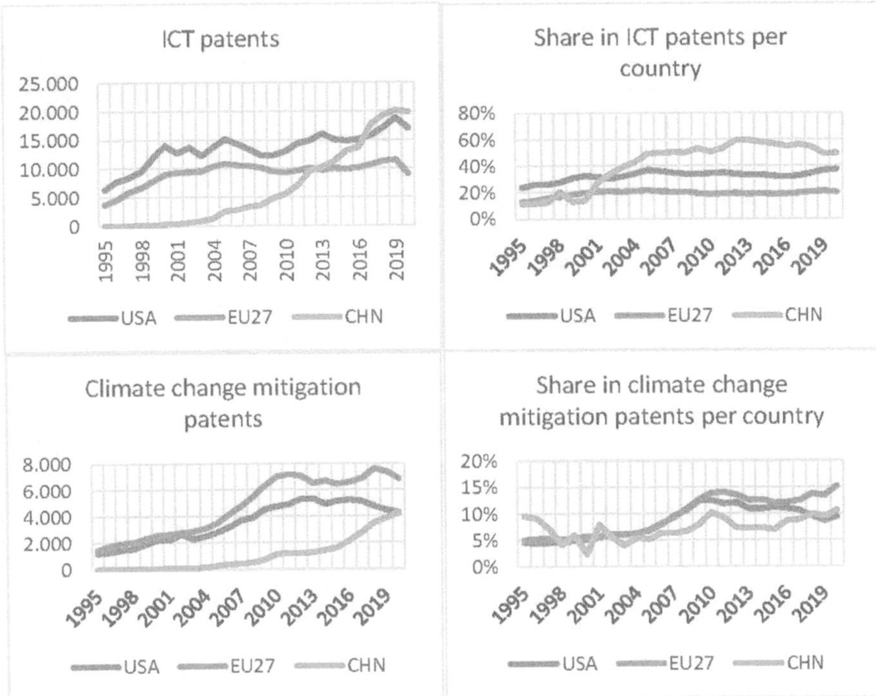

FIGURE 3.2 Patent filings in ICT and climate change mitigation technologies by country and as a share per country, 1995–2020, IP5

Source: Patents in OECD selected technologies.

In semiconductors and artificial intelligence (AI), two technologies which are at the core of debates on digital sovereignty, the EU clearly lags behind and the slower growth rate in AI-related patenting suggests that the EU might be in danger of being further pushed to the technological sideline (Figure 3.3). Semiconductors are an interesting example for the slowly but steady decline of EU involvement in digital technologies. Back in 1980, Philips was the fourth important company in the global semiconductor industry. In 2000, Philips was no longer counted among the top-10 companies, although STMicro, a Swiss-based company, ranked sixth. In 2020, however, no European company is part of the group of the 10 leading semiconductor firms (Bown and Wang, 2024).

For green technologies, the EU leads in energy generation and wind energy and is close to the frontier in battery development, at least in terms of patent output. Yet, in two out of four green technologies, the EU has already been overtaken by China and for energy generation it might happen in the not too distant future. Wind energy represents the only sector where the leading position of the EU in technological development is relatively uncontested. A peculiar aspect in

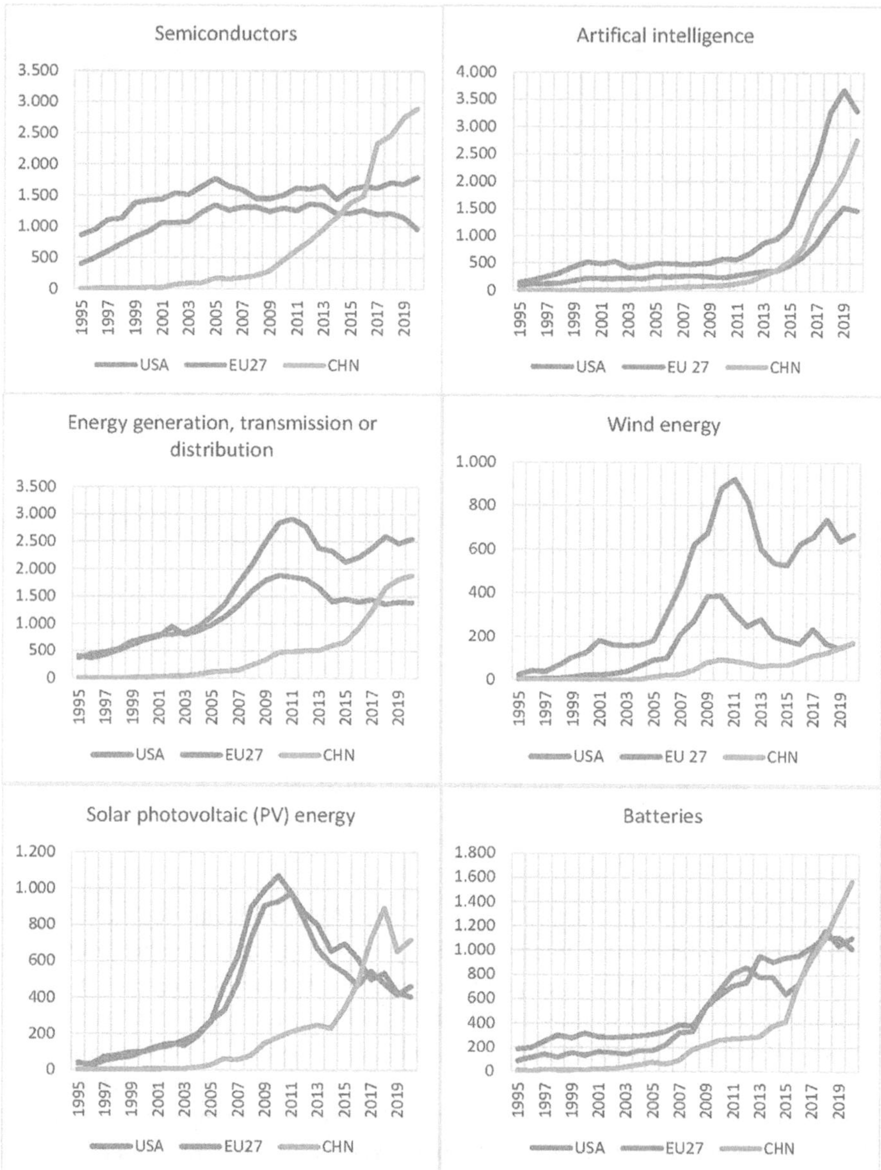

FIGURE 3.3 Patents filings in digital and green technologies, 1995–2020, IP5

Source: Patents in OECD selected technologies.

the development of green patents is the decline of patent output of the EU and the US for energy transition, wind and solar patents after 2010. Instead of ushering in a new era of green growth, the financial and economic crisis of 2008/2009 seems to have caused a break in the hitherto positive dynamics in green technologies. Yet, while the US continued its decline for energy transition and wind till 2020, the EU was able to resume positive growth rates in patenting around 2015. The most dramatic reshuffling occurred in solar photovoltaic, which was originally developed in the EU and in the US but is now dominated by China (Caravella *et al.*, 2024).

3.3.1.3 Production and trade

The relationship between technological capabilities – that is, the mastery of technologies – production capabilities and technological sovereignty is complex, and technology and product-specific. Cantner (2023: 33) points to the problem that '*the knowledge required to create, develop and use the goods and technologies concerned will probably not be built up to the required quality entirely without in-house production*'. Similarly, Guarascio *et al.* (2025: 131) doubt whether 'separating R&D from production represents a viable solution'. This resonates with the work by Pisano and Shih (2012), who argue that deindustrialisation will also erode the ability to innovate because the transformation of R&D into production is intricate and a potent source of tacit knowledge, which in turn is a basis for competitive advantage. Losing learning opportunities 'at the factory floor' will reduce the ability to develop new products and processes (Pisano and Shih, 2012). In addition, mastering technology is important, but what counts in the end is the availability of technology and the products in which the technology is embodied. Hence, production capabilities to manufacture technology-intensive products might be one important element in the strive for technological sovereignty.

Moreover, data on domestic value added suggest a continued decline in the EU's world market share in ICT manufacturing and ICT services industries (Figure 3.4). Declining value-added shares in fast-growing industries (such as ICT industries) signal a loss of competitiveness, though this does not translate one-to-one into growing dependencies. This is shown by the declining world market shares of the US. The main reason why value-added shares may be detached from technological capabilities, and by extension from dependencies, is that US and EU firms could own and control production abroad, that is, they have offshored parts of their production activities abroad. This is especially discernible in ICT manufacturing industries, where also the US has lost market share but managed to maintain its market position in ICT services industries, which is not the case in the EU. Moreover, irrespective of trends, there is a significant difference in market shares, with the US accounting for 38% of global value-added, compared to 20% in the EU.

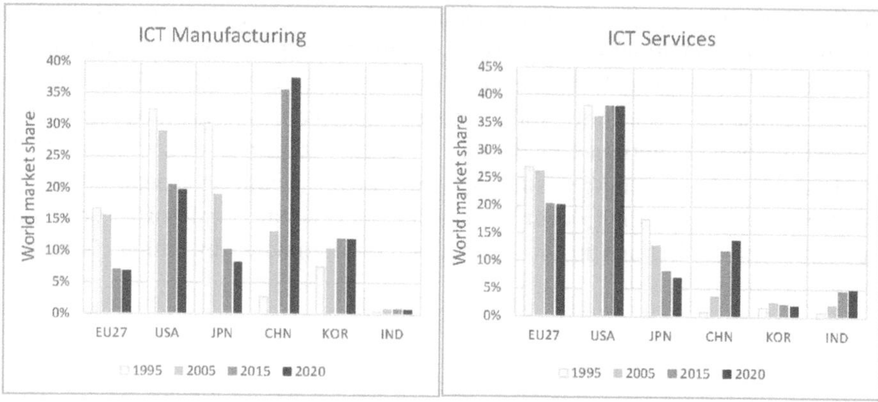

FIGURE 3.4 Comparison of world market shares in value added in ICT manufacturing and services, 1995–2020

Note: Due to data limitations, the world is comprised of the following countries: Australia (AU), Brazil (BR), Canada (CA), Switzerland (CH), China (CN), India (IN), Japan (JP), Korea (KR), Norway (NO), Russia (RU), Taiwan (TW), the United Kingdom (UK) and the United States (US).

Source: Predict database, authors' own calculations.

According to Figure 3.5, the concentration in manufacturing capacities for green technologies is higher than for ICT. A comparison with 2021 suggests that the dominance of China is growing rapidly in almost all green technologies (IEA, 2024). Despite higher output of the EU in terms of patents for wind energy, the EU clearly falls behind in manufacturing capacity, accounting for about 10–20% of output, depending on the considered component. China, meanwhile, produces between 50% and 60% of blades, nacelles and towers. The dominance of China in solar PV manufacturing and batteries is even more pronounced. Overall, the findings suggest an impressive and at the same time problematic global concentration of production capabilities for renewable energy capital goods.

A different insight is provided if we compare EU manufacturing output to EU deployment of the respective green technology. This gives a more accurate indication of dependencies because it shows the ability to serve domestic demand via domestic production (Sgaravatti *et al.*, 2023). Solar PV displays the lowest degree of self-sufficiency with EU manufacturers producing only between 3% (cells) and 22% (modules) of EU final demand. Regarding wind energy technology, EU firms produce on average more than is necessary for domestic use. EU production of batteries could account for about 40% of EU final demand. Yet, a value chain perspective indicates higher vulnerabilities to foreign supply disruptions because EU battery firms are highly dependent upon Chinese imports of cathodes and anodes (European Commission, 2025).

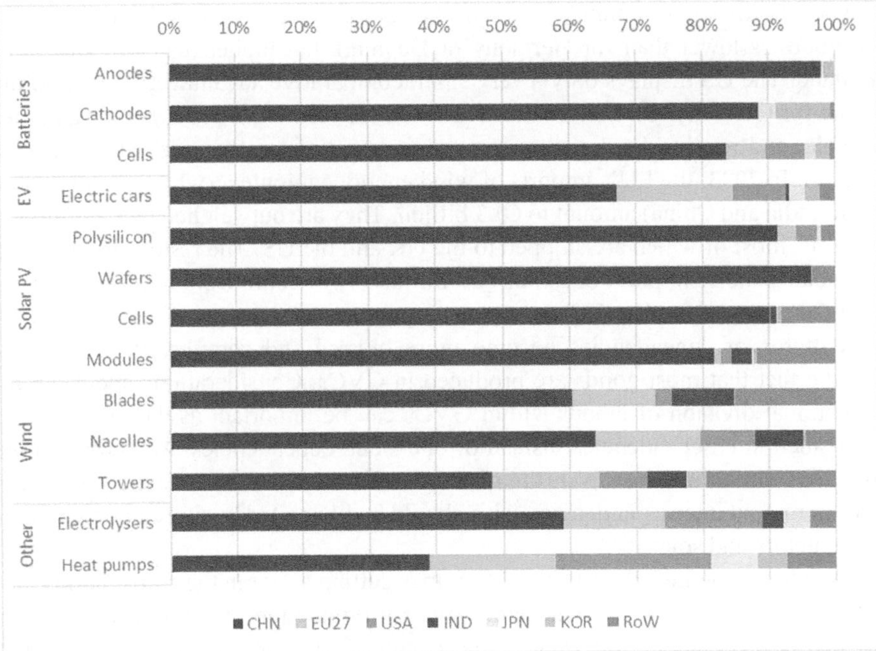

FIGURE 3.5 Installed manufacturing capacity by country/region, 2023

Source: IEA, Energy Technology Perspectives (2024).

Turning to the analysis of trade performance, we start by considering comparative advantages in digital and green technologies. This indicator measures the relative strength of a country in a technology by its revealed comparative advantage in the trade of the respective technology. Empirical analysis reveals that the EU does not possess a comparative advantage in any of the following six key digital technologies: big data, internet of things, artificial intelligence, digital security technologies, microelectronics and digital mobility technologies (German Commission of Experts for Research and Innovations, 2022). China, on the other hand, commands a comparative advantage in all of the six key digital technologies, while the US performs worse than China but better than the EU. In line with this finding, trade statistics in digital high-tech goods indicate that the EU has a persistent trade deficit of the size of 30%–70% as a percentage of imports between 2013 and 2023 (Eurostat, 2024a). Germany, traditionally admired for its prowess in export markets, has run a consistent trade deficit in the aforementioned six digital technologies since 2007 (German Commission of Experts for Research and Innovations, 2022).

Data by the IMF on trade performance in environmental goods[6] show that Germany, the Czech Republic, Denmark, Sweden, Italy, Poland, Austria and Finland have a comparative advantage, while Spain, France, the Netherlands and Ireland are at a disadvantage. China's value for the comparative advantage in environmental goods is lower than for Germany or Denmark but higher than for Austria or Finland. The US displays only a very small comparative advantage, far behind the value for Germany. On a more detailed level, the results for production capacities of solar and wind technology are somewhat corroborated by trade data (Eurostat, 2024a). In 2023, the EU's imports of wind energy equipment (which mainly come from India and China) amount to €0.3 billion. They are outweighed by €2 billion in exports, most of which are shipped to the UK and the US. The results are reversed for solar panels: Imports of about €20 billion (98% come from China) are more than 20 times larger than EU exports.

Patterns of dependencies become more blurred and complex if we account for the fact that most goods are produced in GVCs. Considerations about the international division of labour within GVCs can be important as they may reveal two-sided interdependencies instead of one-sided dependencies. According to the previous discussion, however, the question remains whether there are dependencies or mutual interdependencies. This should be illustrated by two examples: semiconductors and solar PV.

As often lamented, the EU has difficulties getting a foot in the chips market, accounting for just 10% of global semiconductor production. What is typically overlooked in this context, however, is that Dutch ASML and German Siemens EDA are dominant providers of critical inputs for the design and fabrication of chips. ASML, for example, holds a quasi-monopoly in producing lithography systems, which are machines that print patterns onto silicon wafers for the production of the most advanced microchips used for AI. Despite having these technology leaders in the semiconductor value chain, insufficient domestic production capacities and associated dependence on foreign suppliers such as Taiwan and the US have become a problem in the context of an increasingly hostile geopolitical environment. This is aggravated by the fact that import substitution by way of building up domestic capacity for chip production takes quite a long time and requires substantial upfront investment, with the cost of a new foundry amounting to some $20 billion (Bown and Wang, 2024).

Varying degrees of dependency are also emerging along the photovoltaic supply chain. As was mentioned before, China hosts about 90% of production capabilities in solar PV. Apart from the fact that the EU produces cutting-edge scientific publications in some technologically important fields related to solar PV (European Commission, 2025), the EU was able to expand its export shares in the upstream segment of the PV supply chain. While China clearly dominates the midstream and downstream segment, the upstream segment is controlled by the EU, the US and Japan, which have about equal export shares of 25%, much larger than that of China. Caravella *et al.* (2024: 5) interpret this as the '*consolidation of the EU as a supplier of key upstream goods*' in the photovoltaic supply chain. Unrefined silicon and machinery are two important exports of the EU to China in this upstream segment.

3.3.2 *Case study: the success of Galileo*

The insights gained from the previous section are supplemented with a case study of an ambitious high-tech project, which shows that the EU is capable of developing such projects. More specifically, we present a short history of the Galileo project, which was developed during the 1990s and decided upon in 2000 as part of the EU's EU Space Programme. By focusing on Galileo, we do not want to play down the deny the risks and challenges inherent in innovation-oriented industrial policy. Failures, such as the recent stop of Gaia-X, which was intended to build a European cloud solution, clearly show that the success of large-scale innovation and industrial policy endeavours is far from guaranteed. In fact, successful European industrial policy projects of such a scale are rare, which makes studying the feature of these success stories even more insightful.

Satellite positioning constitutes a key digital service incessantly used by private users and across industries. With Galileo, the EU – together with some external partner countries – has established one of the best performing global navigation satellite systems (GNSS). A GNSS consists of a series of satellites which are arranged in a certain constellation to ensure they can provide signals from space to locate objects on earth. Initiated as part of the EU Space Programme, Galileo became operational at the end of 2016 (European Commission, 2024b). While a late-runner compared to the US Global Positioning System (GPS), which as the first mover in this domain has also provided the name for the entire field, and also the Russian GLONASS system, Galileo was successfully established as one of the four GNSS systems which are currently operating. Overall, the Galileo project can be considered a great technological success and even an incidence of technological leapfrogging. The EU was a latecomer in setting up a GNSS system such that path dependencies and network externalities put it in a rather disadvantaged position compared to the incumbent systems, the US GPS and GLONASS. However, the Galileo system excels in terms of technological sophistication (Table 3.3).

The US strongly opposed the creation of a European navigation system arguing that it is economically non-viable as the costs of such a huge infrastructure project would by far outstrip the benefits, given that Europe could rely on GPS for such services (Breeman *et al.*, 2022; Hubert, 2022). In view of the current geopolitical situation, the decision to establish an autonomous European GNSS system[7] has paid off, even if the cost of developing and installing Galileo was substantial[8] at over €20 billion – a huge amount but in line with the expenditure on the Chinese BeiDou system estimated at $25 billion.[9] These numbers show that the expenditure on Galileo is, despite repeated budgetary overruns, not out of tune with comparable large scale investment projects in other countries. Overall, the EU, including member states outlays, however spends much less on the space sector than the US and China (Draghi, 2024).

Turning from costs to benefits, the Galileo system constitutes an essential piece of European infrastructure. There are both economic and security-related benefits.

TABLE 3.3 Comparison of global satellite navigation systems (GNSS)

Name of GNSS	*GPS*	*Galileo*	*GLONASS*	*BeiDou*
Country	USA	EU	Russia	China
Start of services	1993	2005	1993	2015
Launch of the first satellite	1978	2016	1982	2000
Number of active satellites	31	24	24	45
Controlling authority	Military	Civilian	Military	Military
Advantages	High reliability	Most precise, open and collaborative	Similar to GPS	Very precise (3 orbits); open and collaborative, size
Weaknesses	Not the most precise, old technology	Frequent malfunctions, complex governance structure, small size	Similar to GPS, timing based on Moscow War Clock Time	-

Note: Advantages and Weaknesses as assessed by authors based on available literature.
Source: Hubert (2022) and Breeman *et al.* (2022).

Among the economic benefits are improved positioning services to consumers in the EU but also commercial services generating income from the GNSS, as well as protected services to the government (European Commission, 2024b). The European Commission estimates that more than 2.5 billion devices (2021) were able to use Galileo services, giving them up to three times better accuracy when compared to alternative GNSS. Moreover, she estimates that Galileo will generate accumulated revenues of €166 billion from payable services until 2029.

The greatest benefit, however, may be that the EU made itself independent from the US and Russia. The welfare effects from the 'de-risking' implied by making satellite navigation services autonomous are impossible to quantify. Given the current state of geopolitical affairs, we would argue that the vital and diverse services provided by Galileo qualifies it as critical digital infrastructure. Any restrictions or disruptions in the positioning services of GPS and GNSS would be disastrous for the EU economy, but also for military intelligence and operations because modern weapon systems also rely on global positioning systems. This is all the more relevant as Galileo is the sole system which is under the control of a civilian authority (see Table 3.3). Given this and the fact that also services to military actors are provided by GNSS infrastructure services, which just like many modern digital technologies are dual use goods (Coveri *et al.*, 2025), underlines that technological dependencies have both an economic and a security dimension.

3.4 Summary and policy implications

This chapter has shown how the EU's technology gap vis-à-vis the US and China is widening. The last 20 years were characterised by a disruption of the prevailing global technological hierarchy: China is not only catching up but increasingly leap-frogging the EU and the US in digital and green technologies. This development is no longer restricted to production and trade but includes high-quality research output, long believed to be the domain of well-established universities in the US and Europe.

There is, however, a clear difference between the EU's technological dependencies in digital and clean technologies. Unambiguously, the EU has fallen behind in digital technologies and the gap to China and the US tends to widen even further. This holds primarily true for basic and applied research as well as for production and trade. While there are some European hidden champions which dominate niche positions in global supply chains, the overall picture is that European firms lose out in the race for AI, semiconductors and other digital technologies. For green technologies the results are more upbeat, especially with respect to scientific publications and patents in the domains wind energy and energy generation. While the EU is clearly lagging the US in digital technologies, available evidence indicates that it is outperforming the US in clean technologies. Having said this, analysis of production capacity for green technology goods such as batteries or solar PV indicates a strong concentration in China, which may pose a threat to the EU even if it continues to excel in basic and applied research in green technologies.

However, the EU's technological dependence is neither complete nor unresolvable. In contrast to digital technologies, the EU outperforms the US in green technologies and empirical evidence as well as recent political developments suggest that the EU's lead in this domain is likely to increase in the future. Moreover, the science base of the EU is intact, as evidenced by scientific publication records and government-financed R&D. Weaknesses are much more prevalent in the innovation performance of the business sector, especially in digital technologies and at the production stage of green technology goods. The term 'European paradox' has been used to refer to this mismatch between basic and applied research and development. Hence, transforming basic research results into commercial successes more effectively remains one of the challenges for catching up with the US and China in digital technologies (Veugelers, 2024). Using innovation-oriented public procurement and lowering barriers to entry for innovative start-ups are possible remedies.

The EU is well-advised to fill with life the open strategic autonomy it has propagated for some time and to strengthen it efforts in 'de-risking' GVCs via multi-sourcing strategies and strengthening domestic production capabilities as foreseen, for example, in the European Chips Act.

What is more, the Galileo case confirms that despite the identified technology gaps in digital technologies, the EU has a series of strong national innovations systems, including first-class universities, laboratories and other research bodies which enables it to excel in strategically important technology fields (see also Draghi, 2024; Veugelers, 2024). Moreover, it demonstrates that for large-scale infrastructure projects, the state is the central actor providing the funding for projects of that magnitude and high level of risk. Hence, the state has a particularly strong role to play for strengthening industrial capacities, including for defence and space, in the domain of digital infrastructures.

What is needed is mission-oriented innovation and industrial policy at the EU level that is targeting digital technologies of particular relevance for the EU's competitiveness and socio-technological transformation. The Galileo project serves as a case in point. Although it could be argued that the underlying 'intervention logics' (Pellegrin *et al.*, 2019) of such an approach is sector-specific, because it is targeting ICT/AI, such an argument is misleading because the support for ICT/AI is not the goal in itself. Instead, it is a means to respond to the societal challenge posed by the EU's eroding technological sovereignty. Policymakers should formulate mission-oriented policies (Mazzucato, 2013), that aim at zero non-competing imports of technology-intensive goods and services.[10] This does not rule out imports of high-tech products and services, but it requires the EU to be able to produce such products domestically and build capacity to supply them in case of international supply chain disruptions.

Renouncing the ideal of efficiency gains from specialisation and knowledge flows, such a radical shift in the organisation of production will require public investment and will be costly in the short-to-medium term. However, it would increase the EU's autonomy, crisis-resilience and political agency in an increasingly hostile geopolitical environment. In addition, public investment could be justified if EU production follows circular economy principles, thereby not only reducing dependencies on raw material imports but also delivering better outcomes for the environment.

Imperative for the aforementioned proposals is a governance structure that ensures that policies remain manageable and receive sufficient funding. Trivial as these points may seem, the lack of clear objectives and insufficient funding appear to be some of the main problems that haunts industrial policymaking at the EU level at the current juncture.

Notes

1 For a discussion of the origin of the discussion of strategic autonomy in the context of global supply chains among EU member states see Fabry and Veskoukis (2021).
2 Note that there is no consistent terminology in the literature. Cantner (2023), for example, uses the term 'one-sided structural dependency' and 'over-dependence', for what we label simply 'dependence'.
3 No data are available for Germany.
4 Data refer to the average of publications for the years 2017–2019.
5 OECD Bibliometric indicators by field.

6 Environmental goods include both goods connected to environmental protection – such as goods related to pollution management and resource management, and adapted goods, which are goods that have been specifically modified to be more 'environmentally friendly' or 'cleaner'. Most recent values are for 2021. See: https://climatedata.imf.org/datasets/8636ce866c8a404b8d9baeaffa2c6cb3_0/explore
7 While Galileo is an autonomous GNSS, it operates in tandem with the other systems to improve the quality of the positioning services.
8 See budgetary information on the EU space programme from the European Commission at: https://commission.europa.eu/strategy-and-policy/eu-budget/motion/focus/eu-budget-enables-independent-space-and-navigation-policy-europe_en.
9 See: https://www.techinasia.com/gps-rival-china-invests-810-million-build-beidou-products.
10 This refers to Category 3 type of non-competing imports in Gray (1986), which are goods that are unavailable in a certain country due to the lack of proprietary technology required for producing the good.

Bibliography

Bown, C. and Wang, D. (2024) Semiconductors and modern industrial policy. *Journal of Economic Perspectives*, 38(4), 81–110.

Breeman, M. P., Grillo, F., and van de Kaa, G. (2022) Battles in space: De-facto standardization of global navigation satellite systems. *Journal of Engineering and Technology Management*, 65, 1–12.

Bresnahan, T., and Trajtenberg, M. (1995) General purpose technologies: "Engines of growth"? *Journal of Econometrics*, 65(1), 83–108.

Cantner, U. (2023) Industrial policy and technological sovereignty. In S. Tagliapietra & R. Veugelers (Eds.), *Sparking Europe's new industrial revolution: A policy for net zero, growth and resilience* (Bruegel Blueprint 33, July). Bruegel.

Caravella, S., Crespi, F., Cucignatto, G., and Guarascio, D. (2024) Technological sovereignty and strategic dependencies: The case of the photovoltaic supply chain. *Journal of Cleaner Production, 434*, 14022.

Cohen, E. (1992) *Le colbertisme high-tech: Économie du grand projet*. Paris: Hachette Pluriel.

Cohen, W. M. and Levinthal, D. A. (1989) Innovation and learning: The two faces of R&D. *The Economic Journal*, 99(397), 569–596.

Commission of Experts for Research and Innovation (2022) *Report on research, innovation and technological performance in Germany*. Berlin.

Coveri, A., Cozza, C., and Guarascio, D. (2025) Big tech and the U.S. digital–military–industrial complex. *Intereconomics*, 60(2), 81–87.

Draghi, M. (2024) *The Draghi report: In-depth analysis and recommendations (Part B)*. Publications Office of the European Union.

Eaton, J., Gutierrez, E., and Kortum, S. (1998) European technology policy. *Economic Policy*, 13(27), 403–438.

Edler, J., Blind, K., Kroll, H., and Schubert, T. (2023) Technology sovereignty as an emerging frame for innovation policy: Defining rationales, ends and means. *Research Policy*, 52(6), 104765.

Edler, J. and Georghiou, L. (2007) Public procurement and innovation: Resurrecting the demand side. *Research Policy*, 36, 949–963.

European Commission (2020) *The European data strategy: Shaping Europe's digital future* (February). https://ec.europa.eu/commission/presscorner/api/files/attachment/862109/European_data_strategy_en.pdf (accessed 17 October 2025).

European Commission (2021) *Trade policy review: An open, sustainable and assertive trade policy*, (COM(2021) 66 final), Brussels, 18 February 2021.

European Commission (2024a) *The 2024 EU industrial R&D investment scoreboard*. Publications Office of the European Union.
European Commission (2024b) *Galileo: The European Union global navigation satellite system*. Brussels.
European Commission (2025) *Progress on competitiveness of clean energy technologies* (COM(2025) 74 final).
European Parliament (2021) *Key enabling technologies for Europe's technological sovereignty*. Brussels.
Eurostat (2024a) *International trade and production of high-tech products*. https://ec.europa.eu/eurostat/statistics-explained/index.php?title=International_trade_and_production_of_high-tech_products (accessed 17 October 2025).
Eurostat (2024b) *International trade in products related to green energy*. https://ec.europa.eu/eurostat/statistics-explained/index.php?title=International_trade_in_products_related_to_green_energy (accessed 17 October 2025).
Fabry, E. and Veskoukis, A. (2021) Strategic autonomy in post-COVID trade policy: How far should we politicize supply chains? *IAI Papers*, 21(33), 38–66.
Freeman, C. and Perez, C. (1988) Structural crisis of adjustment, business cycles and investment behaviour. In G. Dosi, C. Freeman, R. Nelson, G. Silverberg, & L. Soete (Eds.), *Technical change and economic theory* (pp. 38–66). Pinter Publishers.
Fuest, C., Gros, D., Mengel, P.-L., Presidente, G., and Tirole, J. (2024) *EU innovation policy: How to escape the middle technology trap*. https://iep.unibocconi.eu/sites/default/files/media/attach/2Report_EU%20Innovation%20Policy_upd_240514.pdf (accessed 17 October 2025).
García-Herrero, A., Grabbe, H., and Kaellenius, A. (2023) *De-risking and decarbonising: A green tech partnership to reduce reliance on China* (Policy Brief No. 16). Bruegel. https://www.bruegel.org/system/files/2023-10/PB%2019%202023.pdf (accessed 17 October 2025).
German Commission of Experts for Research and Development (EFI) (2022) *Report on research, innovation and technological performance in Germany 2022*. Berlin.
German Commission of Experts for Research and Development (EFI) (2024) *Report on research, innovation and technological performance in Germany 2024*. Berlin.
Gräbner, C., Heimberger, P., Kapeller, J., and Schütz, B. (2020) Is the Eurozone disintegrating? Macroeconomic divergence, structural polarisation, trade and fragility. *Cambridge Journal of Economics*, *44*(3), 647–669.
Gray, P. H. (1986) Non-competitive imports and gains from trade. *The International Trade Journal*, 1(2), 107–128.
Guarascio, D., Reljic, J., Cucignatto, G., and Simonazzi, A. (2025) Between Scylla and Charybdis: Long-term drivers of EU structural vulnerability. *Review of Keynesian Economics*, 13(1), 112–140.
Hubert, B. (2022, May 15) *How do GPS/Galileo really work & how the galmon.eu monitors all navigation satellites* [Project presentation]. https://www.youtube.com/watch?v=XjRHl2Rr9tQ (accessed 17 October 2025).
IEA (2024) *Energy Technology Perspectives 2024*.
Kaplinsky, R. (2019) Rents and inequality in global value chains. In S. Ponte, G. Gereffi, & G. Raj-Reichert (Eds.), *Handbook on global value chains* (pp. 153–168). Edward Elgar Publishing.
Kvangraven, I. H. (2021) Beyond the stereotype: Restating the relevance of the dependency research programme. *Development and Change*, 52(1), 76–112.
Landesmann, M. and Stöllinger, R. (2020) The European Union's industrial policy. In A. Oqubay, C. Cramer, H. J. Chang, & R. Kozul-Wright (Eds.), *The Oxford handbook of industrial policy* (pp. 621–660). Oxford University Press.
Landesmann, M. A. (2015) Ricardian and Schumpeterian rents: Fundamental ingredients for structural economic dynamics. In M. L. Baranzini, C. Rotondi, & R. Scazzieri (Eds.),

Resources, production and structural dynamics (pp. 186–197). Cambridge University Press.
Mazzucato, M. (2013) *The entrepreneurial state: Debunking public vs. private sector myths*. Anthem Press.
Mazzucato, M. (2018) *Mission-oriented research & innovation in the European Union: A problem-solving approach to fuel innovation-led growth*. Publications Office of the European Union. https://op.europa.eu/en/publication-detail/-/publication/5b2811d1-16be-11e8-9253-01aa75ed71a1/language-en (accessed 17 October 2025).
Pack, H. and Saggi, K. (2006) Is there a case for industrial policy? A critical survey. *World Bank Research Observer*, 21(2), 267–297.
Pellegrin, J., Colnot, L., Prota, F., Ardizzon, F., Delponte, L., Capriati, M., Olechnicka, A., Smith, C. (2019) *How to tackle challenges in a future-oriented EU industrial strategy?* Volume 1. European Parliament.
Pisano, G. and Shih, W. (2012) *Producing prosperity: Why America needs a manufacturing renaissance*. Harvard Business Review Press.
Reuveny, R. and Thompson, W. R. (2001) Leading sectors, lead economies, and economic growth. *Review of International Political Economy*, 8(4), 689–719.
Sgaravatti, G., Tagliapietra, S., and Trasi, C. (2023) Cleantech manufacturing: Where does Europe really stand? *Bruegel Analysis*. https://www.bruegel.org/analysis/cleantech-manufacturing-where-does-europe-really-stand-0 (accessed 17 October 2025).
Stöllinger, R., Foster-McGregor, N., Holzner, M., Landesmann, M., Pöschl, J., and Stehrer, R. (2013) *A "manufacturing imperative" in the EU: Europe's position in global manufacturing and the role of industrial policy* (wiiw Research Report No. 391).
Storm, S. (2019) Lost in deflation: Why Italy's woes are a warning to the whole Eurozone. *International Journal of Political Economy*, 48(3), 195–237.
U.S. National Science Foundation (2025) *Publication output by geography and scientific field*. https://ncses.nsf.gov/pubs/nsb20257/publication-output-by-geography-and-scientific-field# (accessed 4 March 2026).
Van Pottelsberghe de la Potterie, B. (2008) Europe's R&D: Missing the wrong targets? *Intereconomics*, 43(4), 220–225.
Van Veen, E. and Langenberg, R. (2022) Phoenix or Icarus? European strategic autonomy in light of Ukraine. *Clingendael CRU Policy Brief* (February).
Veugelers, R. (2024) An innovation-based industrial policy for the EU. *Intereconomics*, 59(5), 254–261.
Voelsen, D. (2019) 5G, Huawei und die Sicherheit unserer Kommunikationsnetze: Handlungsoptionen für die deutsche Politik. *SWP-Aktuell*, *5* (February).
Wallerstein, I. (1974/2011) *The modern world-system I: Capitalist agriculture and the origins of the European world-economy in the sixteenth century*. University of California Press.
Warwick, K. (2013) Beyond industrial policy: Emerging issues and new trends. *OECD Science, Technology and Industry Policy Papers*, *2*. OECD Publishing.
Xiao, J. and Boschma, R. (2023). The emergence of artificial intelligence in European regions: The role of a local ICT base. *Annals of Regional Science*, 71, 747–773.

PART II

Employment and Labour Market Challenges of the Twin Transformation

4

ON THE WAY TO NET-ZERO

How Progressive Industrial Policy Can Shape Employment Change

Béla Galgóczi

4.1 Introduction

The greening of the economy will continue to have a profound impact on employment and skills. Necessary policies to correct the resource-depleting production and consumption model established during the industrial revolution are having both qualitative and quantitative effects on the world of work. While millions of jobs are being created in the transition to a net-zero carbon economy, millions of jobs will also disappear. The jobs to be created are not necessarily in the vicinity of locations where jobs are being lost. New jobs might replace old jobs in sectors with different patterns of unionisation or collective bargaining coverage. This unprecedented wave of restructuring is intertwined with processes of technological change (digitalisation, automation, and the increasing role of artificial intelligence) and takes place in a new, more conflictual geopolitical context. All this will have unequal effects on many fronts, including skills, gender, age, economic activity, and region (IMF, 2021).

This chapter draws attention to the drivers of employment change in the green transformation. The employment dynamics of this major restructuring process are often viewed and analysed in isolation from other simultaneous economic, technological, and geopolitical trends, as evidenced in optimistic employment forecasts presented by many policymakers and observers.

It is often overlooked that the transition to the low (and zero) carbon economy is redefining comparative advantages. Combustion engine leadership offers no template for the era of electrification, while competencies in carbon-intensive steel production offers little employment security when it comes to green steel. Most of the concerns about possible employment losses are attributed to decarbonisation of industry (or of the entire economy). The more

DOI: 10.4324/9781003745563-7

important question, however, is how a lack of progress in decarbonisation may threaten jobs in a world where competitiveness in clean technologies will be more and more decisive. The talk has been about the fear of 'carbon leakage', where higher environmental and climate standards for industry in the European Union (EU) were thought to result in the relocation of carbon-intensive activities to other world regions. The stakes are higher when the lack of investment in green technologies may result in new low-carbon industrial jobs being created elsewhere.

While change is inevitable, what we see in recent history is that all changes and shocks tend to generate further inequalities. This is particularly true of the dominant model of the green transformation, which is based on the concept of green growth, is technology-driven and includes a key role for the market. Without addressing these inequalities, the existential threat of climate change cannot be averted, because changes might be blocked or slowed down by major social conflict.

This chapter looks at the employment effects of the green transformation in both quantitative and qualitative terms, taking account of the vulnerabilities and challenges of key low-carbon industrial sectors. Section 4.2 scrutinises the concept of 'green jobs', while Section 4.3 analyses forecasts on job creation and skill needs in the green economy. By presenting three case studies of European manufacturing sectors, Section 4.4 takes a broader view of the actual processes of employment change in the green transformation. Section 4.5 looks at the qualitative side (labour protection, job quality, etc.) of emerging green economy jobs, while Section 4.6 concludes with some policy recommendations.

4.2 The contested concept of 'green jobs'

The term 'green jobs' has become mainstream among trade unions, environmental NGOs, the ILO and policymakers. According to the United Nations Environment Programme (UNEP, 2018), green jobs are defined as 'positions in agriculture, manufacturing, R&D, administrative, and service activities aimed at substantially preserving or restoring environmental quality'. 'Green' has become a shorthand term to describe processes, products and services that relate to sustainability and the environment. The term 'green jobs' also serves a positive narrative of the green transformation that puts job creation into focus in an attempt to overcome the jobs versus environment rhetoric. The framing of 'green jobs' is linked to the green growth agenda, largely informed by technology-driven ecological modernisation, where capitalism is seen as compatible with environmental sustainability (Goods, 2014).

However, it is difficult to align the terminology with established statistical classifications, although various attempts had been made. With more or less success, studies and statistical approaches attempt to identify products and services that meet one of several criteria for a green economy.

An expert document by the European Commission (2021a) focuses on 'greening occupations' and identifies structural changes in the labour market that can be linked to the following processes:

- Job creation: new jobs emerge to reduce environmental pressures or increase resource efficiency, and as a result of the development of circular business models (e.g., job creation in renewable energy generation).
- Job substitution: new jobs emerge as a consequence of a shift in economic activity within or across sectors from resource-intensive activities to more circular activities. The automotive sector is one example illustrating this: jobs in combustion engine-related segments are disappearing, while jobs in software development and battery manufacturing are emerging.
- Job destruction: job losses occur with no direct replacement, usually in the sectors with significant adverse environmental effects (e.g., fossil fuel-based energy generation).
- Job redefinition: existing jobs change their day-to-day skillset, work methods, and profiles as part of the transition to a more effective and sustainable economy. The construction industry is a good example as the retrofitting of buildings and low-carbon construction technologies requires new skills-needs and work processes.

The 2024 OECD Employment Outlook (OECD, 2024) distinguishes between 'green-driven occupations' and 'greenhouse (GHG) gas intensive occupations'. The former category includes: (1) Occupations that emerge due to the green transformation and that did not exist before (e.g., Carbon Trading Analysts, or Wind Turbine Service Technicians); (2) green-enhanced skills occupations. These are occupations that are not new, but whose skills and tasks are changing due to the green transformation (e.g., plumbers who now specialise in installing heat pumps); and (3) green-increased demand occupations. These are existing occupations with increasing employment demand in a greening economy but not subject to major changes in performed tasks and worker requirements (e.g., bus drivers and health care workers).

The report stresses that while GHG-intensive occupations are those where most job losses are expected, they share similar skill requirements with other jobs, including green-driven occupations, suggesting that transitions out of these jobs are possible with targeted retraining. It also adds, however, that the move towards the emerging green-driven occupations is more challenging for workers in low-skilled positions than for the high-skilled, calling for urgent policy action to ensure that no one is left behind by the net-zero transition.

As regards estimates for the redistribution of jobs, the report finds that across the OECD more than a quarter of jobs are strongly impacted by the net-zero transition Of these, 20% of the OECD workforce is employed in green-driven occupations, also considering jobs that do not directly contribute to emission reductions but are likely to be in demand because they provide goods and services needed for green activities. Conversely, about 7% of total jobs are in GHG-intensive sectors and are facing shrinking labour market demand.

A more detailed look at the 20% of workers employed in green-driven occupations between 2015 and 2019 yields the following insights:

- About 46% are existing occupations whose skill set is being altered because of the green transformation (referred to here as 'green-enhanced skills occupations').
- About 40% are existing jobs that will be in demand because they provide goods and services required by green activities (referred to here as 'green increased demand occupations').
- Only 14% are what can properly be described as 'green new or emerging occupations'.

4.3 Forecasts on green job creation and skills needs

4.3.1 Forecasts on job creation

The European Commission usually forecasts how the green transformation will be a win-win game with an overall net-positive employment effect. According to these projections (e.g., European Commission, 2021b), the green transformation is expected to have a moderately positive impact on total jobs in the EU. The Commission has simulated the potential employment impact of policies that would deliver a 55% reduction in GHG emissions by 2030 compared to 1990 levels. The simulation used three economic model scenarios with different labour market assumptions. The results projected a net increase in jobs of up to 884,000 or +0.45% by 2030, compared to a business-as-usual scenario.

Ernst and Young (2021) carried out a sectoral analysis of investment projects under the NextGenerationEU Recovery Fund devoted to the green economy (covering energy, transport, buildings, industry, and land use). The study found that these projects together represent an aggregate investment of €200 billion and could create 2.3 million jobs.

Cedefop (2021) estimated that the implementation of the European Green Deal would create an additional 2.5 million jobs (more than +1%) by the year 2030, not only in sectors driving the green transition, but also in administration and support, legal, accounting and consulting services, computer programming, and information services.

With the announcement of the Green Deal Industrial Plan (European Commission, 2023), the Commission's factsheet included the following:

> The green transformation could create up to 1 million additional jobs in the EU by 2030. For example: in 2021 the solar energy sector added 100,000 jobs,

bringing the total to 460,000 jobs. By 2030, solar energy employment could reach 1 million jobs. In the battery sector: approximately 800,000 workers will need to be trained, upskilled, or reskilled by 2025 to meet the demand of this sector for new workers – a staggering 160,000 workers to be trained every year.

The main shortcoming of such forecasts is that they are target-based, assuming that the policy objectives (e.g., 2030 climate policy targets) are being met and that these are also met on the basis of EU manufacturing capacity. These projections do not account for industrial, trade, and investment policy repercussions and regard developments in isolation from the rest of the world.

4.3.2 Labour shortages and skills gaps

Firms in the clean energy sector are starting to report shortages of both workers and sector-specific skills as a result of growth in demand. Trends in online job advertisements indicate that clean energy sectors have some of the highest job vacancy rates (IEA, 2024). Most of the jobs in clean energy are in labour-intensive construction and manufacturing, and these two segments of the value chain account for much of the forecast growth in energy employment up to 2030 in all IEA scenarios. Many clean energy projects are highly reliant on construction workers for building power plants and installing solar panels, yet labour markets are already facing shortages of construction workers and other related professions such as electricians, carpenters, concrete workers, welders, and pipefitters. An analysis by the European Labour Authority (ELA, 2023) revealed that the EU is facing particularly severe shortages in several occupations, including bricklayers, carpenters, machine tool operators, and electricians.

Providing the right regulatory framework for skills development is an important factor in enhancing the competitiveness of a net-zero industry and in addressing labour shortages. Among adopted policies to tackle skills shortages, the EU has provided financial and organisational support for some clean energy industries, including batteries, heat pumps, and wind. While targets are being set, these lack proper monitoring and the required conditionalities on implementing training programmes financed by public resources. As part of the European Skills Agenda (European Commission, 2020), the ambitious target was set to upskill and reskill 120 million adults over the period between 2020 and 2025, with skills partnerships being created to identify how to train new workers. Furthermore, the European Commission launched the European Year of Skills in 2023 to address skills shortages across the continent. The initiative was designed to empower people and companies, especially SMEs, by promoting the reskilling and upskilling of the workers needed to facilitate the green and digital transitions and accelerate innovation and competitiveness. The Green Deal Industrial Plan intends to scale-up the EU's manufacturing capacity for net-zero technologies through various industrial policies. One pillar of these policies centres on reskilling and upskilling strategic industries by establishing dedicated programmes such as the Net-Zero Industry Academies.

In the United States, the Inflation Reduction Act of 2022 mandated that firms seeking tax credits must hire apprentices from registered apprenticeship programmes for at least 15% of the work, support unionisation and the payment of fair wages and must be set-up in deprived or former fossil-heavy regions. No such conditionalities exist in the EU, even though including them in EU public procurement, state aid and investment support programmes is a central trade union demand (ETUC and IndustriAll, 2023; ETUC, 2024).

Poor job quality is also a barrier to skills development, since employers are often unwilling to invest in training employees who are on fixed-term contracts or in agency work arrangements. Often, workers in jobs with only weak or no collective agreements do not have the backing which a sound collective agreement on skills development would supply (ILO, 2019). There is also a need to create new certifications and curricula to reflect emerging skill requirements, especially for new industries like carbon capture, use and storage (CCUS) and low-emission hydrogen. Wherever there is a skills shortage in the range of industries which constitute the clean energy sector, this will hinder competitiveness, since it will hamper innovation, which is a key factor in the sector's ability not only to deliver emission targets but also to gain access to sources of international investment.

4.4 Fragmented evidence on 'green jobs'

Instead of struggling to define what 'green jobs' are, it is more promising to look at the ways how the green transformation (decarbonisation) affects the labour market.

The optimistic forecasts referred to in the previous section were mostly based on the assumption that the huge investments necessary to achieve decarbonisation targets will actually be made and would create European jobs. This might also suggest that the evolving transformation would be smooth and create a win-win situation for all.

Even with all studies projecting a moderate but clear net positive employment effect at the aggregate economy level, differences by regions and sectors can be enormous. There are broadly three main categories of sectors: those where operations will significantly be reduced (fossil energy), those that have to undergo a profound change (e.g., the automotive sector) and those with the biggest potential for job creation (e.g., sectors included in the circular economy).

4.4.1 Employment trends in key green economy segments

As is shown below, while jobs have indeed been created, the rate of job creation in the green economy is muted and uneven. What is more, jobs in key clean technology sectors have been falling in the period between 2017 and 2022. One report on renewable energy jobs revealed that in 2023, there were 16.2 million jobs in the sector globally. The EU had 1.8 million renewable energy jobs in 2023 (Irena, 2024)

Data put together by Bruegel (Jugé *et al.*, 2025) provides a more detailed but still fragmented picture. Accordingly, as of 2022, there were 347,000 jobs in solar energy at the EU27 level, 273,500 in wind and 416,200 in heat pumps (a total of just over 1 million). These jobs were concentrated in the 10 Member States that make up around 80% of total EU jobs in the sector. No net job creation appeared in the last decade in these sectors (Jugé *et al.*, 2025). It is also important to note that Germany, Italy, and Denmark saw job losses in the respective sectors between 2017 and 2022. Based on the Bruegel database, employment in the German wind energy sector had fallen from 140,800 in 2017 to 86,600 by 2022. Over the same period, it fell from 34,200 to 22,400 in Denmark, while it remained at around 37,000 in Spain. Italy, the leader in heat pump employment with 85,000 jobs in 2022 had lost 6,000 jobs by that year, while Spain saw a loss of jobs in heat pump employment from 68,000 in 2018 to 32,000 by 2022. In Portugal, the number fell from 80,000 in 2019 to 25,000 by 2022.

Employment data in the German wind and solar industries (where more detailed data are available for a longer period),[1] illustrates the volatility of employment in these key sectors. Figure 4.1 reveals major employment swings between 2011 and

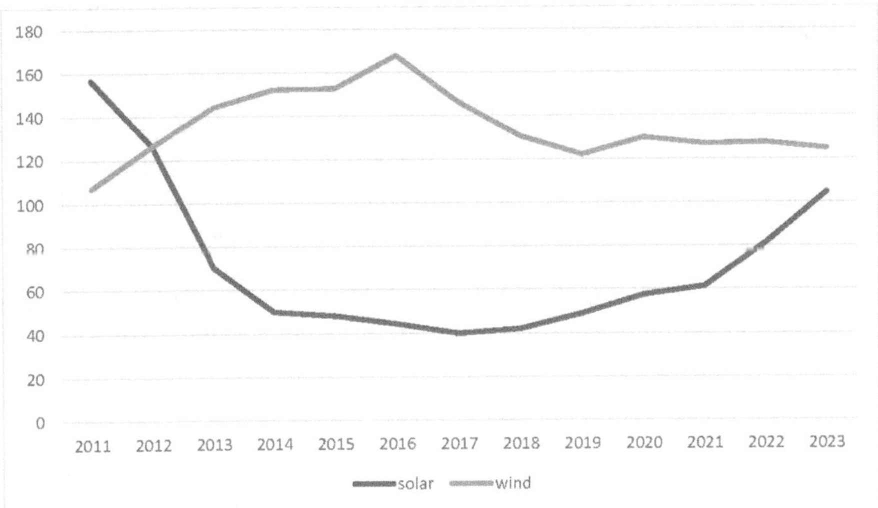

FIGURE 4.1 The development of solar and wind (onshore and offshore) jobs in Germany (in thousands)

Source: German Federal Ministry for Economy (2024).

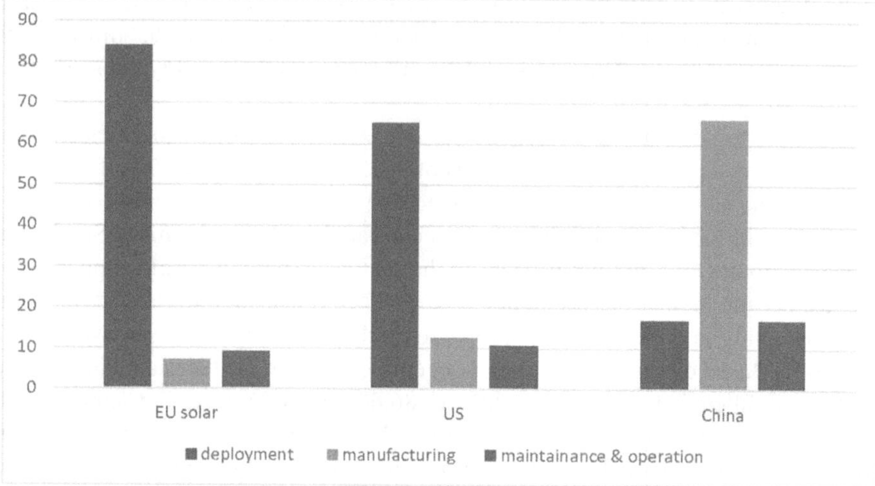

FIGURE 4.2 Distribution of employment by type of activity in the solar sector (in %)
Source: Jugé *et al.* (2025).

2023, with significant overall losses in German solar jobs and a minor increase in wind jobs. These losses and fluctuations point to challenges in terms of both the investment activity that determines the rate of deployment (the demand side for manufacturing) and the market share of European manufacturers in satisfying this demand.

Slow and volatile job creation in key clean manufacturing segments indicates that Europe's transition to net-zero emissions is suboptimal from the perspective of its contribution to employment. Figure 4.2 illustrates what challenges the EU clean industry sector might face. The different characteristics of job distribution within the solar sector between the EU and China reveal that while in China two thirds of solar jobs are in manufacturing, a mere 7% of solar jobs are manufacturing jobs and 84% are in deployment in the EU. In other words, the majority of workers in the European solar sector are installing Chinese solar panels on European roofs. Amid the collapse of the EU solar panel manufacturing sector, this should be seen as a model case scenario that should be avoided in other clean industry segments.

Renewables employment and the creation of clean tech manufacturing capacities depend on the deployment of renewable energy and the related investments, as Figure 4.3 suggests. Whereas installed photovoltaic capacity in the EU tripled between 2015 and 2023, in China it grew 14-fold and was more than 50% higher than the EU and the US combined in 2023.

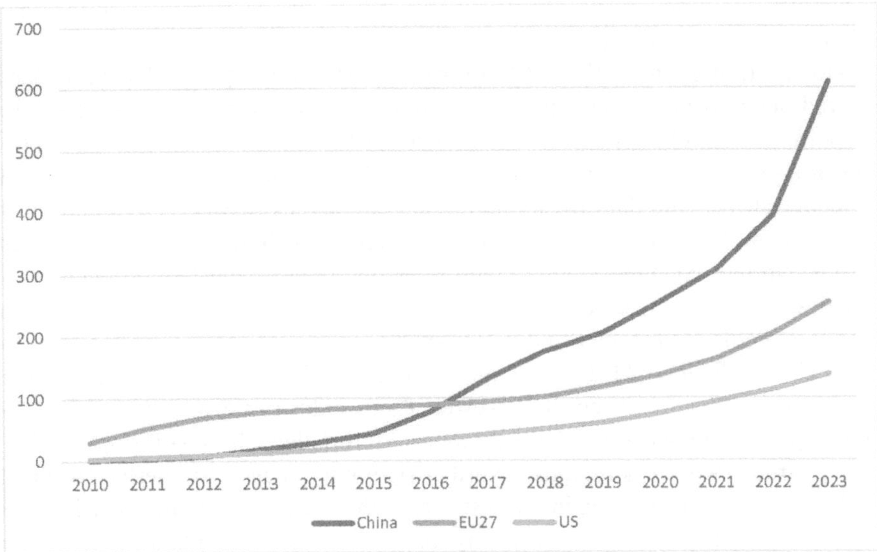

FIGURE 4.3 Installed photovoltaic capacity (2010–2023, GW)

Source: Irena (2024) and Jugé *et al.* (2025).

4.4.2 Case studies

This section takes a look at segments of clean industry manufacturing that are critical for the success of the green transformation. Three case studies allow for deeper insights into challenges and controversial trends that these sectors are facing.

4.4.2.1 Wind industry boom and bust in Bremerhaven

For what the initial green economy boom meant for a structurally weak region, the case of Bremerhaven with the revival of its abandoned service port presents an illustrative example.

The northern German port city of Bremerhaven is a typical case of former shipbuilding centres that have been in crisis for decades. While one in five jobs was lost between 1995 and 2005, with a first wave of wind industry investments a small ecosystem around the offshore wind industry was established by the mid-2000s. With REPower Systems, PowerBlades, WeserWind, and Areva Wind, numerous major players had settled around the former shipyard. Rotor blades, nacelles, foundation structures and offshore transformer stations were manufactured in Bremerhaven at this time. Big research institutions were established, such as the Fraunhofer Institute for Wind Energy and Energy System Technology. The city was also planning the largest base port for offshore wind farms in the world. Thanks to policy incentives and a new wave of investments, 4,000 jobs were created in the early 2010s (Boewe and Schulten, 2023).

However, from the mid-2010s onwards, wind industry developments have slowed down as numerous large wind turbine manufacturers and suppliers withdrew from the market. Industry giants such as REPower (Senvion from 2014) had to cease production completely. Enercon, the largest German wind turbine manufacturer at the time, laid off around 3,000 employees between 2018 and 2021. Several manufacturers relocated production abroad, such as global market leaders Vestas, Nordex, Siemens Gamesa, and Enercon. They established production capacities in countries with lower labour costs and in growth markets such as China, Brazil, or India (Eurofound, n.d.). Nordex relocated rotor blade production from Rostock to India in 2022. The new plant was planned to produce twice as much as the factory in Rostock. According to estimates by industry experts, around 20–30% of companies and operations have disappeared from the value chain since 2017.

For structurally weak regions in northern Germany such as Bremerhaven, which had experienced an upswing in the past decade thanks to wind energy, this development has been fatal. There is hardly anything left of the former wind energy cluster today: with PowerBlades, REPower, and WeserWind, almost all wind turbine and component manufacturers have ceased operations in recent years. The base port for offshore wind farms project has also been terminated. Several factors – a combination of policy failures, market developments and a court judgement – led to this unfortunate outcome. In the early 2010s, it had taken too long for the then federal government to mobilise support for off-shore wind energy developments. The subsequent market down-turn in the industry in the mid-2010s resulted in the suspension of further investment plans for several years. When demand for off-shore wind projects saw a revival by the end of the decade, a court decision blocked the plans for a port extension. It was already too late for Bremerhaven to act from 2022, when off-shore wind became a government priority in wake of Russia's invasion of Ukraine, as nearby ports in the Netherlands, Denmark, and in the German city of Cuxhaven moved faster (Exner and Preuss, 2024).

4.4.2.1.1 The European automotive industry

With a share of nearly 6% of total European employment (equivalent to 13.8 million jobs), the broad automotive sector is a key employer in the EU. It is widely acknowledged that replacing the internal combustion engine with an electric one will require less labour input (Bauer *et al.*, 2020). Changes will take place on a massive scale: up to three million jobs will be fundamentally transformed in terms of skills and competences (BCG, 2021). Decarbonisation and digitalisation will reshape international automotive value chains, posing great uncertainty for the future economic viability of locations across Europe and through global value chains.

The particular challenge for the automotive industry is that besides decarbonisation, digitalisation of both the product and the process, automation of production and the complete reorganisation of automotive value chains are also underway. This paradigm change also means that established incumbent positions are challenged. Newcomers such as Tesla have been able to enter the market in a way that was previously hard to imagine. Chinese brands including BYD, SAIC, and NIO have made significant advances in EU electric car sales. The assumption shared by many industry experts such as, e.g., by the Boston Consulting Group (BCG, 2021) that in the transition to electromobility, apart from changing the engine, 'all other factors remain constant', did not materialise. The main challenge the industry now faces is loss of market share in an overall shrinking market, with significant consequences for employment.

The growth trend in battery electric vehicle (BEV) sales since 2020 was broken in spring 2024 with consecutive double digit drops in the following quarters (ACEA, 2024a). The share of fully electric BEVs, which grew continuously until the end of 2023 to reach a 14.7% share of new car sales, started to fall in 2024 to 12.7% followed by an upswing in the first half of 2025 to reach 17.4% of total European new car sales.

A further concern in Europe, linked also to the discussion on industrial policy, is that China's share in the European electric car market is rapidly increasing. Figure 4.4 shows the share of BEVs made in China in total EU BEV sales between 2020 and 2024 (ACEA, 2024b). This includes western brands such as Tesla, Dacia and Mini that are manufactured in China and exported to Europe, as well as Chinese brands including BYD, SAIC (MG) and Polestar. In 2020, 2.9%

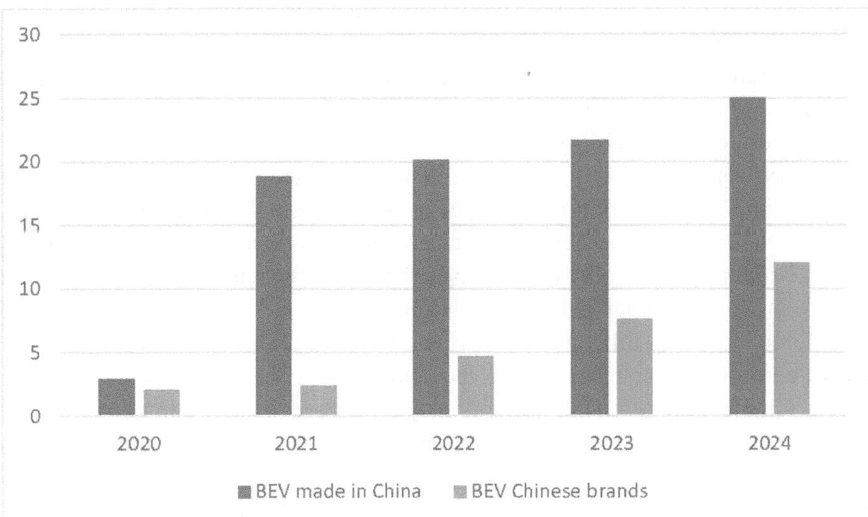

FIGURE 4.4 The share of BEVs made in China in total EU27 BEV sales (2020–2024)

Source: For 2020–2023: ACEA (2024b); for 2024: projection by Transport & Environment (2024).

of BEVs sold in Europe were made in China (2% having been Chinese brands), whereas in 2023 they made up 21.7% (7.6% Chinese brands). A projection by the NGO Transport & Environment (2024) reckoned that in 2024, all China-manufactured BEVs would have reached a quarter of EU27 BEV sales, with the Chinese brands attaining 12%.

Data for the first half of 2025 reveals that new car sales in Europe by Chinese brands have increased by 91% when compared to the same period of 2024, while sales by BYD grew by 311% (JATO, 2025).

This trend also results from the choice of European carmakers to focus their business strategies on premium market segments, abandoning the production of smaller, more affordable entry-level electric cars. If the European automotive industry cannot produce affordable clean cars, this also poses a threat to high-quality jobs in European automotive manufacturing.

Developments in 2024 unfortunately showed that this scenario was not hypothetical. The announcement of Audi management that it would stop the production of its electric car, the Q8 e-tron sports utility vehicle (SUV) puts the future of its Brussels plant and 3,000 quality jobs at risk (De Kerchove Dexaerde, 2024). At the same time, Volkswagen continues to struggle with the transition to electromobility. In an unprecedented move in September 2024, management announced that it was considering two plant closures in Germany, putting aside the employment guarantees contained in its Pact for Future that stood as an example of co-determination and responsible just transition practices. It was about to scrap two crucial model launches: one (a compact SUV) that was seen as the saviour of the Wolfsburg plant; the other being the Trinity model in Zwickau, East Germany, which was seen as a pioneering model with advanced autonomous drive functions (Jolly, 2024).

These trends illustrate that electromobility (with its lower labour demand) as such is less of a threat to EU jobs, than the ability of EU manufacturers to keep up with delivering clean mobility solutions.

From November 2024, the EU has introduced protective countervailing duties on BEVs imported from China. A major question is whether and how the EU automotive industry will be able to benefit from this protective measure. Holding on to the old business model of building ever bigger, heavier and more expensive cars (even if often under hybrid or plug-in hybrid cover) would be a huge failure. Moreover, doing this under the protective umbrella of tariffs would also not benefit consumers while threatening the achievement of road transport emissions targets. Giving up or watering down already binding legislative commitments, like the 2035 exit from the combustion engine, would be the worst option not only for the climate, but also for the medium- and longer-term future of European automotive jobs. Tariffs on electric cars from China will not solve the problems of the EU automotive sector. Instead, the industry needs to reinvent itself, again. The sector will, moreover, be a test case both for the EU's industrial policy awakening and a laboratory for just transition policies and practices.

4.4.2.2 *Northvolt – the failure of Europe's battery hopeful*

Battery manufacturing is a key segment of the electromobility value chain. The Swedish company Northvolt, a homegrown champion capable of competing with Asian giants, was supposed to be Europe's great battery success story. Northvolt was claimed to be able to capture 25% of Europe's battery market by 2030.

In March 2025, however, Northvolt filed for bankruptcy, after months of job cuts, restructuring, and several failed attempts to raise capital (Wikner *et al.*, 2025). The case was a bitter experience, putting Europe's ambitions in lithium-ion battery manufacturing at risk. Ardent competition (in particular from Asia), overspending, the lack of venture capital and state support were seen as the most important factors for the firm's bankruptcy. While a US battery start-up, Lyten has bought out the remaining assets of Northvolt from the bankruptcy, including the manufacturing site in Skellefteå, this does not mean that all previous operations of the former battery hopeful are saved (Connolly, 2025).

The failure of Northvolt does not mean that the fight for a strong European battery ecosystem is over. At the time when Northvolt failed to meet its targets and lost major clients, Chinese battery firms made several deals with European car manufacturers, such as Gotion's partnership with Volkswagen and CATL's joint venture with Stellantis to build a €4.1 billion lithium battery factory in Spain (Meunier and Ponsa Sala, 2025).

Asian battery manufacturers have been steadily expanding their reach into European start-ups, too. Gotion acquired a 25% stake in Slovakia's InoBat in 2023. Founded in 2019, the battery start-up has raised $400 million to date, with Gotion as a major backer. For European start-ups, the appeal of partnering with East Asian battery producers looks attractive, with the latter possessing the technology, scale, and supply chain efficiency that Europe often lacks. According to experts and industry representatives, the EU faces two options: collaborate with Asia's industry giants (Financial Times, 2024), or build a stronghold in the next frontier of battery technology (IEA, 2025).

The dependence on Chinese companies also comes with risks and vulnerabilities, such as possible trade disputes, geopolitical tensions, or sudden export restrictions. Europe should not become an assembly location for Asian battery manufacturers. While partnerships might be unavoidable, industrial policies need to apply proper conditionalities, including technology transfer and local content criteria, as well as labour and environmental standards.

Europe can build an end-to-end value chain for batteries, as batteries are vital components of clean manufacturing technologies. Towards these ends, Europe will need to invest both by mobilising private capital, including venture capital, and through significant public funding.

These case studies illustrate that in order for the green transformation to bring beneficial employment effects, a coherent combination of industrial policies is necessary that fosters innovation, mobilises private and public capital, and leverages supporting trade policy measures.

4.5 The quality of manufacturing jobs in clean technologies

A *just* green transformation requires quality jobs, which is also essential for sustainable competitiveness. This section looks at the qualitative aspects of new jobs in a greening economy. Recent trends and future forecasts make it clear that carbon-intensive sunset industries will shrink (with significant job losses), while low-carbon sunrise industries will offer increasing levels of employment. There is a broad consensus in the literature that decarbonisation might be neutral for total employment or might (even have a slight job creation effect), albeit with huge differences between regions, ages, skills and genders (European Commission, 2022b; Alija and Tatry, 2024). Besides the huge challenge of the transition, it also appears that, even with a neutral employment effect at total economy level, job quality in the transition is tending to deteriorate.

With the caveat that publicly accessible and comparable data are not available, some evidence about the different characteristics of traditional industry jobs and emerging clean industry jobs will be presented below.

Jobs that are expected to be more deeply affected by the green transformation, on the grounds that they are found in more polluting sectors, are generally characterised by having relatively good conditions, with an above-average likelihood of being covered by a collective agreement as well as above-average union density and access to worker representation (Zwysen, 2024). An IG Metall (2024a) survey on wind industry jobs in Germany conducted among works councils in the sector found that only 27.3% of plants were covered by collective bargaining in 2020, with 18.3% covered at the sectoral level, 9% covered at the firm level, and 63.6% had no coverage at all. By 2023, the situation had improved somewhat as coverage at the sectoral level had increased to 25% and at the firm level to 25%, with 50% of plants in the sector still left without coverage. Individual company examples also underline the challenges that workers and trade unions face in emerging sectors involved in the manufacture of clean technologies. Two Danish wind turbine manufacturers, Vestas and Oersted, refused to implement a collective agreement with the German union IG Metall. Protest actions at Vestas are ongoing, while at Oersted, after 15 months of negotiations and a series of warning strikes in 2024, IG Metall managed to establish the first collective agreement in the German offshore wind sector (IG Metall, 2024b). The refusal of Tesla to conclude a collective agreement in Sweden followed by a wide range of solidarity strikes across Europe has been an emblematic case (Bender, 2024).

A recent study by the Somo Institute (Merk *et al.*, 2024) provides an insight into the bleak reality of battery jobs in Hungary, one of the key locations for the EU's emerging battery manufacturing sector. Details of the wage structure and highly flexible working-time schedules reveal high pressures put on workers. Hungary's battery industry also exposes workers to significant health and safety hazards. Between January 2019 and June 2023, Samsung SDI received

57 penalties from the Hungarian authorities for violating fire safety and hazardous material regulations and putting workers' safety at risk. At SK On's Komárom facility, 50 workers were exposed to elevated levels of nickel, a known carcinogen, with some showing nickel concentration levels in their organs three times higher than EU safety thresholds. The operations of the South Korean-owned SungEel Hitech battery recycling firm in Hungary have also been marred by safety violations and fines. In 2023, a grinder explosion at the plant resulted in two worker fatalities.

Moreover, the global battery supply chain is largely controlled by corporations with headquarters in China (CATL and BYD) and South Korea (LGES and Samsung SDI), countries that are known to obstruct unionisation and collective bargaining rights (Merk *et al.*, 2024). Labour standards in battery factories under Chinese ownership are strongly influenced by standards in the low-wage electronics sector, where worker representation and trade unions are characteristically weak. South Korea's Samsung is notorious for its anti-union stance both domestically and internationally, and (according to reports) has obstructed workers' rights at its factory in Göd, Hungary.

Considering this anecdotal evidence, whereas jobs in the shrinking carbon-intensive industries were characterised by higher pay, regulated working time, open-ended regular contracts, relatively high coverage by collective agreements and higher unionisation, many newly created green jobs are of inferior quality in these aspects. It took labour movements a century to fight for labour rights and a secure and decent quality of jobs in the traditional industries. These struggles should not have to be fought again from scratch in the newly emerging green industries, including in solar energy, wind turbines, or battery manufacturing. States must be hold accountable to safeguard job quality in emerging green sectors in Europe's social market economies, since this will not arise by chance or as a result of the operation of the market forces.

4.6 Conclusions

This chapter looked at the main trends and drivers of employment change and job quality in the EU's green transformation. The 'green jobs approach' was briefly discussed with the conclusion that the concept does a poor job when analysing the employment dynamics of this major restructuring process. First, because a green/brown job dichotomy perspective is an oversimplification that does not have an equivalent in statistical classifications. Second, this approach also puts the green transformation in isolation from other economic, technological, and geopolitical trends that take place simultaneously.

There are broadly three types of employment change in the context of the green transformation. Fossil fuel-based energy generation and related activities will be phased out and these jobs – in their present form – will disappear. This makes up a small share of European jobs. Existing industries go through deep decarbonisation while a new clean technology-based manufacturing landscape emerges. These two segments – energy intensive industries on the one hand and clean industry on the other – are deeply intertwined and cannot be separated. The challenge is that as the world does not have a co-ordinated and co-operative decarbonisation approach, those countries and regions that follow a more ambitious path – like the EU – face higher initial costs and suffer a temporary loss of competitiveness. This phenomenon was labelled as carbon leakage and can partially be addressed by creating a level playing field. This is what the EU's carbon border adjustment mechanism (CBAM) aims at. But this is not enough.

This chapter also looked at the main trends of employment change in the decarbonisation process. First, it was shown that employment forecasts about the job creation effect of climate policies are often too optimistic, as these are mostly target based, supposing that the necessary investments would indeed follow and then the delivery will happen on the basis of existing European capacities. In reality, job creation in key clean manufacturing segments of the European economy is slow and volatile, indicating that Europe's transition to net-zero emissions is suboptimal from the perspective of its contribution to employment. It was also shown that the quality of jobs created in the green economy is often inferior when compared to incumbent carbon-intensive sectors.

Thus, a major lessons is that it is not decarbonisation itself that poses a risk to European industrial jobs, but how Europe is able to tap the job creation potential of the green economy. It is no question that workers who lose their jobs in carbon-intensive sectors need sufficient support, both in passive and active forms with skills development equally important. But labour market policy is not sufficient – necessary investments need to be mobilised and industrial and trade policy measures are also key as demonstrated by the case studies from the European automotive and battery industry. The main shortcoming is that the narrative – both in the media and the policy arena – is one-sidedly focused on possible job losses in decarbonising sectors. Industrial and employment policies are currently focused on 'damage control to fend off some of the negative employment effects of decarbonisation in shrinking carbon-intensive sectors. The current policy focus on 'competitiveness' ends up targeting (and subsidising) industrial energy prices. The much bigger part of the employment change, the creation of European quality jobs in a zero carbon economy is being neglected, even if often talked about in numerous policy declarations.

In order to manage the technological transformation of these industries and generate competitive advantages in the mid and longer term, more comprehensive industrial policies are needed. The focus should not be on costs only (either of energy or labour) but also on competences, manufacturing capacity and market share. The upscaled deployment of renewables and energy infrastructure is creating demand for clean technology manufacturing. Both the demand and the supply side of the energy transition need to be developed at the same time, while making sure that as much of this demand as possible is covered by European supply. Massive investment is necessary to achieve these objectives, including public, private, and venture capital investment. The gap between annual current investments and the need to achieve the EU's own 2030 climate policy targets runs in the hundreds of billions of Euros.

Unfortunately, the ambition that appears in the latest industrial policy proposals by the European Commission is not backed by mobilising the necessary resources. The proposal for the EU 2028–2034 multiannual financial framework (MFF) put forward by the European Commission (2025) clearly demonstrates this. Funds for the climate transition and industrial decarbonisation under the European Competitiveness Fund (ECF) are extremely low. The ECF only allocates €67 billion for the climate transition and industrial decarbonisation over a seven-year period, €40 billion of which is to come from the already existing Innovation Fund. This is clearly not enough to bridge the investment gap, but it rightly focuses on strategic activities. Public funding needs for transport cleantech manufacturing alone require €39 billion annually by 2030. Transport & Environment (2025) found that in the battery industry alone, up to 100,000 new jobs that could be created by 2030 are at risk with this proposal.

The central question is how Europe is able to tap the job creation potential of the green economy. If the build-up of new jobs in clean industries happens too slowly and the transformation becomes more protracted and chaotic, international competitors may acquire larger market shares in critical clean industry segments, which in the long-term would cost more jobs. Given the lack of such determined industrial policies, the affected industries resort to calls for reducing the pace of transition (e.g., with respect to the 2035 phase-out of combustion engines, Brussels Watch, 2025), or ease the financial burden (e.g., subsidies for electric energy in Germany, Politico, 2025).

There is no one-size-fits-all just transition policy. A targeted and integrated transformation policy is needed that includes labour market policies, provides social protection to cover transformation risks and secures the necessary investments within a combination of sensible industrial and trade policies. These would include the following main points.

- Industrial, trade, employment and social policies are all relevant in achieving a balanced and fair green transformation. These need to be properly coordinated in a volatile and complex international environment.
- Industrial policies need to mobilise investment (public, private and venture capital) with a focus on innovation and strategic projects of European common interest. Trade policy might help if targeted and temporary, and thus not shielding incumbents from competition, but buying time to catch up. European content and technology transfer criteria should be included.
- Any public funding or procurement needs to be completed by conditionalities in terms of labour and environmental standards.

- Boosting competitiveness cannot be based upon deregulation or putting downward pressure on wages and working conditions. It is also vital that workers have the right to contribute to managing this change with strengthened collective bargaining and stronger information-consultation practices.

Note

1 The difference in the absolute numbers for Germany between the Bruegel database and the German Ministry for Economics and Climate is due to the fact that the former refers to direct jobs, while the latter to direct and indirect jobs (that also includes supporting jobs, as e.g., administration and management).

References

ACEA (2024a) New car registrations. https://www.acea.auto/pc-registrations/new-car-registrations-18-3-in-august-2024-bev-market-share-down-by-almost-one-third/ (accessed 9 July 2025).

ACEA (2024b) ACEA fact sheet 'EU-China vehicle trade'. https://www.acea.auto/files/ACEA_fact_sheet_EU_China_vehicle_trade_June_2024.pdf (accessed 9 July 2025).

Alija, N. and Tatry, L. (2024) Finding a path for younger generations to the energy sector, *European Sustainable Energy Week News Blog*, 04.04.2024, European Commission.

Bauer, W., Riedel, O. and Herrmann, F. (2020) Beschäftigung 2030: Auswirkungen von Elektromobilität und Digitalisierung auf die Qualität und Quantität der Beschäftigung bei Volkswagen, Fraunhofer-Institut für Arbeitswirtschaft und Organisation IAO.

BCG (2021) *Is e-mobility a green boost for European automotive jobs?* Boston Consulting Group, https://web-assets.bcg.com/82/0a/17e745504e46b5981b74fadba825/is-e-mobility-a-green-boost.pdf (accessed 9 July 2025).

Bender (2024) One year on, we know this: Sweden's trade unions are more than a match for Elon Musk. German Bender. *The Guardian*. https://www.theguardian.com/commentisfree/2024/nov/01/one-year-on-we-know-this-swedens-trade-unions-are-more-than-a-match-for-elon-musk (accessed 3 July 2025).

Boewe, J. and Schulten, J. (2023) Mit Rückenwind in die Flaute. In: *Berliner Zeitung*, 01.07.2023. https://netzwerkrecherche.org/wp-content/uploads/2016/03/Boewe_Schulten_BZ.pdf (accessed 9 July 2025).

Brussels Watch (2025) Green groups urge EU to keep 2035 combustion engine ban, Warn Job Losses. https://brusselswatch.org/green-groups-urge-eu-to-keep-2035-combustion-engine-ban-warn-job-losses/ (accessed 9 July 2025).

Cedefop (2021) *The green employment and skills transformation – Insights from a European Green Deal skills forecast scenario. The green employment and skills transformation | CEDEFOP* (accessed 3 July 2025).

Connolly, P. (2025) *Decision: Lyten's purchase of Northvolt approved.* Norran. https://www.norran.se/english/engelska/artikel/decision-lytens-purchase-of-northvolt-approved/jo86ezql (accessed 9 July 2025).

De Kerchove Dexaerde, Y. (2024) *Audi Brussels plant risks closure as car model ceases production after 2025*. Euronews. https://www.euronews.com/business/2024/09/06/audi-brussels-plant-risks-closure-as-car-model-ceases-production-after-2025 (accessed 9 July 2025).

ELA (2023) *Report on labour shortages and surpluses 2022*. Publications Office of the European Union. https://doi.org/10.2883/50704

Ernst and Young (2021) *A clean COVID-19 recovery: The global opportunity*. https://europeanclimate.org/wp-content/uploads/2021/07/final-report-a-clean-covid-19-recovery-the-global-opportunity.pdf (accessed 9 July 2025).
ETUC (2024) Industrial policy for quality jobs – Social conditionalities for social progress. https://www.etuc.org/en/document/industrial-policy-quality-jobs-social-conditionalities-social-progress (accessed 26 June 2025).
ETUC and IndustriAll (2023) ETUC and IndustriAll letter discussion on competitiveness in the framework of the Green Deal Industrial Plan. https://www.etuc.org/en/document/etuc-and-industriall-letter-discussion-competitiveness-framework-green-deal-industrial (accessed 26 June 2025).
Eurofound (n.d.) Restructuring events – European restructuring monitor (ERM). https://apps.eurofound.europa.eu/restructuring-events/detail/106684 (accessed 26 June 2025).
European Commission (2020) European skills agenda. https://employment-social-affairs.ec.europa.eu/policies-and-activities/skills-and-qualifications/european-skills-agenda_en (accessed 26 June 2025).
European Commission (2021a) Greening of the labour market – Impacts for the public employment services. https://op.europa.eu/en/publication-detail/-/publication/a5ce471b-f0dd-11eb-a71c-01aa75ed71a1/language-en (accessed 26 June 2025).
European Commission (2021b) *The future of jobs is green*. Joint Research Centre. https://op.europa.eu/en/publication-detail/-/publication/e3b6064a-4830-11ec-91ac-01aa75ed71a1 (accessed 26 June 2025).
European Commission (2022b) *In focus: Employment in EU's renewable energy sector*. https://commission.europa.eu/news/focus-employment-eus-renewable-energy-sector-2022-05-16_en (accessed 26 June 2025).
European Commission (2023) Green deal industrial plan – Plugging the skills gap. https://year-of-skills.europa.eu/document/download/66dd95df-21b1-44f4-98c3-95af6add-bdd8_en?filename=Skills4Green_factsheet_EN_07022024.pdf (accessed 26 June 2025).
European Commission (2025) The 2028–2034 EU budget for a stronger Europe. https://commission.europa.eu/strategy-and-policy/eu-budget/long-term-eu-budget/eu-budget-2028-2034_en (accessed 26 June 2025).
Exner U. and Preuss O. (2024) „Energiewende ist eine zeitkritische Sache" – Bremens Traum vom Windkraft-Hafen – *WELT*. https://www.welt.de/politik/deutschland/article252148388/Energiewende-ist-eine-zeitkritische-Sache-Bremens-Traum-vom-Windkraft-Hafen.html#:~:text=Der%20Bremer%20Senat%20will%20ein%20Energiewende-Terminal%20bauen.%20In,auf%20Klimaschutz%20fokussierte%20Ampel-Bundesregierung%20bremst%20bei%20dem%20Riesenprojekt (accessed 9 July 2025).
Financial Times (2024) The Northvolt dilemma: Can European EVs avoid relying on Asian batteries? https://www.ft.com/content/8b2a586e-a774-4f9e-9f1b-473691afcaae (accessed 26 June 2025).
German Federal Ministry for Economy (2024) Beschäftigung durch eneuerbare Energien. https://www.bundeswirtschaftsministerium.de/Redaktion/DE/Downloads/E/ee-beschaeftigte-2000-2023.pdf?__blob=publicationFile&v=6 (accessed 26 June 2025).
Goods, C. (2014) *Greening auto jobs: A critical analysis of the green job solution*. Lexington Books.
IEA (2024) *Electricity 2024: Analysis and forecast to 2026*. International Energy Agency. https://www.iea.org/reports/electricity-2024 (accessed 26 June 2025).
IEA (2025) The battery industry has entered a new phase. https://www.iea.org/commentaries/the-battery-industry-has-entered-a-new-phase (accessed 26 June 2025).
IG Metall (2024a) Umfrage unter den Betriebsräten der Windindustrie ausgewählte Ergebnisse der Umfrage im Jahr 2023. https://kueste.igmetall.de/download/2024_09_20_Betriebsraete-Umfrage_Windindustrie_1.pdf (accessed 26 June 2025).
IG Metall (2024b) Ørsted: erster Tarifvertrag für Offshore-Windkraft, 15.04.2024.

ILO (2019, December) Skills for a greener future: challenges and enabling factors to achieve a just transition. *Skills for Employment Policy Brief.*

IMF (2021) Linking climate and inequality. https://www.imf.org/en/Publications/fandd/issues/2021/09/climate-change-and-inequality-guivarch-mejean-taconet (accessed 26 June 2025).

Irena (2024) Renewable energy and jobs – Annual review 2024. International Renewable Energy Agency. https://www.irena.org/Publications/2024/Oct/Renewable-energy-and-jobs-Annual-review-2024 (accessed 26 June 2025).

JATO (2025) Chinese car brands continue their ascent, outselling Mercedes in June and Ford in H1. https://www.jato.com/resources/media-and-press-releases/chinese-car-brands-continue-their-ascent-outselling-mercedes-in-june-and-ford-in-h1 (accessed 26 June 2025).

Jolly, J. (2024) Volkswagen considers German plant closures to save billions in costs. https://www.theguardian.com/business/article/2024/sep/02/volkswagen-vw-germany-plant-closures-cars-electric-vehicles (accessed 26 June 2025).

Jugé M. *et al.* (2025) *European clean tech tracker*. Bruegel. https://www.bruegel.org/dataset/european-clean-tech-tracker

Merk, J., Gonzalez, A. and Cirfusz, M. (2024) Electric dreams, hard realities. What the battery boom means for workers in Hungary? https://www.somo.nl/electric-dreams-hard-realities/ (accessed 19 June 2025).

Meunier, N and Ponsa Sala, C. (2025) A study on Asian electromobility investments in the EU. https://www.transportenvironment.org/uploads/files/2025_01_31_Report-Study-on-Asian-electromobility-investments-1-1.pdf (accessed 19 June 2025).

OECD (2024) OECD Employment Outlook 2024: The net-zero transition and the labour market. https://www.oecd.org/en/publications/oecd-employment-outlook-2024_ac8b3538-en.html (accessed 26 June 2025).

Politico (2025) Germany's energy plans to win EU endorsement as commission unveils new subsidy rules. https://www.politico.eu/article/germany-energy-eu-endorsement-commission-new-subsidy-rules/ (accessed 26 June 2025).

Transport & Environment (2024) To raise or not to raise: how Europe can use tariffs as part of an industrial strategy. *Briefing*, 27.03.2024. https://www.transportenvironment.org/uploads/files/2024_03_TE_EV_tariffs_paper.pdf (accessed 19 June 2025).

Transport & Environment (2025) Europe's automotive industry at a crossroads. https://www.transportenvironment.org/articles/europes-automotive-industry-at-a-crossroads (accessed 19 June 2025).

UNEP (2018) Green jobs: Towards sustainable work in a low-carbon world. https://www.unep.org/resources/report/green-jobs-towards-sustainable-work-low-carbon-world (accessed 26 June 2025).

Wikner, A., Connelly, P. and Lindqist, M. (2025) *Carlsson breaks silence: "It has been terrible living with this"*. Norran. https://www.norran.se/english/skelleftea/artikel/carlsson-breaks-silence-it-has-been-terrible-living-with-this/lqmz4w1r (accessed 26 June 2025).

Zwysen, W. (2024) Green transition and job quality: risks for worker representation. *Technical brief*, 2024.02, ETUI.

5

POLICIES FOR THE GREEN TRANSFORMATION IN EUROPE

The Just Transition Fund in Action

Valeria Cirillo, Marialuisa Divella, Eustachio Ferrulli, and Lidia Greco

5.1 Introduction

The transition to a climate-neutral economy represents one of the most significant policy challenges that the European Union (EU) faces in the 21st century. Among the key instruments designed to support this transformation is the Just Transition Mechanism (JTM), a cornerstone of the European Green Deal, designed to sustain the regions and communities most affected by negative consequences of the shift away from fossil fuels and carbon-intensive industries. The Just Transition Fund (JTF), as the main financial instrument of the JTM, aims to ensure that the benefits and costs of the green transition are distributed fairly across territories, leaving no region behind and strengthening social cohesion throughout the Union.

The JTF marks a significant departure from traditional industrial and cohesion policies in Europe. It can be understood as a form of "third-generation" industrial policy – explicitly focused on reconciling social inclusion, environmental sustainability and structural economic transformation. Whereas earlier industrial policies primarily emphasised competitiveness, technological progress, or market failure correction, the JTF adds a social dimension to avoid that the transition occurs in a socially disruptive manner. It explicitly acknowledges the socio-economic disruptions inherent in the green transition and emphasises the need for proactive measures to support affected communities, thereby safeguarding social cohesion and democratic legitimacy. From its inception, the JTF has been conceived as a fundamentally *territorial policy*: the regions targeted by JTF face substantial job losses and require a fundamental redesign of their development trajectories. In this context, the formulation of effective labour market policies is essential.

Indeed, meeting climate targets entails not only expanding green industries but also transitioning workers and technologies away from environmentally harmful

DOI: 10.4324/9781003745563-8

activities (Hafele *et al.*, 2023). This demands a restructuring of industrial ecosystems (Andreoni, 2022), and carries significant social costs. Governments are therefore called to anticipate sector-specific transition impacts and proactively manage the phase-out of "non-future-fit" sectors, that is, emission-intensive industries with limited long-term viability (Hafele *et al.*, 2023), to avoid cases of harmful deindustrialisation, particularly in regions still reliant on such industries (Feltrin *et al.*, 2022).

Transformation studies advocate for the "active" downsizing of polluting industries while ensuring a just transition for workers (Heyen, 2017). This challenge is intensified in the areas where such industries dominate the economic structure, making structural shifts more difficult due to path dependence (Arthur, 1989, 1990; Malmberg and Maskell, 2002). The phasing out of polluting industries risks severely impacting regional economies, which is why the EU emphasises community involvement in line with ILO principles and the Paris Agreement. Stakeholder engagement, participatory planning, and fostering a shared understanding are essential to mitigate social backlash, although though difficult to implement.

While broad consensus exists on the importance of addressing the social consequences of the transition, especially in the labour market, agreement is more limited regarding how to generate new employment. Evolutionary economic geography (Boschma *et al.*, 2015) and transition studies (Bergek *et al.*, 2008; Geels, 2002; Rip and Kemp, 1998) stress the importance of regional diversification, particularly in areas dependent on unsustainable industries. These approaches argue for developing *related* activities that leverage existing regional capabilities, thus reducing the uncertainty associated with structural change.

Moreover, the mission-oriented industrial policy approach (Mazzucato *et al.*, 2020) highlights the limitations of the private sector in driving transformative change and calls for a proactive role of the state as an "entrepreneurial agent." From this perspective, large-scale, complex "megaprojects" are needed to catalyse systemic transitions (Andreoni *et al.*, 2022). Furthermore, transition strategies must address the political economy of change, considering the power and influence of incumbent industries (Scoones *et al.*, 2015). Understanding these dynamics is key to identifying viable transition pathways (Brauers and Oei, 2020).

Beyond debates on the various approaches to green industrial policy, upskilling and reskilling are widely acknowledged as essential components of a socially just transition. These include vocational training, apprenticeships, and continuing education, tailored to local labour market needs and focused on sectors, such as renewable energy, digital technologies, and sustainable manufacturing. Effective implementation requires collaboration among regional authorities, educational institutions, businesses, and trade unions. This is not an easy task to achieve. The overarching objective is to develop a resilient, adaptable workforce capable of contributing to the green economy in line with the goals of the European Green Deal.

Given this background, this chapter explores the design and state of implementation of the JTF in selected territories of three EU member States – Italy, Spain, and Germany – each characterised by distinct industrial legacies, socio-economic structures, and regional vulnerabilities. By integrating desk research with qualitative analysis, such as semi-structured interviews with key informants,[1] we analyse national programmes and specific territorial cases to understand how the JTF addresses the complex interplay between the ecological transformation, labour market impacts, and social justice. Particular attention is paid to the criteria and mechanisms for regional selection, the role of participatory governance in policy design, and the effectiveness of specific interventions – especially active labour market policies (ALMPs) – in supporting workers and communities throughout the transition process.[2]

The JTF offers a distinctive case for analysis, as it represents a clear departure from traditional industrial and cohesion policies in Europe. It introduces an approach that is explicitly socially inclusive, grounded in the fundamental assumption that the green transition will inevitably create "losers," and that addressing their needs is essential to maintaining social cohesion and democratic legitimacy. An additional aspect sets the JTF apart: this is its strong territorial focus, often targeting sub-regional units. Funding is distributed upon the presentation of Territorial Just Transition Plans (TJTPs), formulated by national and regional authorities in consultation with local stakeholders. These plans are expected to redefine the economic, social, and environmental profile of each region, identify vulnerable sectors, and propose coherent strategies for generating new opportunities. As such, the JTF embodies a *place-based approach* that fosters development, participatory governance, and institutional coordination. Nevertheless, there is a risk that the Fund may evolve into a fragmented and technocratic tool, disconnected from the actual needs and aspirations of local communities.

The remainder of the chapter is structured as follows. The next section provides an overview of the JTF's objectives, eligibility criteria, and allocation mechanisms at the European level. The subsequent section presents detailed case studies of Italy, Spain, and Germany, three countries that illustrate diverse approaches to implementing just transition strategies, followed by a section that further analyses and compares the cases. The penultimate section identifies the main challenges and lessons learned from these national experiences, and offers policy recommendations to improve the effectiveness, inclusiveness, and territorial coherence of just transition policies across Europe. The final section offers critical reflections on the future of the JTF in the context of Europe's evolving policy priorities.

5.2 The EU Just Transition Fund framework

The JTM is one of the tools implemented within the framework of the European Green Deal to finance the EU's 2030 climate target and the EU climate neutral economy by 2050, as established in 2019.[3] It is made up of three pillars (Figure 5.1),

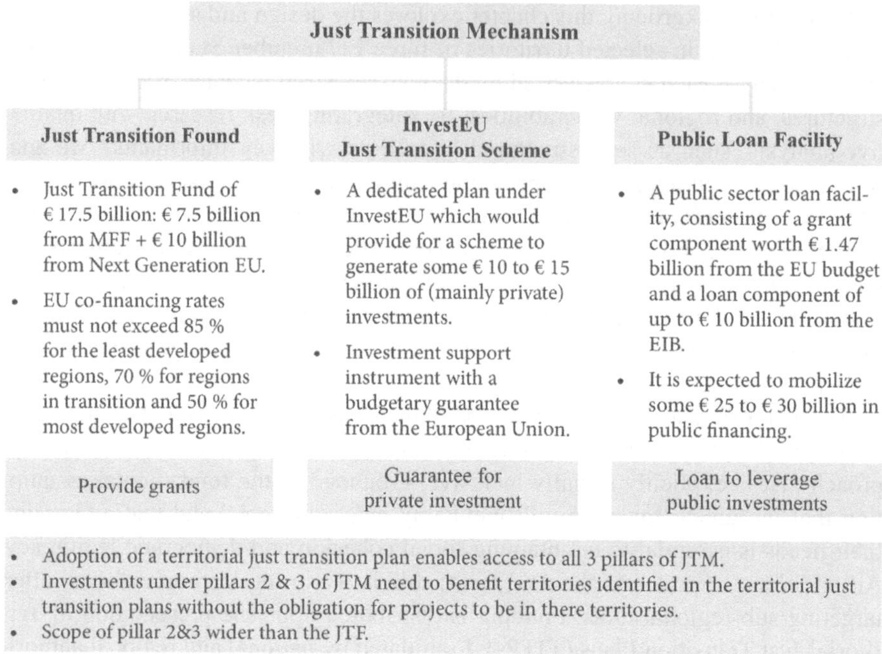

FIGURE 5.1 The scheme of the Just Transition Mechanism

Source: Own adaptation from IndustriALL European Trade Union (2021).

among which there is the JTF, entrusted with more than €17 billion, for the programming period 2021–2027.

The main goal of the JTF is to support policy interventions aimed at mitigating the negative economic and social consequences linked to the shift to green production systems, particularly the negative impact on employment, ensuring that no individual or region is left behind. The fund is thus directed to promote local economic diversification, by fostering new business opportunities and facilitating the upskilling and reskilling of workers affected by the decline of high-carbon sectors and activities.

Access to JTF funding requires Member States to develop "Territorial Just Transition Plans" (TJTPs) aligned with their National Energy and Climate Plans (NECPs) for 2030. These plans are intended to identify the regions and sectors most affected by the green transition. Eligibility criteria for NUTS-3 regions to access the JTF support during the 2021–2027 programming period refer to (a) a significant regional dependence on fossil fuels – such as coal, lignite, peat, oil shale, heavy oil, or diesel – or on greenhouse gas (GHG)-intensive industrial activities; and (b) expected substantial economic and social impacts resulting from the transition to a climate-neutral economy, particularly in terms of job losses and structural changes related to the dismantling of high GHG-emitting industries. Special consideration is given to islands and outermost regions due to their distinct energy transition challenges.

The TJTPs enable regions to allocate JTF resources across a wide range of activities. These include support for SMEs, microenterprises, and start-ups; research and innovation led by universities and public institutions; renewable energy and energy efficiency projects; smart and sustainable local mobility; modernisation of district heating networks; and digital innovation. The fund also finances circular economy initiatives – such as waste prevention and recycling alongside workforce upskilling and reskilling, job search assistance, active inclusion programmes, and investments in social infrastructure, including training centres and care facilities for children and the elderly.

As for the three countries observed in this study (Table 5.1), Italy has received over €1 billion to promote economic diversification and green job creation in Taranto (Apulia) and Sulcis-Iglesiente (Sardinia). Slightly less than €900 millions been allocated to Spain to assist areas affected by the closure of coal mines and power plants, including Asturias, Galicia, Castilla y León, Aragon, Andalucía, and the Balearic Islands. Germany has received almost €2.5 billion to support six key coal-dependent regions, namely, the Lausitzer Revier, Rheinisches Revier, Northern Ruhr area, Mitteldeutsches Revier, and Chemnitz, in their transition to renewable energy industries and broader economic transformation towards climate neutrality.

Focusing explicitly on ALMPs (Figure 5.2), a notable variation in the allocation of JTF resources can be observed. The Mitteldeutsches Revier dedicates nearly 30% of its funding to such initiatives, reflecting a strong emphasis on workforce adaptation. In contrast, some Spanish regions, particularly Córdoba, Cádiz, and Almería,

TABLE 5.1 The allocations of the JTF funding (millions of €) in Italy, Spain, and Germany

Country	*Total JTF funding*	*Of which EU contribution*	*Territories*
Italy	€ 1,211	€ 1,030	Taranto (Puglia), Sulcis Iglesiente (Sardinia)
Spain	€ 1,255	€ 869	Asturias (Asturias), A Coruña (Galicia), León and Palencia (Castilla y León), Teruel (Aragon), Cádiz, Córdoba and Almería (Andalucia), Alcudia (Islas Baleares, Mallorca)
Germany	€ 4,044	€ 2,478	Lausitz Revier (Brandeburg and Saxony) and Schwedt/Oder in Uckermark (Brandeburg); Rhenish district and Northern Ruhr (North Rhine-Westphalia); Mitteldeutsches Revier (Saxony and Saxony-Anhalt) and the city of Chemnitz (Saxony)

Source: Italian, Spanish, and German National JTPs.

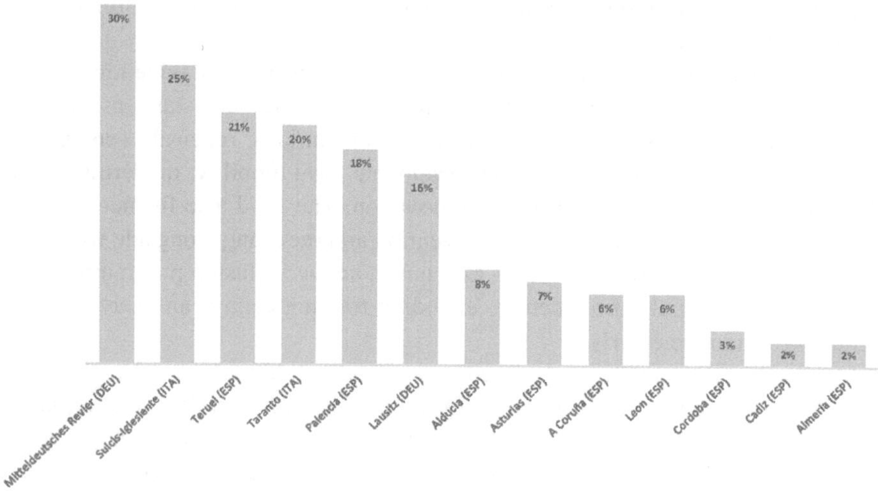

FIGURE 5.2 The share of ALMPs on JTF by "region"

Source: Own elaboration on TJTPs.

allocate a smaller share, while Italian regions like Sulcis-Iglesiente and Taranto also prioritise ALMPs with substantial portions of their JTF resources (about 20%).

5.3 Case analyses

5.3.1 The Italian just transition strategy: economic diversification and workforce reskilling in two priority regions

Approved in December 2022, the National Just Transition Program (NJTP) for Italy designates the Sulcis-Iglesiente area in Sardinia, and the province of Taranto in Apulia as the Italian regions most affected by the shift towards a climate-neutral economy. Of the more than €1 billion allocated to the country – including national co-financing – approximately 30%, just under €400 million, has been earmarked for Sulcis-Iglesiente, while Taranto has received about two-thirds, roughly €800 million. Additionally, €48 million (4% of the total) is earmarked for technical assistance, which plays a crucial role in enabling less developed and transitioning regions to fully benefit from JTF investments. Funds have been received upon presentation of TJTPs developed through participatory processes enhancing social dialogue, especially with workers' representatives, and collaboration with other relevant stakeholders. The respective Executive Plans for the two areas were approved at the beginning of 2025, detailing measures and interventions to concretely reach the planned targets.

Both the TJTPs for Sulcis-Iglesiente and Taranto prioritise three main objectives: (i) increasing renewable energy use, (ii) fostering economic diversification, and (iii) mitigating the social and employment impacts of the green transition. In this regard financial resources are primarily channelled into ALMPs aimed at improving access to employment and supporting workers, businesses, and entrepreneurs in adapting to the structural economic changes linked to the ecological transition.

In the Sulcis plan, Action[4] 1.7 addressed to mitigating the effects of transition (€64 million). It revolves around six strategic priority areas: (i) providing training and reskilling opportunities for unemployed and workers at-risk of job loss; (ii) expanding the educational offer through the creation of new training pathways; (iii) enhancing services for job seekers, including the upgrading of physical infrastructures and facilities; (iv) promoting entrepreneurship and the creation of new businesses by improving labour market services; (v) fostering the active inclusion of job seekers through additional support measures, such as attendance allowances for participants in training activities; and (vi) developing new educational and social inclusion infrastructures, accompanied by continuous monitoring and evaluation throughout implementation (Table 5.2). The plan places particular emphasis on training and education, on vocational training and certifications and on services for enterprise creation. Target groups in Sulcis include unemployed individuals, first-time job seekers, workers at risk of job displacement and aspiring entrepreneurs. These programmes aim to equip participants with skills for the green and blue economy with a focus on vulnerable groups such as women and young people at risk of early school leaving. In spring 2024, the Sardinian regional government launched a call for tenders with

TABLE 5.2 The ALMPs envisaged by the TJTPs of Sulcis and the Province of Taranto

Area	*Type of ALMP*
Sulcis	• Measures for SMEs for upskilling and reskilling activities • Services dedicated to the creation of new businesses or to the adaptation of businesses to new market conditions • Support to Higher Technical Education and Training (IFTS) • Higher professional training for the unemployed, aimed at job placement in large and medium-sized companies operating in the regional territory • Professional training courses aimed at obtaining a qualification and/or certification of skills related to the needs of local production systems in the Green & Blue Economy sectors • Training and Orientation Internships (TFO) aimed at hiring especially women and people with disabilities
Taranto	• Life-long education • Professional qualifications • Training programmes for workers with unemployment benefits • Tertiary, specialised, and professional training programmes for the transition

Source: Own elaboration on TJTPs.

an allocated budget of approximately €6 million to support upskilling and reskilling initiatives in the Sulcis-Iglesiente area.

In the province of Taranto, similar priorities are outlined in Action 2.7 of its TJTP with a budget of €162 million. Measures concern strengthening or reorienting skills to support the economic transition through: (i) continuing education and lifelong learning; (ii) professional training programmes; and (iii) academic tertiary education focusing on the key development drivers identified in the strategy expressed in the Territorial Plan, namely the cultural economy, green transition, and the blue economy. The action also supports academic tertiary education to foster the consolidation of relationships between universities, businesses, and the local community in support of the transition. Target groups are redundant workers, including those in the steel industry and its related industries, with clear retraining objectives for emerging sectors, through strengthening collaborations with accredited institutions to ensure targeted and timely training.

Overall, the initiatives outlined in the TJTPs for Sulcis-Iglesiente and Taranto place ALMPs at the core of their strategies to support the green transition. These measures aim to enhance workforce skills and improve the alignment between labour demand and supply, thereby enabling local communities to better adapt to the socio-economic changes underway (Greco *et al.*, 2023; PCM, 2023).

5.4 Spain's just transition strategy: a coordinated multi-regional framework for decarbonisation and regional revitalisation

Spain has emerged as a global pioneer in promoting a fair and equitable transition to a climate-neutral economy. Already in 2019, it established its Strategic Framework for Energy and Climate based on three pillars: the Climate Change and Energy Transition law, the National Integrated Plan on Energy and Climate (PNIEC) 2021–2030, and the Just Transition Strategy. This integrated approach set the foundation for a coordinated response to the challenges of decarbonisation and sustainable development, especially for the regions severely affected by the closure of coal mines and coal-fired power plants: Asturias, A Coruña, León, Palencia, Teruel, Cádiz, Córdoba, Almería, and Alcudia. Furthermore, in 2020, the national government approved the Spanish Strategy for Science, Technology, and Innovation (2021–2027), highlighting "Climate, Energy and Mobility" as a strategic priority, addressing climate change, decarbonisation, sustainable mobility, and sustainable urban and ecosystem development (MCI, 2020). Following the economic crisis caused by the COVID-19 pandemic, Spain also introduced its National Recovery, Transformation, and Resilience Plan (*Plan de Recuperación, Transformación y Resiliencia*, PNRR), as part of the broader European Next Generation EU initiative. In the same year, the Spanish government established the Institute for Just Transition (Instituto para la Transición Justa, ITJ), which has been coordinating the development and implementation of Spain's national just transition strategy. This strategy mobilises a range of financial resources – including the EU's JTF, the National Recovery and Resilience Plan (NRRP), and other national funding – aimed at revitalising impacted regions.

The Spanish TJTPs for 2021–2027, approved by the European Commission in December 2022, builds therefore upon an integrated policy framework, and was launched well before any European strategy to set the foundation for a coordinated and anticipatory response to the challenges of decarbonisation, sustainable development, and regional equity. A cornerstone of Spain's just transition strategy is the implementation of Just Transition Agreements (*Convenio de Transición Justa*, CTJ).

Until 2024, 15 Just Transition Agreements have been implemented across several Spanish regions, including Asturias, Andalusia, Aragón, the Balearic Islands, Castilla y León, Castilla-La Mancha, and Galicia. These agreements are designed to preserve and stimulate economic activity and employment, stabilise population levels in rural and former coal-mining areas, and support territories affected by the closure of coal-fired power plants or nuclear facilities. They promote economic diversification and specialisation starting from the specific socio-economic characteristics of each region. Interventions target sectors through investments in territorial restoration, support for industrial projects, the promotion of small- and medium-sized enterprises (SMEs), and programmes for worker retraining and reskilling. The agreements are developed through participatory processes that include assessments of potential job losses and the establishment of commitments to maintain employment levels and prevent population decline (ITJ, 2023).

More specifically, the Spanish TJTPs outline several strategic actions in the following areas: (i) ecological transformation of industry, promoting sustainable mobility, circular economy, and energy efficiency; (ii) strengthening the renewable energy value chain, including self-consumption, energy storage, and renewable hydrogen; (iii) supporting SMEs and business projects to drive economic diversification; (iv) fostering research, development, innovation, ICT integration, and digital transformation; (v) environmental rehabilitation, conservation of biodiversity, and promotion of cultural and industrial heritage alongside sustainable tourism; and (vi) enhancing social infrastructure, social economy, and training initiatives. Particular attention is given to vocational training and professional certification programmes for the most vulnerable groups, such as displaced coal workers, unemployed individuals, women, people over 45 years, and individuals with disabilities to promote social inclusion and labour market integration (MTE, 2021: 9).

Figure 5.3 illustrates the distribution of JTF funding across Spanish target areas. Notably, Asturias, Leon and A Coruña have received over half of the total allocation, reflecting their historical reliance on coal mining and heavy industry. Smaller allocations, such as those for Alcudia and Córdoba, have concerned less industrialised or emerging transition territories.

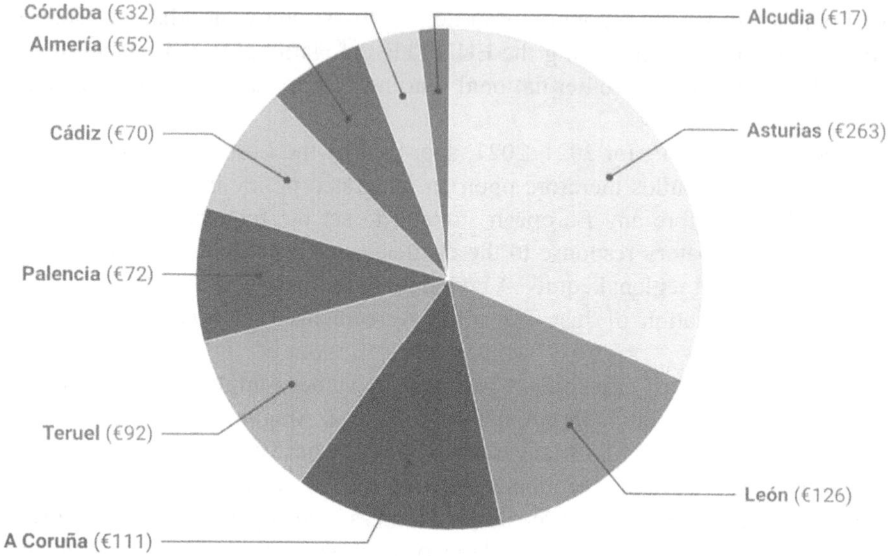

FIGURE 5.3 Spanish JTF overall funding by territory (millions of €)

Source: Spanish NJTP.

The analysis of the Spanish JTF plan, focusing on ALMPs, shows three main investment priorities. First, vocational training infrastructure has received the largest single investment (€15.2 million), particularly in Asturias, indicating a strong emphasis on workforce reskilling. Second, labour market measures account for €25.9 million, with most regions prioritising job placement services. Third, tertiary education infrastructure represents a targeted investment of €11.4 million, though it is concentrated in only two regions. Notably, the plan lacks significant investments in digital transformation and entrepreneurship support, suggesting that these areas may be addressed through alternative funding mechanisms. Overall, the distribution of funds demonstrates a clear prioritisation of human capital development over technological innovation or business-driven strategies, with 78% of resources allocated to education and labour market integration. This focus aligns with the specific challenges faced by coal-dependent regions transitioning their industrial workforces to emerging sectors.

5.5 Just transition in Germany: regional adaptation, workforce transformation and governance challenges in coal-dependent areas

Germany has committed to reducing CO_2 emissions by 65% until 2030 and to achieve climate neutrality by 2045. A critical pillar of this strategy is the planned phase-out of coal by 2038, with the possibility of an earlier exit depending on progress reviews. To support this transition, the European Commission's JTF targets six coal-affected territories: the Lausitzer Revier (Brandenburg and Saxony), Schwedt/Oder in Uckermark (Brandenburg), the Rheinisches Revier and Northern Ruhr area (North Rhine-Westphalia – NRW), the Mitteldeutsches Revier (Saxony and Saxony-Anhalt), and the city of Chemnitz, with a budget of €2.5 billion to facilitate the socio-economic transformation of these regions (Figure 5.4). The initiative operates within the framework of the European Social Fund (ESF) and the European Regional Development Fund (ERDF) for 2021–2027, aiming to improve living conditions and manage the coal phase-out's socio-economic impacts.

In NRW, JTF investments focus on restoring land from lignite mines, expanding SMEs and start-ups in green sectors, such as resource efficiency and circular economy, and providing training to support job retention as lignite mining declines. Brandenburg's funding supports economic diversification, including innovative SMEs, a hydrogen plant to replace lignite production, renewable district heating, an innovation campus, and job training to retain workers and attract youth.

Saxony's allocations target the Lausitzer Revier, Mitteldeutsches Revier, and Chemnitz, emphasising innovation in renewable energy and circular economy, substituting traditional raw materials with green alternatives, and supporting SMEs. The funds also facilitate the reskilling of workers and the expansion of vocational schools, promoting a just transition in these heavily coal-dependent areas.

Saxony-Anhalt is set to receive funding from the JTF to support the greening and gradual phase-out of lignite use in the Mitteldeutsches Revier. The JTF will finance the clean-up of former mining sites, foster the creation of green SMEs and start-ups, and develop new hydrogen infrastructure. Also in this region, training

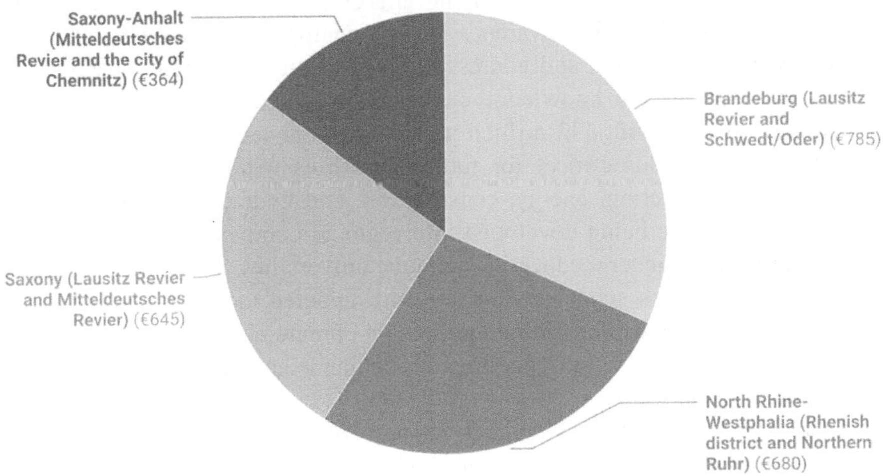

FIGURE 5.4 German JTF founding by territory (millions of €)

Source: German NJTP.

programmes will be enhanced to facilitate the transition of workers from the lignite sector into emerging green economy jobs. The fund will also support initiatives aligned with the New European Bauhaus, such as the use of alternative raw materials to promote sustainable industrial practices.

Despite these plans, there is ongoing debate about the allocation of JTF resources. Regional governments have expressed concerns that the JTF may not provide additional benefits to mining regions but rather serve to finance existing initiatives under the Structural Strengthening Act (SSA) (Klemp and Budke, 2020).

In Brandenburg and Saxony's Lausitz coal region, as well as the Schwedt/Oder refinery area in Uckermark, efforts focus on mitigating economic transition impacts by creating sustainable employment opportunities and improving local infrastructure and education systems. NRW actively supports workers and enterprises through various funding programmes, including those targeting the green economy. The NRW Ministry of Labour manages approximately €120 million from the JTF for employment and social policy measures. These funds support vocational training, continuing education, and retraining for individuals affected by the coal phase-out, with particular attention to SMEs and their employees.

More specifically, in March 2024, NRW has launched the "Coach2Change" programme, providing individualised coaching to help SME employees adapt work structures and processes to meet transformation challenges. EU funds also support Saxony's transition to a greener, low-carbon economy, with €645 million allocated across the region: €375 million for Lausitz, €200 million for Central Germany, and €70 million for Chemnitz.

Active labour market initiatives funded by the JTF in Saxony focus on helping employees adapt to changes in the energy sector and circular economy. These efforts include raising awareness among companies and workers, identifying evolving skills needs, and addressing gaps through targeted consultations, additional training, and knowledge exchange. A key priority is strengthening vocational schools, with €32 million allocated to enhance training quality and attractiveness in fields critical for future industries within JTF regions, such as electrical engineering, energy, construction, and hydraulic engineering. Vocational schools are being developed into regional competence hubs, fostering collaboration with general education schools, universities, and local businesses. This approach equips school authorities with updated technical resources and professional profiles while training teachers on climate policy and regional challenges, aiming to meet future qualification demands and empower educators to lead structural change.

Lastly, the Mitteldeutsches Revier in Saxony-Anhalt, historically shaped by lignite coal mining, has been allocated approximately €364 million in JTF funding, with around €59 million dedicated specifically to ALMPs for the Central German Mining District. These initiatives are designed to support workers affected by the transition, facilitating retraining and employment opportunities.

5.6 The Just Transition Fund in action – comparative assessment

5.6.1 *Insights from interviews with stakeholders*

To gain deeper insights into the implementation of the JTF, we conducted semi-structured interviews in Italy, Spain, and Germany. These interviews focused on the deployment of ALMPs within JT programmes and involved key stakeholders: the Just Transition Platform (JTP) Coordinator at the European Commission's Directorate-General for Regional and Urban Policy (DG REGIO); Managing Authorities (MA) Officers responsible for the JTF in selected regions; and a representative of the German Trade Union Federation, which represents eight trade unions. Although limited in number, these interviews provide valuable perspectives on challenges and progress related to upskilling and reskilling initiatives under the JTF, highlighting areas for further research.

The implementation of upskilling and reskilling initiatives varies significantly across the Just Transition territories examined. In Italy's Sulcis Iglesiente and the Province of Taranto, these actions remain at an early, embryonic stage, as executive plans were finally approved in early 2025 only. The MA are currently engaged in mapping existing local initiatives to avoid policy duplication and design more effective programmes. This mapping is crucial given the availability of funding from multiple sources, including cohesion funds and the NRRP. In the case of Sardinia, however, a tender was published under the ESF using JT resources to test local responsiveness, reflecting cautious implementation steps at the local level.

In contrast, Germany shows more advanced implementation. The German Trade Union Federation representative highlighted ongoing programmes, such as "Fit for Future" and "Coach for Change," which provide coaching and consultancy support to companies and workers for training and business development.

Despite these efforts, the JTP Coordinator at the European Commission confirmed that overall JTF implementation remains slow and uneven. By March 2024, only about 6% of the total JTF budget had been spent across Member States, with upskilling and reskilling actions particularly delayed. Nevertheless, there is optimism at the EU level that implementation will accelerate with time, supported by newly activated assistance mechanisms designed to enhance programme delivery. The latest information suggests that project selection picked up, standings at 38.1% of the total allocation at the end of 2024 (compared to 6.2% in December 2023; including pre-financing, the EU payment rate amounts to 32.2% of the total JTF budget).

Effective planning and implementation of upskilling and reskilling policies require attention to several key aspects, as highlighted by interviewees. They should align with the overall territorial development strategy to support a sustainable societal and economic transition, as emphasised by a MA officer from the Apulia Region. Consequently, coordination between labour market initiatives and broader strategies aimed at strengthening local entrepreneurship and economic diversification towards the green economy is crucial.

Second, qualitative evidence underscores the importance of designing targeted, tailored training interventions that respond to the specific needs of the local workforce and production context. Both Italian MAs prioritise ensuring skill formation matches the demands of private companies, non-profit organisations, cooperatives, and public institutions. Given the low education and training levels in these areas, basic education and foundational skills development are also integral components alongside green skills acquisition.

A representative of the trade unions stressed that interventions should address diverse worker groups, including older individuals, the less educated, low-skilled, and unskilled workers. Italian MAs recognise this challenge, particularly in Sardinia, where the majority of the population has only completed middle school education, often at an advanced age.

Both the EU officer and the union representative highlighted the importance of mapping skill needs, noting that the core issue is not merely skills mismatch but uncertainty about future requirements. Technical Assistance from the EU could support local authorities leading these efforts; however, the JT Platform Coordinator observed that only a few Member States have requested such support.

5.6.2 Challenges and lessons learnt from JTF labour market interventions

Interviewees widely recognise the JTF as a crucial opportunity for economic diversification in regions most affected by the climate transition. The programme provides additional, territorially targeted resources that cannot be reallocated elsewhere. The Apulia MA officer emphasised the importance of this additionality, as well as the EU officer who also observed that the JTF's territorial focus makes its support for upskilling and reskilling distinct from many other funds. More importantly, the JTF is seen as a tool enabling socio-economic transformation in affected areas, offering dedicated resources based on nationally and EU-approved plans. This framework encourages communities to rethink their collective future, with expected long-term impacts.

However, several challenges have emerged. In Italy, the overlap between the JTF and the NRRP – which also finances training programmes like the GOL (Guaranteed Employability of Workers) programme managed by the Ministry of Labour and Social Policies targeting similar beneficiaries – raises concerns about policy duplication and inefficiency, especially as these initiatives are managed by different administrative levels. Local authorities overseeing the JTF are especially careful in safeguarding resources and minimising waste.

Timing is another critical issue: 70% of JTF funds must be spent by 2026, a tight deadline given the programme's ambitious goal. Furthermore, the JTF's territorial scope creates disparities, leaving some regions and sectors unsupported.

The German trade union representative questions the exclusion of industries like automotive, despite facing similar transition challenges.

Concerns also arise with respect to SMEs as the JTF's primary beneficiaries. Unlike large companies, SMEs often struggle to retain workers and plan effective training due to limited capacities and difficulty in identifying skill needs. For this reason, in Germany, the JTF supports hiring HR managers to assist SMEs with training strategies. Additionally, many SMEs' traditional business models limit their demand for innovative skills.

A EU officer identified broader gaps in the assessment of vocational training needs and the involvement of research institutions and academia, which vary across Member States. Although the responsibility for this matter lies with DG Employment and the regional authorities, DG Regio provides toolkits and information on future-proof skills to support implementation.

In conclusion, the JTF offers a crucial opportunity for local communities to move towards sustainable development models by providing dedicated financial resources to regions facing the greatest challenges from the green transition. Upskilling and reskilling interventions are essential components, as workforce quality is a key factor to undertake different development trajectories. Qualitative evidence shows that broad-based skill improvements can coexist with targeted support for specific groups, such as young workers, low-skilled individuals, and women. Nonetheless, a major challenge lies is the clear and context-specific identification of skill needs, which hampers effective planning of ALMPs. Structural issues like brain drain – where young people migrate due to limited job prospects – and difficulties integrating migrant workers, who often require recognition of foreign qualifications beyond training, further complicate the situation. Interviewees emphasise the need for strategic, long-term planning to better understand skill demands across all levels and to attract and retain workers, thereby reducing graduate migration. They also highlight that transitioning to a new socioeconomic model involves more than training; it requires innovation, investor attraction, industrial policy support, sector diversification, and the transformation of legacy industries.

Finally, interviewees suggested to pay greater attention to the cultural aspect of economic transitions, as local communities often display identities tied to those traditional industries that have provided employment for generations. In this respect, including by learning from the past, EU-level policies need to contribute to rebranding these territories and supporting communities in their efforts to diversify their economic and social structures.

5.7 The future of JTF amid Europe's shifting priorities

Despite the JTF's recognised relevance, its future is increasingly uncertain amid rapid political and economic changes in Europe. The EU's response to Russia's invasion of Ukraine – exemplified by initiatives such as *ReArm Europe* and *Readiness 2030* – has shifted the Union's priorities significantly. These defence and security programmes, aimed at enhancing Europe's military capabilities and energy independence, now command substantial financial and political attention, raising concerns about the potential side-lining of climate and social sustainability policies.

Recent data reveal a troubling trend: the surge in global and European military spending threatens to undermine progress towards climate goals. According to EU-News (2025), European military budgets have increased by over 20% since 2022, with member states committing to meet NATO's 2% of GDP defence spending target (some as much as 5%). This shift is reflected in the EU's budget discussions for the next Multiannual Financial Framework (MFF) (2028–2034), where defence and security funding proposals appear to come at the expense of resources allocated to the green transition (EUNews, 2025).

The European Parliamentary Research Service (EPRS) has voiced similar concerns. The European Parliament has repeatedly emphasised that defence spending must not compromise funding for green initiatives, social programmes, and research and development. It warns that reallocating resources towards defence could slow the implementation of the European Green Deal, which is essential for achieving the EU's 2030 and 2050 climate targets (EPRS, 2025).

These geopolitical shifts unfold against a backdrop of economic challenges. Rising inflation, ongoing supply chain disruptions, and monetary tightening have significantly increased the costs of transition projects. What appeared financially feasible in 2020 now faces greater hurdles: the cost of reaching climate neutrality has risen, and without increased funding or adjusted goals, the JTF risks falling short of its mission.

Compounding these difficulties, new U.S. tariffs, especially those on European vehicles, threaten the EU's green transition (EMEA, 2025). These tariffs compromise the competitiveness of key European industries critical to clean energy and low-carbon technologies by undermining investment incentives and risking job losses. As a result, the JTF and broader EU climate strategies risk being deprioritised in favour of short-term economic and security concerns.

Moreover, U.S. tariffs may indirectly bolster China's dominance in electric vehicles and clean technologies. Higher costs and restricted market access for European manufacturers could open the door to cheaper Chinese products – such as solar panels and batteries – flooding the EU market. This would strain local industries and increase Europe's dependence on non-European technologies, heightening strategic vulnerabilities.

Domestically, economic uncertainty fuels political resistance to the Green Deal. Italy's recent call to suspend the initiative (Reuters, 2025) reflects broader concerns about achieving ambitious climate targets amid economic strain. Such opposition risks delaying or weakening emissions reduction commitments as governments prioritise protectionism and economic growth.

The combination of these international factors and the domestic political shifts risk exacerbating existing inequalities, both between regions and across sectors.

The territorial focus of the JTF means that industries located outside designated regions – such as many automotive suppliers – may face significant transition challenges without access to targeted support. SMEs, which often lack the resources for workforce planning and training, are particularly exposed. As a result, there is a real danger that the green transition – and the social justice it is meant to promote – may be side-lined amid competing policy priorities.

Moreover, recent research highlights that the transition to renewable energy is not only a matter of geographic redistribution, but also of sectoral and technological inequalities. As Weko (2024) argues, while renewables have the potential to break the geographic monopolies of fossil fuel resources and redistribute economic benefits, they simultaneously increase the importance of intangible assets, such as data, artificial intelligence, and digital infrastructures. These intangibles are often monopolised by large technology firms, or "Big Tech," which are rapidly expanding their influence in the energy sector (Newell, 2019). For example, companies like Amazon are leveraging their expertise in data harvesting, analysis, and digital infrastructure to enter and shape emerging energy markets. As a result, economic value and power may increasingly flow towards these digital monopolies, rather than being distributed to countries, regions, or local communities. This trend risks creating new forms of sectoral inequality: while some regions and industries may be excluded from transition support, others – particularly those with access to intangible assets and digital capabilities – stand to benefit disproportionately.

5.8 Conclusion

The comparative analysis of the JTF in Italy, Spain, and Germany reveals both the achievements and the persistent challenges of implementing just transition policies within the European Green Deal framework. The JTF has undoubtedly provided vital financial and strategic support to regions most exposed to the risks of decarbonisation, enabling targeted investments in economic diversification, workforce reskilling, and social inclusion. However, the experiences of Italian Sulcis-Iglesiente and Taranto, the Spanish coal regions, and the German coalfields also highlight the complexity of translating ambitious policy objectives into equitable and effective territorial transformation.

First, the territorial focus of JTF has been valuable in steering resources towards the most affected areas and in promoting local mobilisation to define diversification trajectories, based on contextual needs and specificity, thanks to the preparation of detailed TJTPs.

Second, evidence from the case studies highlights a political commitment to positioning ALMPs and skills development initiatives as core pillars of effective just transition strategies. Both Sulcis-Iglesiente and Taranto have prioritised upskilling and reskilling programmes, with particular attention to youth, women, and workers at risk of exclusion. Similarly, Spain's Just Transition Agreements have combined early retirement and compensation for coal workers with significant investments in retraining and local economic development. In Germany, the focus on innovation, research, and the creation of new value chains in renewable energy industries reflects a long-term vision for regional transformation.

Third, participatory governance and social dialogue have emerged as essential components for the legitimacy and effectiveness of transition policies. The Spanish experience demonstrates the value of institutionalising dialogue through dedicated bodies, such as the ITJ.

In Italy the involvement of trade unions, employers, and civil society in the design and implementation of TJTPs has been more formal than substantial, although the commitment of a variety of local actors to support the transition process remains strong. In general, an issue emerges around the difficulty to enhance substantive bottom-up participation; consultation has been more widespread, although it has been still selective for the groups and individuals involved.

Despite these positive developments, several issues and challenges remain. Persistent unemployment, skills mismatches, and low educational attainment continue to undermine the resilience of transition regions. The risk of deepening territorial and social inequalities is heightened by the uneven capacity of local institutions and labour market services, as well as by the limited scale of available resources relative to the magnitude of transformation required. Moreover, the growing importance of intangible assets – such as data, digital infrastructure, and innovation capabilities – raises new questions about sectoral inequalities and the risk of economic value being captured by large technology firms rather than local communities.

Crucially, the success of the green transition hinges on the resilience of workers and communities. Sustained investments in education, vocational training, and lifelong learning are vital to close skills gaps, enable labour mobility, when desired, and support particularly vulnerable groups – such as youth, women, and older workers – who face disproportionate barriers in the labour market. Well-functioning labour market institutions facilitate the implementation of active support measures, enhance job matching efficiency, and enable the delivery of targeted inclusion initiatives.

In this respect the quality of employment in so-called green jobs raises concerns. Most official documents assume that green employment inherently ensures better working conditions. However, this assumption warrants critical reflection: it is not enough to simply create new jobs – care must be taken to ensure they are not precarious or low-quality positions. At the same time, the analysis of the interviewees' responses further underscores that the transition towards a new socioeconomic model cannot be effectively addressed through training policies alone; rather, it necessitates a well-defined and comprehensive industrial policy strategy.

To reduce dependency on carbon-intensive industries, strategies for economic diversification should promote SMEs, entrepreneurship, and the growth of emerging sectors, such as renewable energy, sustainable mobility, and circular economy value chains. Investment in digital infrastructure and local innovation ecosystems is equally essential – not only to spur growth but also to address emerging inequalities tied to digitalisation and intangible assets.

The findings of this chapter highlight that achieving a just transition in Europe requires flexible, inclusive, and territorially sensitive policy interventions: a one-size-fits-all model risks overlooking the distinct socio-economic realities of diverse regions. However, *place-based policies* should support national policies to ensure wider support and secure alignment with wider political strategies.

Financial sustainability remains a cornerstone. The scale of the green transition demands predictable funding that safeguards cohesion objectives, even amid shifting political and economic pressures. Aligning JTF resources with other EU instruments, such as the Recovery and Resilience Facility, can enhance impact while ensuring that climate and social justice remain central to budgetary priorities. Given the upcoming negotiations on the MFF 2028–2034, it is crucial that funding dedicated to the just transition is maintained, if not increased, to support ambitious climate and social objectives in the next EU budget cycle (European Commission, 2025).

Finally, a just transition cannot succeed without inclusive governance. Engaging workers, employers, and civil society through transparent, participatory mechanisms is key to fostering trust, legitimacy, and social cohesion. This should be coupled with robust monitoring and evaluation systems that enable learning, adaptability, and accountability over time.

In a context of rising geopolitical and economic turbulence, the future of just transition policies in Europe remains uncertain. Yet, the experiences of countries like Italy, Spain, and Germany show that social and territorial cohesion can be a driving force for climate ambition. Only by promoting equity and participation can Europe turn the challenges of decarbonisation into pathways for sustainable and inclusive renewal.

Notes

1 Semi-structured interviews focusing on the state of implementation of the active labour market policies in JT programs were carried out with (i) the JTP Coordinator at the European Commission's Directorate-General for Regional and Urban Policy (DG REGIO); (ii) the Managing Authorities (MA) Officers of the JTF for selected regions; (iii) a representative for the German Trade Union Federation, an umbrella organization for eight trade unions in Germany.
2 This analysis builds on previous in-depth research on active labour market policies within Just Transition Programs in Italy, Spain, and Germany, developed by the same authors in a recent comprehensive study – Cirillo *et al.* (2024).
3 The fund is complementary to Structural Funds and the other EU financing programming such as the European Social Fund+ (ESF+), the European Regional Development Fund (ERDF), the European Globalisation Adjustment Fund for Displaced Workers (EGF).
4 "Action" in the context of EU JTF territorial plans refers to a specific operational measure or intervention line within the strategy. Each Action sets objectives, resources, and fields of activity designed to address the territory's transition needs, as formally described in the EU Territorial Just Transition Plans.

References

Andreoni, A. (2022) *Industrial Policy Reloaded: Shaping industrial ecosystems towards sustainable prosperity*. Heinrich-Böll-Stiftung.

Andreoni, A., Cramer, K., Mazzucato, M., and Steyn, G. (2022) How can South Africa advance a new energy paradigm? A mission-oriented approach to megaprojects. *Oxford Review of Economic Policy*, 38(2), 237–259.

Arthur, W. B. (1989) Competing Technologies, Increasing Returns, and Lock-In by Historical Events. *The Economic Journal*, 99(394), 116–131. https://doi.org/10.2307/2234208

Arthur, W. B. (1990) Positive feedbacks in the economy. *Scientific American*, 262(2), 92–99.

Bergek, A., Jacobsson, S., Carlsson, B., Lindmark, S., and Rickne, A. (2008) Analyzing the functional dynamics of technological innovation systems: A scheme of analysis. *Research Policy*, 37(3), 407–429. https://doi.org/10.1016/j.respol.2007.12.003

Boschma, R., and Frenken, K. (2018) Evolutionary economic geography. In: Gordon L. Clark, Maryann P. Feldman, Meric S. Gertler, and Dariusz Wójcik (eds.), *The New Oxford Handbook of Economic Geography* (213–229). Oxford: OUP.

Brauers, H. and Oei, P.-Y. (2020) The political economy of coal in Poland: Drivers and barriers for a shift away from fossil fuels. *Energy Policy*, 144, 111621. https://doi.org/10.1016/j.enpol.2020.111621

Cirillo, V., Divella, M., Ferrulli, E., and Greco, L. (2024) *Active labor market policies in the framework of just transition programs: The case of Italy, Spain, and Germany*, ÖFSE Working Paper 79, Vienna.

Eunews. (2025, May 29). Growth in global (and European) military spending threatens climate goals. Eunews. https://www.eunews.it/en/2025/05/29/growth-in-global-and-european-military-spending-threatens-climate-goals/

Euro-Mediterranean Economists Association (EMEA) (2025). *Trump tariffs could trash climate finance plans*. https://euromed-economists.org/trump-tariffs-could-trash-climate-finance-plans/ (accessed 29 May 2025).

European Commission (2025) *The 2028–34 EU budget for a stronger Europe*. https://commission.europa.eu/strategy-and-policy/eu-budget/long-term-eu-budget/eu-budget-2028-2034_en (accessed 29 May 2025).

European Parliamentary Research Service (EPRS) (2025) *The twin transition and EU security policy*. https://www.europarl.europa.eu/RegData/etudes/BRIE/2025/769566/EPRS_BRI(2025)769566_EN.pdf (accessed 29 May 2025).

Feltrin, L., Mah, A., and Brown, D. (2022) Noxious deindustrialization: Experiences of precarity and pollution in Scotland's petrochemical capital. *Environment and Planning C: Politics and Space*, 40(4), 950–969. https://doi.org/10.1177/23996544211056328

Geels, F. W. (2002) Technological transitions as evolutionary reconfiguration processes: A multi-level perspective and a case-study. *Research Policy*, 31(8–9), 1257–1274. https://doi.org/10.1016/S0048-7333(02)00062-8

Greco, L., Perra, S., and Pruna, M. L. (2023) La sfida della «transizione giusta» in due aree di antica industrializzazione. *Meridiana*, 106, 39–68.

Hafele, J., Le Lannou, L. A., Rochowicz, N., Kuhls, S., and Gräbner-Radkowitsch, C. (2023) *Securing future-fit jobs in the green transformation: A policy framework for industrial policy (ZOE Discussion Papers No. 10)*. ZOE Institute for Future-fit Economies.

Heyen, D. A. (2017) *Governance of exnovation: Phasing out non-sustainable structures (Oeko-Institut Working Paper 2/2017)*. Oeko-Institut.

IndustriALL European Trade Union (2021) *Financing the just transition: An EU overview*. Brussels: IndustriALL.

Instituto para la Transición Justa (ITJ) (2023) *España, 4 años avanzando en una transición energética justa*. Madrid: Gobierno de España. https://www.transicionjusta.gob.es/content/dam/itj/files-1/Documents/Publicaciones%20ES%20y%20EN/Informe%20Transici%C3%B3n%20Justa_4%20a%C3%B1os%20avanzando_def.pdf

Klemp, H. and Budke, R. (2020) *Der Just Transition Fund ist für die Lausitz noch nicht verloren*. B90 Die Grünen Brandenburg. https://gruene-fraktion-brandenburg.de/presse/pressemitteilungen/2020/der-just-transition-fund-ist-fuer-die-lausitz-noch-nicht-verloren (accessed 29 May 2025)

Malmberg, A. and Maskell, P. (2002) The elusive concept of localization economies: Towards a knowledge-based theory of spatial clustering. *Environment and Planning A*, 34(3), 429–449. https://doi.org/10.1068/a3457

Mazzucato, M., Kattel, R., and Ryan-Collins, J. (2020) Challenge-driven innovation policy: Towards a new policy toolkit. *Journal of Industrial and Competition Trade*, 20(4), 421–437. https://doi.org/10.1007/s10842-019-00329-w

Ministerio de Ciencia e Innovación (MCI) (2020) *Estrategia Española de Ciencia, Tecnología e Innovación 2021–2027*. Madrid: Gobierno de España. https://www.ciencia.gob.es/Estrategias-y-Planes/Estrategias/Estrategia-Espanola-de-Ciencia-Tecnologia-e-Innovacion-2021-2027.html

Ministerio para la Transición Ecológica y el Reto Demográfico (MTE) (2021) *Plan de Recuperación, Transformación y Resiliencia: Componente 7 – Plan de Transición Justa (2021–2027)*. Madrid: Gobierno de España. https://planderecuperacion.gob.es/sites/default/files/2023-10/0310203_adenda_plan_de_recuperacion_componente7.pdf

Newell, P. (2019) Trasformismo or transformation? The global political economy of energy transitions. *Review of International Political Economy*, 26(1), 25–48.

Presidenza del Consiglio dei Ministri (PCM) (2023) *Piano Operativo del Just Transition Fund (JTF) – Italia 2021–2027*. Rome: Italian Government. https://www.jtf.gov.it/wp-content/uploads/2023/12/sfc2021-PRG-2021IT16JTPR001-1.1.pdf (accessed 29 May 2025).

Reuters (2025) Italy to ask for immediate suspension of EU Green Deal rules following US tariffs. *Reuters Sustainability*, 3 April. https://www.eunews.it/en/2025/05/29/growth-in-global-and-european-military-spending-threatens-climate-goals/ (accessed 29 May 2025).

Rip, A. and Kemp, R. (1998) Technological change. In: Rayner, S. and Malone, E. L. (eds.) *Human choice and climate change: Vol. II, resources and technology*. Columbus: Battelle Press, 327–399.

Scoones, I., Leach, M., and Newell, P. (2015) *The politics of green transformations*. Abingdon: Taylor & Francis.

Weko, S. (2024) New Sites of Accumulation? Why Intangible Assets Matter for Energy Transitions. *Review of Political Economy*, 1–28. https://doi.org/10.1080/09538259.2024.2391304

PART III

Governance Challenges of Progressive Industrial Policy

6

STRATEGIC OUTLOOK, LEGITIMACY, AND DIRECTIONALITY

Tackling Key Institutional Deficits of EU Industrial Policy

Werner Raza

6.1 Introduction

Industrial policy (IP) is back. This renaissance is perhaps surprising. During the neo-liberal period of the last 30 years, industrial policy was completely banned from economic discourse, though of course it took place under different labels, for instance, innovation and technology policy. While this shift in economic policy discourse in principle is to be welcomed, from a progressive economic and political point of view, it is very important to carefully think about the why, how and for whom of industrial policy. What are the motivations for IP, which objectives shall be achieved, who should be the beneficiaries of IP, who shall sit at the table when it comes to taking decisions, and finally, who will be responsible for implementation?

While the initial motivations for IP in the EU, i.e., the climate crisis and the digital transformation, *aka* the Twin Transformation (TT), seem straightforward, many related critical issues remain unresolved and need to be addressed in the coming years. Since the start of the Russian aggression against Ukraine in early 2022, geo political changes have also become an important motivating factor of IP in the EU. The rivalry between the US and China, and most recently the confrontational policies of the second Trump administration against Europe have made it clear that the age of the liberal international order from which the EU profited so tremendously, has come to an end. As things stand at the moment, the EU is arguably ill-prepared for the incipient age of geopolitical competition and transactional politics. Against pressures emanating both from the international level as well as from domestic politics in the form of rising nationalist-populist political movements, the EU will have to fundamentally revamp its political and economic strategy in the years to come. In the political domain, political integration will have to be strengthened, including in the area of external and security policy. In the economic domain, a

DOI: 10.4324/9781003745563-10

much stronger and pro-active role of the state will be required to increase the resilience of the EU productive system, reduce excessive external dependencies, and mobilise the necessary financial and administrative capacities and capabilities to promote the Twin Transformation. In the social domain, the safeguarding of social and regional cohesion amidst turbulent times will become even more important. IP will undoubtedly acquire a critical role in coping with these multiple challenges.

The geopolitical and security dimension thus adds an additional layer of complexity, against a situation, characterised by multiple implementation deficits when it comes to the green and digital transformations. With respect to the former, while during the last five years progress has been made in many areas, effectively implementing the EU's climate and ecological agenda will necessitate significant additional efforts relative to the EU's (and Member States, MSs) current level of commitments. In fact, a recent study found that of the 154 EU Green Deal targets, 32 are currently "on track" and 64 are identified as "acceleration needed", meaning that significantly more progress is needed to meet the targets on time. Fifteen of the targets are found to be "not progressing" or "regressing", and for 43 of the targets no data are currently available (European Commission, 2025). Thus, in many critical areas the EU is likely to fail its 2030 climate and environmental targets. Given the current political fatigue in all ecological matters, mostly as a consequence of corporate lobbying and far-right propaganda, the coming years will need to see a reinvigoration of the green transformation agenda. Notwithstanding the momentum built up since 2020, the green transformation is a long-term process. With climate change underway, climate science has provided clear-cut evidence that any further postponing of action will increase the economic costs of climate mitigation in the future by a multiple. Above all else, it will take a heavy toll on human life that could have been entirely avoided (Dreyer, 2024; Waidelich *et al.*, 2024).

Digital processes closely interact with the green transformation. While there is a case that the digital transformation has the potential to support the green transformation, the opposite is also true. Digital technologies and applications depend on the expanded availability of certain natural resources and critical raw materials (CRMs). Digital technologies such as Artificial Intelligence (AI) require large amounts of electric energy, the production of which may lead to harmful environmental impacts. Whatever the specific impacts, digital processes are deeply transformative. Their interaction with different social domains, hence, needs political mediation and guidance. IP has a role to play for both enhancing complementarities and for mitigating tensions and remedying trade-offs between the two transformations.

Although the comeback of IP is thus in principle welcome, it is important to situate IP in the wider policy environment and upon that basis define its role in pursuing public policy objectives. This raises questions of legitimacy, directionality and effectiveness. The recently published and highly influential Draghi Report on European competitiveness made the case for IP to be primarily employed for promoting the EU's innovative capacities and capabilities, thereby arguing that without a more productive economy, it will not be possible to pursue other public objectives such as the green transformation or the safeguarding of the welfare state: "If Europe cannot become more productive, we will be forced to choose. We will not be able to become, at once, a leader in new technologies, a beacon of climate responsibility and an independent player on the world stage" (Draghi, 2024: 01). The statement thus implies that, if push comes to shove, trade-offs between competitiveness and environmental sustainability need to be resolved to the benefit of the former. Though to his credit, the Draghi Report makes proposals to foster areas of complementarity, reversing the order of priorities in this way would be problematic. Complementarities should be exploited to the extent possible. The overarching importance of the green transformation must however not be sacrificed at the altar of competitiveness. Precisely, because the priority-setting between conflicting policy goals during a process of profound structural change is of such importance, IP must be embedded in inclusive democratic forms of deliberation and debate. It is the central hypothesis of this chapter that the key deficit of the current approach to EU IP is one of legitimacy. Moreover, European IP lacks a coherent strategic outlook and is prone to short-term and opportunistic adjustments. This in turn creates conceptual contradictions, leads to political resistance, as well as ineffective implementation. The governance of EU IP is thus in need of a more inclusive setup that gives both strategic outlook, democratic legitimacy and long-term directionality to the transformation process.

In developing this argument, the remainder of this chapter proceeds as follows: Section 6.2 provides a critical assessment of EU IP since the beginning of the decade, identifying key deficits of the prevailing approach. In Section 6.3, the key deficits of both the lack of strategic outlook and the issue of legitimacy are addressed. The latter matters not only for reasons of social support for IP, but is particularly important for lending directionality and effectiveness to the process. We introduce the issue of conditionality as a means to enhance legitimacy. Section 6.4 provides concluding remarks.

6.2 Assessing EU industrial policy initiatives for the twin transformation

Since the 1990s, the prevailing approach to European economic policymaking had pushed back government involvement in the economy and reduced the role of public intervention. With the Single Market, the early 1990s saw an acceleration of European integration. The European Monetary Union and the Maastricht Treaty limited state capacities for IP. A new consensus saw the role of the State as that of market "regulator". Selective policies, targeting particular fields, were to be abandoned as the market knew best which industries and firms were most efficient.

Only in the aftermath of the Eurozone crisis the European Commission exhibited a renewed interest in IP, stressing the centrality of manufacturing for Europe's future (European Commission, 2012, 2014, 2017). In response to stagnating investment in Europe, in late 2014, the EU Commission launched the "Juncker Investment Plan", with the aim of supporting the recovery of public and private investment in Europe. In 2015, the European Fund for Strategic Investments (EFSI), the main tool of the Juncker Plan, was created and institutionally embedded in the European Investment Bank (EIB) (European Union, 2015). EFSI was set up with rather limited EU funds (€21 billion), the underlying idea being that via public funds private financial resources could be leveraged.

By December 2020, EFSI had approved €102.1 billion in financing, which was expected to generate €540.3 billion in total investments.[1] The EFSI programme thus illustrated the seriousness of Europe's investment gap and the mismatch between public investment needs and idle private financial resources. The success of EFSI in leveraging private money notwithstanding, an independent evaluation concluded that EFSI failed to meet expectations in the financing of more innovative start-ups and early stage growth small and medium enterprises (SMEs). Designed as a "demand driven instrument" with no goal of economic convergence amongst MSs, funds were concentrated in a few major EU countries. At the end of 2017, France, Italy, and Spain had received 44.5% of total investment (European Commission, 2018).

Overall, although IP in the 2010s acquired a new significance, the approach by, and large remained orthodox. With the focus put on horizontal policies, funding prioritised research and innovation, infrastructure, as well as SMEs (Cimoli *et al.*, 2015; Pianta *et al.*, 2020). Under the existing fiscal rules, public funding remained circumscribed and focused on leveraging private capital. EFSI was arguably the role model for what was later characterised by the critical academic literature as the de-risking approach, where the State tried to attract private capital to investment ventures by assuming most of the economic risks (Gabor, 2023; Gabor and Braun, 2023; Skyrman, 2024). Though programmes like EFSI were relatively successful, in comparison to peer competitors like the US and China, overall investment activity (public and private) in the EU, however, remained below potential.

When confronted with a new pan-European wave of environmental activism in 2018/2019, in December 2019, the incoming Von der Leyen-Commission launched its proposal for a European Green Deal (EGD), a wide-ranging package of legislation with the aim (i) to reduce emissions of greenhouse gases in the EU to net-zero by 2050, (ii) decouple economic growth from resource use, and (iii) ensure a "just and inclusive" transition in the European Union by "leaving no place and no person behind". Related to IP more specifically, the initial policy focus of the EGD was on promoting a circular economy via a Circular Economy Action Plan, including efforts to ecologically design products and facilitate the repair of products. With the 2020 EU Industrial Strategy (and its update in 2021 following the COVID-19 pandemic), the EC, however, aimed at fostering the resilience of the Single Market and the Open Strategic Autonomy of the EU, including by the monitoring of strategic dependencies and the promotion of industrial alliances. To date, 11 industrial alliances have been formed (e.g., on Batteries,

Clean Hydrogen, Photovoltaic Industry, Plastics, Processors and Semiconductors, Raw Materials). The alliances are essentially consultative bodies, with no funding or decision-making powers. With respect to the stated aim of accelerating the Twin Transformation, the Strategy promoted, amongst others, (i) the decarbonisation of steel production, and (ii) the promotion of joint research projects under the Horizon Europe partnerships.

However, with the outbreak of the energy crisis following the Russian war in Ukraine as well as the IP initiatives of the Biden administration (in particular the Inflation Reduction Act), IP increasingly moved to the core of EU policymaking in the context of the EGD. In February 2023, the Commission published the *Green Deal Industrial Plan (GDIP)* with the aim to create a more supportive environment for scaling up the EU's manufacturing capacities for net-zero technologies and products required to meet Europe's ambitious climate targets (European Commission, 2023a). The Strategy rests on four pillars (i) a predictable and simplified regulatory environment; (ii) faster access to funding; (iii) enhancing skills; and (iv) open trade for resilient supply chains. With respect to the first pillar, the Commission introduced a number of initiatives, in particular the Net Zero Industry Act (European Commission, 2023c). The latter provides a simplified regulatory framework – e.g., via shorter lead times for permitting processes and the one-stop-shop principle for administrative processes – in order to increase the manufacturing capacities of technologies and products that are key to meet climate neutrality goals, such as batteries, windmills, heat pumps, solar, electrolysers, as well as carbon capture and storage technologies. With respect to the second pillar on funding, the Strategy does not introduce any new funding programmes, but the aim is to facilitate the use of existing EU funds for financing clean tech innovation, manufacturing and deployment, with a focus on REPowerEU, InvestEU, and the Innovation Fund. It is against this background that the EC Investment Needs Assessment concluded that "while funding possibilities have recently increased, the current EU budget has insufficient possibilities for supporting the objectives of the Net-Zero Industry Act and for ensuring a level-playing field between MSs, relative to the identified public investment needs" (European Commission, 2023b: 3). With respect to pillar three, the skills agenda, the GDIP by and large refers to already existing initiatives, e.g., the European Skills Agenda and the European Pact for Skills, as well as to existing support programmes for skills acquisition under the Just Transition Mechanism (JFT), the European Regional Development Fund, and the European Social Fund. Besides referencing existing trade policies, new measures under Pillar 4 (Trade) include initiatives for promoting secure, sustainable and affordable global supply of raw materials via the promotion of a Critical Raw Materials Club, Clean Tech/Net-zero Industrial Partnerships, and a new export credit strategy. At the time of writing (October 2025), only limited progress had been achieved on these initiatives.

With respect to CRMs, more concrete steps have been taken with the *European Critical Raw Materials Act (CRMA)* of May 2024 (European Union, 2024). As part of Pillar 1 of the GDIP, its objective is to enhance the supply of CRMs for relevant industries and strategic technologies by fostering extraction, processing, and recycling within the EU. While for the first time it sets concrete and ambitious benchmarks, they are legally non-binding. Key elements of the CRMA include legal changes to expedite permitting processes for strategic projects linked to strategic raw materials (SRMs). The regulation aims to streamline approval procedures by granting strategic projects "public interest" status and by imposing stricter permitting timelines. Since the approval process represents only a fraction of the overall lead time required to establish mining projects, it remains unclear whether the Act will significantly reduce the total time required to implement a project. The CRMA also introduces obligations related to recycling and circularity, national exploration programmes, data collection, risk monitoring, and increased transparency. These measures serve various aims, including securing CRMs from secondary sources, gaining a better overview of potential supply shortages, and fostering public acceptance of raw material projects.

Though not formally a part of the EGD, *Important Projects of Common European Interest (IPCEIs)* have been promoted by the EC as a complementary tool of IP to promote the green and digital transformation. On the basis of Article 107(3)(b) of the Treaty on the Functioning of the European Union (TFEU), public financial support to promote the execution of an important project of common European interest may be considered compatible with the internal market. In 2014 (with an update in 2021), the Commission published a Communication specifying the criteria for the compatibility with the internal market of State aid to promote the execution of IPCEIs. Since IPCEIs have to be supported from national budgets (though under the Recovery and Resilience Fund (RRF) also EU funds were made available for IPCEI funding), MSs are however in the driving seat to form an IPCEI, identify the scope of the projects and select participating companies and projects. For the time being, a centrally managed EU IPCEI fund does not exist, though the Commission supports a platform – the Joint European Forum for IPCEI – facilitating their establishment. At the end of 2024, 10 IPCEIs were in operation. With a focus on the microelectronics value chain (2 IPCEIs), the hydrogen value chain (4 IPCEIs), the battery value chain (2 IPCEIs), cloud computing (1 IPCEI) and the health value chain (1 IPCEI), the large majority is focused on supporting research and development as well as projects of first industrial deployment. One IPCEI (the Fehmarn Belt fixed rail-road link) is dedicated to infrastructure. With participation of 22 MSs, IPCEIs have mobilised some €91 billion in investments so far, of which €37.5 billion is state aid, the rest being expected private co-funding.[2] Recent assessments (Eisl, 2022; Schmitz *et al.*, 2024) identify two principal problems with the existing IPCEI structure: (i) the lack of common European funding for IPCEIs, particularly as the RFF funds will be phased-out in 2026, and thus funding will depend on national fiscal space, which is highly divergent amongst MSs; and (ii) the high administrative burden associated with the approval process, with stringent eligibility and compatibility criteria to be met by project applicants.

Initially proposed in February 2022 and adopted in September 2023, the *European Chips Act* (ECA) intends to reinforce the semiconductor ecosystem in the EU, ensure the resilience of supply chains and reduce external dependencies. Its specific objective is to ensure Europe meets its digital decade target of doubling its global market share in semiconductors to 20% by 2030. Thus, a crucial difference between the Chips Act and the microelectronics IPCEIs is that IPCEI rules require novelty beyond the global state-of-the-art. The ECA introduced noteworthy initiatives, including in particular a strategic mapping of the semiconductor sector; a virtual design platform to lower the barriers to entry to chip design, especially for SMEs and start-ups; different equity and debt solutions for SMEs and startups under the Chips Fund; competence centres in each MS to facilitate access to the virtual design platform and pilot lines; and a European Semiconductor Board comprising EU MSs, which advises the European Commission (Kleinhans, 2024). Most of these activities refer to ECA Pillars I (Chips for Europe Initiative promoting R&D) and III (Coordination & Monitoring). Pillar II incentivises public and private investments in manufacturing facilities for chipmakers and their suppliers. The Chips Act foresees a total funding volume of €43 billion, of which €11 billion will be provided for R&D and innovation (mostly through existing funds supplied via Horizon Europe and the Digital Europe Programme). The remaining volume for investments in new manufacturing capacity (Pillar II) is expected to come from the MSs and private companies. In addition, the EU will also set up a Chips Fund to facilitate access to debt financing and equity, in particular for start-ups, scale-ups, SMEs and small mid-caps. This will be implemented by the European Innovation Council and InvestEU (though implementation was still pending by the end of 2024).

Initial assessments of the ECA have pointed to a number of shortcomings: firstly, for state aid exemptions under Article 107 TFEU to be applicable, national funds must be directed to "first-of-kind" manufacturing facilities. Consequently, a bias to promote leading-edge semiconductor production (2–3 nm) has been introduced, which does not necessarily fit the needs of downstream European producers (e.g., in the car industry), which typically need chips that are produced at larger sizes above 10 nm. Moreover, chips made in Europe will likely be more expensive than the products of Asian competitors and may find it difficult to find a market.[3] Secondly, the target of a 20% world market share will not necessarily reduce external EU dependencies, given the highly diversified technologies produced in the semiconductor global value chain with transnational division of labour, low levels of substitutability, and strong customer–supplier alliances. Instead, from a geopolitical perspective, the EU should more specifically look at which elements of its domestic semiconductor value chain are of strategic importance for others, i.e., at reverse dependencies and indispensability. Thirdly, institutional capacities and capabilities for market monitoring, formulation of policies and coordination between EU MSs and with international partners are severely lacking in the EU, while the existing governance structure of support programmes is complex and non-transparent (Dachs, 2023; Kleinhans, 2024).

The aforementioned analysis can be summarised by three main conclusions:

1 *Many initiatives at the expense of coherence and strategic outlook*: what is perhaps most apparent is the plethora of programmes and instruments that have been enacted during the last five years. Given the sequence of exogenous shocks and challenges hitting the EU, it is arguably not surprising that EU policymakers have reacted to each of these events by enacting specific policy responses. This consisted of both establishing new initiatives and programmes, while also adapting existing instruments to the latest policy challenge. This mode of crisis politics also affected the implementation of the EGD, the latter arguably representing a rather coherent set of policies with a clear objective. On the one hand, the EGD profited from the emergency measures, e.g., by the significant RRF funds diverted to promote the energy transformation. On the other hand, the original EGD objectives became gradually superseded by new objectives with a geopolitical motivation, in particular supply chain resilience, strategic autonomy and technological sovereignty.
2 *A complex institutional structure with demanding processes*: while the EGD's approach prioritised sector regulations and the deployment of price instruments, in particular carbon-pricing within the Emission Trading Scheme (ETS), more systematic IP became prioritised as a consequence of the Pandemic and the Ukraine crisis. Most notably, besides the focus on energy security, this triggered new efforts to promote green and digital technologies. The policy approach thus shifted to one favouring incentive mechanisms via grants, loans and public guarantees. In contrast to peer countries such as the US and Japan, given the EU institutional structure, the enacted subsidy programmes and instruments are rather complex in nature, with a variegated distribution of competences between the EU and MSs in accordance with the EU *acquis*. As a consequence, policy coherence suffered, and implementation has been uneven, critically depending on the institutional capacities of national bodies. This is particularly pertinent in cases where access to funds has been conditional upon the presentation of national plans by MSs before project funding could start (e.g., in the case of the RRF and the JFT). Access to project financing is typically based on application and monitoring processes with strict formal conditionalities requiring significant upfront resources from applicants. Programme and project administration within the competent bodies, including coordination between bodies at national and EU level, are generally time-consuming and results in considerable lead-times between project application and kick-off. Given the dominant co-financing model in many programmes, programme uptake also depends on the financial powers of MSs, thus increasing heterogeneous implementation across the EU.

3 *A fragmented and non-transparent funding structure*: with the exception of NextGenerationEU (NGEU) as a temporary emergency funding mechanism, EU-level funding remained circumscribed. It essentially consisted of reshuffling regular budgetary resources and ETS funds for the purposes of the Twin Transformation, which then went into diverse existing and new funds supplemented by NGEU money. Large disbursements of public resources happened at the level of MSs, particularly in those with significant fiscal power (e.g., Germany and France), while thanks to the NGEU the lack of own funds in most MSs was temporarily remedied. Incentives for private investors via EU guarantees and co-funding under the de-risking approach, as well as green finance reforms did raise money, but in overall quantitative terms, private investment for the Twin Transformation remained below expectations. For an overview of funding programmes, see Table 6.1.

Thus, while funding remains an important issue, especially for the coming years, our preliminary analysis points to institutional issues as the major shortcomings of the prevailing approach. It is to these that we will turn in the next section

TABLE 6.1 Non-exhaustive overview of EU funding programmes relevant for the Twin Transformation

Funding initiative/ programme	*Time frame*	*Budget (€ billion)*	*Source of funding and funding instruments*	*Objectives*
NextGeneration EU (NGEU)	2021–2026	750	Grants and loans financed through common debt (EU bonds)	Support the EU's COVID-19 recovery, green transition, and economic resilience
Recovery and Resilience Fund (RRF)	2021–2026	724	The RRF is the operational arm of the NGEU	Digitalisation, green transition, energy infrastructure
REPowerEU	2022–2026	300	Mainly RRF	Reduce Europe's energy dependence on Russia
Horizon Europe	2021–2027	93.5	Grants mainly (EU budget)	Research and Innovation
The European Regional Development Fund	2021–2028	226	Grants (EU budget)	Ameliorate regional imbalances
The Cohesion Fund	2021–2029	48	Grants (EU budget)	Ameliorate regional imbalances

(*Continued*)

TABLE 6.1 (Continued)

Funding initiative/ programme	*Time frame*	*Budget (€ billion)*	*Source of funding and funding instruments*	*Objectives*
European Structural and Investment Funds (ESIF)	2014–2020	535	Various	Execute European economic, innovation, agricultural, and cohesion policy
Strategic Technologies for Europe Platform (STEP)	2021–	15	Reshuffling of existing funds	Support technological upgrading (incl. digitalisation, decarbonisation, and biotech)
European Fund for Strategic Investments (EFSI)	2015–2020	33.5	Guarantees, Loans, Equity, Venture Debt (EU budget, EIB, EIF)	Revive European investments to boost growth and competitiveness
InvestEU	2021–2027	26	Similar to EFSI	Similar to EFSI
Net-Zero Industry Act (NZIA)	2023–2030	16–18	No additional EU funds, proposed member state spending	Strengthen the European manufacturing capacity of net-zero technologies
Social Climate Fund	2026–2032	86.7	25% of ETS-2 revenues (max. €65 bn) plus 25% national co-financing	Support households and firms impacted by climate policies
Innovation Fund	2020–2030	40	Monetisation of 530 million ETS allowances, assuming a carbon price of €75/tCO_2	Finance "innovative low-carbon technologies"
The EU Chips Act	2023–2030	NA	Mostly private and MS funding; reshuffling of EU resources (e.g., Horizon, RRF)	Support Europe's semiconductor manufacturing
Important Projects of Common European Interest (IPCEI)	2018–	NA	Member States, private co-funding	Strengthen open strategic autonomy by enabling breakthrough innovation and infrastructure projects
Just Transition Mechanism	2021–2027	55	EU grants and loans	Ameliorate the regional impact of decarbonisation

Source: Own adaptation, based on Skyrman (2024: 12).

6.3 Key deficits of and challenges for EU industrial policy

Based upon the survey of the previous section, two key deficits of the current EU approach to IP will be discussed in this chapter. These are: (i) the lack of a coherent definition and strategic outlook of IP, (ii) the legitimacy problems of the current approach, and (iii) the strengthening of directionality of IP.

6.3.1 The lack of a coherent definition and of strategic outlook

IP may be conducted for different purposes. While most obvious in the case of late industrial development in emerging economies, industrial policies have been a pervasive feature of the economic policies of high-income countries as well. They have though come under different labels. As various scholars have shown (see e.g., Block and Keller, 2009; Mazzucato, 2015), the US government has for instance systematically promoted research and development particularly in high-tech sectors (including the military-industrial complex) through state-sponsored programmes such as Defense Advanced Research Projects Agency (DARPA) and others throughout the last decades. The underlying motivations may vary and depend on the respective political-economic context. They may include national security concerns, the promotion of (public) health, or the security of supply with essential goods and services to increase crisis resilience. Evidently, the motivations underlying IP are of critical importance not only in terms of generating public support domestically. In a world that after more than three decades of hyper-globalisation (Rodrik, 2011) has become highly interrelated, they also have important foreign policy implications. IP for rearmament coupled with protectionism might provoke retaliatory action from other countries and *in extremis* trigger an arms race, thereby generating a security dilemma.[4] Alternatively, an IP to promote the green transformation coupled with green technology transfer and largely open trade in green products and services might lead other countries to cooperate and thus promote a green transformation at the global level. IP motivations are thus crucial and should be carefully specified.

Looking back at the last five years, the debate on the motivations and objectives of IP in the European Union went through basically three phases. As a consequence of the commitments assumed by the EU under the Paris Climate Accord in 2015, and triggered by the emergence of large-scale climate activism in European civil society during 2018 and 2019, the first phase featured the quest for a green transition. The objective underlying the EGD presented by Commission President Ursula von der Leyen as her lighthouse project in December 2019 was to decarbonise the European economy and make it climate-neutral until 2050. To that end, the first von der Leyen Commission introduced a large package of programmes and regulations to put the European economy on the path to sustainable development (see Chapter 2 for an overview). Though the EU had been engaged in environmental policy for decades, the EGD elevated the policy field to a strategic level and represented the most comprehensive and ambitious policy initiative to date. Arguably, the prime motivation was to deliver on international commitments given the EU's self-image as a global leader on climate issues, while also reacting to increasingly widespread and profound concerns amongst large segments of the EU population, in particular the younger generation.

A second and partially overlapping phase came with the outbreak of the COVID-19 pandemic in March 2020. Against the backdrop of disruptions in global supply chains and the quest for the development of an effective vaccine, a second motivation for IP emerged, whose aim was to increase the security of supply for essential goods and services. The pandemic was the starting point for a rising awareness in policymaking circles that the European economy was dependent on other countries in quite substantial ways, when it came, for instance, to medical equipment and pharmaceutical substances, which were mostly produced in China, India or other non-European countries (Raza *et al.*, 2021). What is more, in such situations, the governments of producer countries of essential goods (including the EU) tended to – at least temporarily – prioritise domestic consumption and thus restrict exports, as happened, e.g., in the case of COVID-19 vaccines and other needed medical equipment during the pandemic (Bollyky and Bown, 2020). In response, EU policymakers started to reflect on the EU's "Open Strategic Autonomy" and the need to increase the resilience of global supply chains led by European firms. As a consequence, the EU and MSs enacted a number of policies to diversify supply chains, promoted near- and onshoring of essential production (e.g., in the pharmaceutical sector and semiconductors) and the build-up of stockpiles of essential pharmaceutical substances and medical goods. The basic motivation of these policy initiatives was to increase the EU's crisis preparedness, by guaranteeing a certain level of security of supply for essential goods given turbulences in the global economy in the immediate aftermath of a shock. Arguably, the EU crisis response was thus by and large defensive in nature, though the reluctance of the EU to share novel vaccine technology – *aka* its "vaccine nationalism" – was severely criticised by the countries of the Global South at the time (Kampmark and Kurečić, 2022).

Against the background of the growing geopolitical confrontation between the US and China, a third phase came with the outbreak of the war against Ukraine in February 2022. While the pandemic had already pointed political attention to specific vulnerabilities, the perception that the EU was in fact suffering from a much broader set of dependencies, including CRMs, green and digital technologies, as well as energy, that could be "weaponised" against it (Farrell and Newman, 2019), now became widespread. As these dependencies were typically concentrated on countries, the EU had increasingly tense relations with – e.g., CRMs, green technologies and pharmaceutical substances from China, natural gas and oil from Russia – the motivation for promoting industrial policies became increasingly "securitized" (Buzan *et al.*, 1998). That is, the principal rationale for conducting different kinds of industrial policies became increasingly motivated by national security concerns. The issue of technological sovereignty in tandem with (more) local manufacturing, i.e., the ability to control the capacities and capabilities needed to produce strategic products, moved onto the centre stage of EU industrial policymaking. In response, different policy instruments were applied. These included geographical diversification of supply, where domestic production was impossible and insufficient, respectively (e.g., buying liquified natural gas (LNG) from the US and UAE instead of Russian pipeline gas), a strategic reorientation of trade policy to serve security purposes (e.g., via export restrictions, Foreign Direct Investment (FDI) screening, trade sanctions), as well as the promotion of re- and onshoring of strategically important advanced technologies (e.g., via the ECA, the IPCEIs on batteries).

Most recently, external dependencies particularly in high-tech sectors have led to a renaissance of the debate about the EU's competitiveness. Based on the perception that the EU economic model suffers not only from a number of dependencies, but in particular from insufficient innovation dynamics, a number of recent strategy documents, e.g., the Letta Report (Letta, 2024), the Strategic Agenda 2024–2029 (European Council, 2024), and most recently the Draghi Report (Draghi, 2024), diagnose a competitiveness gap of the European economy vis-à-vis its global peers. Consequently, a large number of both horizontal and sectoral measures to close this gap has been proposed, and the European Commission is working on implementing a new competitiveness agenda with policy proposals forthcoming in 2025 et seq.

The strategic orientation has thus shifted from environmental and crisis resilience objectives to promoting EU competitiveness and security, with a focus on increasing productivity and innovation via a mix of deregulation and regulatory simplification, the creation of a single market for energy, finance and telecommunications, public and private investment in high-tech, as well as more assertive foreign economic policies. Twenty-four years after the notorious 2000 Lisbon Agenda, which had introduced a number of neoliberal reforms based on labour market flexibilisation, deregulation and liberalisation, competitiveness – though in a somewhat modified form – is thus re-enthroned as the overarching objective of EU economic policy. As a consequence, the conventional view on the hierarchy of economic goals has been re-established: the first priority is growth based on productivity and innovation, everything else, including decarbonisation and social welfare, is relegated to second place.

Though the Draghi Report states that competitiveness should not be understood as a zero-sum game pitting the EU against other countries, it nevertheless explicitly refers to the EU's growth and productivity gap vis-à-vis the US and China as the problem to be tackled by its proposed agenda. The report also cites statistics in support, for instance the EU's falling share of world gross domestic product (GDP), falling EU shares in global trade, or the small number of EU companies amongst the world's top 50 tech companies and their falling share of global tech revenues (Draghi 2024, 7 et seq.). As Paul Krugman already observed some 30 years ago (Krugman, 1994), to elevate the concept of competitiveness from the company level to the macroeconomy is however dangerous. If one follows the Draghi Report and defines productivity as the essential measure of a country's competitiveness, Krugman's main argument was that in large advanced economies productivity basically depends on domestic factors, as the relative weight of the international sector in the national economy remains circumscribed. One might argue that after three decades of neoliberal globalisation this argument does not hold any longer, as the EU has been increasingly integrated into the world economy. However, this has happened to a limited extent only. The share of total trade (extra-EU exports + imports of goods) to EU GDP grew from approx. 23% in 2002 to roughly 29% in 2023, i.e., an increase of roughly one quarter.[5] One might thus assume that international factors, such as e.g., exchange rate movements, unfair competitive practices of trade partners, etc. might have played a stronger role in determining EU economic performance. However, a look at the EU trade balance (goods and services) reveals, that since the mid-1990s the trade balance has always shown a surplus with a significant growth tendency since 2009 (except for 2022 due to the Ukraine shock). In 2023, net export of goods and services stood at 3.70% of EU GDP, i.e., a significant surplus. Whatever negative impacts the world economy might have had on the EU economy, the EU seemed to have managed well with respect to its external position.[6]

The EU's slower growth dynamics relative to the US and China thus should be primarily explained by domestic factors. The Draghi Report cites relevant factors such as relatively low Research & Development (R&D) dynamics, low investment levels (both public and private), and the lack of risk-taking private investment capital. It however fails to fully account for the dysfunctional macroeconomic framework of the EU, which via fiscal austerity and restrictive monetary policies has had a strong contractionary effect on effective demand during most of the last 25 years. The latter is arguably the most pronounced difference compared to the US and China, which over the same time period have both followed much more expansionary fiscal and monetary policies. However, insofar as the Draghi Report focuses on domestic measures to increase productivity dynamics and labels this a competitiveness agenda, it might be considered an otherwise harmless misnomer. To the extent, however, that the policy agenda puts the emphasis on reacting to perceived external threats to EU competitiveness, it might quickly turn into a "dangerous obsession", leading to skewed policies that might threaten the international economic system and ultimately be self-defeating (Krugman, 1994).

The latter happens precisely through the securitisation of economic relations propagated by the Draghi Report as well as the new EC's Strategic Agenda. This is particularly problematic, since it tends to introduce a zero-sum logic into EU policymaking. Either the EU gains access to critical raw-materials "in the new scramble for Africa" or its peer competitors; Either the EU controls advanced photolithography technology by introducing export restrictions for EU producers like ASML, or China will acquire these technologies, misuse them to enhance its military capabilities and "weaponize" them against the EU. Either the EU produces batteries and electric vehicles, or Chinese competition will displace EU companies from the global market. As Krugman (1994) lucidly observed, "The rhetoric of competitiveness turns out to provide a good way [...] to justify hard choices", as it appeals to national unity and sacrifice in the face of external threats. If others put their national interest first, the EU needs to follow suit. Needless to say, the second Trump administration with its America-first rhetoric and coercive trade policy has exacerbated this stance amongst EU policymakers.

What such a motivation overlooks, is that increased international economic competition will have broader repercussions upon international politics more generally. The political climate between countries and thus the willingness to engage in cooperation to arrive at mutually beneficial solutions for pressing global problems must necessarily suffer. Little surprise that multilateralism and global governance is considered to be in deep crisis by many observers (see e.g., Eggel and Galvin, 2020). Under such conditions, mutual distrust reigns and virtually every IP is perceived by other countries as an unwarranted act of protectionism that must be answered by retaliatory action. The shift to such a security-oriented competitiveness agenda that pits the EU against other countries should thus be considered an ambivalent and potentially self-damaging development. Precisely because of the increase of geopolitical rivalries, and the subsequent risk of self-damaging tit-for-tat trade retaliation and economic warfare between countries, the motivation for IP should be strictly defensive in nature and oriented towards achieving legitimate social objectives such as climate neutrality or enhancing societal resilience in crisis situations, by e.g., expanding domestic production capacities for essential goods and services such as essential medicines. In other words, IP needs to be embedded into a vision of "Defensive Regionalism" (Buzan, 1984), instead of "malevolent mercantilism" (Gilpin, 1975). While the latter employs economic statecraft to secure access to raw materials, energy, technology or export markets, with a mixture of economic and political coercion, while at the same time protecting its domestic market from foreign competition, the former approach is oriented towards promoting domestic welfare. It is based, in particular, on (i) a principled definition of what constitutes a legitimate argument for (protective) industrial policies, (ii) builds on a careful case-by-case analysis instead of reliance on a generic principle (of e.g., free trade, or expanding state power), and (iii) is open to addressing the concerns of trade partners through a process of cooperation with the aim of finding mutually beneficial solutions.

Given the EU's relatively high external dependencies on, e.g., energy, technology, and CRMs, and its lack of hard power in international relations, the "assertive" foreign economic policy agenda propagated by the Draghi Report and recent Commission documents should be avoided. The EU has an obvious right to economic self-defence, if coerced by others. In an increasingly multi-polar world, the focus of the EU's external policy approach, particularly given the new Commission's priority on economic security, should otherwise focus on promoting cooperative international economic relations. This runs however counter to the new competitiveness agenda, with the latter aiming to increase the EU's competitive leverage on world markets, that is, markets that are increasingly protected by tariff walls. Instead, a strategy based on Defensive Regionalism would be more inward-looking, with economic dynamism being generated as a consequence of a public sector-led investment strategy for the green and digital transformation.

6.3.2 *The legitimacy problems of the current IP approach*

Whatever the specific motivation, for IP programmes to be accepted by societal stakeholders, they have to be considered legitimate. While economists typically focus on the technical aspects of economic policy, and thus tend to neglect legitimacy issues, such an approach is fundamentally flawed in the case of policies for the Twin Transformation. The latter will produce deep changes to our modes of production and consumption, indeed our way of life. Along the way, some segments of society will profit, while others and potentially large parts of the population will find themselves negatively affected, at least during the transitory period up to 2050. Given the fundamental uncertainty of the process and the associated social concerns, sustained political support critically depends upon a positive, if not optimistic vision of the future. Citizens will have to be convinced that (i) the Twin Transformation is not only necessary but indeed desirable; (ii) that they are stakeholders in this process and have a chance to co-shape it; and (iii) that their aspirations and concerns are taken onboard, so that the distribution of benefits and costs during the transformation is fair and balanced.

These three requirements of a legitimate political approach to managing the Twin Transformation can be substantiated by three concepts of political theory, namely, hegemony, input legitimacy and output legitimacy. Hegemony is here interpreted in the Gramscian sense and refers to the requirement for a vision of change (or grand narrative) underlying the political management of the Twin Transformation to convince people and garner active support from civil society (Figure 6.1). It should inspire hope and optimism for a better future. Apart from this ideational element, support is more likely if it is combined with two further elements: (i) people are given a stake in the process, such that they have a chance to voice their interests and concerns (input legitimacy); (ii) the instruments and policies employed deliver on the promises of the transformation process, and social costs arising along the way are managed in an effective and balanced manner (output legitimacy). Input and output legitimacy are complementary. Though the balance between them may shift during the process, both should be employed to secure legitimacy.[7]

While climate science has provided a convincing case for the necessity of the green transformation, the same has not happened with respect to the desirability of the process.[8] Though one might argue that given the existential threat of the climate crisis to human survival, its desirability should be self-evident, this is not entirely convincing. Surveys, for instance, typically confirm that a large majority of citizens is aware of the threats posed by climate change and support policies to tackle it. However, in-depth questions reveal that different segments (or milieus)

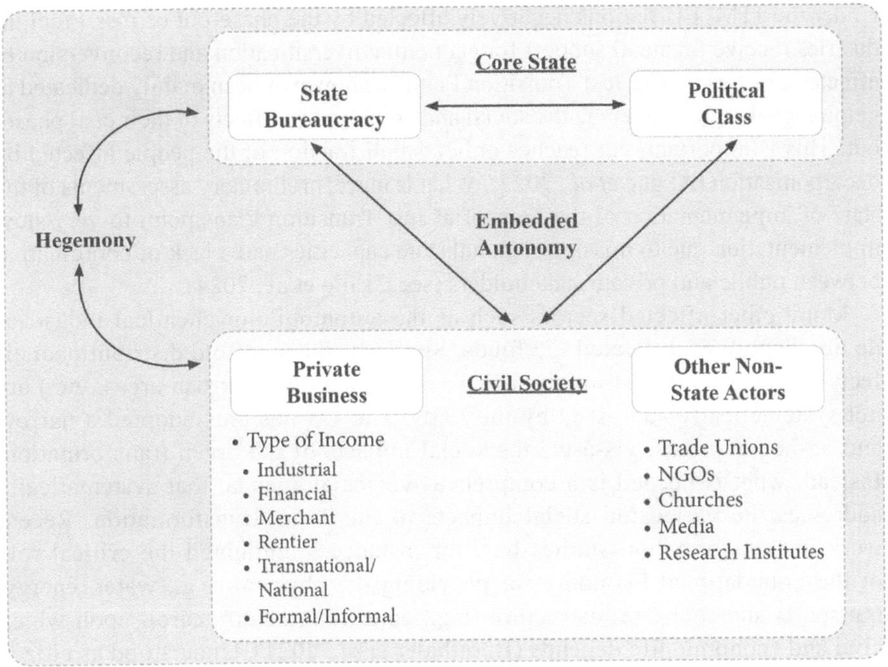

FIGURE 6.1 Inclusive state – society relations

Source: Own adaptation, based on Grumiller and Raza (2025).

of the population have diverging views as to the specific policies to be employed, and what is more, are unwilling to change their cherished yet unsustainable personal lifestyles in more profound ways (Schleer *et al.*, 2024). In other words, while in general people understand the threat posed by climate change, their desire to change their current lifestyle in exchange for some diffuse future benefit is limited. To this, one has to add that other social drivers such as vested interests in the fossil economy also hinder decarbonisation policies. Studies indicate that under the current constellation of social forces, the EU will likely not be able to reach its climate targets in time (Engels *et al.*, 2024).

The pace as well as effectiveness of decarbonisation policies, including green industrial policies, is thus severely curtailed by a lack of (active) support by important segments of society. Indeed, the recent electoral success of populist far-right parties across Europe upon the basis of, amongst others, a climate-sceptic message suggests that popular support for the green transformation is indeed receding.

To its credit, the European Commission has understood that the green transformation needs to be complemented by a social pillar. In proclaiming that "not one is left behind", Ursula von der Leyen introduced the JTM as an element of the EGD in 2019, which became operational in 2021 in the context of the Fit-For-55 package.

Under the JTM, EU regions negatively affected by the phase-out of fossil fuel industries receive financial support for economic diversification and reconversion of affected territories. The Just Transition Fund has however been mainly dedicated to helping coal regions manage the social and employment effects of their coal phase-out. This is important, but reaches only a small fraction of the people affected by decarbonisation (Akgüç *et al.*, 2022). What is more, preliminary assessments of the state of implementation of the Territorial Just Transition Plans point to very slow implementation due to missing regional state capacities and a lack of coordination between public and private stakeholders (see Cirillo et al., 2024).

Many other affected sectors such as the automobile or chemical industries do not dispose of dedicated EU funds. Similarly, the manifold distributional effects of the green transformation (e.g., on workers, rural/urban areas, etc.) are not systematically addressed by the EGD. The EU has thus adopted a narrow and ad-hoc approach vis-à-vis the social impacts of the green transformation. Instead, what is needed is a comprehensive social agenda, that systematically addresses the variegated social impacts of the Twin Transformation. Recent work in transformation studies has, for instance, highlighted the critical role of the Foundational Economy for providing the physical (e.g., water, energy, transport) and social infrastructure (e.g., education, health, care), upon which civil and economic life depends (Bärnthaler *et al.*, 2021). Understood as citizen rights, the provision of these basic public services will be of particular importance for sustaining social reproduction and societal stability during the transition period. Their expanded development during the transition would not only meet the social needs of ageing societies for care services, but could become an important source of new employment, given that a significant number of jobs will be lost in both carbon-intensive sectors and economic activities taken over by digital technologies.

With respect to the digital transformation, the latter will foreseeably impact both production and consumption quite profoundly, thus generating winners and losers along the way. The digital transformation, however, requires a different answer as to its necessity and desirability. While the socio-ecological transformation is a politically induced (and thus exogenous) process in order to put capitalist society onto a different, i.e., ecologically sustainable, trajectory, the digital transformation is a process endogenous to capitalist society. Thus, in the latter case, the objective is not to induce the process but to manage it in socially beneficial directions. Though it is premature to make a conclusive judgement of the economic benefits and costs of the digital transformation, some studies expect sizable job losses, particularly in routine tasks (Acemoglu and Restrepo, 2019; Frey and Osborne, 2017), while others emphasise negative skills-related effects on the income of workers (see e.g., Baldwin, 2019). Thus, to the extent that digitalisation displaces labour or necessitates new skills, the government has, for instance, a role to play to support skills acquisition and training, as emphasised by the Draghi Report (Draghi, 2024).

As technology is not neutral but can be used for both socially useful and detrimental purposes, the critical engagement with technological change as, e.g., promoted by Critical Theory (Horkheimer and Adorno, 1944; Marcuse, 1991), however points to the need for a more systematic political regulation of the digital revolution. More recent work, in particular on the rapid expansion of digital technologies, especially in the form of social media, surveillance technology, biometric tracking, or artificial intelligence, has raised concerns about privacy, freedom, and loss of political control. Also, the power of digital platforms and of big tech companies not only in the economic realm, but in expanding its influence on politics is cause for concern (Rikap *et al.*, 2024; see e.g., Zuboff, 2020). It is thus difficult to argue that the digital transformation as such is desirable. Instead, the political management of the digital transformation is necessary and indeed desirable to guarantee individual freedoms and civil rights, as well as to promote the employment of digital technologies to socially beneficial ends. While acknowledging that the approach of the EU to regulating digital technologies has traditionally been motivated by the desire to protect individual freedoms and rights, in the recent debate on promoting the digital revolution, other motivations related to national security and competitiveness have become more prominent. It has been argued, in particular, that against the background of increasing geopolitical rivalries, the EU cannot afford to lack behind its peer competitors in advanced technologies including artificial intelligence, cloud computing or semiconductors. Thus, support programmes for these industries have been designed (e.g., the EU Chips Act, the Microelectronics IPCEIs), which have handed out significant amounts of money to often large multinational companies without apparently imposing any social conditionalities and regulations. To this one has to add external pressure from the US government to weaken EU digital rights regulations in the interest of US tech giants.

The debate on the necessity as well as desirability of the digital transformation thus remains contradictory. On the one hand, EU policymakers increasingly justify significant financial support for the digital transformation on grounds of national security and the EU's competitiveness. Upon this basis, the Draghi Report goes so far as to suggest that the EU actively supports the formation of European based big tech companies. In contrast, the social and political impacts of the digital transformation are increasingly relegated to second place. This risks to create a situation, in which corporate interests, including US-based big tech companies, increasingly dictate the political agenda of the EU digital transformation. Instead, the case for the desirability of the digital transformation should be based on a distinct European approach to the digital sphere, that is motivated by promoting the EU's digital sovereignty. This approach should (i) strengthen the political regulation of digital technologies on the basis of a strong commitment to civil liberties and fundamental rights; (ii) promote forms of public digital infrastructures, including public sub-stacks and universal platforms, such as search engines and foundation AI models, which are organised as a commons governed by new public institutions with state and civil society representation; (iii) provide financial support to tech companies only upon the basis of strong transparency and information-sharing as well as social conditions; (iii) not shy away from a more stringent competition policy, including if necessary the dismantlement of companies with a dominant market position (see Rikap *et al.*, 2024).

By way of conclusion, for industrial policies promoting the Twin Transformation to achieve legitimacy, they must be based on a new inclusive European social contract (Ricz, 2020). This contract must involve three elements: (i) a new narrative outlining the contours of a future European society based on a sustainable production and consumption model, (ii) social equity by way of an enlarged welfare model of foundational economy, that is comprehensive as well as effective in providing a social safety net for the entire population, as well as (iii) a political model including enhanced democratic participation of affected stakeholders to co-shape the twin transformation.

6.3.3 Enhancing the directionality of IP through (social) conditionalities

IP interventions come in different forms, but can be roughly categorised into (i) financial transfers (grants, preferential loans, guarantees, public equity), (ii) taxes and tariffs, and (iii) regulation (disciplines, prohibitions). The predominant neoliberal policy framework during the last four decades, as, e.g., codified in EU competition and state aid rules, by and large displayed a restrictive stance towards public transfers to the private sector. Subsidies needed special justification, and were only allowed for a number of exemptions, including R&D, regional development and specific social purposes. The main economic arguments levelled against subsidisation emphasised competitive distortions, rent-seeking behaviour, and moral hazard (e.g., in the case of state-financed bail-outs of "too big to fail" corporations).

At latest with the arrival of the Corona Pandemic in 2020 and the effects of the war in Ukraine since 2022, this state of affairs has markedly changed. Both the EU and most MSs have initiated large-scale funding programmes including hefty hand-outs to private companies. Motivated by the challenges of the Twin Transformation as well as geopolitical security concerns, large IP programmes have been initiated in many industrialised countries, including the US, the EU, China, Japan, amongst others. The programmes typically target certain strategic sectors, e.g., semiconductors, green technologies, or telecommunications.

The principal rationale for mobilising significant public financial resources for the twin transformation has to do with influencing the directionality of private investment, against a situation of existential threats emanating either from climate change or from geopolitical risks. For instance, to build-up domestic productive capacity in strategic products like semiconductors, or for switching to energy production based on renewables. Predominantly, this is not done through command and control measures, but indirectly by offering the corporate sector financial incentives under the condition that the public funds are used – and possibly matched by private funds – to achieve a defined objective. Thus, ideally, a desired process of change, such as the decarbonisation of the economy, can be catalysed, if not accelerated. Underlying this approach is an implicit social contract that given the scale of the needed transformation, the necessary adjustment requires a collective effort encompassing all members of the political society, with each making its contribution according to his/her abilities. Adjustment burdens exceeding individual possibilities are shared throughout the community, in particular by offering public financial support. Receiving public money thus obliges the recipient to honour his/her part of the implicit social contract. This includes to use the money for the defined purpose, in conformity with the respective legal framework conditions, and to share any benefits eventually accruing from the investment, be it with the direct stakeholders of the company (i.e., owners, workforce), or with the general public at large (e.g., via tax contributions, free licensing of new technical knowledge, etc.).

With the government in a liberal democracy acting as the collective agent of society, it is its obligation to serve as the guarantor of the social contract. In legal terms, the government concludes a funding agreement with the respective company, which stipulates the conditions under which the latter is entitled to receive the financial transfer. Such conditions may come in multiple forms, including through performance standards, i.e. targets to be achieved by the beneficiary relating to production, investment or employment; In addition, process conditions might be employed, that oblige the beneficiary to accept or introduce changes to its corporate governance system, for instance public (co-)ownership, introduction of collective bargaining, or special transparency or reporting mechanisms (see Table 6.2 for overview).

TABLE 6.2 Industrial policy conditionalities

Performance standards	*Corporate control*
Production, investment, employment, and export quotas	Public or domestic ownership
Environmental and safety standards	Promotion of intra-firm or intra-sectoral cooperation
Training and skill programmes	Acceptance of collective-bargaining rules
Technological or local content requirements	Accepting joint ventures
Geographical location	Inclusion of independent directors
	Disclosure of pollution information
	Regulation of intellectual property rights

Source: Author's elaboration, based on Bulfone *et al.* (2024).

TABLE 6.3 Indicative taxonomy of social conditionalities

Performance standards	*Corporate control*
Location guarantees	Establishment of Works Councils
Employment quotas	Consultation/Co-decision rights for Work Councils
Skill upgrading programmes	Information and monitoring rights for Work Councils
Sharing of new technology (e.g., compulsory licensing requirements)	Mandatory seats for trade unions/Work Councils on boards
Domestic content and sourcing requirements	Labour standards (minimum wages, collective bargaining)
	Health and safety standards
	Prohibition of stock buy-backs and of dividends
	Sharing of profits (e.g., upside profit sharing)

Source: Author's elaboration.

A specific sub-category refers to social conditionalities. These include both measures targeting the affected labour force, e.g., via employment and labour standards, skills acquisition, the establishment of works councils or collective bargaining, and extend to measures that benefit society at large, e.g., the sharing of new technology, the sharing of (excess-)profits, or domestic content requirements (see Table 6.3 for an overview).

While there is widespread agreement that the green – and to some extent also – the digital transformation pose extraordinary challenges that require this collective effort including the transfer of significant amounts of public money to the private sector, the danger of corporate welfarism is clearly looming in the background (Bulfone *et al.*, 2023). In other words, the corporate beneficiaries might see the availability of public money as a windfall opportunity for increasing profits via rent-seeking or for moral hazard behaviour, e.g., by pocketing public money for ailing business activities. In addition, as currently not only the EU, but many other countries have set up massive financial support programmes, particularly large transnational corporations might try to play off governments against each other in order to extract the highest possible subsidy.

The scholarly literature on corporate welfarism emphasises that the privatisation of many state-led activities (e.g., public services) during the neoliberal period has resulted in a marked shift of structural power in favour of the corporate sector (Busemeyer and Thelen, 2020; Culpepper, 2010). As mentioned above, in many respects the state has lost its capacity to directly take care of certain activities, and in fact depends on the private sector to perform such tasks. This literature thus warns against the prevailing view, that the return of IP should be interpreted as a sign of renewed state power (see e.g., Iversen and Soskice, 2019). Instead, the prevalence (or not) of strong conditionalities attached to financial handouts to private firms should be the indicator, upon the basis of which to assess the power balance between the state and private capital.

Preliminary comparative assessments of conditionality policies of the EU and other countries, in particular the US, highlight the following aspects that merit particular attention:

(a) the US has been more proactive in including (social) conditionalities than the EU, using a wide array of different instruments (Blue Green Alliance, 2023; Estevez, 2023);
(b) coalition-building, in particular with trade unions and civil society, and a broadly shared motivation (in the US primarily the geopolitical threat of China to US supremacy) have been critical for successful implementation and monitoring in the US case (Bulfone *et al.*, 2024);
(c) government monitoring and enforcement during implementation is difficult due to capacity constraints and lacking access to information, but is facilitated by including monitoring provisions that grant corporate stakeholders, e.g., works councils and trade unions, access to information (Blue Green Alliance, 2023); and
(d) the legal room to define and include conditionalities into funding agreements is relatively wide, even under EU competition and state aid law. It is ultimately constrained by fundamental constitutional rights (e.g., protection of private property) only (Damjanovic, 2024; Zenke *et al.*, 2024).

To the extent that information is publicly available, the EU and MSs have used conditionalities only selectively, and not with a focus on social conditionalities. Examples include, amongst others (Bulfone *et al.*, 2024):

(a) conditionalities to prevent fraud within the framework of the Recovery and Resilience Facility (RRF);
(b) in the Microelectronics IPCEI, a "claw-back" profit-sharing mechanism was introduced, under which companies may be required to redistribute extra profits obtained as a result of EU funding. In the case of a supply chain crisis, the Commission can require semiconductor companies that have received financial support under the EU Chips Act to share information about their production capacities and, if necessary, to prioritise domestic orders for critical products. If companies do not comply with these requirements, the Commission can impose fines or other sanctions; and
(c) within the framework of the European Defence Fund, access to funding is restricted to companies established in at least two EU MSs, or associated members part of the European Economic Area. Intellectual property rights resulting from funded projects should not be controlled by any third countries or third-country entities. Otherwise, the Commission can claw back the initial funding.

Various reasons have been proposed in the literature, as to why the conditionality regime in the EU appears relatively weak (Bulfone *et al.*, 2024; Cooiman, 2023; Ducastel *et al.*, 2024). Amongst them are (i) the lack of financial power of the EU and its dependency on MSs to extend funds, (ii) administrative capacity constraints both at EU, but particularly at the level of MSs, and (iii) a comparatively weak security dispositive, including opposing views on the "China-threat". With respect to the low profile of social conditionalities, the already relatively high level of labour and social standards in the EU as well as the exclusion of trade unions from industrial policymaking in the EU serve as the main explanations. In contrast to the US, where trade unions have played an important role in co-designing social conditionalities, and thus have put considerable pressure upon the Biden administration, the calls of European trade unions to introduce stronger social conditionalities have been mostly ignored by the Commission as well as MS governments (ETUC, 2024).

By way of conclusion, conditionalities, including in particular social conditionalities, can serve as an important mechanism for guaranteeing the desired directionality of investment, i.e., for making sure that financial transfers to the private sector are effective in pursuing specific objectives of the Twin Transformation. Weak or no conditionality invites indeed the kind of adverse behaviour emphasised in the mainstream economics literature, such as rent-seeking, moral hazard or anti-competitive behaviour. Given the relatively weak bargaining position of many EU institutions as well as governments vis-à-vis the private sector, and in particular large transnational corporations, it is precisely through (social) conditionalities that the public purpose of financial transfers can be safeguarded. The adoption of a more inclusive approach to IP, that mobilises the support of trade unions and civil society at large for such an approach, is thus of high political urgency, as it would provide more autonomy to IP policymakers relative to the corporate sector, and thus facilitate the implementation of conditionalities greatly.

6.3.4 Concluding remarks

IP in the European Union is here to stay. The present juncture will determine whether EU IP will be directed towards promoting economic security and competitiveness at the expense of social justice and environmental sustainability, or an inclusive and broadly supported project of transformation will be pursued.

The experience since 2020 points to the importance of social mobilisation for promoting more inclusive forms of IP. Due to both exogenous shocks such as the pandemic and the Ukraine war, and strong political resistance from corporate interests as well as authoritarian populism, the EU political system has started to backtrack from its environmental agenda under the EGD.

Under the changed geopolitical situation, the dysfunctionality of the EU governance system has however become glaringly obvious. Protracted consensus-building, weak coordination, binding funding constraints under the revised Stability and Growth Pact, and strong external dependencies are all contributing to a situation characterised by political paralysis. The push to further centralisation and technocratic governance led by the EC is resisted by in particular the large EU MSs. However, in programmatic terms a new power bloc is emerging composed of liberals, conservative as well as authoritarian populist forces, that promotes the new economic security and competitiveness agenda, where IP is increasingly repurposed to promote militarisation, while social and environmental standards as well as civic rights are progressively dismantled.

From a progressive perspective, what is instead necessary is a re-founded social contract combining social safety with environmental sustainability and a good life for all. IP should be put into the service of a defensive regionalism that responds to social needs, strengthens economic resilience and autonomy, and guides technological change to the benefit of society at large. Such a project can only be initiated and sustained by broad societal support, which in turn is predicated upon an inclusive and participatory approach to industrial policymaking and a fair sharing of benefits and costs. Turning IP from an elite-driven top-down venture to a bottom-up project, is something progressive forces need to urgently engage with.

Notes

1 See EIB website on EFSI: https://www.eib.org/en/products/mandates-partnerships/efsi/index?utm_source=chatgpt.com (accessed 23 October 2025).
2 For more information see DG Competition dedicated IPCEI website: https://competition-policy.ec.europa.eu/state-aid/ipcei_en (accessed 23 October 2025).
3 The moratorium declared by INTEL in September 2024 on the construction of large manufacturing sites in Magdeburg and in Poland despite €10 billion in subsidies granted by the German government are seen by some experts as suggesting the economic non-viability of large-scale production in the EU (INDUSTRIEMAGAZIN, 2024; Jahn *et al.*, 2024).
4 A security dilemma describes a situation in which the actions of a country to increase its security (e.g., through rearmament) create a situation that ultimately undermines its security. The reason for this is that as other countries do not know whether rearmament serves defensive or offensive objectives, they will react by retaliatory action. This in turn can further escalate tensions and ultimately lead to (armed) conflict (see Herz (1950) for the original formulation of the concept).
5 Own calculation, based on AMECO data tables DMGE, DXGE and UVGD.
6 Own calculations, based on AMECO data tables UBGS and UVGD.
7 In this, we do not follow the conventional view that given the multi-level governance structure of the EU including its democratic deficit output legitimacy is of higher importance (Scharpf, 2002). Given the fundamental importance of the Twin Transformation, its legitimacy needs an approach involving both dimensions. To sustain the process of transformation over the required timespan of at least three decades in the face of ups and downs, i.e., resistance from vested interests, adverse outcomes from electoral cycles etc., it needs to be supported by a broad social base, with an active stake in the process.
8 See 6th IPCC Assessment Report at: https://www.ipcc.ch/report/sixth-assessment-report-cycle/ (accessed 23 October 2025).

References

Acemoglu, D., and Restrepo, P. (2019) 'Automation and New Tasks: How Technology Displaces and Reinstates Labor'. *Journal of Economic Perspectives*, 33(2), 3–30. https://doi.org/10.1257/jep.33.2.3

Akgüç, M., Arabadjiewa, K., and Galgóczi, B. (2022) 'Why the EU's Patchy "Just Transition" Framework Is Not up to Meeting Its Climate Ambitions'. *ETUI Policy Brief 2022.06*. https://www.etui.org/publications/why-eus-patchy-just-transition-framework-not-meeting-its-climate-ambitions (accessed 17 October 2025).

Baldwin, R. E. (2019) *The Great Convergence: Information Technology and the New Globalization*. First Harvard University Press paperback edition. Cambridge, MA: The Belknap Press of Harvard University Press.

Bärnthaler, R., Novy, A., and Plank. L. (2021) 'The Foundational Economy as a Cornerstone for a Social–Ecological Transformation'. *Sustainability*, 13(18), 10460. https://doi.org/10.3390/su131810460

Block, F. and Keller, M. R. (2009) 'Where Do Innovations Come from? Transformations in the US Economy, 1970–2006'. *Socio-Economic Review*, 7(3), 459–483. https://doi.org/10.1093/ser/mwp013

Blue Green Alliance (2023) *Best Practices for Implementation: How the Lessons from the Bipartisan Infrastructure Law Can Ensure the Inflation Reduction Act Delivers Good Jobs and Community Benefits*. Minneapolis.

Bollyky, T. J. and Bown, C. P. (2020) 'The Tragedy of Vaccine Nationalism Only Cooperation Can End the Pandemic'. *Foreign Affairs*, 99(5), 96–108.

Bulfone, F., Ergen, T., and Kalaitzake, M. (2023) 'No Strings Attached: Corporate Welfare, State Intervention, and the Issue of Conditionality'. *Competition & Change*, 27(2), 253–276. https://doi.org/10.1177/10245294221101145

Bulfone, F., Ergen, T., and Maggor, E. (2024) *The Political Economy of Conditionality and the New Industrial Policy*. Köln: Max Planck Institute for the Study of Society.

Busemeyer, M. R. and Thelen, K. (2020) 'Institutional Sources of Business Power'. *World Politics*, 72(3), 448–480. https://doi.org/10.1017/S004388712000009X

Buzan, B. (1984) 'Economic Structure and International Security: The Limits of the Liberal Case'. *International Organization*, 38(4), 597–624.

Buzan, B., Wæver, O., and de Wilde, J. 1998. *Security: A New Framework for Analysis*. Boulder, CO: Lynne Rienner Pub.

Cimoli, M., Dosi, G., Landesmann, M. A., Mazzucato, M., Page, T., Pianta, M., Stiglitz, J. E., and Walz, R. (2015) 'Which Industrial Policy Does Europe Need?' *Intereconomics*, 50(3), 120–155.

Cirillo, V., Divella, M., Ferrulli, E., and Greco, L. (2024) *Active Labor Market Policies in the Framework of Just Transition Programs: The Case of Italy, Spain, and Germany*. Vienna: ÖFSE *Working Paper no. 79*. https://doi.org/10.60637/2024-wp79

Cooiman, F. (2023) 'The Limits of Derisking. (Un)Conditionality in the European Green Transformation'. *Competition & Change*, 10245294231224137. https://doi.org/10.1177/10245294231224137

Culpepper, P. D. (2010) *Quiet Politics and Business Power: Corporate Control in Europe and Japan*. 1st edn. Cambridge University Press. https://doi.org/10.1017/CBO9780511760716

Dachs, B. (2023) *The European Chips Act*. Vienna: FIW POLICY BRIEFS. https://www.fiw.ac.at/publications/fiw-policy-brief-no-58-the-european-chips-act/ (accessed 17 October 2025).

Damjanovic, D. (2024) 'Rechtliche Stellungnahme Zur Möglichkeit Der Formulierung von Beteiligungskonditionalitäten Des Staates an Einem Privaten Unternehmen Im Rahmen Der Industriepolitik'.

Draghi, M. (2024) 'The Future of European Competitiveness Part A | A Competitiveness Strategy for Europe'.

Dreyer, C. (2024) 'The Cost of Inaction'. *Climate Policy Initiative*. https://www.climatepolicyinitiative.org/the-cost-of-inaction/ (accessed 17 October 2025).
Ducastel, A., Rivière, C., and Ferlazzo, E. (2024) 'The European Investor State Has No Clothes. Generic Promises and Local Weaknesses of Green Public Subsidies in France'. *Competition & Change*, 28(3–4), 454–473. https://doi.org/10.1177/10245294231213413
Eggel, D. and Galvin, M. (2020) 'Multilateralism Is in Crisis – Or Is It? Global Challenges, No. 7, April 2020.' *Global Challenges*. https://globalchallenges.ch/issue/7/multilaterism-is-in-crisis-or-is-it (accessed 17 October 2025).
Eisl, A. (2022) *EU Industrial Policy in the Making. From Ad Hoc Exercises to Key Instrument: How to Make IPCEIs Fit for the Long Run*. Paris: Jacques Delors Institute. POLICY PAPER.
Engels, A., Marotzke, J., Ratter, B., Gonçalves Gresse, E., López-Rivera, A., Pagnone, A., and Wilkens, J. (eds.) (2024) *Hamburg Climate Futures Outlook 2024: Conditions for Sustainable Climate Change Adaptation*. 1. Auflage. Bielefeld: Transcript.
Estevez, I. (2023) *Multi-Solving, Trade-Offs, and Conditionalities in Industrial Policy*. Washington, DC: The Roosevelt Institute. https://rooseveltinstitute.org/publications/multi-solving-trade-offs-and-conditionalities-in-industrial-policy/ (accessed 17 October 2025).
ETUC (2024) 'Industrial Policy for Quality Jobs: Social Conditionalities for Social Progress | ETUC'. https://www.etuc.org/en/document/industrial-policy-quality-jobs-social-conditionalities-social-progress-0 (accessed 17 October 2025).
European Commission (2012) 'A Stronger European Industry for Growth and Economic Recovery. COM(2012) 582 Final'.
European Commission (2014) 'For a European Industrial Renaissance. COM (2014) 14 Final'.
European Commission (2017) 'Investing in a Smart, Innovative and SUSTAINABLE INDUSTRY. A Renewed EU Industrial Policy Strategy. COM(2017) 479 Final'.
European Commission (2018) 'Independent Evaluation of the EFSI Regulation, Final Report, Directorate-General for Economic and Financial Affairs'.
European Commission (2023a) 'A Green Deal Industrial Plan for the Net-Zero Age. Communication from the Commission to the European Parliament, the European Council, the Council, the European Economic and Social Committee and the Committee of the Regions; COM (2023)62 Final'.
European Commission (2023b) *Investment Needs Assessment and Funding Availabilities to Strengthen EU's Net-Zero Technology Manufacturing Capacity*. Brussels. COMMISSION STAFF WORKING DOCUMENT. https://single-market-economy.ec.europa.eu/system/files/2023-03/SWD_2023_68_F1_STAFF_WORKING_PAPER_EN_V4_P1_2629849.PDF (accessed 17 October 2025).
European Commission (2023c) COM(2023) 161 *final Proposal for a REGULATION OF THE EUROPEAN PARLIAMENT AND OF THE COUNCIL on Establishing a Framework of Measures for Strengthening Europe's Net-Zero Technology Products Manufacturing Ecosystem (Net Zero Industry Act)*. https://eur-lex.europa.eu/resource.html?uri=cellar:6448c360-c4dd-11ed-a05c-01aa75ed71a1.0001.02/DOC_1&format=PDF (accessed 17 October 2025).
European Commission (2025) *Delivering the EU Green Deal: Progress towards Targets*. Luxemburg: European Commission, Joint Research Centre. https://data.europa.eu/doi/10.2760/3105205
European Council (2024) 'Strategic Agenda 2024–2029'. www.consilium.europa.eu/media/4aldqfl2/2024_557_new-strategic-agenda.pdf (accessed 17 October 2025).
European Union (2024) 'Regulation (EU) 2024/1252 of the European Parliament and of the Council of 11 April 2024 Establishing a Framework for Ensuring a Secure and Sustainable Supply of Critical Raw Materials and Amending Regulations (EU) No 168/2013, (EU) 2018/858, (EU) 2018/1724 and (EU) 2019/1020'.

Farrell, H. and Newman, A. L. (2019) 'Weaponized Interdependence: How Global Economic Networks Shape State Coercion'. *International Security*, 44(1), 42–79. https://doi.org/10.1162/isec_a_00351
Frey, C. B. and Osborne, M. A. (2017) 'The Future of Employment: How Susceptible Are Jobs to Computerisation?' *Technological Forecasting and Social Change*, 114, 254–280. https://doi.org/10.1016/j.techfore.2016.08.019
Gabor, D. (2023) The (European) Derisking State. *SocArXiv*. Preprint. https://doi.org/10.31235/osf.io/hpbj2
Gabor, D. and Braun, B. (2023) 'Green Macrofinancial Regimes'. https://doi.org/10.31235/osf.io/4pkv8
Gilpin, R. (1975) 'Three Models of the Future'. *International Organization*, 29(1), 37–60. https://doi.org/10.1017/S0020818300017896
Grumiller, J. and Raza, W. (2025) 'Towards an Institutional Setup for Industrial Policy in Late Industrialization in the 21st Century'. *Development Policy Review*, 43(2), e70004. https://doi.org/10.1111/dpr.70004
Herz, J. H. (1950) 'Idealist Internationalism and the Security Dilemma'. *World Politics*, 2(2), 157–180. https://doi.org/10.2307/2009187
Horkheimer, M. and Adorno, T. W. (1944) *Dialectic of Enlightenment: Philosophical Fragments*. Nachdr. Stanford, CA: Stanford Univ. Press.
INDUSTRIEMAGAZIN (2024) 'Europäische Halbleiter-Industrie: Intel stoppt Bau in Magdeburg: Verzögerung des Chip-Werks trifft Europa hart'. *INDUSTRIEMAGAZIN*. https://industriemagazin.at/news/intel-stoppt-bau-in-magdeburg-verzoegerung-des-chip-werks-trifft-europa-hart/ (accessed 17 October 2025).
Iversen, T. and Soskice, D. W. (2019) *Democracy and Prosperity: Reinventing Capitalism through a Turbulent Century*. Princeton, NJ and Oxford: Princeton University Press.
Jahn, T., Olk, J., and Volkery, C. (2024) 'Chipfabrik: Stoppt Intel das Werk in Magdeburg? Konzern vertröstet Scholz'. https://www.handelsblatt.com/unternehmen/chipfabrik-stoppt-intel-das-werk-in-magdeburg-konzern-vertroestet-scholz/100065948.html (accessed 17 October 2025).
Kampmark, B. and Kurečić, P. (2022) 'Vaccine Nationalism: Competition, EU Parochialism, and COVID-19'. *Journal of Global Faultlines*, 9(1), 9–20.
Kleinhans, J.-P. (2024) 'The Missing Strategy in Europe's Chip Ambitions'. *Interface*. https://www.interface-eu.org/publications/europe-semiconductor-strategy (accessed 17 October 2025).
Krugman, P. (1994) 'Competitiveness: A Dangerous Obsession'. *Foreign Affairs*, 73(2), 28. https://doi.org/10.2307/20045917
Letta, E. (2024) 'Much More than a Market. Speed, Security, Solidarity. Empowering the Single Market to Deliver a Sustainable Future and Prosperity for All EU Citizens'. https://www.consilium.europa.eu/media/ny3j24sm/much-more-than-a-market-report-by-enrico-letta.pdf (accessed 17 October 2025).
Marcuse, H. (1991) *One-Dimensional Man: Studies in the Ideology of Advanced Industrial Society*. Boston, MA: Beacon Press.
Mazzucato, M. (2015) *The Entrepreneurial State: Debunking Public vs. Private Sector Myths*. New York, NY: PublicAffairs.
Pianta, M., Lucchese, M., and Nascia, L. (2020) 'The Policy Space for a Novel Industrial Policy in Europe'. *Industrial and Corporate Change*, 29(3), 779–795. https://doi.org/10.1093/icc/dtz075
Raza, W., Grumiller, J., Grohs, H., Essletzbichler J., and Pintar, N. (2021) *Post Covid-19 Value Chains: Options for Reshoring Production Back to Europe in a Globalised Economy*. Study for the European Parliament's Committee on International Trade.
Ricz, J. (2020) 'Developmental States in the Twenty-First Century: New Wine into Old Bottles?' *İstanbul Üniversitesi Sosyoloji Dergisi*, 40(2). https://doi.org/10.26650/SJ.2020.40.2.0056

Rikap, C., Durand, C., Paraná, E., Gerbaudo, P., and Marx, P. (2024) 'Reclaiming Digital Sovereignty A Roadmap to Build a Digital Stack for People and the Planet'. https://www.ucl.ac.uk/bartlett/public-purpose/sites/bartlett_public_purpose/files/reclaiming-digital-sovereignty.pdf (accessed 17 October 2025).

Rodrik, D. (2011) *The Globalization Paradox: Why Global Markets, States, and Democracy Can't Coexist*. Oxford, UK and New York, NY: Oxford University Press.

Scharpf, F. W. (2002) *Governing in Europe: effective and democratic?*. Oxford, UK: Oxford University Press.

Schleer, C., Wisniewski, N., and Reusswig. F. A. (2024) *Shaping the Social-Ecological Transformation: How Social Barriers Can Be Overcome and How Resonance Potentials Can Be Utilised*. Heidelberg und Potsdam: Friedrich Ebert Stiftung. https://www.sinus-institut.de/media-center/studien/fes-sozialoekologische-transformation (accessed 17 October 2025).

Schmitz, L., Seidl, T., and Wuttke, T. (2024) 'The Costs of Conditionality. IPCEIs and the Constrained Politics of EU Industrial Policy'. https://doi.org/10.31219/osf.io/f63gd

Skyrman, V. (2024). *Industrial Policy, Progressive Derisking, and the Financing of Europe's Green Transition. Vienna, ÖFSE Working Paper No. 78*. https://doi.org/10.60637/2024-wp78

Waidelich, P., Batibeniz, F., Rising, J., Kikstra, J. S., and Seneviratne, S. I. (2024) 'Climate Damage Projections beyond Annual Temperature'. *Nature Climate Change*, 14(6), 592–599. https://doi.org/10.1038/s41558-024-01990-8

Zenke, I., Heymann, T., and Arnold, N. (2024) *Rechtliche Zulässigkeit Einer Verknüpfung Staatlicher Zuwendungen Mit Sozialen Vorgaben*. Berlin: Kurzgutachten erstellt im Auftrag des DGB Bundesvorstands.

Zuboff, S. (2020) *The Age of Surveillance Capitalism: The Fight for a Human Future at the New Frontier of Power*. First trade paperback edition. New York, NY: PublicAffairs.

7

PAST, PRESENT, AND FUTURE OF INNOVATION AGENCIES IN EUROPE

Rainer Kattel

7.1 Introduction[1]

> Innovation agencies do not innovate.
>
> (Dan Hill, former Director of Strategic Design at Vinnova, Sweden)

The economist Hyman Minsky once quipped that there are as many types of capitalism as there are varieties of Heinz pickles – namely, 57. While there are perhaps not as many types of innovation agencies in Europe or globally, it is still important to note that there is a great variety of public and often also public-private hybrid organisations supporting innovation activities in societies. Innovation agencies form an evolving ecosystem of organisations that changes over time, co-evolving with technology, innovation and public policies.

Today, innovation agencies are often autonomous organisations that implement core elements of science, technology, and innovation (STI) policies. This specific form of innovation agency is relatively recent, emerging in the late 1980s and 1990s, predominantly focusing on supporting entrepreneurship in emerging technologies, innovation and technology development infrastructure, and various collaborations within innovation ecosystems. Today, the European network of leading innovation agencies, TAFTIE, counts 40 member organisations across Europe and globally.[2] Also, many countries have multiple agencies or units within larger organisations at the national and regional levels. European Commission organisations and activities complement these agencies.

However, as the concept of innovation is expanding to include institutional, social, public sector, and similar innovations, particularly as a response to create SDGs-relevant policies, this chapter assumes that the universe of innovation agencies is also expanding with organisations such as policy labs and similar

DOI: 10.4324/9781003745563-11

organisations, and ad hoc activities, focusing on creating, testing, and scaling innovations across all sectors and activities of societies.

While there is a growing body of literature on the expanding scope of innovation policy, there needs to be a greater focus on innovation agencies and their development. This chapter synthesises the latest academic research on innovation policy, innovation agencies, policy labs, and similar organisations, emphasising the emerging capacities and capabilities for effective innovation policy-making in this broad context.

In Europe, policymakers realised by the early 2000s that the union of quite diverse member states requires stronger coordination of national initiatives, as otherwise it will be challenging to compete with the more dynamic US and emerging Asia, especially in ICT, but also in future technologies. As a result, policymakers recognised the need for more proactive coordination, trying to improve the European Research Area governance both via stronger top-down coordination of European Research Area initiatives and, probably more successfully, via bottom-up initiatives such as the European Strategy Forum on Research Infrastructures, which created and opened up pan-European research infrastructures and the joint programming and technology initiatives between the EU, intergovernmental funding schemes, and national schemes and strategies. As the framework programmes continue to be one of the main investment vehicles on the European level, the governance landscape of such EU-wide efforts is loosely experimentalist in nature: broad targets/goals (e.g., twin transition) and policy logics (e.g., smart specialisation or missions) are set on the European level, and the member states and regions/cities have the autonomy to develop context-relevant policy solutions that are assessed and refined through peer learning. While ideally, this should lead to contextual learning and experimentation, the implementation guidance developed by the EU is often quite rigid, hampering learning in policy organisations. The latter is usually replicated on the member state level. Perhaps ironically, on the regional and city levels, we experience almost the opposite: a bonfire of pilots rarely scaled into full-blown policies, again diminishing learning of what works and why in innovation. While many pilots aim to destabilise existing unsustainable systems (e.g., in mobility), without learning from the pilots and scaling, the trust in policymakers' ability to tackle key challenges is bound to diminish. Furthermore, there are considerable differences between European countries regarding their capacities (e.g., levels of investment and other resources) and capabilities (e.g., speed and agility in updating policies and relevant organisations) in innovation. Equally importantly, the impact of public administration reforms (such as new public management [NPM]) is not evenly distributed across European administrations.

Furthermore, Europe's innovation landscape has been increasingly influenced by geopolitical shocks and systemic vulnerabilities. Russia's war in Ukraine, rising US–China technological rivalry, and the fragility of global supply chains have all emphasised Europe's reliance on external actors for critical technologies, raw materials, and defence capabilities. These developments have prompted the European Union to prioritise *strategic autonomy* and *technological sovereignty* in its policy agenda, linking research and innovation (R&I) not only to competitiveness and sustainability but also to security and resilience. In this context, innovation agencies face rising expectations: they must function not only as mission-focused and market-shaping bodies but also as essential intermediaries in enhancing Europe's capacity to act independently amid uncertainty and geopolitical pressures.

In this context, European innovation agencies face today two broad challenges: first, they are tasked with, or engaged in, transforming socio-technical systems (e.g., food, mobility); and second, socio-technical systems fall under over-lapping systems of governance (e.g., food system includes elements from energy, waste management, health, and other policy areas), typically governed by the EU, national and local-level regulations and institutions. The transformation challenge indicates that innovation agencies require a broad spectrum of new capabilities across multiple systems. The governance challenge indicates the need for inter-organisational or distributed capabilities (e.g., division of labour and its coordination between multiple organisations). This chapter discusses how innovation agencies are responding to this dual challenge and what could be critical steps to increase their capabilities to tackle the challenges effectively.

By combining these perspectives, the chapter contributes to two interconnected debates: the governance of innovation agencies and the pursuit of European strategic autonomy. While research on innovation agencies has focused on their diversity of forms and roles – from technology transfer offices to mission-driven ecosystem builders – less attention has been paid to how these agencies operate under geopolitical stress. At the same time, policy discussions of strategic autonomy have emphasised industrial competitiveness and defence procurement but have rarely engaged with the institutional capacities required to deliver on these ambitions. Bringing these strands together, the chapter argues that the future of European innovation agencies lies in their ability to develop dynamic capabilities that cut across missions and security domains. In doing so, the chapter reframes agencies as central to Europe's resilience, not just its competitiveness.

The chapter is structured as follows: Section 7.2 discusses how, historically, innovation agencies have had a dual purpose: first, to provide stable support to businesses and other actors such as universities and, at the same time, to experiment with cutting-edge, emerging technologies. This ambidextrous need has led to continuous organisational innovation and renewal. Today's focus on grand challenges is spurring a new wave of such changes. This is followed by Section 7.3 looking at the rise of challenge-driven policies (such as missions, for instance) and how this has led to the rapid expansion of instruments for how innovation is being supported and in the number of organisations engaging in innovation. This section gives an overview of such instruments and organisations. In Section 7.4, the report discusses how innovation agencies are developing (new) dynamic capabilities in attempting to tackle grand challenges. However, these capabilities could be better conceptualised and distributed across innovation agencies. This section offers a way to conceptualise such capabilities and examples of how innovation agencies develop them. Section 7.5 briefly discussed how innovation agencies interact with the strategic autonomy debates. And finally, Section 7.6 offers ideas on how governments could speed up the development of dynamic capabilities within innovation agency ecosystems.

7.2 Delivering agile stability: the expanding universe of innovation agencies

Innovation agencies, in the broadest sense, are as old as capitalism. Supporting innovation is one of the core activities of governments in market economies. However, looking at the history of innovation agencies, or "innovation bureaucracy",[3] we witness the following organisational sequence and evolution over the past few centuries: new agile (often small at the outset, led by charismatic and entrepreneurial leaders and networks of actors, and acting in the liminal space between public and private sectors) public innovation organisations are established to deal with new emerging technological or socio-economic challenges, and over time these organisations, or rather the tasks they fulfil, are "socialised" or institutionalised into existing public sector practices. Once new practices and organisations become the new normal.

One way to make sense of this dynamic is to use analytical lenses developed by Max Weber more than a century ago. Weber was interested in ways in which authority, or legitimacy, is generated and exercised, as well as how one type of authority (charismatic) becomes another type (legal-rational or bureaucratic), only to be challenged again by the initial type (charismatic). In the context of innovation agencies, their historical evolution can be described through two ideal-typical categories of organisation – *charismatic networks* and *expert organisations* – and that their evolution is often an oscillation between the two extremes, within the same organisation, or leads to the emergence of new ones. Dan Breznitz and colleagues have aptly called the charismatic networks Schumpeterian agencies.[4]

Importantly, these two ideal types of organisation possess rather different capabilities and skill sets, and they perform different functions. The charismatic networks provide agility and dynamism for innovation agencies to search for new directions and ways of doing things, while expert organisations bring long-term focus, predictability and stability to deliver needed policies and results. This "agile stability" is key to the success of innovation systems as through it public innovation agencies complement private sector activities and capabilities in innovation. Innovation agencies create conditions, through various policy options, for the private sector and society as a whole to further explore and exploit existing technological and innovation potentials (e.g., through applied research grants for private companies or public vocational education training) to converge on and advance the (global) best practices and the socio-technological frontier. This often involves weighing competing policy subjects and their potential and needs. Policy makers ask whether they should support an existing electronics company or a new startup in services. Is one sector or economic activity more important than another? These questions tend to be oriented towards mid-term challenges and solutions, spanning a typical electoral cycle or two, and summarised in national development and innovation strategies. They are also often about using existing resources effectively and are representations of the existing political and economic landscape.

On the level of innovation systems (regions and countries), agile stability means constantly balancing multiple timeframes and policy cycles: on the one hand, mitigating the risks of the short- and mid-term exploitation strategies of existing industries and economic sectors and on the other hand, managing the uncertainties of radical innovation, as well as the search for new competitive advantages through new directions of innovation. On the level of specific industries or sectors, agile stability is expressed perhaps more directly. Take cars as an example. While in the late nineteenth century, cars were an open-ended new technology competing with horse-drawn carriages and trains, the industry matured considerably over the twentieth century, only to face in the twenty-first century the new challenge of electric and self-driving cars. Throughout the evolution of the car industry over the past 150 years, public organisations have played diverse roles, from regulator (of safety and standards) to educator (from technical production skills to public safety awareness), to infrastructure builder (streets, highways), to research funder (electric and self-driving cars). Diverse organisations have played these roles with diverse political and economic networks, administrative cultures, funding mechanisms and evaluation criteria. Yet without these organisations, it is safe to say, cars would not be as ubiquitous, relatively reliable and safe as they are today. In other words, the mid- and long-range questions policy makers face are answered by diverse organisations that often work in parallel, compete for political and financial resources and go through internal management reforms.

In sum, the fluid and ambidextrous nature of innovation agencies within innovation systems and sectors shows that quite different kinds of organisations are dealing with diverse tasks, and the latter evolve over time. Equally importantly, innovation agencies can go about fulfilling their tasks in quite different ways: some organisations can be involved in directly creating new technologies (e.g., government research institutes), others can support private companies (e.g., funding agencies through grants) and yet others can act as intermediaries of knowledge (e.g., engineering or business associations). As argued by Kattel et al. (2022), innovation agencies can take the shape of the following ideal typical organisational types according to *how* the organisations go about dealing with innovations[5]:

1 *Creators*: organisations directly involved in creating new knowledge and technologies, often in codified form (such as scientific publications), for instance, public research institutes;

2. *Doers*: organisations involved in creating and delivering actual new products or services, for instance, state-owned companies or specialised agencies (e.g., for space exploration or agriculture);
3. *Funders*: organisations that fund private or public entities involved in innovations, for instance, STI funding agencies or development banks;
4. *Intermediaries*: organisations that act as knowledge and interest intermediaries, such as engineering or business associations or technology parks and clusters; and
5. *Rulers*: organisations that create and constrain the legitimacy and space (through politics, policy and regulations) for others and give direction to their missions and tasks, such as ministries, cabinet offices or specialised offices for innovation.

However, the organisational dynamic is accompanied by policy dynamics. In the context of Western countries, innovation policy is typically periodised through three frames:

- The post–World War II era of industrial policy in which countries mixed mission- and diffusion-oriented innovation policies;
- The era of competitiveness-focused innovation policies, which developed in the late 1980s as diffusion-oriented or horizontal policies became dominant, with complementary macro-economic policies focusing on trade liberalisation and price stability; and
- The (re-)emergence of mission- or challenge-oriented innovation policies in the late 2000s.[6]

The latest frame around grand challenges as a "normative turn" in STI policies has been reinforced by COVID-19 responses that promised to build back better and the various implications of the war in Ukraine. The key driver behind "normative" STI policy initiatives is the ambition of achieving a particular type of economic growth (e.g., smart, inclusive and sustainable). As argued by Mazzucato (2017, 2021), this constitutes a direct admission that economic growth not only has a rate but also a direction, which means that it can have multiple different directions. Policymakers have a choice, for instance, of how and how quickly they aim to decarbonise certain economic sectors. These alternative pathways include diverse trade-offs, spillovers and dynamic efficiency changes across sectors. Thus, as Stirling (2009) argues, modern-day challenges or missions are not about picking the one and only direction of change but a wider directionality that includes and enables multiple competing and complementary pathways and experimentation along the way.[7]

The European Union has arguably been the leading policy actor in bringing directionality discussions to the centre of innovation policy through its renewed focus on missions. For over a decade, the EU has attempted to reorient its STI agenda towards grand challenges (Soete *et al.*, 2017). In 2021, the EU's Horizon Europe R&D funding programme commenced, and with it, the EU has committed to providing €53.5 billion in funding through Horizon Europe's second pillar, "Global Challenges and European Industrial Competitiveness", and its five mission areas by 2027. Another aim of the programme is to encourage member states – and regions and cities – to refocus their STI policies according to the mission-oriented approach. However, while the EU and other leading economies have promised to increase public spending on various challenges they face, the debate on effectively aligning and absorbing these funds is in the early stages.

While mission-oriented policies have taken Europe by storm, missions are being implemented in widely different ways, depending on contextual factors in most cases. The widespread application of this approach is vindicating the decision to place missions at the heart of the normative turn in STI and public policymaking at large. However, to date, it needs to be clarified that this normative focus on directionality is accompanied by organisational changes to deliver on such promises. While there are some interesting practical examples of this shift in actual missions, most missions are implemented through existing institutions and policy schemes, with the result that missions are understood through existing organisational capabilities and epistemological and analytical tools. As such, many missions are constrained to business-as-usual practice and incremental changes in both policies and organisations.[8] Indeed, there is a risk that the concept of missions as a shift towards understanding policymaking as a bottom-up experimentation aimed at solving the deeper challenges societies face will be overrun by political events such as inflation, the cost-of-living crisis and the return of more traditional, mercantilist industrial policies, such as tariffs on advanced industrial goods.

Arguably, one of the main missing pieces in implementing missions, and other similarly challenge-focused policies, is the organisational development that innovation agencies need to undertake (Mazzucato and Kattel, 2024). The current challenge for European countries can be summed up in this evolving policy context as follows: what the EU has missed so far is complementing the policy of directionality with an organisational ecosystem to operate effectively within the set directionality. The current generation of STI policies needs to be complemented by an evolution in innovation agencies.

7.3 Tackling grand challenges with innovation agencies

Next to the normative turn towards framing innovation policies through specific challenges or directionality, we also increasingly witness an epistemic turn in some innovation agencies.[9] The adoption of working practices from (strategic and user-centred) design and agile software development is driving the emergence of new, often peripheral, public organisations (such as various policy and innovation labs) and networks (task forces, ad hoc events such as hackathons, swat and crisis teams, volunteer movements). These working practices focus on agile processes such as prototyping and experimentation, relying on epistemological frameworks from action research and ethnography rather than economics or public policy analysis. These new innovation agencies have brought experiential, experimental and techno-solutionist "hacker" routines to public organisations, in an attempt to formalise within organisations what can be called bureaucracy hacking (Kattel *et al.*, 2022). These new routines can also be seen as responding to the need to simplify existing, but often overly complex and technical, policy design and engagement practices, particularly in the aftermath of NPM reforms (Kattel *et al.*, 2023). The key challenge for innovation agencies is what kind of new practices to pick up and socialise, and which practices can remain in the mostly – and often intentionally – peripheral labs and networks (Begovic *et al.*, 2021).

There is an emerging STI (and beyond) policy landscape where normative approaches to goals meet agile organisational practices; for brevity, we can call them challenges-based policies and practices. Such challenge-based policies and practices are highly diverse, including large, powerful, well-funded programmes, as well as small, lightly funded ones, and respective organisational forms, as summarised in the Table 7.1. There is considerable variation in the design of challenge-based policies and practices.

Table 7.1 exemplifies how innovation agencies are evolving by either incorporating new agile practices or collaborating in networks where such practices are used. This new, emerging shape of innovation agencies could be called neo-Weberian as it aligns well with the idea of the Neo-Weberian State (NWS). In public administration literature, there has been a discussion of the NWS' emergence over the last decade, particularly focused on the European context. Conceived by Pollitt and Bouckaert in the early 2000s, it has been at the forefront of debate since the explicit discussion in the 2011 edition of their paradigmatic *Public Management Reform* textbook (Pollitt and Bouckaert, 2011; see also Bouckaert, 2023, Pollitt *et al.*, 2008/09).

The NWS posits that a new paradigm of the state has emerged in the era of post-NPM reforms. The NWS emphasises the importance of public organisations in providing public services and, at the same time, recognises the need for more citizen engagement in the design and delivery of public services. In innovation policy, neo-Weberian agencies can be characterised by the emergence of long-term societal goals (e.g., climate goals) as core elements of policies which are accompanied by the incorporation of new methods and analytical tools such as user-centred design, foresight and policy labs.

The neo-Weberian innovation agency is an ideal-typical simplification and synthesis of such conceptual discussions and empirical developments. It serves as a heuristic to understand ongoing changes in innovation policy and its implementation. Yet, we should not see them super agencies solving societal challenges on

TABLE 7.1 Typology of challenge-based policies and practices

Type	*Features*	*Institutional form*
Foresight and futures thinking	Raise awareness and readiness for future challenges and scenarios	Both as established organisations and ad hoc processes
Digital teams/agencies	Rapid transformation of key public services, agile way of working	Both centralised and decentralised teams, mostly outside existing organisations
(Policy) labs	Encourage user-centric approaches, testing, experimentation, and quick iteration	Typically, new organisations outside existing systems/ organisations compete for projects (in-house consulting)
Sandboxes	Encourage risk-taking and experimentation	Time-bound, separate legislation, within existing organisations
Hackathons	Mobilise stakeholders and trial multiple solutions, induce experiments	Ad hoc unique events
Technology prizes	Solve specific technological challenges, create market awareness	Ad hoc unique events
Challenge prizes	Mobilise stakeholders around issues, increase awareness	Ad hoc unique events
Purpose-oriented procurement (innovative, sustainable solution)	Create markets and increase capabilities for new solutions	Part of the routine procurement processes and organisation
Missions	Tackle socio-economic challenges through multi-stakeholder cross-sectoral collaborations	High-level political leadership, lead agencies (innovation, development banks)

Source: Maldonado and Kattel (2024); see also Goulden and Kattel (2024).

their own, quite to the contrary. The neo-Weberian agencies understand that part of their role is also to utilise the wider organisational configuration of public agencies in developing new capabilities in driving innovation in society.

Let us briefly look at some examples.[10] The Swedish innovation agency Vinnova has attempted to change its ways of working over the last few years by creating, among other things, the new post of strategic design director.[11] This is an attempt to bring in new capabilities nested in human-centric design and, as a result, Vinnova's work is being reframed, from focusing primarily on technological issues to tackling socio-economic challenges and transforming related socio-technical systems. This has meant considerably enlarging the circle of key stakeholders and changing the way of working at Vinnova. For instance, one of the missions it has chosen is rethinking food systems to provide healthy, sustainable food in Swedish schools.

To deliver this, Vinnova is working with the entire food delivery value chain, or food system, from producers to users (children and parents) and spurring innovations (via funding), helping to shape markets and to transform existing systems from energy production and transportation to waste management.

Thus, it is an attempt to combine a relatively long-term view of investing into new technologies with short-term changes in day-to-day habits around eating. One can argue that what Vinnova is trying to do is to develop capacities and capabilities for agile stability. While Vinnova is only at the beginning of its transformation, its blueprint is becoming increasingly copied by other Nordic countries and beyond. Importantly, Vinnova – created in 2001 through a merger of seven research councils as a traditional innovation funder/intermediary – is part of a larger ecosystem of innovation organisations that provide complementary capacities and capabilities. What we are witnessing are attempts to redefine and redesign the borders of this ecosystem for delivering its more complex policy missions, such as transforming food systems. In the era of competitiveness and growth policies, nobody would have thought that schools and pupils are important parts of an innovation agency's ecosystem, but delivering sustainable food systems may depend most on how kids and schools behave and collaborate with the likes of Vinnova. And these new forms of collaboration and co-creation, in turn, help Vinnova to learn and design new routines and capabilities for supporting new forms of sustainability innovations.

Another example comes from the digital government. The UK's Government Digital Service (GDS), created in 2011, has become a global gold standard in public sector digital agencies (Clarke, 2019), and it is another fascinating example of a neo-Weberian agency and of agile stability in action. Perhaps the most fundamental change brought on by GDS is the reform of public digital procurement through spending controls on procurement contracts and creating a new digital marketplace for bids (Kattel and Takala, 2023). This has enabled thousands of SMEs to bid and win public tenders and to break existing oligopolistic markets and create new, more open, IT markets around government digital transformations. At the same time, GDS also radically changed the government's digital presence by creating a unified gov.uk website. Through this, the entire user experience of the UK government was transformed. Both reforms were based on user research and design practices to make information and services readily available and digitally usable. The capabilities that GDS brought into government formed around a redefinition of value proposition (a focus on user needs) which was achieved by an influx of people who could deliver towards this new notion of value. It is worth noting that many of the people hired by GDS outside the civil service did not come from the private sector but were from the BBC and other similar public or third-sector organisations.

In the last few years, GDS has become the standard-bearer for the digital and design profession within the UK government. It now focuses on professionalising digital skills across the UK government. The hackers and doers have become the new mandarins. Its initial new capabilities around user-centred design have become increasingly part of the routine skills many departments and agencies have in-house, rather than relying on a central agency.

Importantly, in both cases, various new capabilities and skills are interacting with the existing institutional and political infrastructure. The new capabilities evolve in interactions with other public sector actors of the broader innovation ecosystem and often also in partnerships with private actors and citizens. Indeed, as seen in the examples above, new capabilities are pivotal for more direct engagement with the private sector and citizens and for reframing the purpose of such engagements. This indicates different relationships with stakeholders and, accordingly, changing requirements for skills and capabilities.

In the European context, as mentioned above, its current framework programme for STI relies heavily on the idea of missions, and its implementation offers an interesting example of how and why new capabilities are needed for such ambitious polices. In terms of implementation, national-level mission-oriented policies are predominantly implemented by existing R&D and innovation agencies and mostly through upgrading existing policy instruments (Kattel and Mazzucato, 2023). While European missions often target wide democratic engagement practices to build a renewed legitimacy for transformational policies, there is still little evidence that overall policy practices have changed fundamentally. Rather, we see many European countries building missions incrementally into their existing policy and organisational landscapes. Thus, for instance, the Netherlands introduced the so-called Topsectoren approach in 2012 to strengthen coordination and collaboration between various R&D system actors. While originally the primary goal of this approach was to improve the match between the knowledge demands of innovative firms and the activities of research institutes, it gradually shifted towards more transformative goals such as "Mission-Oriented Topsector and Innovation Policy" (MTIP), now containing 25 missions within 4 themes. While much of the Topsector governance has evolved into MTIP governance, perhaps the most marked difference is the creation of mission teams as cross-sectoral steering bodies for missions. Similar incremental approaches can be found in most European countries that implement missions. However, what is clearly missing in most cases is the focus on new organisational capabilities and developing the overall organisational landscape of innovation agencies.

7.4 The emerging dynamic capabilities in innovation agencies

The chapter started with the assumption that innovation agencies face today two broad challenges: first, they are tasked with, or engaged in, transforming socio-technical systems (e.g., food, mobility); and second, socio-technical systems fall under over-lapping systems of governance (e.g., food system includes elements from energy, waste management, health, and other policy areas, typically governed from different ministries). In the previous section, the chapter discussed emerging neo-Weberian agencies that attempt to tackle both challenges by developing novel capabilities for internal practices and outward engagement with the ecosystem. The new capabilities are predominantly dynamic; they aim to change existing ways of working and engagement. This section sketches what these emerging capabilities are. Importantly, given the double challenge described above, innovation agencies are not only striving to build these new capabilities internally, but, as this section argues, a "meta-governance" of multiple innovation agencies working in the same ecosystem is needed.

A quick search in Google's Ngram viewer shows that the use of state capacity – as perhaps the broadest proxy for public sector capacities and capabilities – in published books has experienced exponential growth since the late 1980s. It is, however, not a coincidence that the focus on state and public sector capacities emerges more broadly in the shadow of NPM, neoliberal governance, and policy reforms. Rather than understanding governance as a collaborative effort between all sectors, these reforms gave normative preference to business practices (Kattel and Mazzucato, 2020). Increasing focus on public sector capacity as a concept should thus be understood as an attempt to rebalance our understanding of how change happens in societies – through cross-sectoral co-creation – and as an effort to build the muscles in public organisations to work together to tackle socio-economic challenges.

When we look at academic conceptualisations of public sector capacities and capabilities over the past decades, we can summarise these discussions through three interconnected layers (Kattel *et al.*, 2025):

- state capacities,
- organisational routines, and
- dynamic capabilities of the public organisations.

7.4.1 State capacity

The concept of state capacity emerged in writings on "developmental states" from the mid-1980s onwards to describe the ability of national governments to "implement official goals, especially over the actual or potential opposition of powerful social groups or in the face of recalcitrant socioeconomic circumstances" (Skocpol, 1985). More generally, researchers using the concept have understood state capacity as resulting from the development of coherent bureaucratic institutions staffed by civil servants with relevant expertise to their roles, building on the ideas of Max Weber, and the political "autonomy" of the state or its ability to act without undue interference from other economic actors and interest groups (Evans and Rauch, 1999). Both of these aspects require raising and deploying financial resources, including taxation and investment. Thus, state capacity can be seen as a structural capacity of the state, encompassing many of its institutions and organisations as a structure upon which its activities rest.

In the context of European innovation policy and agencies, we can detect somewhat of paradox in the state capacity dimension: on the one hand, European policies provide ample space for member state-level experimentation (e.g., there is no single blueprint or even guidance on how to interpret and design mission-oriented policies); on the other hand, once the EU is funding policies and helping with the implementation, it tends to focus on the ability to absorb EU funds and on the ability to provide administrative transparency (e.g., member states create or change existing agencies into implementation agencies for EU funds, separating policy and implementation). We can argue that such an imbalanced understanding of autonomy is the key feature of state capacity in Europe. Importantly, such a view of state capacity is forming organisational routines in many innovation agencies across Europe.

7.4.2 *Organisational routines*

The idea of organisational routines originates from evolutionary economics, particularly from the seminal work by Nelson and Winter (1982), who describe the idea of routines as follows:

> We use this term to include characteristics of firms that range from well-specified technical routines for producing things, through procedures for hiring and firing, ordering new inventory, or stepping up production of items in high demand, to policies regarding investment, research and development (R&D), or advertising, and business strategies about product diversification and overseas investment. In our evolutionary theory, these routines play the role that genes play in biological evolutionary theory. They are a persistent feature of the organism and determine its possible behavior (though actual behavior is determined also by the environment); they are heritable in the sense that tomorrow's organisms generated from today's (for example, by building a new plant) have many of the same characteristics, and they are selectable in the sense that organisms with certain routines may do better than others, and, if so, their relative importance in the population (industry) is augmented over time.

Importantly, routines are not good or bad: there is no ideal routine to obtain or learn. In brief, organisational routines can be defined as the abilities necessary to activate the set of resources (including financial resources, tangible and intangible assets, and staff skills) that an organisation needs to achieve organisational goals. In public organisations, they are embedded within formal and informal routines or "tasks", and can be grouped along six types that are required to perform policy functions: analytical, planning, coordination, evaluation, policy and participation (Karo and Kattel, 2018). Generally, the focus of these capabilities is on the stable and durable working and performance of organisational functions.

In the European policy context, long-term planning is the overarching routine expressed through multi-year policy cycles formulating agreements on priority areas, specific policy programmes (e.g., Horizon Europe) and respective expenditures. One of the key problems of such programmes is their limited space to pivot in the middle of policy and funding programmes. Such a rigid approach undermines the ability to learn from implementation; policy cycles become drawn out over multiple years, with key learning occurring at the end of such cycles. Such a paradox – long-term planning without agile learning – almost guarantees that most learning and adaption occurs on the level of policies. If a policy is ineffective, we need a new policy rather than different implementation practices and organisational development. The problem is that the analysis that says a policy is not working is often outdated. The effectiveness of such policies gets lost in bureaucratic inertia which in turn become the dominant organisational routine. Such relatively stable routines can be, and some argue should be, complemented by short-term adaptability and the introduction of new processes. This complementarity is achieved through a subset of organisational capabilities: dynamic capabilities.

7.4.3 Dynamic capabilities

As we can see from above, one of the key challenges public organisations face is their ability to learn from their own policies and their ecosystem. European innovation policy development and evaluation are typically practised as a waterfall: new initiatives are rolled out as finished programmes and evaluated after a few years or even at the end of the policy cycle. Such an approach makes it more difficult for the main public organisations responsible for the policy (e.g., a ministry) and implementing agency (e.g., an innovation agency) to know about the effectiveness of their current instruments and policies. Policy analysis and evaluation is time and resource consuming but separating it from day-to-day activities diminishes learning within existing teams and organisations. Accordingly, innovation agencies find it challenging to pivot towards socially relevant issues, to discontinue ineffective activities, or to quickly scale new effective practices and instruments. In other words, European innovation agencies tend to be poor at dynamic capabilities and the emergence of neo-Weberian innovation agencies can be understood as an attempt to create these dynamic capabilities.

Dynamic capabilities are specific abilities embedded in routines that enable organisations to adapt their resources, processes and skills in response to an evolving strategic environment. The concept first emerged in the 1990s from the strategic management literature to identify "firm's ability to integrate, build, and reconfigure internal and external competencies to address rapidly changing environments" (Teece *et al.*, 1997). In the last decade, it has been increasingly used to analyse the public sector's ability to adapt in the face of new and ever more complex societal challenges.

There is yet to be a consensus on the number and content of public-sector dynamic capabilities. Kattel *et al.* (2025) propose to typologies these capabilities as follows:

- Strategic awareness: the ability to spot, understand, and organise around emerging problems and opportunities by using data, foresight, and community insights.
- Adjusting priorities: the capacity to re-evaluate focus and reallocate resources in response to shifting needs, crises, or new opportunities.
- Building coalitions: the ability to work across silos and sectors to align shared goals, mobilise partners, and unlock collective resources.
- Learning and experimentation: the capability to test new ideas, learn from experience, and embed lessons into policies, programmes, and organisational culture.
- Reconfiguring delivery: the ability to mobilise people, structures, and resources to deliver strategic priorities and sustain innovation.

In sum, dynamic capabilities identify the set of specific abilities that enable the renewal of existing public organisations and their dominant organisational routines. Ultimately, dynamic capabilities should enable a (re-)alignment to produce stronger policy design, better policy implementation, and successful policy outcomes.

Examples of neo-Weberian agencies such as Vinnova and GDS can be analysed through the lens of dynamic capabilities. In both cases, the organisations developed a novel set of capabilities, particularly around sense-making approaches and tools (strategic design for missions and user-centred agile design for digital solutions, respectively), seizing (experimentation) and learning (diffusing new practices across the organisation). But equally importantly, both organisations attempted new ways of orchestrating the ecosystem (Vinnova through a massive outreach campaign; GDS through the professionalisation of key digital skills across the government) and focused on reshaping some of the core routines such as procurement. In both cases, the dynamic capabilities enable the rethinking of main organisational routines and, as is evident, particularly in the case of GDS, feed back into state capacity via re-establishing the government's autonomy in the digital markets and led to much better use of existing financial resources.

Importantly, while dynamic capabilities apply to individual organisations, it is also key to understand how organisations such as innovation agencies working in the same ecosystem complement each other. Thus, some of the dynamic capabilities can also be distributed across multiple organisations working together. For instance, going back to Vinnova's school food and sustainable street missions, it is clear that Vinnova alone cannot deliver on these ambitious goals, no matter how strong its dynamic capabilities are. It needs a broad coalition of public and private actors to collaborate with. The latter requires many of these organisations to build their own dynamic capabilities and change their predominant organisational routines.

When we look at the European Union and the member states, there is no "meta-governance" of building and developing dynamic capabilities across multiple innovation agencies in various socio-technical systems. Moreover, in any given socio-technical system, innovation agencies are bound to be on different governance levels (central, regional, local) and of different types. Thus, we can again detect a somewhat paradoxical situation: on the one hand, the European Commission encourages experimentation within broad goals and practices (e.g., smart specialisation, twin transitions, missions), but this gets stuck with bureaucratic inertia of EU funding administration on the level of member states; on the other hand, particularly regions and cities are carrying out pilots after pilots, establishing all sorts of policy labs. Thus, as Radosevic and Zoretic (2024) argue about smart specialisation strategy,

> particularly in institutionally less developed countries and regions, there is often a clash between the requirements for experimental governance and the public policy demand for predominantly procedural accountability. Our central argument is that the experimentation dimension cannot be added to the conventional policy cycle without altering it.

Pilots can be seen both as expressions of an experimentalist approach but also as results of NPM-inspired projectification: particularly EU-funded pilots tend to be tied to deliverables and milestones set in contracts that leave little room for pivoting when context or learning from the ground would require doing so. Thus, paradoxically, pilots become "a new form of iron cage, with a relative lack of flexibility and action space" (Mukhtar-Landgren, 2021). The experimental policy frameworks die by thousands of pilots.

7.5 Innovation agencies and strategic autonomy: defence R&D as a capabilities challenge

The recent geopolitical upheavals, particularly Russia's war in Ukraine, have brought the question of *strategic autonomy* to the centre of European policy debates. Concepts such as open strategic autonomy and technological sovereignty, which initially emerged in relation to economic competitiveness and technological dependencies, now increasingly hinge on defence capabilities and the governance of defence-related research and development (Edler *et al.*, 2023; Bria *et al.*, 2025). For European innovation agencies, this introduces a new set of challenges and opportunities: how to integrate defence innovation into the broader mission-oriented and challenge-driven policy landscape without reverting to narrow mercantilist industrial strategies (Kattel and Soete, 2024). At present, Europe faces several structural weaknesses in its defence R&D and innovation ecosystem. First, spending is drastically lower than in the US, with the EU investing roughly 17 times less in defence R&D than the US Department of

Defense. Second, the European defence market is fragmented both operationally and politically: divergent procurement rules, competing national authorities, and insufficient coordination between member states undermine efforts at creating interoperable systems. Third, the institutional infrastructure for defence R&D remains underdeveloped compared to the US, lacking a centralised or distributed set of organisations capable of delivering high-risk, high-reward innovation. These weaknesses are particularly consequential when viewed through the lens of technological sovereignty: Europe's reliance on external suppliers in critical areas such as semiconductors, AI, and cybersecurity directly undermines its ability to act autonomously in crisis situations. Historically, the importance of defence R&D for broader innovation systems is well documented. In the US, agencies like DARPA have not only produced critical military technologies but also catalysed general-purpose innovations with transformative civilian spillovers. This reflects the so-called "supermultiplier" effect of defence R&D, with particularly strong crowding-in of private investment and industrial scaling effects (Deleidi and Mazzucato, 2021). In contrast, European defence R&D remains both underfunded and poorly integrated into wider socio-economic missions such as the twin green and digital transitions. The danger is that rising defence expenditures will be captured by a narrow military-industrial complex, reinforcing path dependencies rather than supporting Europe's broader mission-oriented ambitions. For innovation agencies in Europe, the defence challenge underscores two interrelated governance questions. First, how can defence R&D be aligned with wider societal missions and transitions rather than treated as a siloed domain? Second, what kind of organisational ecosystem is needed to enable high-risk, high-reward (HRHR) research while ensuring spillovers across sectors? Here, the US experience with DARPA provides inspiration but not a blueprint (Mowery, 2010). As multiple analyses stress, there is no singular "DARPA model" that can be copied wholesale (Fuchs, 2010; Bonvillian and Van Atta, 2011; Bonvillian *et al.*, 2019). Instead, DARPA's effectiveness stems from a unique institutional and political environment that sustains risk-taking, buffers agencies from short-term demands, and embeds them in a supportive network of military, industrial, and academic actors (Kattel and Entsminger, 2025). The key lesson for Europe is not to replicate DARPA but to emulate some of its critical capabilities across a variety of organisations. This resonates with the broader argument of this chapter: innovation agencies should be viewed as an ecosystem of diverse, complementary organisational forms rather than as singular "super-agencies". In defence R&D, this means creating a distributed European landscape of high-risk, mission-oriented programmes and managers who can take on transformative challenges while being supported by dedicated structures for procurement, contracting, and regulatory flexibility. Rather than building a monolithic "EU DARPA", Europe would be better served by developing a networked system of defence innovation agencies that interact with existing policy agendas, including missions in climate, energy, and digital transformation.

Five capability-building lessons emerge that echo the broader dynamic capabilities framework discussed earlier. First, Europe should create a European-wide network of high-risk programme managers, fostering collaboration, shared expertise, and secondments across agencies. Second, defence R&D organisations need to cultivate a culture of *strategic amnesia* (Kattel and Entsminger, 2025) – the willingness to disregard past failures and entrenched routines in order to pursue novel, risky directions. Third, HRHR programmes must be shielded by specialised support structures – agile contracting, adaptive procurement, and legal expertise – to avoid being suffocated by bureaucratic inertia. Fourth, annual defence innovation challenges could broaden awareness of strategic needs, draw in a wider range of actors (SMEs, start-ups, civil society), and explicitly link defence innovation to the twin green and digital transitions. Finally, high-level policy coherence is essential: defence innovation must be integrated with broader European missions, ensuring that investments in autonomy and security reinforce, rather than compete with, sustainability and cohesion agendas.

For European innovation agencies, the strategic autonomy agenda thus crystallises the broader argument of this chapter: building *dynamic capabilities* requires both organisational change and ecosystem-level governance. Defence R&D is not merely a sectoral issue but a litmus test of Europe's ability to combine long-term stability with agile responsiveness, to balance national fragmentation with supranational coordination, and to channel mission-oriented investments into transformative socio-technical change. Unless innovation agencies can be empowered to engage with these dual demands, Europe risks reproducing the very vulnerabilities that the rhetoric of strategic autonomy seeks to overcome.

7.6 Conclusion: what can be done to make innovation agencies more effective?

In their 1971 article on public choice, Ostrom and Ostrom argue that "Perhaps a system of public administration composed of a variety of multiorganisational arrangements and highly dependent upon mobilising clientele support will come reasonably close to sustaining a high level of performance in advancing the public welfare" (Ostrom and Ostrom, 1971). In the context of innovation agencies, the first part of their argument seems particularly relevant today: rather than thinking of innovation agencies as a single type of organisation, policymakers should aim to develop a landscape of diverse innovation agencies with varying strengths and dynamic capabilities. Thus, what becomes pivotal is the overall governance of diverse agencies and distributed capabilities. However, such a design of institutions is almost entirely absent in European, and indeed global, thinking and practice about innovation agencies.

Innovation agencies in Europe stand at a critical juncture. Their historical evolution – from industrial support organisations to mission-oriented and ecosystem-building bodies – has given them a prominent role in shaping markets, fostering capabilities, and driving transformative change. Yet the pressures of the current geopolitical moment mean that their remit is expanding further. Strategic autonomy debates reveal both the vulnerabilities of Europe's innovation system and the importance of agencies as coordinators of high-risk, high-reward research and as brokers across fragmented national and sectoral boundaries. The DARPA experience demonstrates that institutional design matters, but not in the form of simple organisational imitation. Instead, Europe needs a distributed ecology of agencies capable of experimenting, absorbing risk, and linking defence and civilian innovation with mission-oriented societal goals. The five capability lessons drawn from defence R&D – strategic amnesia, agile contracting and support structures, empowered programme management, annual challenge mechanisms, and policy coherence – are equally relevant for climate, digital, and social missions.

The future of European innovation agencies therefore lies not in consolidating into a single "super-agency", but in cultivating dynamic capabilities across a diverse ecosystem. If agencies can combine stability with agility, align missions with autonomy, and embed experimentation within democratic governance, they can become pivotal institutions for Europe's resilience and renewal. In this sense, the search for strategic autonomy is not only a defence imperative but also a broader test of Europe's capacity to govern transformative innovation.

Notes

1 The chapter draws heavily on my previous academic work, most of it captured in the book I co-authored with Wolfgang Drechsler and Erkki Karo: *How to make an entrepreneurial state. Why innovation needs bureaucracy, Yale, 2022*, and in my working paper (Kattel, 2024). These sources contain most of the relevant academic literature and discussions. I am grateful to Werner Raza, Wolfgang Polt, Peter Kaufmann, and the participants in the ÖFSE and AK Wien-organised seminar in June 2024 for their feedback and comments on an earlier version of this report.
2 Further details: https://taftie.eu/.
3 For more details on these historical patterns of evolution, see Kattel *et al.* (2022).
4 See, for instance, Breznitz and Ornston (2014) and Breznitz *et al.* (2018).
5 In their 2016 report, Glennie and Bound (2016) offer a similar if narrower typology of today's innovation agencies: first, *Market and System Fixers*: seek to address failures in markets and networks that impede business innovation and investment in R&D, often without preference for specific technologies or sectors; second, *Industry Builders*: focus on transforming an economy or creating new sources of economic competitiveness by investing in the development of a set of new sectors or technologies; third, *Mission Drivers*: aim to induce innovations that address major societal and economic challenges, often in policy areas of significant traditional R&D spending such as defence, energy, the environment or health; and fourth, *System Optimisers*: work towards ensuring continuous global competitiveness and creating more effective and enabling innovation systems by experimenting with different policy and programme mixes.
6 Key references include Ergas (1986), Foray *et al.* (2012), Schot and Steinmueller (2018), and Kattel and Mazzucato (2018).
7 See also his recent excellent discussion of "innovation democracies", Stirling (2024).
8 See also succinct discussion by Piret Tõnurist, "13 reasons why missions fail", (2023), https://oecd-opsi.org/blog/13-reasons-why-missions-fail/.

9 For more detailed arguments, see Kattel and Mazzucato (2023).
10 More detailed discussion in Kattel *et al.* (2002).
11 For a critical reflection, see Rohracher et al. (2023).

References

Begovic, M., Kattel, R., Mazzucato, M., and Quaggiotto, G. (2021) *COVID-19 and the need for dynamic state capabilities: An international comparison.* UCL Institute for Innovation and Public Purpose and United Nations Development Programme. https://www.ucl.ac.uk/bartlett/public-purpose/publications/2021/apr/covid-19-and-need-dynamic-state-capabilities-international-comparison (accessed 25 October 2025).

Bonvillian, W.B. and Van Atta, R. (2011) 'ARPA-E and DARPA: Applying the DARPA model to energy innovation', *Journal of Technology Transfer*, 36, 469–513. https://doi.org/10.1007/s10961-011-9223-x

Bonvillian, W. B., Van Atta, R., and Windham, P. (eds.) (2019) *The DARPA model for transformative technologies: Perspectives on the U.S. Defense Advanced Research Projects Agency.* Cambridge, UK: Open Book Publishers.

Bouckaert, G. (2023) 'The Neo-Weberian state: From ideal type model to reality?', *Max Weber Studies*, 23(1), 13–59. https://doi.org/10.1353/max.2023.0002

Bria, F., Timmers, P., and Gernone, F. (2025) *EuroStack – A European alternative for digital sovereignty.* Gütersloh: Bertelsmann Stiftung. https://www.euro-stack.info

Breznitz, D. and Ornston, D. (2014) 'Scaling up and sustaining experimental innovation policies with limited resources: Peripheral Schumpeterian development agencies', in Dutz, M. et al. (eds.) *Making innovation policy work: Learning from experimentation.* Paris: OECD Publishing, 235–260. https://doi.org/10.1787/9789264185739-12-en

Breznitz, D., Ornston, D., and Samford, S. (2018) 'Mission critical: The ends, means, and design of innovation agencies', *Industrial and Corporate Change*, 27(5), 883–896. https://doi.org/10.1093/icc/dty027

Clarke, A. (2019) 'Digital government units: What are they and what do they mean for digital era public management renewal?', *International Public Management Journal*, 22(4), 1–31.

Deleidi, M. and Mazzucato, M. (2021) 'Directed innovation policies and the supermultiplier: An empirical assessment of mission-oriented policies in the US economy', *Research Policy*, 50(2). https://doi.org/10.1016/j.respol.2020.104151

Edler, J., Blind, K., Kroll, H., and Schubert, T. (2023) 'Technology sovereignty as an emerging frame for innovation policy: Defining rationales, ends and means', *Research Policy*, 52(6). https://doi.org/10.1016/j.respol.2023.104765

Ergas, H. (1986) *Does technology policy matter?* Brussels: Centre for European Policy Studies.

Evans, P. and Rauch, J. E. (1999) 'Bureaucracy and growth: A cross-national analysis of the effects of "Weberian" state structures on economic growth', *American Sociological Review*, 64(5), 748–765. https://doi.org/10.2307/2657374

Foray, D., Mowery, D. C., and Nelson, R. R. (2012) 'Public R&D and social challenges: What lessons from mission R&D programs?', *Research Policy*, 41(10), 1697–1702. https://doi.org/10.1016/j.respol.2012.07.011

Fuchs, E. R. H. (2010) 'Rethinking the role of the state in technology development: DARPA and the case for embedded network governance', *Research Policy*, 39(9), 1133–1147.

Glennie, A. and Bound, K. (2016) *How innovation agencies work: International lessons to inspire and inform national strategies.* London, UK: Nesta. https://www.nesta.org.uk/documents/496/how_innovation_agencies_work.pdf (accessed 25 October 2025).

Goulden, A. and Kattel, R. (2024) *Designing and implementing mission-oriented policies: Tools and resources from the field.* UCL Institute for Innovation and Public Purpose,

Policy Report 2024/01. https://www.ucl.ac.uk/bartlett/public-purpose/publications/2024/feb/designing-and-implementing-mission-oriented-policies (accessed 25 October 2025).
Karo, E. and Kattel, R. (2018) 'Innovation and the state: Towards an evolutionary theory of policy capacity', in Wu, X., Howlett, M. and Ramesh, M. (eds.) *Policy capacity and governance*. Cham: Palgrave Macmillan, 123–150.
Kattel, R. (2024) *Past, present and future of innovation agencies in Europe*. Working Paper 80, Austrian Foundation for Development Research, Vienna. https://www.oefse.at/fileadmin/content/Downloads/Publikationen/Workingpaper/WP80_innovation-agencies-in-Europe.pdf (accessed 25 October 2025).
Kattel, R. and Entsminger, J. (2025) Open strategic autonomy through defence innovation? Lessons from the US defence innovation systems. *JRC Working Paper Series for a Fair, Innovative and Sustainable Economy, 16/2025*. Seville: European Commission.
Kattel, R. and Mazzucato, M. (2018) 'Mission-oriented innovation policy and dynamic capabilities in the public sector', *Industrial and Corporate Change*, 27(5), 787–801. https://doi.org/10.1093/icc/dty032
Kattel, R. and Mazzucato, M. (2020) 'COVID-19 and public-sector capacity', *Oxford Review of Economic Policy*, 36(Supplement_1), S256–S269. https://doi.org/10.1093/oxrep/graa031
Kattel, R., Drechsler, W., and Karo, E. (2022) *How to make an entrepreneurial state. Why innovation needs bureaucracy*. Yale: Yale University Press.
Kattel, R. and Mazzucato, M. (2023) *Mission-oriented innovation policies in Europe: From normative to epistemic turn?* UCL Institute for Innovation and Public Purpose, Working Paper Series (IIPP WP 2023-09). https://www.ucl.ac.uk/bartlett/public-purpose/wp2023-09 (accessed 25 October 2025).
Kattel, R. and Soete, L. (2024) *European security in a changing geo-political context: From the European Research Area to the European Defence Research and Innovation Area and from cohesion to European territorial security policy*. UCL Institute for Innovation and Public Purpose, Policy Report 2024/12.
Kattel, R., Haverkamp, K., Kalema, N., and Kofler, J. (2023) *New public management and innovation policy: A systematic literature review*. UCL Institute for Innovation and Public Purpose, Working Paper Series (IIPP WP 2023-05).
Kattel, R. et al. (2025) *Dynamic capabilities for transformative change in city governments*. UCL Institute for Innovation and Public Purpose, Working Paper Series (IIPP WP 2025-03).
Kattel, R. and Takala, V. (2023) 'The case of the UK's government digital service: The professionalisation of a paradigmatic public digital agency', *Digital Government Research and Practice*, 4(4), 1–15. https://doi.org/10.1145/3630024
Maldonado, M. and Kattel, R. (2024) 'How can policymakers address today's complex crises? Insights from the IIPP's work with Peru and the UK's innovation agencies', *IIPP Blog*. https://medium.com/iipp-blog/how-to-design-challenge-based-instruments-fce95a7d52ca (accessed 25 October 2025).
Mazzucato, M. (2017) *Mission-oriented innovation policy: Challenges and opportunities*. UCL Institute for Innovation and Public Purpose. https://www.ucl.ac.uk/bartlett/public-purpose/publications/2017/sep/mission-oriented-innovation-policy-challenges-and-opportunities (accessed 25 October 2025).
Mazzucato, M. (2021) *Mission economy: A moonshot guide to changing capitalism*. London, UK: Allen Lane.
Mazzucato, M. and Kattel, R. (2024) 'What mission-driven government means', *Project Syndicate*, 7 May. https://www.project-syndicate.org/commentary/mission-driven-government-what-it-means-and-common-misconceptions-by-mariana-mazzucato-and-rainer-kattel-1-2024-05 (accessed 25 October 2025).
Mowery, D.C. (2010) 'Military R&D and innovation', in Hall, B. H. and Rosenberg, N. (eds.) *Handbook of the economics of innovation*, Vol. 2. Amsterdam: Elsevier, 1219–1256.

Mukhtar-Landgren, D. (2021) 'Local autonomy in temporary organizations: The case of smart city pilots', *Administration & Society*, 53(10), 1485–1511. https://doi.org/10.1177/00953997211009884

Nelson, R. R. and Winter, S. G. (1982) *An evolutionary theory of economic change*. Cambridge, MA: Belknap Press of Harvard University Press.

Ostrom, V. and Ostrom, E. (1971) 'Public choice: A different approach to the study of public administration', *Public Administration Review*, 31(2), 203–216. https://doi.org/10.2307/974676

Pollitt, C. and Bouckaert, G. (2011) *Public management reform: A comparative analysis – New public management, governance, and the Neo-Weberian state*. Oxford, UK: Oxford University Press.

Pollitt, C. et al. (2008/09) 'A distinctive European model? The Neo-Weberian state', *The NISPAcee Journal of Public Administration and Policy*, 1(2).

Radosevic, S. and Zoretic, T. (2024) 'EU smart specialisation policy between experimentation and accountability: Dynamic policy cycle perspective', *European Planning Studies*, 32(8), 1693–1712. https://doi.org/10.1080/09654313.2024.2359669

Rohracher, H., Coenen, L., and Kordas, O. (2023) 'Mission incomplete: Layered practices of monitoring and evaluation in Swedish transformative innovation policy', *Science and Public Policy*, 50(2), 336–349. https://doi.org/10.1093/scipol/scac071

Schot, J. and Steinmueller, W. E. (2018) 'Three frames for innovation policy: R&D, systems of innovation and transformative change', *Research Policy*, 47(9), 1554–1567. https://doi.org/10.1016/j.respol.2018.08.011

Skocpol, T. (1985) 'Bringing the state back in: Strategies of analysis in current research', in Rueschemeyer, D., Evans, P. B. and Skocpol, T. (eds.) *Bringing the state back in*. Cambridge, UK: Cambridge University Press, 3–38.

Soete, L. et al. (2017) *Towards a mission-oriented research and innovation policy in the European Union: An ESIR memorandum*. European Commission. https://doi.org/10.2777/715942

Stirling, A. (2009) *Direction, distribution and diversity! Pluralising progress in innovation, sustainability and development*. Brighton: STEPS Centre. https://opendocs.ids.ac.uk/opendocs/handle/20.500.12413/2458 (accessed 25 October 2025).

Stirling, A. (2024) 'Responsibility and the hidden politics of directionality: Opening up "innovation democracies" for sustainability transformations', *Journal of Responsible Innovation*, 11(1). https://doi.org/10.1080/23299460.2024.2370082

Teece, D. J., Pisano, G., and Shuen, A. (1997) 'Dynamic capabilities and strategic management', *Strategic Management Journal*, 18(7), 509–533. https://doi.org/10.1002/(SICI)1097-0266(199708)18:7<509::AID-SMJ882>3.0.CO;2-Z

PART IV

Funding Challenges for Progressive Industrial Policy

8

FINANCING THE EUROPEAN UNION'S PROGRESSIVE INDUSTRIAL POLICIES

Strategies Beyond Financial Derisking

Viktor Skyrman

8.1 Introduction

> Is it possible to deploy industrial policies that strengthen green growth and economic security without hurting competition, economic openness and cohesion in the EU? Is it possible to do so without stronger EU-level governance, backed by financial resources? To me, the answer to the first question is 'yes', and to the second, 'no'.
>
> *(Jeronim Zettelmeyer, Director of Bruegel; Aghion et al., 2023: 11–12)*

With the rise of industrial policy (IP) in recent years (Breznitz and Gingrich, 2025), the climate crisis is increasingly defined as an investment problem rather than a pricing problem. Amid ambitious IP in the US and China, European policymakers agree that carbon pricing alone will not bring about the several €trillions needed for Europe's green transformation (Jakob and Overland, 2024). As the annual green investment gap exceeds 2% of the EU's gross domestic product (GDP), of particular relevance is *how* the EU's green industrial programmes will be financed. Amid scarce fiscal resources and public sector austerity, the paradigmatic idea of *de-risking*[1] aims to "escort" private finance to green and societally important but otherwise unprofitable destinations, instead of directly carrying out investments by fiscal means and public investment banks (UNCTAD, 2019: 143–166; Kedward *et al.*, 2022a). Exemplified by the European Fund for Strategic Investments (EFSI) and InvestEU programmes, policymakers have seen derisking as a cheap and attractive financing alternative under Europe's austerity framework. The Letta report similarly proposes the launch of a "European Green Guarantee" with a supposed multiplier of 12 (Letta, 2024: 31). Meanwhile, critics argue that derisking

DOI: 10.4324/9781003745563-13

reinforces commodification, contributes to carbon lock-in and undermines market-shaping approaches where states take more central roles (Gabor, 2023).

This chapter discusses how derisking measures has largely failed to bring about the investments needed to reach the EU's twin transformation goals. Drawing on heterodox and mainstream academic and policy-oriented discussions, the chapter discusses alternative public financing measures for the expanded EU-level industrial policies discussed in this volume. The chapter also elaborates on "progressive derisking", i.e., requirements to make derisking compatible with progressive approaches of European industrial policy.

The next section reviews Europe's green and digital investment gap. The ensuing section discusses the hegemonic fiscal programme of derisking, while providing an account on the extent of derisking in major EU investment programmes. The subsequent section discusses ways to increase public funding for the twin transformation, including increased EU-level taxation particularly on financial transactions, wealth and capital gains; the permanent issuance of EU bonds; a permanent EU investment fund; and further leveraging of development banks (DBs) for scaled-up credit allocation and equity funding. The penultimate section discusses "progressive derisking" as alternative derisking policies that may be compatible with progressive approaches of European industrial policy. The chapter ends with a summary.

8.2 The growing European investment gap

The investment gap grows the more green investment is postponed. One study estimates the EU's yearly climate investment needs to €813 billion, or 5.1%, of EU GDP. With around €407 billion being spent in 2022, the study estimated a €406 billion (2.6% of EU GDP) annual green investment deficit in Europe (Calipel *et al.*, 2024: 2). Meanwhile, there is an annual €620 billion investment gap needed to meet the objectives of REpowerEU and the European Green Deal until 2030 (Lagarde, 2024 based on EC, 2023: 7), while the digital transformation would need additional investments of €125 billion (Lagarde, 2024). In relation to the EU's economy, with a nominal GDP of €19.35 trillion in the beginning of 2024 (IMF, 2024), €620 billion amounts to 3.2% of the EU's nominal GDP. Furthermore, to reach the 90% target by 2040, the EC "estimates that between 2030 and 2040, investment needs will increase to €1.5 trillion per year" (Strategic Perspectives, 2024: 38). The gap, meanwhile, for the EU to reach net-zero by 2050 is estimated to average €360 billion per year, 2.3% of the current EU-27 GDP, according to one think tank (Institut Rousseau, 2024: 172). By comparison, estimations of direct and indirect fossil fuel subsidies in the EU range between €290 billion (Strategic Perspectives, 2024: 40) to €359 billion annually (Institut Rousseau, 2024: 33). Meanwhile, yearly shareholder dividends from European listed firms amounts to €410 billion, while EU-27 fossil fuel subsidies amounted to some €359 billion (Institut Rousseau, 2024). When adding investments needed for further geopolitical and structural goals, the

Draghi report calls for €750–800 in additional yearly investments, corresponding to around 4.5% of EU GDP as of 2023 (Draghi Report, 2024: 59). For summaries of additional estimations, see Raza (2024: 52) and Skyrman (2024a: 8–9).

8.3 Derisking – an overview of the European case

Radical uncertainty makes risk incalculable and renders pricing mechanisms (e.g. interest rates and uniform carbon prices) blunt tools to stimulate investment in risky sectors and radical innovations, where path dependency, technological inertia, institutional feedbacks and lengthy high-risk lead times are at play. Moreover, as green investments are "widely considered a relatively risky, volatile, and often not profitable asset class" (Babic, 2024: 3; see Tagliapietra *et al.*, 2023: 52–53). In this context, derisking aims to increase private investment to green and societally important but otherwise unprofitable destinations (Kedward *et al.*, 2022a). This is achieved by public sector institutions absorbing private sector risk by tinkering on risk/return profiles through guarantees, public-private partnerships and blended finance and thereby implicitly guaranteeing profits for private investors, which in turn has significant political, economic, environmental and social implications (Gabor, 2021a). At its core, derisking strategies aim to mobilise and "crowd-in" private investment and make green sectors increasingly investible, instead of steering financial flows to preferred sectors directly through fiscal means, DBs and other public sector institutions (UNCTAD, 2019: 143–166). In contrast to the developmentalist literature that emphasises the disciplining of private capital, with states on top in state-capital hierarchies, derisking strategies position the private sector and "institutional investors, rather than domestic governments, as the leading actors in a global sustainable transition" (Kedward and Ryan-Collins, 2022: 283).

Critics argue that derisking reinforces commodification and contributes to carbon lock-in, is especially exposed to regulatory capture, arbitrage (Kedward et al., 2022b: 1) and greenwashing (Dafermos *et al.*, 2021: 244, Cooiman, 2023: 9–11), while it undermines policy-steer (Griffith-Jones *et al.*, 2022: 200, Gabor, 2023: 23) and conditionalities on private investments. Derisking approaches have thereto failed to shift financial flows away from brown and towards green activities in much of the Global South (Ameli *et al.*, 2021; Kalinowski, 2023) as well as in Europe (Kedward and Ryan-Collins, 2022: 284). Moreover, EU derisking programmes usually lack transparency, partly due to protecting clients' commercial confidentiality, which makes scrutiny, climate impact assessment and public control measures difficult to implement (Mack and Findeisen, 2023: 8).

Out of Table 8.1, EFSI and InvestEU can be distinguished as having the most inflated nominal multipliers. While most of the assessments and evaluations of EFSI have been carried out by European Investment Bank (EIB) itself, most scholars have taken these at face value (cf. Griffith-Jones and Naqvi, 2020; Mertens and Thiemann, 2022; Mazzucato, 2023: 15). The supposedly unlocked €500 billion of private investments through €26 billion of EU guarantees and €7.5 billion

TABLE 8.1 17 important European programmes or financing mechanisms

Investment initiative/ programme	*Time frame*	*Budget (€ billion)*	*Explicit estimated private sector additionality?*	*Source of funding and instruments*	*Objective*
NextGeneration EU (NGEU)	2021–2026	750	No	Grants and loans financed through common debt (EU bonds)	Support the EU's COVID-19 recovery; green transition; economic resilience
Recovery and Resilience Fund (RRF)	2021–2026	724	No	The RRF is the operational arm of the NGEU	Digitalisation, green transition, energy infrastructure
REPowerEU	2022–2026	300	No	Mainly RRF	Reduce Europe's energy dependence on Russia
Horizon Europe	2021–2027	96	No	Grants mainly (EU budget)	Research and Innovation
The European Regional Development Fund	2021–2028	226	No	Grants (EU budget)	Ameliorate regional imbalances
The Cohesion Fund	2021–2029	48	No	Grants (EU budget)	Ameliorate regional imbalances
European Structural and Investment Funds (ESIF)	2014–2020	535	Yes. 731 (including from the EU budget). Multiplier -1.37	Various	Execute European economic, innovation, agricultural and cohesion policy
Strategic Technologies for Europe Platform (STEP)	2021–	15	Yes. 160. Multiplier – around 10.	Reshuffling of existing funds	Support technological upgrading (incl. digitalisation, decarbonisation, and biotech)
European Fund for Strategic Investments (EFSI)	2015–2020	33.5	Yes. 500. Multiplier of around 15	Guarantees, Loans, Equity, Venture Debt (EU budget, EIB, EIF)	Revive European investments to boost growth and competitiveness
InvestEU	2021–2027	26	Yes. 372. Expected multipliers range from 11 to 14.3	Similar to EFSI	Similar to EFSI

(*Continued*)

TABLE 8.1 (Continued)

Investment initiative/ programme	*Time frame*	*Budget (€ billion)*	*Explicit estimated private sector additionality?*	*Source of funding and instruments*	*Objective*
Net-Zero Industry Act (NZIA)	2023–2030	16–18	Yes. 92 billion. Multiplier of around 5.4	No additional EU funds, proposed member state spending	"strengthen the European manufacturing capacity of net-zero technologies"
Social Climate Fund	2026–2032	NA	Yes. "at least € 86.7 billion"	25 % of ETS-2 revenues (max. € 65 bn) plus 25 % national co-financing	Support households and firms impacted by climate policies
Innovation Fund	2021–2027	NA	Yes. 40 billion	Monetisation of 530 million ETS allowances, using a carbon price of € 75/ tCO2.	Finance "innovative low-carbon technologies"
The EU Chips Act	2023–2030	NA	Yes. Public and private investment expected to mobilise a total of € 43 billion	Mostly private and MS funding; reshuffling of EU resources (e.g. Horizon, RRF)	Support Europe's semiconductor manufacturing
Important Projects of Common European Interest (IPCEI)	2018–	NA	34.8 in public investments; 56.8 in private investments (and growing)	Member states, private co-funding	"strengthen open strategic autonomy, by enabling breakthrough innovation and infrastructure projects"
Just Transition Fund	2021–2027	17.5	Yes. 30 billion	EU grants and loans	Ameliorate regional imbalances
InvestAI	2025–	50	200 billion	NA	Boost AI investment

Note: The light grey area indicates programmes where no explicit additionality figures are stated (no or weak derisking). The dark grey area indicates programmes with explicit derisking estimations/targets (strong derisking). The European Competitiveness Fund is a recent investment proposal not mentioned in the list.

Sources: Own elaboration, based on Demertzis *et al.* (2024) (mainly); Heimberger and Lichtenberger (2023b: 211–212), Seidl and Schmitz (2023: 16), and the European Commission.

of EIB's own resources, reaching a multiplier of 15. The EIB thereto reports that EFSI projects were riskier than its typical projects. Yet as of 2022, only a modest €184 million in guarantees were called. The low default rate might indicate that these projects were not as risky as presumed, and that EFSI guarantees have not contributed to riskier investments (Demertzis *et al.*, 2024: 20). EFSI's guarantees also did poorly in stimulating investments related to climate change adaptation (as opposed to climate change mitigation), "which may reflect the specific difficulties in preparing bankable adaptation investments" (ECA, 2021: 39). The high leverage of InvestEU, the successor of EFSI, has likewise limited policymakers' "capacity to turn innovative projects with transformative potential into propositions for private and market-based finance as it limits their capacity to provide direct and balance-sheet-intense support" (Mack and Findeisen, 2023: 7). In summary, "EFSI highlighted the difficulties of unlocking transformative investments with indirect financial instruments" (Mack and Findeisen, 2023), while InvestEU's high leverage "prevents it from taking the risks necessary to provide truly additional green investment" (Mack and Findeisen, 2023: 2). EU derisking programmes has largely failed to increase high-tech investments or high-tech R&D investments – partly because several of these programmes, such as InvestEU, mainly target large-scale infrastructures projects (Gros *et al.*, 2025). Current financing strategies thus do little to ameliorate Europe's "the middle-technology trap", as the continent's corporate sector is considerably less high-tech, less R&D-intensive, and increasingly uncompetitive compared with that of the US or China (Gros *et al.*, 2025; Whitfield and Wuttke, 2025).

8.4 The need for public financing

Research on the actual private/public ratio of green investments is inconclusive. Some estimate public money to finance 17% of green investments, while other studies show that the number surpasses 5%, i.e. are larger than private investments (Heimberger and Lichtenberger, 2023a: 11). While European policymakers reiterate that the majority of climate finance should come from the private sector, one think tank contrarily propagates that the public sector should fund 70% of the European green investment gap to reach net zero by 2050 (Institut Rousseau, 2024: 172).

Moreover, despite the price-drop of solar and wind manufacturing, private investments into these mature green technologies are lacking – the European wind sector "has a cumulative annual shortfall of approximately €74 billion" (Strategic Perspectives, 2024: 38). Therefore, fossil fuel-fired power plants still generated 61% of global electricity in 2022, compared to 64% in 1985 (Christophers, 2024: 6). Especially large-scale loans to mature technologies with limited technological uncertainty, such as wind and solar, are well-suited to be conducted by public institutions. Moreover, much infrastructure is publicly owned, so private finance cannot be crowded in towards these ends anyway (Mack and Findeisen, 2023: 6).

The feasibility of large-scale public financing for societal challenges is enhanced from a historical perspective, as the 2–3% green investment gap to GDP can be perceived as a fairly small number for an advanced continent. The costs of wars and economic crises often surpass these numbers by far. US federal spending increased from 10% to 43% in the 1940s (Sachs, 2019). Moreover, the "cumulative increase in public debt in the three years following a banking crisis" have averaged 86.3% in the postwar era (Reinhart and Rogoff, 2009: 471). Yet, the EU controls only ~1% of GNI, compared to 40–45% at the national level, limiting its ability to finance large-scale, cross-European projects. As a result, common strategies often rely on unequal national funding which run the risk of exacerbating uneven economic development within the Union. Many economists now call for expanding the EU budget by 1–2% of GDP (Landesmann, 2025: 35).

Some core components of how to increase supranational funding for industrial policies discussed in this volume are thus presented below, including issuance of EU bonds; a permanent investment fund; progressive European taxation; "progressive" derisking; and a network of expanded supranational and public DBs.

8.4.1 EU bonds and the RRF

As the centrepiece of the NextGenerationEU programme (2021–2026), the RRF was launched to alleviate the economic hardships during COVID-19. Authorising the EC to borrow up to €672.5 billion (Hodson and Howarth, 2023), the RRF raises €723.8 billion through EU bonds issued by the EC, of which around half (€338 billion) are dispersed to Member States (MSs) in grants and the other rough half (€385.8 billion) in repayable loans. MS receive grants or loans based on their National Recovery and Resilience Plans (NRRPs) that are evaluated by the EC and approved by the council. Grants are distributed based on criteria including the magnitude of the economic downturn during the COVID-19 pandemic, average unemployment, GDP per capita and need for structural reforms. The total size of grants thereby ranges between from 9% of GDP for the EU's poorest MSs to less than 1% of GDP for its richest MSs. At least 37% of disbursed amounts should be dedicated to climate investments and at least 20% should be spent on digitalisation.

Scholars have referred to the RRF as an innovative European investment model (Heimberger and Lichtenberger, 2023a: 13); a landmark agreement (Mazzucato, 2023: 9) as well as an ambitious "institutional innovation" (Mazzucato, 2023: 32), and reports of positive growth effects (FT, 2024). For a more critical account, see Reimer et al. (2025). Moreover, EU bonds issued under the RRF represent a paradigm shift in European fiscal policy. EU debt increased 10-fold from €50 billion in 2020 to €500 billion in 2024, is projected to reach €900 billion by 2026 and will by then only trail four sovereign EU bond markets of (France, Italy, Germany, and Spain) in terms of volume (FT, 2023a). Unlike conventional government debt, EU bonds are not passed on to domestic public debt ratios, which alleviates fiscal constraints at the same time as necessary structural investments are carried out

(Heimberger and Lichtenberger, 2023a: 21). Given its overall track record, EU bonds should become permanent. Firstly, there is a lack of MS fiscal space given the (reformed) Stability and Growth Pact (see Heimberger in this volume). Secondly, there is a risk of increased regional imbalances of a financing strategy for the twin transition solely based on MS spending. Thirdly, EU bonds could provide a safe asset that enhances stability and liquidity on a unified EU capital market. Fourthly, borrowing costs would likely be lower on permanent and more liquid bonds, compared to the temporary nature of the RRF (FT, 2023a).

8.4.2 A permanent EU investment fund

The time-limited timespans of instruments such as the RRF and InvestEU are not conducive to the long-term goals of the twin transformation. A legally simple option to permanently generate public investment would be through a permanent European investment fund. The European Competitiveness Fund, proposed in July 2025 by the European Commission, is one of the newest proposals of such a fund and deserves special attention (Jarlebring, 2025). Similar to the RRF, per capita allocation of the fund's resources could be based on the need for reaching specified performance targets, such as emission reduction plans. This would render higher per capita investments in Eastern and Southern Europe than in Western and Northern MSs (Heimberger and Lichtenberger, 2023b: 207). A permanent investment fund could provide "at least 1% of EU economic output per year" to address climate and energy-related investment needs (Heimberger and Lichtenberger, 2023a). This would amount to €1.65–1.8 trillion from 2026 to 2035 in 2024 prices.

The fund could be set up in multiple ways, including having one component for long-term structural investments, and one counter-cyclical "rainy day fund" to be used in economic downturns (Schmidt, 2023: 39–40). Pointing to an International Monetary Fund (IMF) study, Heimberger and Lichtenberger (2023a: 19) reiterate a hypothetical example where MSs would dedicate 0.35% of GDP to such a rainy-day fund (Heimberger and Lichtenberger, 2023b: 210). The fund would contribute to net investment regardless of business cycles or MS' fiscal situations. As future generations would benefit from these investments, having them participating in the financing through long-term EC-issued debt instruments (Aghion *et al.*, 2023: 39) would be another option.[2] The fund could also be financed through taxation, issue its own bonds, and/or be augmented through additional voluntary contributions from MSs (Griffith-Jones and Carreras, 2021: 28). Or as alluded to by Letta (2024: 26–27), MSs could be required to allocate a portion of their state aid towards a pan-European fund as to counter fragmentation. The EIB, with its experience and technical expertise, is a suitable candidate to manage such a fund (Griffith-Jones and Carreras, 2021: 28; Demertzis *et al.*, 2024: 30). For further discussion on a permanent investment fund, see chapter Heimberger's chapter in this volume.

8.4.3 EU-wide taxation

As the burden of taxation has been increasingly transferred from capital to labour the last decades (Guzzardi *et al.*, 2023: 173), EU-wide capital taxes would reduce economic inequality, increase tax system fairness, likely enhance European cross-border investments, reduce negative-sum tax competition between MS, increase efficiency and simplicity and reduce administrative burdens for firms, and, above all, significantly improve Europe's fiscal space (Mazzucato, 2023: 10–11, Mazzucato and Macfarlane, 2023: 23–24). In addition, partial pooling enforcement agency resources could better counter some forms of tax evasion and avoidance (Skyrman, 2024a: 20). More specifically, Guzzardi *et al.* (2023: 182–184) provide details for the size and makeup of EU-wide wealth, capital gains and corporate tax rates. In addition, the EC's previous ambition to introduce a common financial transaction tax (FTT), which would raise around half of the EU budget (Table 8.2), should re-enter the agenda. An FTT proposal by the EC in 2013 was estimated to generate revenues corresponding to 0.4–0.5% of the GDP of participating MSs (European Commission, 2013).

Aside from capital taxes,[3] "only 11 EU member states have some form of carbon tax, and those that do tax carbon below the levels recommended by economists" (Aghion *et al.*, 2022: 3). Against this backdrop, some scholars propose a transnational carbon taxation system instead of a globally regressive EU carbon border scheme (Gallagher and Kozul-Wright, 2021), both as a means to generate taxation revenues, but crucially to stimulate green investments at the expense of brown investments (Aghion *et al.*, 2022: 26–27). A European broad-based carbon tax,[4] based on the "social cost of carbon", would generate between 0.5% to 5% of GDP in tax revenue annually (Breckenfelder *et al.*, 2023: 25).

Table 8.2 gives an overview of some of these taxes and their estimated revenues. Several other EU-wide taxes have been proposed, and the EuroMemo Group (2024: 15) calls for "an enlarged EU budget corresponding to 5% of GNI, financed by new fiscal resources, including taxation of the super-wealthy and of the windfall profits

TABLE 8.2 Yearly tax revenues of proposed EU taxes

	Tax revenues, % of EU GDP
EU wealth tax	1
EU financial transaction tax	0.5
EU capital gains tax	0.4
EU corporate tax (25%)	1.5
Total capital taxes	**3.4**
EU carbon tax	0.5–5
EU digital services tax	0.2
Total	**4.1–8.6**

Sources: EC (2013), Guzzardi *et al.* (2023: 182–184), Breckenfelder *et al.* (2023: 25), and Thomadakis (2025).

of corporations which had benefitted from the crisis, such as energy companies and banks". For a discussion of a European re-insurance system as a de facto alternative to a fiscal union, see Schelkle (2023). Lastly, one should note that the electoral appeal of several tax measures mentioned here is growing (Brachet, 2025).

8.5 Progressive derisking

Although state lending and investment could provide a much larger share of green financing on a technical level, political constraints for such strategies are obvious. The large majority of economists and policymakers would agree that it "is neither realistic to expect that 'the market' [… nor …] public balance sheets … [alone] can create and allocate the volume of capital required for the Green Transition" (Murau *et al.*, 2024). This begs the question: amid the critique of derisking, are all forms of derisking necessarily unwarranted?

This section defines "progressive derisking" (PDR) proponents as those who do not oppose derisking per se, but rather the way it is currently executed. Instead of subsidising private capital with little or no strings attached (which risks IP failure and corporate welfare), progressive deriskers argue that the public sector can and should mobilise private investments as long as risks and rewards, knowledge, and other outputs are shared equitably between private subsidy recipients and the state, and that civil servants can impact how goods and services are produced and distributed.

PDR proponents highlight that markets are co-created by private and public sector actors. By acting as investors of first resort, co-creating and shaping markets, and financing general-purpose technologies such as the internet, nanotechnology, biotechnology and emerging clean-tech sectors, states have remained core (albeit latent) contributors to radical innovation in the neoliberal era (Cypher, 1987; Block and Keller, 2009; Demertzis *et al.*, 2024: 28). Thus, rather than to merely "de-risk private risk-takers" (Mazzucato, 2021: 123), the public sector should be more engaged in innovation-specific risk-taking. Mazzucato's emphasis on a virtuous state-capital interplay is echoed by prominent IP scholars such as Rodrik (2014, 2023: 46–48), who similarly describes IP as a mode of cooperation between government bureaucrats and firms, rather than top-down state command-and-control processes. Similarly, "industrial policy should be about institutionalised collaboration and dialogue between governments, the private sector and civil society" according to Tagliapietra et al. (2023: 53; see also Veugelers *et al.*, 2024: 16).

8.5.1 Conditionalities

A key difference between EU derisking programmes and PDR is that the latter emphasises that the public sector should not subsidise the private sector without performance related conditionalities. Conditionalities imply the ability of policymakers to affect business conduct, even if it interferes with short-term profitability.

They come in the form of "rules, governance structures, benchmarks and ownership agreements that align the preferences of state and corporate actors thereby limiting the scope for rent-seeking behavior and strategic failures", and can be used to steer private investments, co-create markets and foster innovation. Historically, conditionality scholarship includes Wade's (1990) categorisation of states in positions of "leadership" and "followership" vis-à-vis industry, Amsden's (1989) notion about "performance standards" and Rodrik's (2009) conception of both "carrots" (rewards) and "sticks" (restrictions) in industrial policies. Successful IP requires ways to monitor recipients receiving subsidies and castigate those who digress from stated goals (Bulfone *et al.*, 2024: 3, 2025).

Areas covered by the conditionalities include requirements that subsidy recipients reinvest profits into R&D, worker training, or other productive activities; public sector profit sharing via royalties or partial government equity ownership; access, i.e. that government will have access to for example products at low cost or intellectual property rights it helps to co-finance (Mazzucato and Macfarlane, 2023: 18). By way of example, conditionalities in US IP programmes have been extensive. The Biden government has prohibited subsidised firms to expand in China or conduct "joint research or technology licensing [involving] sensitive technologies". The CHIPS partly forbids dividend or stock buyback, while the Inflation Reduction Act (IRA) puts a 1% excise tax on stock buybacks. Meanwhile, a "prevailing wage clause" stipulates receiving firms to pay out decent wages and benefits to employees.

An example of equitable access is the Oxford/AstraZeneca vaccine, Vaxzevria. Under the UK government Vaccine Task Force, the UK government secured 100 million doses in advance, offering a demand guarantee to AstraZeneca. In exchange, AstraZeneca was required to sell the vaccine at cost during the pandemic (Mazzucato, 2022: 8). In 2021, Vaxzevria was priced at $2.15 per dose for the EU, much lower than Pfizer's and Moderna's mRNA vaccines, which cost $19.50 and $25.50, respectively (Kollewe, 2021). For a more detailed account of conditionalities, readers are referred to Bulfone *et al.* (2025), Mazzucato and Rodrik (2023: 8–9), and Raza (2024), as well as Raza's chapter in this volume.

In comparison, current EU programmes, the European Central Bank's asset purchase programmes as well as the RRF lack many conditionalities integrated to the US IRA and CHIPS act (Cohen *et al.*, 2019; Gabor, 2023; Letta, 2024: 39–40), including decent wages, job creation, right to collective bargaining, taxes on excess profits, profit sharing and bans on excessive shareholder remuneration, including on dividends and share buybacks (Mazzucato, 2022: 13; Mazzucato and Macfarlane, 2023: 19; Schmidt, 2023: 39). Clearly, practical and legal challenges, as well as trade-offs regarding the volume of investments, have to be faced (Griffith-Jones and Carreras, 2021: 27). As 100% of EIF (the EU's multilateral DB for financial intermediation; for a critical overview, see 2023) and about one third of the EIB activities are carried out via private actors, these EU institutions have an important role to apply conditionalities (Griffith-Jones and Carreras, 2021: 27). Where it is impossible to impose conditionalities, direct financing from DBs might be more suitable (Griffith-Jones and Naqvi, 2020: 22). Moreover, while guarantees limit the Commission's ability to tie performance criteria or conditionalities to financial support, grants give the EC direct control over profit sharing and performance-related conditionalities (Mack and Findeisen, 2023: 7).

8.5.2 Public development banks – key tools for public investment and progressive derisking

Public financial institutions are often prescribed to provide patient capital to emerging industries (Dziwok and Jäger, 2021). Even American policymakers have

> found it desirable to have active state provision of credit: the Small Business Administration plays a major role in the provision of small business loans, the Export-Import Bank is a major provider of lending support, especially for exporters like Boeing, and, in recent years, more than 90% of all mortgages have been underwritten by the federal government.
>
> *(Noman and Stiglitz, 2015: 13–14)*

More than 40% of banking assets are currently state-owned in Germany, compared to 65% in India, 60% in China, while less than 10% in the UK, France, Spain, Italy, Japan, and the US (DiPippo *et al.*, 2022: 15). In the postwar period, many states required state pension funds and private institutional investors to hold large parts of their assets in prioritised sectors, such as government bonds or mortgage credits (Skyrman, 2024b: 212).

Yet, in liberal financial systems, the most efficient means by which states can steer finance and investment is through DBs. In the early 2020s, the 25 largest development finance institutions, 7 of which are European, had $9 trillion in assets, or 78% of all development finance assets (Gallagher and Kozul-Wright, 2021: 110), while state-owned DBs and development finance institutions held $20.2 trillion in assets in 2023. Due to their already important footprint and large size, multilateral DBs account for over one third of climate finance to developing countries (UN DESA, 2022: 88), and 10% of global investments annually (UN DESA, 2022: 20). As of 2020, the EIB funded 40% of offshore wind capacity in Europe (Griffith-Jones and Naqvi, 2020: 13).

In addition to conditionalities, progressive deriskers highlight DBs (DBs) as key tools for PDR (Griffith-Jones and Carreras, 2021: 26; Griffith-Jones *et al.*, 2022; Mazzucato and Macfarlane, 2023; Mazzucato, 2023). Derisking is legitimised and deemed progressive as long as DBs reap some of the profits "where feasible" (Griffith-Jones and Carreras, 2021: 4), while retaining policy steer, rather than outsourcing too much influence over industrial policy to private actors (e.g. Dafermos *et al.*, 2021: 244; Kedward *et al.*, 2022b: 1; Griffith-Jones *et al.*, 2022: 200; Gabor, 2023: 23). As benchmarking and anchor institutions, DBs mainly utilise four types of funding instruments: loans (ordinary and concessional), guarantees, grants and equity investments[5] (Griffith-Jones *et al.*, 2022: 203), as well as providing consultancy services. For example, the EIB "mainly operates through lending, borrowing on capital markets, steering and de-risking private funds, and advising" (Mertens and Thiemann, 2022: 73). Progressive deriskers highlight that different sectors, type of investments and end-goals require different instruments, or a mix of instruments (Griffith-Jones *et al.*, 2022: 213), as "[i]t is important to stress that DBs can involve private finance in different ways, some of which will be more desirable in terms of maximising development impact, and minimising future contingency risk" (Griffith-Jones *et al.*, 2022: 200).

Progressive deriskers have been sympathetic to some derisking programmes executed by the EIB. While derisking sceptics discredits the EFSI-executed InvestEU as derisking "per excellence" (Gabor, 2023), progressive deriskers have contrarily voiced some mild praise to the InvestEU's predecessor EFSI (e.g. Griffith-Jones and Naqvi, 2020: 3, 7; Mertens and Thiemann, 2022: 89; Mazzucato, 2023). Mazzucato *et al.* (2023: 15) argue that among the

> best practices and results achieved by the EFSI, two key points deserve major attention. First, additionality played a great role as it enabled the triggering of private investments at a national level … for an amount of resources up to 15 times of that received by countries as part of the programme. Second, the role of the EIB Group has been crucial for the successful crowding-in of additional financial resources and implementation of the plan.
>
> *(For details, see Mertens and Thiemann, 2022: 86. For a critical discussion, see Demertzis et al., 2024: 20)*

Importantly, DBs play a crucial role in current neoliberal capitalism, and have been promoted as public "off-balance sheet" institutions that surpass fiscal limitations before, during and in the aftermath of the GFC and the COVID-19 crisis. While increased public spending and regulation are prone to political backlash, DBs already have an impressive track record and essentially do not clash with neoliberal policy prescriptions (Mertens and Thiemann, 2019, 2023). Given their green and safe (usually triple A-rated) profile, large amounts of institutional capital already flow to DB bonds. Importantly, they help to overcome fiscal constraints as DB liabilities do not register towards the Maastricht criteria (Adler *et al.*, 2019: 32). Hence, the further leveraging of DBs to address public underinvestment could be done without challenging the Union's fiscal orthodoxy, and an EIB that leads a coalition of European DBs would essentially not add much to EU or individual member budgets (Adler *et al.*, 2019; UNCTAD, 2019: 163).

As the public sector plays a key role in radical innovation[6] (Mazzucato, 2013; Bofinger, 2025), the EIB should take a more proactive and market shaping approach rather than to respond to private sector demand, market failures, and financing conventional technology (Griffith-Jones and Carreras, 2021: 26; Mertens and

Thiemann, 2022: 89; Mazzucato and Macfarlane, 2023: 17; Demertzis *et al.*, 2024: 20). While loans and guarantees are important, equity and quasi-equity instruments should become more common as "debt finance seems to be ineffective in stimulating green innovation" (cf. Aghion *et al.*, 2022: 27; Padoan, 2023: 110). Equity stakes avoid unsustainable leveraging of firms, increases policy steer, and let public actors capture rewards along with risk-taking stemming from successful financing of innovative firms (Griffith-Jones and Carreras, 2021: 27; Griffith-Jones *et al.*, 2022: 200; Mack and Findeisen, 2023: 7).

To increase their potential, DBs can be further capitalised by being granted "autonomous borrowing powers", i.e., letting them issue their own bonds and equity; taking savings and deposits from savers; receive central bank financing or manage public pension or social security funds (Mazzucato and Macfarlane, 2023: 20); obtain increased refinancing from existing MSs and/or accept new MSs (UN DESA, 2022: 89). Central bank[7] seigniorage profits, DB profits and Special Drawing Rights have also been promoted as means to finance DBs (UN DESA, 2022: 78, 83–84; UNCTAD, 2022: 175). MSs' paid-in capital to the EIB could increase – preferably double, as was done in 2012 (Griffith-Jones and Carreras, 2021: 26–27). National DBs should also be leveraged through several of the aforementioned options, as the efficiency of supranational DBs is enhanced when working closely with domestic and regional DBs and public sector institutions with better knowledge of local economic circumstances and networks (Griffith-Jones *et al.*, 2022: 220–221). New ways of domestic-supranational DB cooperation, including co-investing or co-lending, should thereto be enhanced, not least when financing cross-border projects and European public goods (Mertens and Thiemann, 2022: 87; Griffith-Jones *et al.*, 2022: 213).

8.6 Conclusions

The EU's austerity-prone export-oriented growth model is ill-suited for the pending de-globalisation and increased geopolitical strife we may likely witness into the 2030s (Karas, 2024; Alami *et al.*, 2025; Frauenlob, 2025). Reduced external demand can and should be replaced by strengthening internal demand – especially in wealthier MSs with fiscal space that run significant export surpluses. Progressive IP is key towards such stimulus, revitalisation and greening of the continent (Bärnthaler *et al.*, 2025), but this requires significant sources of enlarged funding. Yet, EU strategies for increased financial capacity building remain limited. Boosting securitisation, a hot topic among EU policymakers to increase investments, are obviously a crisis-prone alternative, as was shown during the 2008 global finance crisis. Moreover, Europe's largely conservative banking sectors have tended to avoid engaging with securitisation instruments (Skyrman, 2024b). Additional strategies than securitisation or solely bringing forward a European Capital Markets Union are thus needed.

This chapter has thus discussed alternative strategies to finance EU-level industrial policy proposals brought forward in this volume. Such proposals include expanding the EU budget for 2028 and onwards through increased EU-level taxation on (for example) wealth and the financial sector; the permanent issuance of EU bonds; a permanent EU investment fund; and the continued leverage of DBs. Many of these financing options are rather mutually supportive than exclusive on a technical level. The targeting of European public goods would be key in enhancing the political feasibility of increased public supranational funding.

While direct public financing may be a paramount alternative for ameliorating the climate crisis, this option remains politically difficult. Most scholars and policymakers hold the view that "It is neither realistic to expect that 'the market' [… nor …] public balance sheets … [alone] can create and allocate the volume of capital required for the Green Transition" (Murau *et al.*, 2024). Meanwhile, adverse social, economic and environmental side-effects have been related to derisking, including regulatory capture, arbitrage, greenwashing and corporate welfare. Yet, should all forms of derisking be discarded? This chapter has differentiated between different forms of derisking, highlighting that some scholars support an implicit form of "progressive derisking" where public policy steer is maintained, the state-capital relationship is "symbiotic" and not "parasitic" (Mazzucato, 2021: 167), and as long as risks and profits are shared through conditionalities. Further research into the potential and pitfall of "progressive" forms of derisking is warranted. Lastly, as finance has been one important component of China's successes in the realm of IP, innovation and green energy investments, some policy implications are likely relevant for the EU (for an EU-China financial statecraft comparison, see Li and Ban, 2025; Larsen, 2025; FT, 2025).

Notes

1 That is, financial derisking, not to be misunderstood as "geopolitical derisking". From a Western standpoint, the latter implies the partial near-shoring and decoupling of supply chains and trade diversification vis-à-vis Russia and China.
2 This would not have any adverse effect on MSs' fiscal budgets.
3 Other studies have estimated revenues from an EU-wide wealth tax to correspond to between 1.5% and 11% of GDP (Kapeller *et al.*, 2021, 2023; Heimberger and Lichtenberger, 2023b: 207).
4 "Carbon taxes are indeed typically regressive, hitting more the poorest income classes, possibly triggering social protests as in the case of French Gillets Jaunes" (Guzzardi *et al.*, 2023: 183).
5 "… there is a loose hierarchy of involving private finance in development funding in terms of impact, with most impactful mechanisms being DBs borrowing on private capital markets to offer direct loans; private lenders and investors co-lending or coinvesting with DBs; on-lending to commercial institutions; and complex opaque financial engineering products least attractive in terms of development impact, while also creating contingent liabilities" (Griffith-Jones *et al.*, 2022: 200).
6 According to one op-ed, "if you want to know what's worth investing in, look at what US federal research funding organisations … [e.g. NIH, DARPA] are investing in today, and then go long 30 years. In the 1950s, the big thing was transistors, which gave us the microelectronics revolution in the 1980s. In the 1960s, it was digital processing, which gave us personal computers in the 1990s. In the 1970s it was biotech, which started to

come on line in the 2000s. And in the 1980s, it was the beginnings of machine learning and big data" (FT, 2017).

7 "[V]irtually all central banks have [at some point] engaged in 'industrial policy' or 'selective targeting'". This was still widespread practice until the central banking revolution of the 1980s. Even today, despite their rhetoric to the contrary, many central banks, including many across the OECD, are effectively directing lending and investment. Epstein, cited by Volz (2017: 13). For policies on how the European Central Bank can undergird EU progressive IP, see the contribution by Bronstering, Smolenska, and Barmes in this volume as well as Jäger and Dziwok (2024) and Skyrman (2024b: 16–19).

Bibliography

Adler, D., Wargan, P., and Prakash, S. (2019) *Blueprint for Europe's just transition*. The Green New Deal for Europe.

Aghion, P., Ahuja, K., Bown, C. P., Cantner, U., Criscuolo, C., Dechezleprêtre, A., and Zysman, J. (2023) *Sparking Europe's new industrial revolution – A policy for net zero, growth and resilience*. Bruegel.

Aghion, P., Boneva, L., Breckenfelder, J., Laeven, L., Olovsson, C., Popov, A. A., and Rancoita, E. (2022) Financial markets and green innovation. *The European Central Bank Working Paper Series*, No 2686/July 2022.

Alami, I., Taggart, J., and Chodor, T. (2025) Rebuilding the ladder? Contemporary contests over industrial policy. *Global Policy*.

Ameli, N., Kothari, S. and Grubb, M. (2021) Misplaced expectations from climate disclosure initiatives. *Nature Climate Change*, 11(11), 917–924.

Amsden, A. H. (1989) *Asia's next giant: South Korea and late industrialization*. Oxford University Press, USA.

Babic, M. (2024) Green finance in the global energy transition: Actors, instruments, and politics. *Energy Research & Social Science*, 111, 103482.

Bärnthaler, R., Mang, S., and Hickel, J. (2025) Toward a post-growth industrial policy for Europe: Navigating emerging tensions and long-term goals. *Globalizations*, 1–25.

Block, F. and Keller, M. R. (2009) Where do innovations come from? Transformations in the US economy, 1970–2006. *Socio-Economic Review*, 7(3), 459–483.

Bofinger, P. (2025) A New Schumpeterian Growth Theory (NSGT): The way out of Europe's middle-technology trap. *European Journal of Economics and Economic Policies*, 22(2), 252–273.

Brachet, I. (2025) Will Denmark lead Europe towards a super-rich tax? Social Europe. https://www.socialeurope.eu/will-denmark-lead-europe-towards-a-super-rich-tax (accessed 17 October 2025).

Breckenfelder, J., Maćkowiak, B., Marques-Ibanez, D., Olovsson, C., Popov, A. A., Porcellacchia, D., and Schepens, G. (2023) The climate and the economy. *The European Central Bank Working Paper Series*, No 2793/March 2023.

Breznitz, D. and Gingrich, J. (2025) Industrial policy revisited. *Annual Review of Political Science*, 28.

Bulfone, F., Ergen, T., and Maggor, E. (2024) The political economy of conditionality and the new industrial policy (No. 24/6). *MPIfG Discussion Paper*.

Bulfone, F., Ergen, T., and Maggor, E. (2025) Regulating via conditionality: The instruments of the new industrial policy. *Regulation & Governance*.

Calipel, C., Bizien, A., Pellerin-Carlin, T., Paris, (2024) European Climate Investment Deficit report An investment pathway for Europe's future. I4CE.

Cherif, R. and Hasanov, F. (2019) *The return of the policy that shall not be named: Principles of industrial policy*. International Monetary Fund.

Christophers, B. (2024) *The price is wrong: Why capitalism Won't save the planet*. Verso Books.
Cohen, L., Gómez-Puig, M., and Sosvilla-Rivero, S. (2019) Has the ECB's monetary policy prompted companies to invest, or pay dividends? *Applied Economics*, 51(45), 4920–4938. https://doi.org/10.1080/00036846.2019.1602715
Cooiman, F. (2023) The limits of derisking. (Un)conditionality in the European green transformation. *Competition & Change*, 10245294231224137.
Cornago, E. and Springford, J. (2021) Why the EU's recovery fund should be permanent. *Policy Brief*, July 14, Centre for European Reform (CER)
Cypher, J. M. (1987) Military spending, technical change, and economic growth: A disguised form of industrial policy? *Journal of Economic Issues*, 21(1), 33–59.
Dafermos, Y., Gabor, D., and Michell, J. (2021) The Wall Street Consensus in pandemic times: What does it mean for climate-aligned development?. *Canadian Journal of Development Studies/Revue canadienne d'études du développement*, 42(1–2), 238–251.
De Baer, M., Campiglio, E., and Deyris, J. (2021) It takes two to dance: Institutional dynamics and climate-related financial policies. *Ecological Economics*, 190, 107210.
Demertzis, M., Pinkus, D., and Ruer, N. (2024) *Accelerating strategic investment in the European Union beyond 2026*. Bruegel.
DiPippo, G., Mazzocco, I., and Kenedy, S. (2022) *Red Ink: Estimating Chinese industrial policy spending in comparative perspective*. Center for Strategic & International Studies (CSIS), Washington, DC.
Dittrich, P. J. and Ständer, P. (2017) A European agency for disruptive innovation: How could it look like and what would it do?
Dossche, M., Slacalek, J., and Wolswijk, G. (2021) 'Monetary Policy and Inequality'. ECB Economic Bulletin No. 2.
Dziwok, E. and Jäger, J. (2021) A classification of different approaches to green finance and green monetary policy. *Sustainability*, 13(21), 11902.
EC (2013) *Taxation of the financial sector*. https://taxation-customs.ec.europa.eu/financial-transaction-tax_en (accessed 17 October2025).
EC (2021) *A Global Green Deal. op-ed article by Ursula von der Leyen, President of the European Commission, and Werner Hoyer, President of the European Investment Bank*. European Commission, Brussels.
EC (2023) 2023 Strategic Foresight Report – Sustainability and people's wellbeing at the heart of Europe's Open Strategic Autonomy.
ECA (2021, September 20) Special Report 22/2021: Sustainable finance: More consistent EU action needed to redirect finance towards sustainable investment.
ECB (2022) 'ECB Takes Further Steps to Incorporate Climate Change into Its Monetary Policy Operations'. Press release. Available at: https://www.ecb.europa.eu/press/pr/date/2022/html/ ecb.pr220704~4f48a72462.en.html (accessed 17 October 2025).
EIB (2023, February 28) Investment Report 2022/2023.
EuroMemo Group (2024) How should the EU cope with the polycrisis? European Economists for an Alternative Economic Policy in Europe.
Frauenlob, M. (2025) The return of industrial policy in the United States and the EU: A comparative perspective. *Wirtschaft und Gesellschaft*, 51(2), 55–73.
FT (2017, August 24) America tampers with the Chomsky trade at its peril. *The Government and Taxpayers Are the Key Investors in Basic Scientific Research*.
FT (2023a) EU becomes 'real player' in debt markets but faces investor scepticism. October 12 2023.
FT (2023b) The EU's plan to regain its competitive edge. November 5, 2023.
FT (2024) The EU's recovery fund is already shaping its future. April 7, 2024.
FT (2025) The lessons from China's dominance in manufacturing. May 28, 2025.
Gabor, D. (2021a) The Wall Street Consensus. *Development and change*, 52(3), 429–459.

Gabor, D. (2021b) Revolution without revolutionaries: Interrogating the return of monetary financing. *Transformative Responses to the Crisis*.

Gabor, D. (2023) The (European) derisking state.

Gallagher, K. P. and Kozul-Wright, R. (2021) *The case for a new Bretton Woods*. John Wiley & Sons.

Griffith-Jones, S. and Carreras, M. (2021) The role of the EIB in the Green transformation.

Griffith-Jones, S. and Naqvi, N. (2020) Industrial policy and risk sharing in public development banks: Lessons for the post-COVID response from the EIB and EFSI (No. 143). *GEG Working Paper*.

Griffith-Jones, S., Spiegel, S., Xu, J., Carreras, M., and Naqvi, N. (2022) Matching risks with instruments in development banks. *Review of Political Economy*, 34(2), 197–223.

Gros, D., Mengel, P. L. and Presidente, G. (2025) The EU investment gap is really an R&D gap. *Journal of Industrial and Business Economics*, 52(3), 667–682.

Guzzardi, D., Palagi, E., Faccio, T. and Roventini, A. (2023) In search of lost time: An ensemble of policies to restore fiscal progressivity and address the climate challenge (No. 2023/28). LEM Working Paper Series.

Heimberger, P. and Lichtenberger, A. (2023a) RRF 2.0: A permanent EU investment fund in the context of the energy crisis, climate change and EU fiscal rules (No. 63). *Policy Notes and Reports*.

Heimberger, P. and Lichtenberger, A. (2023b) Options for a Permanent EU Sovereign Fund: Meeting the climate-investment challenge and promoting macroeconomic stability. *Financing Investment in Times of High Public Debt*. 2023 European Public Investment Outlook.

Hodson, D. and Howarth, D. (2023) The EU's recovery and resilience facility: An exceptional borrowing instrument?. *Journal of European Integration*, 46(1), 69–87.

IMF (2024) *Datamapper, Profile*, EU.

Institut Rousseau (2024, January) *Road to net zero: Bridging the green investment gap*. Greens/European Free Alliance. https://www.greens-efa.eu/en/article/study/road-to-net-zero (accessed 17 October 2025).

Jäger, J. and Dziwok, E. (2024) *Understanding green finance. A critical assessment and alternative perspectives*. Edward Elgar Publishing.

Jakob, M. and Overland, I. (2024) Green industrial policy can strengthen carbon pricing but not replace it. *Energy Research & Social Science*, 116, 103669.

Jarlebring, J. (2025) *One fund to rule them all: An analysis of the proposed European Competitiveness Fund (European Policy Analysis, 2025:13epa)*. Swedish Institute for European Policy Studies. https://sieps.se/en/publications/2025/one-fund-to-rule-them-all/ (accessed 17 October 2025).

Jones, C. I. and Williams, J. C. (1998) Measuring the social return to R&D. *The Quarterly Journal of Economics*, 113(4), 1119–1135.

Juhász, R., Lane, N. J., and Rodrik, D. (2023) The new economics of industrial policy. *Annual Review of Economics*, 16.

Kalinowski, T. (2023) The Green Climate Fund and private sector climate finance in the global south. *Climate Policy*, 24(3), 281–296.

Kapeller, J., Leitch, S. and Wildauer, R. (2023) Can a European wealth tax close the green investment gap? *Ecological Economics*, 209, 107849.

Kapeller, J., Wildauer, R. and Leitch, S. (2021, March) *A European wealth tax for a fair and green recovery – Foundation for European progressive studies*. Policy Paper Foundation of European Progressive Studies/Karl-Renner Institute.

Karas, D. (2024) *A regulationist perspective on industrial policy in the US & EU*. Second Cold War Observatory.

Keating, D. (2023, October 25) The EU is offering as much green funding as the US IRA. *So Why Aren't Innovators Getting It? Energy Monitor*. https://www.energymonitor.ai/

policy/green-deals/eu-green-funds-match-us-ira-but-harder-to-access/?cf-view (accessed 17 October 2025).

Kedward, K., Gabor, D., and Ryan-Collins, J. (2022a) Aligning finance with the green transition: From a risk-based to an allocative green credit policy regime. Available at SSRN 4198146.

Kedward, K., Gabor, D., and Ryan-Collins, J. (2022b) A modern credit guidance regime for the green transition. The European Money and Finance Forum. *SUERF Policy Note* Issue No 294.

Kedward, K., Gabor, D., and Ryan-Collins, J. (2024). Carrots with(out) sticks: Credit policy and the limits of green central banking. *Review of International Political Economy*, 1–25. https://doi.org/10.1080/09692290.2024.2351838

Kedward, K., & Ryan-Collins, J. (2021). A green new deal: Opportunities and constraints. In *Economic policies for sustainability and resilience* (pp. 269–317). Cham: Springer International Publishing

Kollewe, J. (2021, August 11). COVID 19 vaccines: The contracts, prices and profits. *The Guardian*. Retrieved from https://www.theguardian.com

Lagarde, C. (2024) Speech by Christine Lagarde, President of the ECB, at the plenary session of the European Parliament Strasbourg. 26 February 2024.

Landesmann, M. (2025) EU industrial policy in the evolving geo-political and geo-economic environment (No. 96). The Vienna Institute for International Economic Studies, wiiw.

Larsen, M. (2025) The archetype of a 'big green state'? What China tells us about green macrofinancial regimes. *Review of International Political Economy*, 32(6), 2115–2146.

Lee, B. and Lee, Y. W. (2022) Experience, communication, and collective action: Financial autonomy and capital market development in East Asia. *New Political Economy*, 27(5), 731–753.

Letta, E. (2024) Much more than a market-speed, security, solidarity: Empowering the Single Market to deliver a sustainable future and prosperity for all EU Citizens.

Li, X., & Ban, C. (2026). Financing technological innovation in China: Neo-developmental financial statecraft through government guidance funds. *Review of International Political Economy*, 33(1), 131–161.

Mack, S. and Findeisen, F. (2023) Do more with more–How the EU can improve funding for the European Green Deal.

Mazzucato, M. (2013) The entrepreneurial state: Debunking public vs. private sector myths.

Mazzucato, M. (2021) *Mission economy: A moonshot guide to changing capitalism*. Penguin UK.

Mazzucato, M. (2022) *Rethinking the social contract between the state and business: A new approach to industrial strategy with conditionalities*. UCL Institute for Innovation and Public Purpose, Working Paper Series (IIPP WP 2022–18).

Mazzucato, M. (2023) Financing the Sustainable Development Goals through mission-oriented development banks: UN DESA Policy Brief Special Issue.

Mazzucato, M., Carreras, M., and Mikheeva, O. (2023). Steering economic recovery in Europe. Lessons for governing the Recovery and Resilience Facility.

Mazzucato, M. and Macfarlane, L. (2023) Mission-oriented development banks: The case of KfW and BNDES.

Mazzucato, M. and Rodrik, D. (2023) Industrial policy with conditionalities: A taxonomy and sample cases. UCL Institute for Innovation and Public Purpose *IIPP Working Paper Series*, 7.

Mertens, D. and Thiemann, M. (2019) Building a hidden investment state? The European investment bank, national development banks and European economic governance. *Journal of European Public Policy*, 26(1), 23–43.

Mertens, D. and Thiemann, M. (2022) Investing in the single market? Core-periphery dynamics and the hybrid governance of supranational investment policies. *Journal of European Integration*, 44(1), 81–97.

Mertens, D. and Thiemann, M. (2023) 5. The European investment bank: The EU's climate bank?. *Handbook on European Union Climate Change Policy and Politics*, 68.
Murau, S., Haas, A., and Guter-Sandu, A. (2024) Monetary architecture and the green transition. *Environment and Planning A: Economy and Space*, 56(2), 382–401.
Nölke, A. (2022) *Post-corona capitalism. The alternatives ahead.* Bristol University Press.
Noman, A. and Stiglitz, J. E. (Eds.) (2015) *Industrial policy and economic transformation in Africa.* Columbia University Press.
Padoan, P. C. (2023) 6. Escaping Fragmentation and Secular Stagnation. The EU Policy Mix and Investment Financing. Financing Investment in Times of High Public Debt, 101.
Perez, C. (2012) Financial bubbles, crises and the role of government in unleashing golden ages. *FINNOV Milton Keynes*, UK: Open University.
Pisani-Ferry, J., Tagliapietra, S., and Zachmann, G. (2023) A new governance framework to safeguard the European Green Deal (No. 18/2023). *Bruegel Policy Brief.*
Raza, W. (2024) Towards a progressive industrial policy for the twin transformation in the European Union: Synthesis report (No. 21/2025). Vienna: *ÖFSE Research Report* no. 21. https://doi.org/10.60637/2025-rr21
Reimer, F., Guter-Sandu, A., Haas, A. and Murau, S. (2025) Schrödinger's off-balance-sheet fiscal agency: The recovery and resilience facility and the limits to incremental fiscal integration in Europe. *Journal of European Integration*, 48(1), 137–158.
Reinhart, C. M. and Rogoff, K. S. (2009) The aftermath of financial crises. *American Economic Review*, 99(2), 466–472.
Rodrik, D. (2009) Industrial policy: Don't ask why, ask how. *Middle East Development Journal*, 1(1), 1–29.
Rodrik, D. (2014) Green industrial policy. *Oxford Review of Economic Policy*, 30(3), 469–491.
Rodrik, D. (2023) Productivism and new industrial policies: learning from the past, preparing for the future. SPARKING EUROPE'S NEW INDUSTRIAL REVOLUTION, 41.
Sachs, J. (2019) *Getting to a carbon-free economy.* The American Prospect.
Sastry, P., Verner, E. and Marques-Ibanez, D. (2024) Business as usual: Bank climate commitments, lending, and engagement.
Schelkle, W. (2023) *When all else fails: European re-insurance of member states.* European University Institute.
Schmidt, V. A. (2023) Making EU economic governance fit for purpose: Investing in the future and reforming the fiscal rules while decentralizing and democratizing. In *EconPol forum.* Vol. 24, No. 4, 38–44. Munich: CESifo GmbH.
Seidl, T. and Schmitz, L. (2023). Moving on to not fall behind? Technological sovereignty and the 'geo-dirigiste' turn in EU industrial policy. *Journal of European Public Policy*, 31(8), 2147–2174.
Skyrman, V. (2024a) *Industrial policy, progressive derisking, and the financing of Europe's green transition.* Vienna: *ÖFSE Working Paper* no. 78. https://doi.org/10.60637/2024-wp78
Skyrman, V. (2024b) *The financialization of the Swedish growth model: Four essays on capitalist regulation and institutional change.* Viktor Skyrman.
Skyrman, V. (2024c) Why didn't Europe securitise more? The institutionalisation of covered bonds as an efficient instrument for financialisation. *New Political Economy*, 29(1), 144–158.
Strategic Perspectives (2024) *Forging economic security and cohesion in the EU.* Brussels.
Tagliapietra, S., Trasi, C., and Veugelers, R. (2023) Europe's Green Industrial Policy. *ICE, Revista de Economía*, 932, 52–53.
Thomadakis, A. (2025) Towards a European digital services tax: Renewing the momentum for a fair contribution (CEPS In-depth Analysis). European Capital Markets Institute. https://www.ecmi.eu/sites/default/files/2025_04_fmi-toward-a-european-digital-tax-1.pdf (accessed 17 October 2025).

UN DESA (2022) Financing for Sustainable Development Report 2022. Inter-agency Task Force on Financing for Development.
UNCTAD (2019) *Trade and Development Report 2019: Financing a Global Green New Deal.* United Nations Publication.
UNCTAD (2022) *Trade and Development Report 2022: Development prospects in a fractured world: Global disorder and regional responses.* United Nations Publication.
Veugelers, R., Tagliapietra, S. and Trasi, C. (2024) Green Industrial Policy in Europe: Past, present, and prospects. *Journal of Industry, Competition and Trade*, 24(1), 4.
Volz, U. (2017, February) On the role of central banks in enhancing green finance. *The UN Environment Inquiry.*
Whitfield, L. and Wuttke, T. (2025) Opportunities for latecomer technological catch-up in the era of renewables capitalism: Possible pathways out of the periphery. *Development and Change*, 56(4–5), 783–812.

9

BOOSTING PUBLIC SPENDING FOR THE TWIN TRANSITION UNDER THE NEW EU FISCAL RULES

A Proposal

Philipp Heimberger

9.1 Introduction

New EU fiscal rules came into force on 30 April 2024 (EU Regulation, 2024). This represents the most comprehensive reform of the fiscal framework since policymakers tightened the rules in the aftermath of the financial crisis (e.g. Claeys *et al.*, 2016; Heimberger *et al.*, 2020). Although the targets of a fiscal deficit of 3% of gross domestic product (GDP) and a 60% public debt ratio have remained unaltered, there are important changes to the old framework. The new framework establishes key technical elements for the negotiation of multi-year fiscal consolidation plans between individual national EU governments and the European Commission, where fiscal adjustment is supposed to ensure that the public-debt-to-GDP ratio is on a plausibly downward trajectory (e.g. Darvas *et al.*, 2024; Heimberger *et al.*, 2024).

This chapter introduces the key elements of the new EU fiscal rules (Section 9.2) and discusses them critically, with a focus on the question of how much scope the framework provides for member countries to address the challenges of the green and digital transition (Sections 9.3 and 9.4). The existing literature shows that there is a need for additional public investment to meet the climate goals (e.g. Pisani-Ferry and Tagliapietra 2024; Heimberger and Lichtenberger, 2024), as current policy actions are inadequate to set the EU on a trajectory compatible with limiting global warming to 2°C (Batut *et al.*, 2024). There are incentives for national governments to include an investment and reform package in the context of a multi-year fiscal adjustment path, and policymakers have allowed governments to activate national escape clauses to exempt additional defence spending (Council of the EU, 2025a). However, the reformed framework falls well short of providing adequate fiscal space, since governments would typically have to achieve an

DOI: 10.4324/9781003745563-14

expansion of public expenditure on the green and digital transition either by reining in other spending items or by raising taxes. Meeting the new EU fiscal rules will require major Euro area member countries to move from their currently sizeable primary deficits to primary surpluses in the medium term (Darvas *et al.*, 2024). While the temporary exemption for defence spending will make the overall fiscal stance more expansionary over the next years than it would otherwise have been, the higher interest payments to service the debt incurred on defence spending and the aversion to higher fiscal deficits will likely exert downward pressure on public spending on the twin transition. I discuss three main options to provide additional fiscal space to expand public expenditure on the twin transition (Section 9.5): (i) changes to certain key assumptions in the technical substructure of the new framework; (ii) expanded national co-financing of EU programmes; and (iii) the establishment of an EU investment fund.

9.2 Key elements of the new EU fiscal rules

The new EU fiscal rules are supposed to bring the fiscal deficits of EU member countries to below 3% of GDP and their public-debt-to-GDP ratios to below 60% of GDP. This implies that the major deficit and debt targets have not changed from the previous framework. However, the old framework's annual budgetary targets, based on meeting a 'structural' (cyclically adjusted) deficit limit (e.g. Heimberger and Kapeller, 2017; Heimberger *et al.*, 2020), are no longer relevant. Furthermore, the previous debt reduction rule, according to which the public debt ratio had to fall to 60% of GDP within 20 years, has been scrapped. The new framework shifts the focus from the annual development of public finances to a medium-term view spanning four to seven years. There is an enhanced role for bilateral technical discussions and negotiations between each national government and the European Commission on country-specific multi-annual fiscal consolidation paths (Darvas *et al.*, 2024).

One major change is that the new rules replace multiple operational targets from the old framework with a single indicator: *net expenditure growth.* Net expenditure is defined as total government spending net of discretionary revenue measures (e.g. tax hikes would provide more room for a growth in expenditure), interest payments, expenditure on EU programmes that fully matches EU funds, national expenditure on co-financing of EU programmes, cyclical elements of unemployment spending, and one-offs and other temporary measures (EU Regulation, 2024).

Under the new framework, when public debt exceeds the 60% reference value, or when the fiscal deficit rises above the 3% reference value, the European Commission will put forward a so-called *reference trajectory*. This trajectory is supposed to ensure that by the end of a fiscal adjustment period of at least four years, the public debt ratio is on a *plausibly downward path* (e.g. Darvas *et al.*, 2024). The reference trajectory can be understood as pre-plan guidance on how much fiscal adjustment each member country would have to implement over a multi-year adjustment period to keep the public debt ratio on a plausibly downward path in the ten years following the fiscal adjustment. Adjustment requirements are translated into a net expenditure path. The European Commission will use a control account to track annual and cumulative upward and downward deviations from the plan in actual net expenditure growth. Temporary deviations from the net expenditure path will only be allowed in exceptional circumstances. If a member state deviates from the plan markedly (by either 0.3 percentage points of GDP annually or 0.6 percentage points of GDP cumulatively), the European Commission may open an excessive deficit procedure, whereby the government in question will need to take corrective measures within 6 months (EU Regulation 2024).

Multi-year budget plans covering at least four years are negotiated between the European Commission and national governments against the background of the reference trajectory, rooted in an analysis of the sustainability of a member country's public debt (Heimberger, 2023; Darvas *et al.*, 2023; Heimberger *et al.*, 2024). Hence, the country-specific nature of the fiscal adjustment requirements is an important change from the old framework. The new framework includes a general EU escape clause and national escape clauses that can be triggered in the event of some serious occurrence that justifies temporary non-compliance with the rules.

Importantly, member states can commit to a range of investments and reforms, extending the fiscal adjustment path from four years to a maximum of seven years, provided the European Commission agrees that the package of investment and reform meets a set of criteria. They must be (i) growth-enhancing; (ii) be consistent with debt sustainability; (iii) address common EU priorities (e.g. Green Deal, digitalisation, security); (iv) account for country-specific recommendations in the European Semester; and (v) keep the national investment level at least constant (EU Regulation, 2024). Notably, the reformed framework does not provide any broad exemption for public investment at the national level, irrespective of the co-financing of EU programmes.

To extend the fiscal adjustment period and reduce the need for annual adjustment, there are incentives for national governments to submit a package of investment and reform to the European Commission. The package should include government spending on common priorities regarding the twin transition. However, member countries have to make the case that the planned measures are growth-friendly and consistent with debt sustainability (e.g. European Commission, 2025a).

Since there are no broad-based exemptions, if a member country wants to increase green and digital spending, it will have to make room by restricting other spending items in order to comply with the technical requirements to limit the growth of net expenditure. There are already examples of this. Italy revised its National Recovery and Resilience Plan in late 2023 reallocating €11.8 billion to RePower EU at the expense of other missions. Notably, the largest cuts were made to the supply of educational services and social infrastructure – affecting families, communities, and the third sector – with budget reductions of €360 million and €2.85 billion, respectively (Reljic and Zezza, 2025: 11).

The insistence by Germany, Austria and some other countries on stricter fiscal rules during the reform process has further led to the introduction of so-called 'safeguards' for minimum fiscal consolidation. A new 'deficit resilience safeguard' will be applied when the multi-year path is set. This will require a government to continue with fiscal consolidation – even after it has reached the 3% fiscal deficit target – until the 'structural' fiscal deficit falls below 1.5% of GDP. The 'debt sustainability safeguard' requires the government in a country with a public debt ratio above 90% of GDP to plan a reduction in the debt ratio of at least 1 percentage point of GDP per year over the course of the adjustment period; and 0.5 percentage points of GDP per year for a government that faces a public debt ratio of between 60% and 90%. These 'safeguards' will lead to harsher fiscal adjustment requirements for several member states in the future (e.g. Darvas *et al.*, 2023).

9.3 Fiscal consolidation requirements to meet the new EU fiscal rules

The European Commission uses Debt Sustainability Analysis (DSA) for its assessment of whether the public debt ratio will decline even under adverse scenarios. The DSA shows how the public debt ratio will evolve in the future, given assumptions on GDP growth, interest rates, inflation and fiscal policy (e.g. Van Dijk *et al.*, 2022; Heimberger, 2023; Heimberger *et al.*, 2024; Erce, 2025).

As described above, the new EU fiscal rules set net expenditure paths. However, net expenditure is derived from an interim variable: the structural primary fiscal balance (i.e. the cyclically adjusted fiscal balance net of interest payments). Since it is not very intuitive to present the adjustment requirements in terms of restrictions on the growth rate of net expenditure, we will follow previous contributions (Darvas *et al.*, 2024; Heimberger *et al.*, 2024; Heimberger, 2025) and provide a discussion of how much the structural primary balance of an individual country will have to improve annually as a percentage of GDP for it to meet the requirements of the new framework. We will focus on the 11 member states that joined the Euro area (EA) in 1999,[1] plus Greece, which joined 2 years later, in 2001. We will refer to this group as the EA12.

Figure 9.1 presents the fiscal adjustment requirements to meet the new EU fiscal framework for the EA12 countries, based on the reference trajectories submitted to the individual governments by the European Commission in June 2024 (Darvas *et al.*, 2024). The DSA-based criteria of fiscal consolidation are binding for 8 of the EA12 countries. This means that the safeguards were typically not a significant constraint in the first round of application of the new EU fiscal rules, because the DSA-based criterion was stricter for the vast majority of EU member states (Darvas *et al.*, 2024). However, the safeguards must be expected to lead to harsher fiscal adjustment requirements in future rounds of application of the new EU fiscal rules, in particular for member countries with high public debt levels.

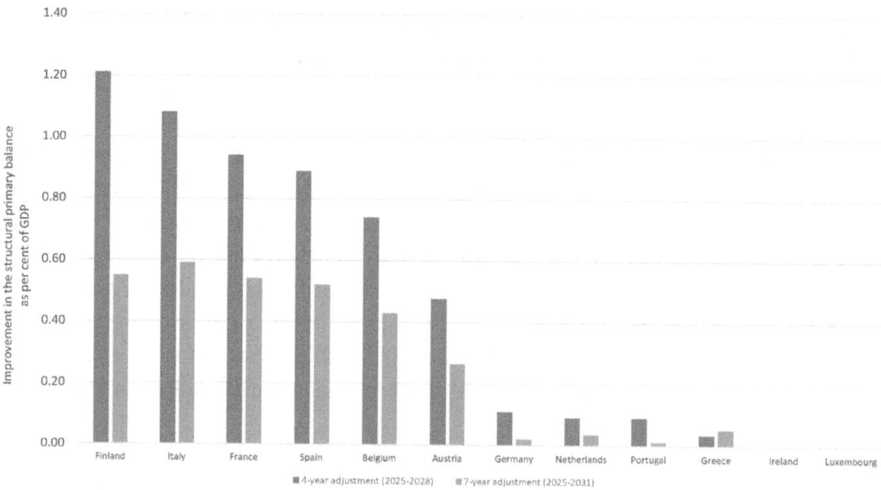

FIGURE 9.1 Technical trajectories submitted in June 2024: fiscal consolidation requirements to meet reformed EU fiscal rules (annual improvement in the structural primary balance as per cent of GDP)

Source: Darvas *et al.* (2024).

Over the 4-year period from 2025 to 2028, the average annual fiscal consolidation requirement in the EA12 is slightly below 0.5% of GDP per year. For a 7-year adjustment – for which governments must submit an acceptable investment and reform package – the average annual adjustment requirement in the EA12 is halved, to 0.25% of GDP. However, the fiscal consolidation effort varies significantly from country to country. In the 4-year (7-year) adjustment case, the average annual adjustment for Finland amounts to 1.2% of GDP (0.6%); Italy: 1.1% (0.6%); France and Spain: 0.9% (0.5%); Belgium: 0.7% (0.4%); Austria: 0.5% (0.3%); Netherlands: 0.1% (0.04%); Germany: 0.1% (0.02%); Portugal: 0.1% (0.01%); Greece: 0.03% (0.05%); Ireland; and Luxembourg: 0% (0%). France, Italy, Spain, and Belgium represent about half of the overall EA12 GDP. The addition of Finland and Austria (where the governments are also set to implement substantial fiscal consolidation) brings the GDP share of Euro area countries conducting contractionary fiscal policies to well over 50%.

Heimberger (2025) shows that countries such as Italy and France are set to implement fiscal consolidation that is historically large – comparable to the time of the Euro crisis.[2] Against this background, the outlook for the coming years will be one of austerity: Europe will witness a multi-year period of simultaneous fiscal cutbacks in many EA12 member countries representing a major share of the overall Euro area economy.

However, in the first quarter of 2025, developments surrounding the war in Ukraine and the Trump administration's strategy of withdrawing financial support have put large-scale defence spending high up on the European political agenda. European policymakers have allowed 16 EU member countries to activate their national escape clauses for defence spending (Council of the EU, 2025b). That said, there is a flexibilisation limit, as the maximum exemption for additional defence spending is 1.5% of GDP. Furthermore, the exemption under the national escape clause is only for four years, although the political commitment to raise military expenditure extends much further into the future. Hence, there will be pressure to finance additional defence spending through national budgets in the medium term by raising taxes and/or by cutting back on social spending.

In any case, exempting additional military spending from the current EU fiscal rules will lead to at least a short-term deterioration of the fiscal balance, although the overall impact on the economy and public finances will depend on how much additional military spending increases economic output (e.g. Ilzetzki, 2025). Importantly, defence spending at present is mostly current spending on military personnel and equipment, while many studies on defence spending focus on R&D spending. R&D expenditure delivers considerably stronger overall positive economic effects than military expenditure on personnel and equipment. However, R&D is only a small fraction of military expenditure. Zezza and Guarascio (2024) provide evidence for Italy that digital and green public spending comes with a high fiscal multiplier of, on average, just below two. This indicates that, if governments were to focus on positive and long-lasting investment on the twin transition, the additional spending could contribute substantially to an increase in economic activity and tax revenue, whereas an increase in current military expenditure on personnel and equipment would not raise economic activity in the longer run.

The deadline for individual national governments to submit their fiscal-structural plans based on the European Commission's reference trajectories was October 2024.[3] The national governments submitted their multi-annual fiscal policy plans, and the European Commission (2024a) published an assessment of the submitted plans. Eight of the medium-term plans assessed by the European Commission did it recommend an extension of the fiscal adjustment period from four to seven years, based on the packages of investment and reform submitted (Finland, France, Italy, Romania, Spain, Austria, Belgium, and Germany). All the other countries assessed entered the shorter (typically four-year) adjustment period (European Commission, 2025c).[4]

Examples of investment and reform accepted as part of the packages submitted in a bid to extend the adjustment horizon included (European Commission, 2024c): reform of unemployment allowance, national health, social assistance and social security (Finland); reform of unemployment insurance, acceleration of renewable energy production, spending reviews, simplification of the business environment (France); reforms in the area of civil justice, tax administration, business environment, public administration and investment in childcare (Italy); reform of the pension system, the minimum wage, public-sector remuneration, taxation of micro-enterprises and tax administration (Romania); investment in the digital transformation of education, promotion of renewable energy generation, reform of taxation and education (Spain). While this list does include some elements that are relevant to the green and digital transition, it is apparent that many other items do not address – either directly or indirectly – the priorities of the twin transition.

9.4 A critical assessment of the new EU fiscal rules

The new EU fiscal rules will be less restrictive than would have been the case had the old framework been reactivated. The abolished public debt reduction rule, requiring governments to bring down the public debt ratio to 60% of GDP within 20 years, would have been harsher, in particular for member countries with a high public debt level (e.g. Eichengreen and Panizza, 2016; Balboni, 2024). After the rise in public deficits and public debt due to the pandemic, the old framework would have been so harsh as to be virtually unenforceable.

The key idea of the new framework remains that governments have to demonstrate that they have sufficient fiscal discipline to bring public debt ratios down over the medium term. However, if the negative growth effects of fiscal consolidation turn out to be greater than anticipated by the European Commission's DSA framework, public debt ratios will also turn out to be higher than expected (Heimberger *et al.*, 2024).

The focus on multi-annual fiscal consolidation strategies comes with significant political risks, as existing research highlights that adjustments typically lead to a decline in government approval and a corresponding rise in political instability (e.g. Jacques and Haffert, 2021), while they tend to increase electoral abstention and boost the electoral outcome of populist parties, especially in economically vulnerable regions (Gabriel *et al.*, 2026; Baccini and Sattler, 2024).

There is a political push for additional deficit-financed defence spending. However, this must be expected to lead to a rising share of government interest payments in total tax revenue. Furthermore, one has to expect political aversion to increased government spending other than on defence, because that would lead to even higher fiscal deficits. Taken together, these developments will likely exert downward pressure on national public spending on the twin green and digital transition. If fiscal adjustments to spending other than on defence end up burdening the economy – or, in the case of cuts to social spending, if they hit larger parts of the population – voters may react with dismay, while some bond investors could also show concern if there are signs of political instability (Born *et al.*, 2020). More volatile financial markets may increase the pressure on the European Central Bank to backstop government bond markets, which would likely be politically contentious.

As the EU fiscal framework focuses on the medium-term reduction in public liabilities relative to output, it becomes unlikely that public assets can be increased during the twin transition. The new EU fiscal framework does not take account of the build-up of public assets through public (infrastructure) investment. Ball *et al.* (2021), in an article published on the International Monetary Fund's website, argue that countries with stronger government net worth – calculated as total public assets minus liabilities – enjoy greater economic stability and stronger macroeconomic development. From this perspective, public assets are also key to ensuring sustainable public finances in the long run. However, considerations of government net worth are not part of the new EU fiscal framework, as the focus is on public liabilities. The green transition, in particular, requires the capital stock to be replaced and extended over the coming decades (e.g. Shayegh *et al.*, 2023; ECB, 2025). The EU fiscal rules' focus on a reduction in public liabilities will constrain the expansion of public assets.

The reformed EU fiscal framework is inadequate when it comes to promoting public investment in climate and energy. It provides incentives for governments to submit investment and reform plans to the European Commission. If the Commission accepts the package of measures, it does not grant a broad-based exemption for the financing of these investments; instead, it only extends the fiscal adjustment horizon to up to seven years, which typically does not change the overall fiscal consolidation requirements substantially, but reduces the need for annual adjustment (Darvas *et al.*, 2024). The level of public investment at least has to be kept constant. However, to meet the net expenditure rule, governments have to make room for an increase in national spending on public investment in the green and digital transition by restraining other spending items, for example social protection, health, or education. Governments could also raise taxes, although this may prove unpopular, in particular if the tax hikes were to affect large sections of the population. Furthermore, the current geopolitical context is characterised by pressures to increase military spending.

Keeping the level of public investment constant will not be enough to meet the ambitious climate targets over the next decade(s). Furthermore, an analysis by Boivin and Darvas (2025) of the multi-year budget plans submitted by EU member states to the European Commission shows that the nationally financed public investment rate is projected to be cut in more than a third of countries. Hence, the Commission's conclusion that EU countries will maintain or increase investment over the plan horizon is exaggerated. The EU target of becoming climate neutral by 2050, and thus achieving net-zero greenhouse gas emissions, will require significant additional investment, e.g. in transport and energy infrastructure and more energy-efficient housing (Wildauer *et al.*, 2020; Pisani-Ferry, 2021; Abraham *et al.*, 2023; Stöllinger, 2023). Much of the additional investment will have to be launched by the public sector to attract further private investment, pointing to a need to increase public investment by at least 1% of EU GDP per year (Heimberger and Lichtenberger, 2023; Raza, 2024; Skyrman, 2024). The first round of multi-year plans submitted to the European Commission does not meet the requirements for additional public investment.

The rise in defence spending, in combination with fiscal consolidation pressure on other spending items from 2025 onwards, will make it impossible for national governments to sufficiently boost public investment in the twin transition – although this is necessary if climate and digitalisation targets are to be met. Existing research shows that public investment can be reduced or postponed more easily than other government spending components, especially when the pressure to cut back on government spending increases (Jacques, 2021). National EU governments' fiscal plans to meet the new EU fiscal rules from 2025 onwards show that harsher fiscal consolidation measures correlate with deeper public investment cuts (Boivin and Darvas, 2025).

9.5 Options for providing additional space for higher public spending on the green and digital transition

In what follows, I discuss three options to increase the fiscal space available for public spending on the twin transition in the context of the new EU fiscal rules: changes to the European Commission's DSA framework; national co-financing of EU programmes; and an EU investment fund for climate and digitalisation.

Changes to the European Commission's DSA framework. While debt sustainability is the key element of the new regulatory framework, studies on the European Commission's DSA show that fiscal consolidation requirements can be significantly altered by making minor changes to a few DSA assumptions (Heimberger *et al.*, 2024). Hence, changes to the DSA assumptions could reduce the DSA-based fiscal adjustment requirements. This may include allowing for a different treatment of ageing costs in some countries (Paetz and Watzka, 2024).

However, the most sensible change may involve the treatment of investments and reforms within the DSA framework. As explained above, the new fiscal rules aim to incentivise governments to submit investment and reform plans in order to extend the adjustment period. However, the European Commission's DSA framework currently does not consider the potential for positive economic growth effects stemming from investment and reform. One way forward could be to implement changes to the DSA framework, so that the effects of increased investment and new reforms are explicitly taken into consideration. For example, one could use public investment multipliers from the existing empirical literature (e.g. Fournier, 2016; Suresh *et al.*, 2024) to allow for higher potential growth rates in the medium term. In similar fashion, one could assess the effects of structural reform (e.g. Campos *et al.*, 2025) on growth and public debt ratios (European Macro Policy Network, 2025). Higher growth rates in the DSA lead to more favourable simulations of how the public debt ratio will develop over time, thereby reducing DSA-based fiscal adjustment requirements.

Changing the DSA methodology would be possible without further legislative reform, as the legislative texts do not regulate the DSA assumptions. The application of the DSA was left to the discretion of the European Commission, which decided to use its existing DSA framework (European Commission, 2024b) for the first round of reference trajectories. A DSA working group is supposed to review the underlying methodology. One limitation is that the new EU fiscal rules also include safeguards that stipulate minimum adjustment requirements, in particular for countries with high structural fiscal deficits and high public debt ratios. The reduction of the DSA-based consolidation requirements may make a safeguard binding. Furthermore, there is a minimum fiscal consolidation requirement of 0.5% of GDP per year for EU member states in an EU excessive deficit procedure. Currently, 8 of the 27 EU member states are in an excessive deficit procedure. Hence, the minimum adjustment requirements in the preventive and corrective arms of the fiscal regulation framework place limits on how much additional fiscal space can be gained by implementing sensible changes to the DSA framework. Furthermore, the room for manoeuvre that may arise from changes to the DSA framework is not earmarked for spending on the twin transition. Nevertheless, by taking into account the positive growth effects of investment and reform in the context of the European Commission's DSA would support the latter's goal of incentivising national governments to submit investment and reform plans by making potential growth policy dependent (European Macro Policy Network, 2025). And modifications to the technical substructure of the EU fiscal rules that do not require changes to the legal text come with the potential of extra fiscal space when the DSA-based adjustment requirements are binding.

National co-financing of EU programmes. When assessing whether individual member states comply with their fiscal plans submitted under the new framework, the European Commission will exclude national spending on the co-financing of EU funded programmes from government expenditure. In the short term, this will not have a major impact, since most national co-financing relates to spending on EU regional funds. In the longer run, however, it will provide incentives to channel extra money through the EU budget, and may increase the scope for steering national fiscal spending into EU policy priorities in order to increase co-financing expenditure.

Using national co-financing under EU programmes does not count towards net expenditure in assessing compliance with the new EU fiscal rules. In the future, an expanded use of national co-financing may enable governments to meet the fiscal targets more easily and to align them more closely with EU policy goals, including green and digital transition efforts. By leveraging EU funds, national governments could enhance their ability to achieve national objectives, while also contributing to the EU's broader strategic priorities. However, the potential for co-financing will depend on what EU programmes are available in the future and how much national co-financing they require or allow. Hence, the next Multiannual Financial Framework (MFF, 2028–2034) will be crucial. If the EU were to step up its co-funding for Important Projects of Common European Interest (IPCEIs), national governments would have more fiscal space and motivation to earmark resources for these projects, despite the tight budget (Di Carlo *et al.*, 2024).

The European Commission has proposed making the MFF significantly more flexible: instead of fixed programmes, there should be a general budget pot that addresses broadly defined EU objectives (European Commission, 2025b). The governments of individual member states could then set their own priorities in light of the EU objectives. Consequently, EU funds could be leveraged much more easily than before, and they could also be combined more easily and effectively with the exemption of national co-financing from EU fiscal rules.

Heimberger and Schratzenstaller (2024) argue that expenditure under the MFF should be reallocated to finance additional public climate investment. This would include enhancing the climate-friendliness of cohesion and agricultural policy and increasing the current target of 30% of EU spending related to climate targets. Furthermore, Heimberger and Schratzenstaller (2024) suggest that, while the MFF is currently primarily financed by the national contributions of EU members, the introduction of new sustainability-oriented own resources could provide additional financing for climate investment and support the EU's strategic goals. Revenue from EU emissions trading and the carbon-border adjustment mechanism are suitable as green 'own resources'. Further potential sources of funding for the next MFF include taxes on shipping traffic, international air traffic and cryptocurrencies.

A new EU investment fund. As explained above, the necessary investment in the green and digital transition is difficult to finance with national funds alone, if the new EU fiscal rules are to be adhered to. One option that would enable a substantial increase in public investment would be the introduction of a permanent investment fund for climate and digitalisation at the EU level (Heimberger and Lichtenberger, 2023, 2024).

The key aspects of such a new EU investment fund could be based on the experience gained with the Recovery and Resilience Facility (RRF). The RRF was adopted during the COVID-19 crisis to support the economic recovery of EU member states from that crisis, in tandem with the implementation of investments and reforms to better achieve climate and digital goals. The RRF is not large enough to address investment demands adequately, especially since the grants will only flow until 2026. Cornago and Springford (2021) argue that achieving the EU climate target by 2030 would require an expansion of public investment in the order of ten times the green investment share of the RRF.

Following the example of the RRF, the European Commission would issue bonds on behalf of the EU to raise the funds on financial markets for the new EU investment fund to promote the green and digital transition. While member states would not be individually liable for the EU bonds issued, there is still the question of how to service the debt in the context of the overall EU budget. In this regard, member states could either agree on additional EU own resources in order to generate a revenue stream from which the EU bonds could be serviced, or they could allow for the build-up of an EU debt stock (Heimberger and Lichtenberger, 2023).

Investments financed by such a permanent EU investment fund could focus on genuinely European public goods projects in the field of energy and transport system transformation, as well as digital infrastructure, to create EU added-value (Beetsma and Buti, 2024). For example, Creel et al. (2020) propose investment in a European high-speed rail system that could reduce CO_2 emissions in the transport sector over the long term. In addition, in the area of energy and decarbonisation, they recommend the introduction of an integrated electricity grid for the transmission of 100% renewable energy and support for complementary battery and green hydrogen projects. When it comes to digital infrastructure, genuine EU projects could focus on significant cross-border benefits for multiple member states that align with the EU-wide digital strategy and foster EU integration in the digital space, including a high-speed, ultra-broadband network connecting all EU regions, an EU-wide 5G network, EU cloud infrastructure, cross-border digital identification systems, European digital health infrastructure, and an EU high-speed data transport network.

9.6 Conclusions

The design of the new EU fiscal rules demonstrates that policymakers have learnt little from past mistakes, including when lack of fiscal policy coordination among member states exacerbated the Euro crisis in the period 2011–2013 (Heimberger, 2017). Large fiscal consolidation will be required in a number of (big) Euro area countries from 2025 onwards in order to comply with the reformed fiscal rules. However, the move towards exempting a (sharp) rise in military spending in the EU from fiscal rules over the next four years will make fiscal policy in the EU member states overall more expansionary than it would otherwise have been. It is to be expected that the rise in military expenditure, in combination with fiscal consolidation pressure on other spending components, will lead to key policy goals related to the targeting of climate change and digital challenges being missed.

The new EU fiscal rules will increase the pressure for fiscal consolidation. To make room for additional defence spending in the medium term, governments will have to raise taxes and/or cut other spending on social protection, education, and health. However, other long-term financing solutions for the twin green and digital transition should be considered. In light of the new EU fiscal rules, this chapter provides three options to expand the fiscal space for additional public expenditure on the green and digital transition: (1) An expansion of the national co-financing of EU programmes, which is not counted when assessing compliance with net expenditure restrictions in the reformed fiscal rules. (2) Changes to key assumptions in the technical substructure of the new rules that will lead to an overall reduction in fiscal adjustment requirements. (3) A permanent EU investment fund for climate and digitalisation that provides funding at the European level, possibly focusing on genuinely European projects that deliver EU value added – e.g. investment in an integrated electricity grid, high-speed trains across the EU, an EU-wide 5G network or an EU cloud infrastructure.

Notes

1 This group includes: Belgium, Germany, Finland, France, Ireland, Italy, Luxembourg, Netherlands, Austria, Portugal, and Spain.

2 Paetz and Watzka (2024) also highlight the fact that some of the required fiscal adjustments in EA12 countries are substantial in historical perspective.

3 For countries that did not meet the October 2024 deadline, a new reference trajectory (based on updated macroeconomic and fiscal projections) is to be used. For example, Austria had elections in late September 2024 and did not meet the October deadline for submitting a multi-year fiscal plan, since the plan needed to be submitted by the new government. As a consequence, the European Commission submitted an updated reference trajectory in December 2024, which took the deterioration in fiscal and macroeconomic forecasts into account and led to considerably stricter adjustment requirements.
4 Other EU member countries did not apply for an extension of the adjustment period from four to seven years, especially those where the adjustment requirements are comparatively low.

References

Abraham, L., O'Connell, M., and Oleaga, I. (2023) The legal and institutional feasibility of an EU Climate and Energy Security Fund. *ECB Occasional Paper*, 2023/313.

Baccini, L. and Sattler, T. (2024) Austerity, economic vulnerability, and populism. *American Journal of Political Science*, 69, 899–914. https://doi.org/10.1111/ajps.12865

Balboni, F. (2024) New EU fiscal rules: How they work and do they matter? *HSBC Global Research report*, 2 January. https://www.research.hsbc.com/C/1/1/320/gQ9NWDN (accessed 24 January 2025).

Ball, I., Detter, D., Manuelides, Y., and Yan, W. (2021) *Why public assets are key to debt sustainability: A moral goal*. IMF PFM Blog Public Financial Management. https://blog-pfm.imf.org/en/pfmblog/2021/04/why-public-assets-are-key-to-debt-sustainability-a-moral-goal (accessed 19 March 2025).

Batut, C., Kaiser, J., Surun, C., Daumas, L., Kekenbosch, T., Leonard, C., Malliet, P., and Pommeret, A. (2024) *Executive summary of the report on climate debt*. Institut Avant-garde, https://www.institutavantgarde.fr/executive-summary-of-the-report-on-climate-debt/ (accessed 6 March 2025).

Beetsma, R. and Buti, M. (2024) Promoting European public goods. *EconPol Forum*, 25(3), 37–41.

Boivin, N. and Darvas, Z. (2025) The European Union's new fiscal framework: A good start, but challenges loom. *Bruegel Policy Brief* No. 06/25.

Born, B., Müller, G., and Pfeifer, J. (2020) Does austerity pay off? *Review of Economics and Statistics*, 102(2), 323–338.

Campos, N., De Grauwe, P., and Ji, Y. (2025). Structural reforms and economic performance: The experience of advanced economies. *Journal of Economic Literature*, 63(1), 111–163.

Claeys, G., Darvas, Z., and Leandro, A. (2016) A proposal to revive the European fiscal framework. *Bruegel Policy Contribution* No. 2016/07.

Cornago, E. and Springford, J. (2021) Why the EU's recovery fund should be permanent. *Policy Brief*, 14 July, Centre for European Reform (CER).

Council of the EU (2025a) Council activates flexibility in EU fiscal rules for 15 member states to increase defence spending, Press release 8th July 2025, https://www.consilium.europa.eu/en/press/press-releases/2025/07/08/council-activates-flexibility-in-eu-fiscal-rules-for-15-member-states-to-increase-defence-spending/ (accessed 6 October 2025).

Council of the EU (2025b) National escape clause for defence expenditure, https://www.consilium.europa.eu/en/policies/national-escape-clause-for-defence-expenditure-nec/ (accessed 7 October 2025).

Creel, J., Holzner, M., Saraceno, F., Watt, A., and Wittwer, J. (2020) How to spend it: A proposal for a European Covid-19 recovery programme. *wiiw Policy Report* No. 38, wiiw, Vienna.

Darvas, Z., Welslau, L., and Zettelmeyer, J. (2023) A quantitative evaluation of the European Commission's fiscal governance proposal. *Bruegel Working Paper* 16/2023.

Darvas, Z., Welslau, L., and Zettelmeyer, J. (2024) The implications of the European Union's new fiscal rules. *Bruegel Policy Brief*, 20 June.

Di Carlo, D., Eisl, A., and Zurstrassen, D. (2024) Together we trade, divided we aid: Mapping the flexibilization of the EU state aid regime across GBER, IPCEIs and Temporary Frameworks. Joint *JDI-LUHNIP Policy Paper, Economics and Finance* No. 307.

ECB (2025) Green investment needs in the EU and their funding. *ECB Economic Bulletin*, (1/2025).

Eichengreen, B. and Panizza, U. (2016) A surplus of ambition: Can Europe rely on large primary surpluses to solve its debt problem? *Economic Policy*, 31(85), 5–49.

Erce, A. (2025) Assessing the Debt Sustainability Analysis methodology in the EU's new economic governance framework, in-depth analysis requested by the ECON committee of the European Parliament (February).

EU Regulation (2024) Economic governance review: Council adopts reform of fiscal rules. https://www.consilium.europa.eu/en/press/press-releases/2024/04/29/economic-governance-review-council-adopts-reform-of-fiscal-rules/ (accessed 24 January 2025).

European Commission (2024a) 2025 European Semester: Bringing the new economic governance framework to life. Communication from the Commission to the European Parliament, the Council and the European Central Bank, *COM*(2024) 705 final.

European Commission (2024b) Debt sustainability monitor 2023. *Institutional Paper* No. 271.

European Commission (2024c) 2025 European Semester: Bringing the new economic governance framework to life, Communication from the Commission to the European Parliament, the Council and the European Central Bank, *COM*(2024) 705 final.

European Commission (2025a) Accommodating increased defence expenditure within the Stability and Growth Pact. *Communication from the Commission, COM*(2025) 2000 final.

European Commission (2025b) The road to the next multiannual financial framework. Communication from the Commission to the European Parliament, the European Council, the Council, the European Economic and Social Committee and the Committee of the Regions, *COM*(2025) 46 final (accessed 11 February 205).

European Commission (2025c) National medium-term fiscal-structural plans, https://economy-finance.ec.europa.eu/economic-and-fiscal-governance/stability-and-growth-pact/preventive-arm/national-medium-term-fiscal-structural-plans_en (accessed 7 October 2025).

European Macro Policy Network (2025) Making fiscal space policy-responsive: Reform proposal for potential output estimation in the DSA. Policy Brief, November. https://empn.eu/wp-content/uploads/2025/11/EU-Fiscal-Rules-Reform-121125.pdf (accessed 2 March 2026).

Fournier, J. (2016) The positive effect of public investment on potential growth. *OECD Economics Department Working Paper* No. 1347.

Gabriel, R., Klein, M., and Pessoa, A. (2026) The political costs of austerity. *Review of Economics and Statistics*, 108(1), 145–161. https://doi.org/10.1162/rest_a_01373

Heimberger, P. (2017) Did fiscal consolidation cause the double-dip recession in the Euro area? *Review of Keynesian Economics*, 5(3), 539–558.

Heimberger, P. (2023) Debt sustainability as an anchor in EU fiscal rules: An assessment of the European Commission's reform orientations, in-depth analysis requested by the ECON committee of the European Parliament (March).

Heimberger, P. (2025) Fiscal consolidation and its growth effects in Euro area countries: Past, present and future outlook. *Review of Evolutionary Political Economy*, 6, 589–617. https://doi.org/10.1007/s43253-025-00146-4

Heimberger, P. and Kapeller, J. (2017) The performativity of potential output: Pro-cyclicality and path dependency in coordinating European fiscal policy, *Review of International Political Economy*, 24(5), 904–928.

Heimberger, P. and Lichtenberger, A. (2023) RRF 2.0: A permanent EU investment fund in the context of the energy crisis, climate change and EU fiscal rules. *wiiw Policy Report* No. 63, wiiw, Vienna.

Heimberger, P. and Lichtenberger, A. (2024) A permanent EU investment fund to promote the green transition in light of EU fiscal rules. *European Journal of Economics and Economic Policies: Intervention*, 22(2), 181–188. https://doi.org/10.4337/ejeep.2024.0134

Heimberger, P. and Schratzenstaller, M. (2024) Shaping the EU's financial architecture for the future. *Heinrich-Böll-Stiftung Policy Paper*, July.

Heimberger, P., Huber, J., and Kapeller, J. (2020) The power of economic models: The case of the EU's fiscal regulation framework. *Socio-Economic Review*, 18(2), 337–366.

Heimberger, P., Welslau, L., Gechert, S., Guarascio, D., and Zezza, F. (2024) Debt sustainability analysis in reformed EU fiscal rules: The effect of fiscal consolidation on growth and public debt ratios. *Intereconomics*, 59(5), 276–283.

Ilzetzki, E. (2025) Guns and growth: The economic consequences of defense buildups. *Kiel Report* No. 2 (February).

Jacques, O. (2021) Austerity and the path of least resistance: How fiscal consolidations crowd out long-term investments. *Journal of European Public Policy*, 28(4), 551–570.

Jacques, O. and Haffert, L. (2021) Are governments paying a price for austerity? Fiscal consolidations reduce government approval. *European Political Science Review*, 13(2), 189–207.

Paetz, C. and Watzka, S. (2024) The new fiscal rules: Another round of austerity for Europe? *IMK Policy Brief* No. 176.

Pisani-Ferry, J. (2021) Climate policy is macroeconomic policy, and the implications will be significant. *PIIE* (Peterson Institute for International Economics) *Policy Brief* No. 20/21.

Pisani-Ferry, J. and Tagliapietra, S. (2024) An investment strategy to keep the European Green Deal on track, *Bruegel Policy Brief* No. 31/24.

Raza, W. (2024) Towards a progressive industrial policy for the twin transformation in the European Union: Synthesis report (21/2025).Vienna: *ÖFSE Research Report no. 21*. https://doi.org/10.60637/2025-rr21

Reljic, J. and Zezza, F. (2025) Breaking the divide: Can public spending on social infrastructure boost female employment in Italy? *Economic Modelling*, 143, 106974.

Shayegh, S., Reissl, S., Roshan, E., and Calcaterra, M. (2023) An assessment of different transition pathways to a green global economy. *Communications Earth & Environment*, 4, 448.

Skyrman, V. (2024) Industrial policy, progressive derisking, and the financing of Europe's green transition. Vienna: *ÖFSE Working Paper* no. 78. https://doi.org/10.60637/2024-wp78

Stöllinger, R. (2023) Advancing the European Green Deal with industrial policy. *FIW Policy Brief* No. 59.

Suresh, N., Ghaw, R., Obeng-Psei, R., and Wickstead, T. (2024) Public investment and potential output. *Office for Budget Responsibility Discussion Paper* No. 5.

Van Dijk, J., Schuster, F., Sigl-Glöckner, P., and Ziesemer, V. (2022) Building on the proposal by the EU-Commission for reforming the Stability and Growth Pact. *Dezernat Zukunft and Instituut voor Publieke Economie*.

Wildauer, R., Leitch, S., and Kapeller, J. (2020) *How to boost the European Green Deal's scale and ambition*. Policy Paper, Foundation of European Progressive Studies/Karl-Renner Institute/Austrian Federal Chamber of Labour (June).

Zezza, F. and Guarascio, D. (2024). Fiscal policy, public investment and structural change: A P-SVAR analysis on Italian regions. *Regional Studies*, 58(6), 1356–1373.

10

BUILDING A COHERENT EUROPEAN GREEN MACROFINANCIAL REGIME

How the ECB Can Leverage the EU's Sustainable Finance Framework to Secure Climate Objectives and Price Stability

Gaston Bronstering, Agnieszka Smoleńska, and David Barmes

10.1 Introduction

Accelerating the sustainability transition is the major challenge of our times. It requires collaboration and comprehensive policy intervention across public and private sector institutions underpinned by a central bank policy that supports both consistent integration and management of risks related to climate change as well as, within the scope of the mandate, alignment of capital flows and investment with the transition to net zero. As we discuss in this chapter, EU sustainable finance regulation and the calibration of the ECB's monetary policy should be mutually reinforcing, supporting a positive feedback loop, accelerating the transition. In this way, EU policymakers may support the emergence of a truly green EU macrofinancial policy regime (Downey and Blyth, 2025; Gabor and Braun, 2025; Smoleńska, 2025). Following Gabor and Braun (2025), a macrofinancial regime is defined as the system of policies, institutions and rules that governs the interaction between a country's macroeconomy (including inflation, growth and employment) and its financial system (including banks, markets and capital flows), shaping how financial and economic stability are maintained over time.

Over the past few years, the European legislators erected a comprehensive set of sustainability objectives and legislation horizontally cutting through various policy realms. The European Climate Law (Regulation 2021/1119) translated the Paris Climate Agreement into the concrete obligation of reducing greenhouse gas emissions by at least 55% by 2030 and 90% by 2040, and achieving climate neutrality by 2050 (European Commission, 2025). To reach these objectives, the European Green Deal introduced sustainability policies such as the Emission Trading Scheme (ETS) across a range of different economic policy areas. The 2024 Clean Industrial Deal reoriented European green industrial policy towards competitiveness and

DOI: 10.4324/9781003745563-15

strategic autonomy, e.g. by restricting the scope of corporate governance regulation and postponing the latter's application.

The EU Sustainable Finance legislation has created a complex framework that seeks to ingrain sustainability considerations across the financial market. It includes definitions of sustainable activities (EU Green Taxonomy), corporate governance and disclosure (the Corporate Sustainability Reporting Directive (CSRD) and the Corporate Sustainability Due Diligence Directive (CSDDD)), product and service standards (e.g. Green Bond Standard and Paris-aligned and Transition-aligned benchmarks), and prudential reforms. In the current phase of its implementation, the Sustainable Finance Framework faces serious challenges due to concerns over excessive administrative burden, political reprioritisations due to a shifting geopolitical landscape, and a more general backlash against sustainability policy. This trend is epitomised by the recent Omnibus package aiming at reducing administrative burden by 25% by amending among other policies the CSRD and CSDDD. The effects of this policy reversal undermine not only the goals of the EU Green Deal but also challenges the overall macrofinancial regime in the EU.

As this chapter argues, with the EU Sustainable Finance Framework regulating definitions, data provision and corporate governance rules governing firm behaviour, it has direct relevance and should be consistently integrated in the discharge of central banking tasks, related to monetary policy and supervision, among others. The way in which the ECB integrates the Sustainable Finance Framework into its activities importantly shapes how the latter is perceived by market participants and ultimately enforced. Put differently, the ECB can contribute to building a coherent European Green Macrofinancial Regime by leveraging the Sustainable Finance Framework for its various activities and most importantly its monetary policy operations. While a strong alignment with the Sustainable Finance Framework would mainstream and consolidate the mentioned elements by sending a strong signal to market participants, a persisting disconnect could seriously undermine its credibility and thereby put at risk not only the ECB pursuit of price stability but also the Sustainable Finance Framework as well as the green transition more generally. The importance of the Sustainable Finance Framework for ECB policy is made evident in the latter's opinion on the Omnibus package, where the likely negative impact on financial stability is highlighted (ECB, 2025a).

Consequently, this chapter investigates the legal as well as practical pathways to further align ECB activities and more specifically its monetary policy operations – i.e. credit operations, collateral policy, and asset purchases – with the Sustainable Finance Framework. We find that there is ample space within the ECB's primary mandate and secondary objectives to further integrate the Sustainable Finance Framework. Furthermore, we discuss three practical pathways of how this could be done. First, differentiate interest rates between sustainable and unsustainable economic activities based on a Green Targeted Longer-Term Refinancing Operation (Green TLTRO). Second, effectively green the collateral framework. Finally, continue tilting the ECB's balance sheet on a stock-based approach. While this chapter focuses on the monetary policies of the European Central Bank, our findings can be generalised to central banks and their functions more broadly.

At this crossroad, in deciding between an ambitious or weak green macrofinancial regime, the ECB is not powerless. All the contrary. The ECB can participate in enforcing the Sustainable Finance Framework by leveraging it in its activities. This matters not only for the pursuit of its mandate but also for the general achievement of the Union's sustainability objectives.

10.2 The crucial interdependencies between the ECB and climate change (policy)

To begin with, climate and environmental change matter for monetary policy. Consequently, one of the conclusions from the ECB's 2021 monetary policy strategy review was that climate change and transition policies are likely to affect the conduct of monetary policy and the ECB's ability to deliver on its price stability mandate (Drudi *et al.*, 2021). For instance, climate change directly causes supply shocks through extreme weather events (Cantelmo *et al.*, 2024), and disorderly transition policies could have inflationary effects in the short to medium term (van't Klooster, 2025). In her speech on 17 March 2022, ECB Executive Board Member Isabel Schnabel (2022) outlined three mechanisms through which climate change influences price stability. First, climate-related disasters affect economic activity and price levels (climateflation). Second, prices increase due to the legacy cost of the dependence on fossil energy sources, as recently highlighted by the Russian attack on Ukraine (fossilflation). Third, prices also rise due to the increasing demand for a limited quantity of resources needed for the green transition (greenflation). Most recently, Christine Lagarde has reaffirmed the importance of climate change for the ECB, responding to a letter from Members of the European Parliament: "Climate change has profound implications for price stability through its impact on the structure and cyclical dynamics of the economy and financial system" (Lagarde, 2025).

In addition to climate and environmental change, the policies to mitigate the latter also matter for the ECB and its various activities. Evidently, EU climate and environmental policies set the pace of the green transition and therefore provide an important risk benchmark against which to assess the transition of institutions under the ECB's supervision (Smoleńska and van't Klooster, 2022). Furthermore, the Sustainable Finance Framework and more specifically its elements on sustainability disclosures constitute an important source of information for the ECB's monetary policy, as elaborated in the ECB's own Opinion on the Omnibus package. At the same time, although streamlining sustainable finance rules might mitigate the inconsistencies, overlaps, and complexities of the current framework, the Omnibus package is unlikely to significantly ease administrative burden and risks undermining green investment and the management of climate-related risks by reducing the scope of EU sustainability rules (Mack, 2025), for instance with regards to scope of data available through disclosures and transition plan requirements. Meanwhile, the Sustainable Finance Framework and especially the CSRD and CSDDD constitute crucial inputs for the ECB's activities in terms of monetary policy implementation, prudential supervision of credit institutions, financial stability, and statistical data collection (ECB, 2025a). Borrowing from (Lagarde, 2025), "to adequately consider the implications of climate change and nature degradation, the Eurosystem requires sufficient high-quality climate data". Limiting the availability of firm-level data, weakens the Eurosystem's ability to perform granular assessments of climate-related financial risk on its balance sheet and within its collateral framework (ECB, 2025a). Consequently, the burden alleviation should not come at the expense of the scope nor the ambition of the Sustainable Finance Framework (ECB, 2025a). Beyond the availability of climate data, the amendments to the CSRD and CSDDD and delays in the transposition of the CSRD into the national laws of euro area member states could hinder the Eurosystem's ability to implement measures (ECB, 2025a). The prospective impact of the Omnibus package demonstrates the urgent need for alignment between the Union's climate, financial, and monetary policy.

Ultimately, the ECB's activities also matter for climate and environmental change. To start with, the ECB has acknowledged that "market neutrality" approaches in monetary policy and financial frameworks negatively interact with sustainability targets (Dafermos *et al.*, 2020). For instance, Isabel Schnabel recognised that the ECB's monetary policy had a carbon bias, favouring carbon-intensive activities as its environmental externalities are not priced in (Schnabel, 2021). Furthermore, the contractionary monetary policy in response to rising price levels following the Russian invasion of Ukraine and the opening of economies after the COVID-19 pandemic was criticised for negatively affecting the green transition and, most notably, the financing of renewable energy (Krahé and Heilmann, 2024; van't Klooster and Weber, 2024). Indeed, higher interest rates affect different sectors of the economy in a heterogenous way and renewable energy investments are particularly vulnerable due to their higher up front capital intensity compared to fossil energies (IEA, 2023). The higher vulnerability of renewable energies to changes in interest rates was confirmed by many empirical studies (Monnin, 2015; Polzin *et al.*, 2021; Schmidt *et al.*, 2019). This negative effect of (contractionary) monetary policy on the green transition undermining price stability on the longer term demonstrates the insufficient consideration of climate in the ECB's monetary policies and a lack of alignment with the EU's climate objectives and policies more generally. Isabel Schnabel (2023a) acknowledged that "[t]he insight that the effects of interest rate changes are not symmetric across economic sectors is not new and it is empirically well-documented", referring to Auer *et al.* (2021) who find a non-linear relationship between corporate leverage and the sensitivity of industrial production to monetary policy shocks across euro-area manufacturers. In addition, Durante *et al.* (2022) document a higher sensitivity to monetary policy shocks for firms that are more leveraged, younger, and operating in specific industries.

In sum, there are crucial interdependencies between climate change, climate change policy, and the various activities of the European Central Bank. As we will see in the following, the acknowledgement of these interconnections has started a process of alignment that is still in its early stages and requires more effort.

10.3 Missed opportunities of the EU's sustainable finance framework

Over the past few years, the ECB has taken first steps to integrate the EU's sustainability goals including the sustainable finance framework into its various activities and supported the rising awareness of the financial sector of issues related to climate change. While the ECB was even quicker in the greening of its supervisory policy as a result of legislative intervention (Smoleńska and van't Klooster, 2022), this chapter focuses on monetary policy, where the interplay between the Sustainable Finance Framework and policy operationalisation is less explored and less consistent. Already in September 2020, the ECB decided that bonds with coupons linked to a performance target referring to one or more of the environmental objectives set out in the EU Taxonomy Regulation and/or the United Nation Sustainable Development Goals (UN SDGs) (relating to climate change or environmental degradation) will become eligible as collateral for Eurosystem credit operations and also for Eurosystem outright purchases for monetary policy purposes starting in January 2021 (ECB, 2020; Lagarde, 2025). While this policy change may seem highly technical, it is telling of the depth of interactions between sustainable finance policies, including those that seek to promote particular types of financing products, and various ECB policies. Collateral eligibility is after all well established as one of the important ways in which the central bank may influence financial market behaviour and risk perception.

Building on the 2021 monetary policy strategy review, the Governing Council presented a roadmap to incorporate climate change in the ECB's monetary policy framework and operations, including the areas of disclosure, risk assessment, collateral frameworks, and corporate asset purchases (ECB, 2021). On 4 July 2022, the Governing Council decided to take further steps to include climate change into its monetary policy operations, leveraging various elements of the EU sustainable finance framework (ECB, 2022).

First, building on the carbon bias of "market neutral" asset purchases, the ECB decided to align its corporate bond holdings with the Paris-Climate Agreement by reinvesting the proceeds from maturing bonds into more sustainable new ones (ECB, 2022). The selection of new bonds would be based on an internal climate scoring that is strongly guided by the requirements for the EU Climate Transition Benchmarks and EU Paris-aligned Benchmarks. Tilting was motivated by the ECB's primary mandate and secondary objectives (Elderson, 2022). First, tilting was considered essential for pursuing price stability as carbon-intensive issuers are more vulnerable to both physical and transition risks associated with climate change. Substantial holdings of such bonds therefore pose significant financial stability risks to the Eurosystem's balance sheet. In February 2023, the Governing Council decided the remaining reinvestments of the Eurosystem's holdings of securities under the Asset Purchase Program (APP) will be "tilted more strongly towards issuers with a better climate performance", supporting the "gradual decarbonisation of the Eurosystem's corporate bond holdings, in line with the goals of the Paris Agreement" (ECB, 2023a). In contrast, the ECB's Governing Council decided in June 2023 to discontinue the greening of the Corporate Sector Purchasing Program (CSPP) starting in July 2023 with the ending of all net purchase programmes following the return to the normalisation of monetary conditions – only nine months after it had started – putting an end to one of the flagship measures of the ECB's sustainability agenda (ECB, 2023b).

Second, the ECB announced that it would limit shares of assets issued by high-carbon footprint entities that can be pledged as collateral by individual counterparties when borrowing from the Eurosystem and consider climate risk when reviewing haircuts applied to corporate bonds used as collateral (ECB, 2022). Beyond the carbon footprint of an asset, a reference to the Sustainable Finance Framework and its sustainability definitions would have been useful here. Moreover, the ECB announced it would make the eligibility of companies' marketable assets and credit claims as collateral in Eurosystem credit operations dependent on whether the latter complies with the CSRD (ECB, 2022).

In March 2024, the ECB announced that the design of its operational framework will aim to incorporate climate-related considerations into the structural monetary policy operations to the extent that the operational framework ensures the effective implementation of the monetary policy stance and does not cause prejudice to the ECB's primary objective of price stability (ECB, 2024a). This commitment was reiterated in the conclusions of the 2025 monetary policy strategy review. The Governing Council will "continue to adapt the design of its monetary policy operational framework in relation to disclosures, risk assessment, corporate sector asset purchases and the collateral framework" (ECB, 2025b: 16). Furthermore, the 2025 monetary policy strategy review extended the time horizon for the objective of price stability in the presence of supply shocks, significantly paving the way for a stronger integration of climate and environmental determinants of longer-term price stability (ECB, 2025b).

While the ECB has taken initial steps to integrate climate-related considerations into its various policies since its 2021 Roadmap, there is insufficient clarity about how it relies on definitions, data and methodologies underpinning the Sustainable Finance Framework in the calibration of its policies. Furthermore, the ECB has backtracked on its commitments, as in the case of the tilting of its corporate bond holdings. More generally, we observe a gap between the ECB's analytical perspective on climate change and its implications for its monetary policy and its operational implementation. Aligning the ECB activities with the Sustainable Finance Framework is crucial to effectively integrate climate and environment-related risk and to consistently impact the behaviour of financial market actors, who are questioning the credibility of EU climate ambitions, especially given the regulatory rollback in Brussels. The incertitude around the green transition evidently threatens the rollout of necessary climate mitigation and adaptation actions and, by extension, also the stability of the financial system. At this critical juncture, clearly outlining how central bank policies may be reliant on the Sustainable Finance Framework also has the potential to strengthen the latter and contribute to a coherent and ambitious European Green Macrofinancial Regime, more generally.

10.4 Support a coherent European macrofinancial regime

Building on the understanding of macrofinancial regimes as the systems of policies, institutions, and rules that govern the interaction between a country's macroeconomy and financial system, shaping the maintenance of financial and economic stability (Gabor and Braun, 2025), central banks represent crucial and influential actors. Consequently, the ECB and its various activities contribute to shaping the overall macrofinancial regime of the euro area with respect to sustainable finance. Here central banks may either develop dedicated policies to support consistent integration of climate change considerations from a risk-based or promotional perspective or not. When they do, especially with regard to central bank communication and monetary policy calibration, these developments are highly consequential for market development and bank choices (Smoleńska, 2025). In other words, the ECB's framework is material to shaping actors' decisions, creating incentives for European finance to promote sustainable finance products and practices.

Likewise, precisely how the ECB will integrate and use the definitions, data points, and methodologies developed under the Sustainable Finance Framework will impact the latter by either reinforcing or weakening it. Specifically, this relates to how the Sustainable Finance Framework may support the ECB in the process of consistently integrating sustainability factors in the operationalisation of its policies. There are two ways of doing this. First, as in the case of the eligibility of collateral criteria to sustainability-linked bonds, the ECB may expand the scope of existing requirements to include new SFF-aligned instruments. Second, the ECB may differentiate SFF-aligned instruments by introducing dedicated policies such as green Targeted Longer-Term Refinancing Operations to support the development of the market segment (Smoleńska, 2025).

The logic of expansion is relevant with reference to the interpretation of the ECB's mandate and would suggest considering climate and environmental change as part and parcel of the primary mandate. Furthermore, the ECB already acknowledges an array of sustainable finance products and practices – see, for instance, the previously mentioned inclusion of green bonds into the ECB's collateral framework. Here, the Sustainable Finance Framework supports the calibration of ECB policies by ensuring that data related to the climate change risks to which the economic actors are exposed to is available and that the understandings of sustainability and transition goals are aligned. Where the EU sustainable finance framework is oriented towards increasing transparency around climate change-related risk exposures, the integration of this approach into the ECB's monetary policies will support adequate risk management and financial sector resilience. Meanwhile, the logic of differentiation appears much more helpful for thinking of how the ECB could align its activities with the Sustainable Finance Framework in a more proactive way. Favourable treatment of products considered aligned with the EU Taxonomy or EU Green Bond Standard in force will support market development and facilitate accelerated financing of such activities, supporting long term alignment of the economy with the transition. Such an approach further enhances the effectiveness of policy intervention, where in specific cases SFF-aligned instruments may support risk mitigation, including mitigation of risk of misalignment with the transition or physical risk in the context of adaptation activities. Conversely, the absence of coherence between EU sustainable finance policies and the ECB's monetary policy operationalisation in particular risks undermining the objectives of both.

While the importance of sustainability disclosures associated with the EU sustainable finance framework for the successful integration of sustainability-related risks was already highlighted in its recent Opinion on the Omnibus package (ECB, 2025a), the ECB should also consider the appropriateness of consistently using the sustainability definitions under the EU Taxonomy Regulation and the Sustainable Finance Disclosure Directive for calibration of its policies. The mainstreaming of SFF-aligned sustainability definitions, rather than the development of bespoke ones for the purpose of central banking activities, would support a more coherent implementation of the transition among market participants and EU institutions. In the alternative, there is the risk that the progress achieved in terms of climate change risk management and the increased deployment of capital for transition investments will be undermined (Platform on Sustainable Finance, 2025).

In the context of increasing geopolitical tensions and the emergence of distinct and sometimes even opposed green macrofinancial regimes, the endorsement of the Sustainable Finance Framework by the ECB represents an important step to consolidate the European green macrofinancial regime and affirming its distinctiveness from other competing macrofinancial regimes such as the US, currently turning its back to the green transition (Blyth, 2025). At the same time, other central banks such as the Bank of Japan and the People's Bank of China have begun to implement climate policies in a more promotional manner rather than focusing on managing climate risk. For instance, the Bank of Japan introduced a green loans scheme, providing zero-interest financing to lenders that support action to address climate change (Clarke, 2022; Kuroda, 2021). Similarly, the People's Bank of China has introduced the carbon emission reduction facility, a structural monetary policy instrument aiming at mobilising capital to promote climate and environmental objectives (People's Bank of China, 2021). Between these two approaches and under the ECB's mandate, there is still broad scope for further alignment of its policies with the Sustainable Finance Framework.

10.5 Room for alignment within the ECB's mandate

As previously discussed, there are crucial interconnections between climate and environmental change, climate policy, and the ECB's various activities. Consequently, the 2025 monetary policy strategy states that while governments bear the primary responsibility and tools to address climate change, its mandate would require the ECB to

> assess the impact of climate change and nature degradation and to further incorporate climate considerations into its policy framework, since physical and transition risks related to climate change have implications for both price and financial stability and affect the value and the risk profile of the assets held on the Eurosystem's balance sheet.
>
> *(ECB, 2025b: 16)*

But what are the exact legal grounds on which the ECB could further integrate its monetary policy operations with the EU's sustainability goals and the EU Sustainable Finance Framework? As we will see in the following, both the ECB's primary mandate as well as its secondary objectives provide ample space to further align its activities with the EU's sustainability goals and more concretely the sustainable finance framework.

First, the ECB pursues the primary objective of maintaining price stability as set out in the first sentence of Article 127(1) of the Treaty on the Functioning of the European Union (TFEU). Building on the previously mentioned conceptualisation of climateflation, fossilflation, and greenflation, Christine Lagarde (2020) stated that including climate change into the ECB's activities would not represent a "mission creep" as the former clearly poses a risk to price stability. This argument can be made in a similar fashion for nature-related risks (O'Connell, 2024). However, climate change is not only directly relevant for the ECB's primary mandate. Following the European Court of Justice (ECJ), and more specifically its decision in the Case C-62/14 *Gauweiler*, the exercise of the ECB's primary objective also extends to the preconditions of the latter (Zilioli and Ioannidis, 2022). For instance, actions intended to preserve the functioning and reliability of the transmission mechanism, i.e. the uniform transmission of monetary policy signals across the Eurozone, may be regarded as pertaining to the primary objective and therefore fall within the mandate of the ECB (ECJ, 2015). Consequently, climate change could also be deemed relevant for the ECB's primary objective if it undermined the preconditions of the exercise of the latter. Van't Klooster (2025) adds that the ECB's insufficient consideration of climate change and environmental factors relevant to price stability would be due to its "myopic" medium-term monetary policy horizon, which spans two to five years. The quasi extension of the monetary policy horizon in the presence of supply shocks in the 2025 monetary policy strategy represents an important step towards fully capturing the longer-term effects of climate and environmental change. Yet a disconnect remains between the ECB's policy horizon and market participants, who are expected to transition to a net-zero economy by 2050. A potential next step could be to align the time horizon of the ECB's monetary policy strategy with the EU microprudential framework, i.e. ten years and above (EBA, 2025).

Second, a legal basis to further integrate the sustainable finance framework into the ECB's activities can also be found in its secondary objectives. According to the second sentence of Article 127(1) TFEU, the ECB is to support the general economic policies of the Union without prejudice to the objective of price stability. The latter are laid down in Article 3 of the Treaty on the European Union (TEU) and include, amongst other elements, "full employment and social progress" and "the quality of the environment". On the place of climate action among the secondary objectives, Frank Elderson stated that "it is irrefutable that the EU's climate policy constitutes part of the general economic policies in the EU" (ECB, 2024b). More concretely, Elderson described how the Sustainable Finance Framework creates an "ecosystem" of EU legislation that links nature degradation, the economy and the financial sector – and thus central banks and supervisors – and leaves no doubt that central bankers have the duty and tools at their disposal to take nature-related risks into account when exercising their mandate (ECB, 2024b). The prioritisation of climate policy in the Union's economic policy is also reflected in the Paris Climate Agreement and the European Climate Law (Regulation 2021/1119). Financial stability is an intermediate objective that underpins the ability of ECB to pursue its primary objectives (Smoleńska and Beukers, 2023). Likewise, climate and environmental considerations as both are included in the primary mandate as a precondition of price stability and as a secondary objective standing for themselves (ECB, 2023c; Heynen, 2022). Moreover, Article 11 TFEU states that "environmental protection requirements must be integrated into the definition and implementation of the Union's policies and activities, in particular with a view to promoting sustainable development" (Zilioli and Ioannidis, 2022). This translates into an obligation for the ECB to consider and support the objectives of the Climate Law when performing its tasks (Elderson, 2022). As mentioned by the NGFS (2021), and especially following the opinion of the International Court of Justice (e.g. Carbon Brief, 2025) this obligation also implies a growing litigation risk for central banks if they fail to convincingly support the green transition. Furthermore, Article 7 of the TFEU represents another transversal treaty provision stating that the activities and policies of the ECB must be consistent with EU law, including, for instance, the EU law on nature and biodiversity as well as other environmental legislation. In this context, the ECB's consistent integration of the Sustainable Finance Framework could further support proportionality of implemented policies (Smoleńska and Tokarski, 2022).

While the ECB's interference with the principles of an open market economy with free competition (third sentence of Article 127(1) TFEU) must meet proportionality standards, actions such as the differentiation between green and brown assets could be justified using EU standards like the EU Taxonomy or the EU Green

Bond Standard (Zilioli and Ioannidis, 2022). But, as previously mentioned, the ECB seems to already have "turned away from considering market neutrality as a binding legal instrument" (Heynen, 2022) and recognised the "carbon bias" of its monetary policies (Schnabel, 2021).

In sum, both the ECB's primary mandate and secondary objectives provide ample justification for further aligning its activities with the EU's sustainable finance policies, particularly those related to risk management, sustainability definitions, and corporate governance requirements. However, one would be mistaken to understand the ECB's climate-related activities from a purely legal perspective. Analysing how the ECB has legitimised its green monetary policies over time, Aguila and Wullweber (2025) identify three distinct narratives. First, environmental issues would be understood as a financial risk that is to be mitigated. Second, green monetary policy would contribute to closing the green investment or financing gap. Third, the ECB would integrate climate change into its activities as the latter poses a risk to price stability. While the first narrative was dominant until 2021, the third one gained increasing traction and eventually became dominant, while the second one remained marginal. Despite a growing recognition that climate change requires increasing central bank intervention, the latter would be constrained by the ECB's mandate, which is grounded in a market liberal institutional structure, thus precluding a truly effective and encompassing green monetary policy (Aguila and Wullweber, 2025).

In other words, resistance to green monetary policies would be less related to the ECB's mandate per se, but in the historically and institutionally rooted narrow interpretation of the latter. Oman *et al.* (2024) provide a complementary analysis of "tales" of central banking and financial supervision for the ecological transition. Hence, the interpretation of the EC's mandate does not happen in a legalistic vacuum but has the potential to be shaped by exterior forces such as civil society organisations demanding climate action and progressive scholars providing solutions for the latter. This raises the question of how an alignment of the ECB's monetary policy operations with the Sustainable Finance Framework might look like in practical terms.

10.6 Pathways to leverage the sustainable finance framework

In the following, we outline three practical pathways of how the ECB could leverage the Sustainable Finance Framework in its monetary policy operations. First, by differentiating interest rates via a Green Targeted Longer-Term Refinancing Operation. Second, by a renewed tilting of the ECB's balance sheet. Third, by an effective greening of the ECB's collateral framework.

10.6.1 A green targeted longer-term refinancing operation

As previously discussed, the recent episode of contractionary monetary policy in response to surging inflation was criticised for negatively impacting investments into sustainable economic activities (e.g. renewable energies), and therefore to endanger both the green transition as well as longer-term price stability (Altaghlibi *et al.*, 2024; Egli *et al.*, 2018; Hashmi *et al.*, 2022; Razmi *et al.*, 2021; Zhang *et al.*, 2023). In response, the idea was brought up to differentiate interest rates to shield sustainable activities from the negative effects of contractionary monetary policy and secure their longer-term positive effect for price stability (Altaghlibi *et al.*, 2024; Jourdan *et al.*, 2024). As the Sustainable Finance Framework provides a classification of sustainable economic activities in the form of the EU Sustainable Finance Taxonomy, a differentiated rate could be implemented via a Taxonomy-based Green Targeted Longer-Term Refinancing Operation (Green TLTRO) (Altaghlibi *et al.*, 2024; Jourdan *et al.*, 2024).

The latter would provide banks with a lower interest rate that corrects for the unintended negative impact on pricing of transition-aligned investments. Given that banks and corporations started reporting on their alignment with the EU Taxonomy under the new disclosure regime, data on green lending should now be available. However, the implementation of the Omnibus package will very likely decrease the availability of important climate metrics, necessary for the effective implementation of a Green TLTRO. Nevertheless, banks will continue to report their exposures to climate change and environmental risks, as well as their transition risk mitigation measures (including Taxonomy-aligned investments) following the Pillar 3 reporting framework (Smoleńska and van't Klooster, 2022). If the Sustainable Finance Framework was to be evaluated insufficient to effectively integrate climate-related risk, the ECB could also envision a penalty rate to be imposed on climate-relevant and transition-misaligned activities based on extensions of the Sustainable Finance Framework such as the EU's transition finance framework (European Commission, 2021; Miller and Dikau, 2022). Whether it is the EU Taxonomy or another element of the Sustainable Finance Framework or the EU Green Bond Standard, the ECB should explicitly consider the appropriateness of using existing regulatory definitions when assessing and integrating sustainability into its various activities.

While the People's Bank of China and the Bank of Japan certainly operate within unique economic, political, and financial environments, their recent policies integrating climate change considerations into central banking operations offer useful lessons for policy choices supporting efficiency and consistency of requirements across a macrofinancial regime (Waite, 2022). Beyond the management of climate risk, the EU's sustainable finance framework could indeed be further leveraged in a promotional manner to support credit allocation to activities contributing to the green transition in more generally, in line with the twin goals of long-term financial stability and supporting economic policies in the Union (Kedward *et al.*, 2022). While more generous conditions of credit operations in terms of longer maturity and programme duration could, for instance, maximise the impact of a Green TLTRO, it could also interfere with the contractionary policy stance in the short term. Giovanardi *et al.* (2023) also warn that interest rate differentiation based on sustainability criteria may, if improperly implemented, lead to negative effects on the debt sustainability and more specifically the leverage ratio of green firms. However, these trade-offs can, however, be mitigated through smart design choices, such as flexible or limited lending envelopes, scope reductions of eligible lending, and a hard cap on the size of the Green TLTRO programme (Jourdan *et al.*, 2024).

10.6.2 Tilting the ECB's balance sheet

As previously mentioned, the tilting of the ECB's corporate bond holdings as part of the (APP and CSPP) relied on an internal climate score that partly drew on the Sustainable Finance Framework and more specifically the EU Climate Transition Benchmark and the Paris-aligned Benchmark. Going beyond the previous flow-based approach, tilting the stock of the ECB's outstanding corporate bond holdings could leverage more recent sustainability definitions included in the Sustainable Finance Framework, such as the Green Bond Standard or the Taxonomy Regulation (Schnabel, 2023b). This would ensure that such instruments are adequately represented in the ECB's policies, also in the context of transition risk management. Beyond the tilting of its corporate bond holdings, the mentioned sustainability definitions should also be integrated into the ECB's broader policies, including collateral policies. Of course, as Giovanardi *et al.* (2023) argue, while the preferential treatment of green bonds in the central bank's collateral portfolio can effectively mitigate underestimated transition and physical risks, one should not expect this policy to effectively contribute to filling the financing gap for the green transition. However, a macrofinancial perspective on integrating climate change factors in central banking policy allows such policy choices to be seen in their wider, systemic context. In particular, explicit communication of such policies would further support consistent interpretation of SFF by market participants, beyond monetary policy interactions.

10.6.3 Greening the collateral framework

Another pathway to further align the ECB's monetary policy operations with the Sustainable Finance Framework would be to leverage sustainability definitions for the greening of the collateral framework via collateral eligibility or haircut differentiation. On 29 July 2025, the ECB announced the introduction of a climate factor to adjust the value assigned to assets pledged as collateral (and the maximum amount the Eurosystem is willing to lend against them) based on their climate-related risk after the application of standard risk-based haircuts (ECB, 2025c). This measure is said to align with the ECB's climate and nature plan and aims to enhance the management of climate risk on the Eurosystem's balance sheet as well as within the collateral framework (Lagarde, 2025). As studies indicate that carbon-intensive assets have in general lower haircuts (EIU, 2024), the climate factor has the potential to correct this mispricing of climate risk, if correctly implemented.

The climate score is generally composed of backwards-looking climate metrics such as carbon intensity and the decarbonisation rate, forward-looking climate metrics such as the decarbonisation targets, and the quality of climate disclosures (ECB, 2025d). More concretely, the climate factor builds on two elements of the Sustainable Finance Framework. First, the 2024 climate stress test of the Eurosystem's balance sheet provides information for the sector-specific stressor inputs. Second, the climate score from the Corporate Sector Purchasing Program (CSPP) – the methodology used for tilting the ECB's corporate bond holdings – provides information for the issuer-specific exposure inputs. Consequently, with the current operationalisation of the climate factor, there remains much more potential for further alignment with the Sustainable Finance Framework and, more specifically, sustainability definitions such as the Taxonomy Regulation.

Furthermore, the scope of the climate factor is currently restricted to marketable assets issued by non-financial corporations and their affiliated entities, i.e. approximately 10% of all outstanding eligible collateral (Erlandsson, 2025) or only about 5% of collateral pledged by banks (Martin, 2025), the most important financial actors in the Eurozone. The announcement of the climate factor already includes the regular review by the Governing Council to reflect the increasing availability of data and models as well as relevant regulatory developments and advances in risk management capabilities (ECB, 2025c). A more ambitious and therefore more impactful operationalisation would expand the scope to other asset classes such as bank deposits and sovereign bonds. Further criticism includes the focus on relative measures of climate performance and the exclusion of absolute measures such as total emissions, the lack of consideration for companies' plans to expand fossil fuel-related and other equally environmentally harmful activities such as deforestation, as well as the favouring of short-term perspectives via the penalisation of assets based on maturity (Martin, 2025). Consequently, an improved climate factor aligned with the Sustainable Finance Framework could for instance lean on institutions transition plans to adjust the risk associated with their assets pledged as collateral.

10.7 Conclusion

While the ECB has recently started to align some of its policies with the EU sustainable finance framework, there remains much room for increasing coherence between the two. This integration follows from the secondary mandate of the ECB, in particular. However, in this article we also discussed the broader context of developing an EU green macrofinancial policy regime, that is underpinned by consistent sectoral and financial policies.

From this perspective, the recent process of policy rollback on the green transition represents a challenge but also an opportunity to showcase the importance of policy consistency and coherence. The so-called burden alleviation introduced by the Omnibus package highlights the extent to which the ECB depends on the

Sustainable Finance Framework for the effective integration of climate and environment-related risks into its various activities. While this dependence demonstrates that the ECB cannot fully rely on the Sustainable Finance Framework for its monetary policy and should continue to develop its risk-based approach, there is still scope for the former to be more consistently integrated in central bank policies. Data availability is not the only reason the ECB should align its monetary policy operations with the Sustainable Finance Framework. Beyond that, alignment with the EU's financial policy would contribute to a more coherent and therefore impactful European Green Macrofinancial Regime that supports systemic change and credibility of transition policies and EU's industrial policy (Skyrman, 2024). Building on the Sustainable Finance Framework is not only useful in terms of coherence and mainstreaming of sustainability definitions but also gives a clear signal to market participants that the green transition is not just of symbolic value but something material to their day-to-day operations. Conversely, insufficient alignment with the Sustainable Finance Framework could severely question the credibility of the latter and thereby of the European sustainability agenda more generally. The latter scenario is furthermore detrimental to primary objectives of central banking policy, namely price stability.

Both the ECB's primary mandate and secondary objectives provide ample space to further align its monetary policy operations with the Sustainable Finance Framework. Thus, progressive actors should continue to push for the latter given the embeddedness of the legal interpretation of the mandate in the broader European political economy. At the same time, the operationalisation of the 2025 Monetary Policy Strategy represents a good opportunity for the ECB to start contributing to a more coherent European Green Macrofinancial Regime. Practically, this could take the form of a Green Targeted Longer-Term Refinancing Operation based on the Taxonomy Regulation, a renewed tilting of the ECBs corporate securities portfolio based, for instance, on the Green Bond Standard, and an updated climate factor for greening the collateral framework. The ECB can and should take these steps – both to ensure longer-term price stability and to contribute to the emergence of a strong and coherent European Green Macrofinancial Regime.

References

Aguila, N., and Wullweber, J. (2025) Legitimising green monetary policies: Market liberalism, layered Central Banking, and the ECB's ongoing discursive shift from environmental risks to price stability. *J. Eur. Public Policy*, 32, 665–696. https://doi.org/10.1080/13501763.2024.2317969

Altaghlibi, M., van Tilburg, R., and Bronstering, G. (2024) *The impact of a Green LTRO on the energy transition*. ABN Amro, Sustainable Finance Lab.

Auer, S., Bernardini, M., and Cecioni, M. (2021) Corporate leverage and monetary policy effectiveness in the euro area. *Eur. Econ. Rev.*, 140, 103943. https://doi.org/10.1016/j.euroecorev.2021.103943

Blyth, M. (2025) *Burning down the house: Carbon politics, American Power and the almighty dollar*.

Cantelmo, A., Fatouros, N., Melina, G., and Papageorgiou, C. (2024) Monetary policy under natural disaster shocks. *Int. Econ. Rev.*, 65, 1441–1497. https://doi.org/10.1111/iere.12694

Carbon Brief (2025) ICJ: What the world court's landmark opinion means for climate change. *Carbon Brief*. https://www.carbonbrief.org/icj-what-the-world-courts-landmark-opinion-means-for-climate-change/ (accessed 17 October 2025).

Clarke, D. (2022) *BoJ green loans scheme gets underway*. Green Cent. Bank. https://greencentralbanking.com/2022/01/20/japan-green-loans-scheme/ (accessed 17 October 2025).

Dafermos, Y., Gabor, D., Nikolaidi, M., Pawloff, A., and van Lerven, F. (2020) *Decarbonising is easy, beyond market neutrality in the ECB's corporate QE*. NEF.

Downey, L., and Blyth, M. (2025) 'Macrofinance and the green transformation: nudging, attracting, and coercing capital towards decarbonization'. *Review of International Political Economy*, 32(3), 529–541. https://doi.org/10.1080/09692290.2025.2493797

Drudi, F., Moench, E., Holthausen, C., Weber, P.-F., Ferrucci, G., Setzer, R., Nino, V. D., Barbiero, F., Faccia, D., Breitenfellner, A., Faiella, I., Farkas, M., Bun, M., Fornari, F., Ciccarelli, M., Darracq Paries, M., Giovannini, A., Papadopoulou, N., Parker, M., Petroulakis, F., Hebbink, G., Piloiu, A., Hlásková, S. J., Ploj, G., Popov, A. A., Kapp, D., Lopez-Garcia, P., Lozej, M., Lydon, R., Manninen, O., Roos, M., Manzanares, A., Santabárbara, D., Schotten, G., Mikkonen, K., Sotomayor, B., Stracca, L., Mongelli, F. P., Montes-Galdón, C., Müller, G., Nerlich, C., Osiewicz, M., Cruz, L. V., Page, A., Avgousti, A., Diez-Caballero, A., Aubrechtova, J., Mendoza, A. F., Téllez, M. D., Grüning, P., Garcia-Sanchez, P., Isgro, L., Bua, G., Kashama, M. K., Queiroz, R., Rognone, L., Röhe, O., McInerney, N., Meinerding, C., Tsalaporta, P., Van Den End, J. W., Theofilakou, A., Weth, M., Osorno-Torres, B., and Ouvrard, J.-F. (2021) Climate change and monetary policy in the Euro area. *SSRN Electron. J.* https://doi.org/10.2139/ssrn.3928292

Durante, E., Ferrando, A., and Vermeulen, P. (2022) Monetary policy, investment and firm heterogeneity. *Eur. Econ. Rev.*, 148, 104251. https://doi.org/10.1016/j.euroecorev.2022.104251

ECB (2020) ECB to accept sustainability-linked bonds as collateral.

ECB (2021) ECB presents action plan to include climate change considerations in its monetary policy strategy.

ECB (2022) ECB takes further steps to incorporate climate change into its monetary policy operations.

ECB (2023a) Monetary policy decisions.

ECB (2023b) Combined monetary policy decisions and statement.

ECB (2023c) The role of financial stability considerations in monetary policy and the interaction with macroprudential policy in the euro area.

ECB (2024a) Changes to the operational framework for implementing monetary policy.

ECB (2024b) ESCB legal conference 2024.

ECB (2025a) Opinion of the European Central Bank of 8 May 2025 on proposals for amendments to corporate sustainability reporting and due diligence requirements (*CON*/2025/10).

ECB (2025b) An overview of the ECB's monetary policy strategy.

ECB (2025c) ECB to adapt collateral framework to address climate-related transition risks.

ECB (2025d) FAQ on the climate factor in the Eurosystem collateral framework.

ECJ (2015) Case C-62/14.

Egli, F., Steffen, B., and Schmidt, T. S. (2018) A dynamic analysis of financing conditions for renewable energy technologies. *Nat. Energy*, *3*, 1084–1092. https://doi.org/10.1038/s41560-018-0277-y

EIU (2024) ECB collateral policy threatens EU's path to net zero. *Econ. Intell. Unit*. https://www.eiu.com/n/ecb-collateral-policy-threatens-eus-path-to-net-zero/ (accessed 13 September 2025).

Elderson, F. (2022) *The European climate law and the European Central Bank.*
Erlandsson, U. (2025) ECB: necessary, not at all sufficient [*WWW Document*]. https://anthropocenefii.org/blog/ecb-necessary-not-sufficient (accessed 9 September 2025).
European Commission (2021) *Strategy for financing the Transitio to a Sustainable Economy.*
European Commission (2025) 2040 climate target – European Commission [*WWW Document*]. 2040 Clim. Target. https://climate.ec.europa.eu/eu-action/climate-strategies-targets/2040-climate-target_en (accessed 4 July 2025).
Gabor, D., and Braun, B. (2025) Green macrofinancial regimes. *Rev. Int. Polit. Econ.*, 1–27. https://doi.org/10.1080/09692290.2025.2453504
Giovanardi, F., Kaldorf, M., Radke, L., and Wicknig, F. (2023) The effectiveness of green collateral policy as an instrument of climate policy [*WWW Document*]. CEPR. https://cepr.org/voxeu/columns/effectiveness-green-collateral-policy-instrument-climate-policy (accessed 6 July 2025).
Hashmi, S. M., Syed, Q. R., and Inglesi-Lotz, R. (2022) Monetary and energy policy interlinkages: The case of renewable energy in the US. *Renew. Energy*, 201, 141–147. https://doi.org/10.1016/j.renene.2022.10.082
Heynen, P. (2022). The ECB going green: Impact on the interrelationship between monetary policy and banking supervision? *Maastricht J. Eur. Comp. Law*, 29, 667–684. https://doi.org/10.1177/1023263X231158219
IEA (2023). *World Energy Investment 2023.*
Jourdan, S., van Tilburg, R., Kramer, B., Simić, A., and Bronstering, G. (2024) *A green interest rate for the Eurozone: Evaluating the design choices. SSRN Electron. J.* https://doi.org/10.2139/ssrn.5015926
Kedward, K., Gabor, D., and Ryan-Collins, J. (2022) A modern credit guidance regime for the green transition (No. 294). *SUERF The European Money and Finance Forum.*
Krahé, M., and Heilmann, F. (2024) *Fossil fuel to the fire: Energy and inflation in Europe.* Dezernat Zukunft e.V., Berlin.
Kuroda, H. (2021) *Opening remarks by governor KURODA at the TCFD summit 2021 [WWW Document].* Bank Jpn. https://www.boj.or.jp/en/about/press/koen_2021/ko211005a.htm (accessed 17 October 2025).
Lagarde, C. (2020) *Remarks on the occasion of receiving the Grand Prix de l'Économie 2019 from Les Echos.*
Lagarde, C. (2025) *Re: Your letter* (QZ-012).
Mack, S. (2025) *Don't throw it under the Omnibus – The EU needs to make sustainability reporting more effective.* Hertie School, Jacques Delors Centre.
Martin, L. (2025) *Understanding the ECB's new "climate factor."* Reclaim Finance. https://reclaimfinance.org/site/en/2025/09/09/understanding-the-ebcs-new-climate-factor/ (accessed 13 September 2025).
Miller, H., and Dikau, S. (2022) Preventing a "climate Minsky moment": Environmental financial risk and prudential exposure limits, exploring the case study of the Bank of England's prudential regime.
Monnin, P. (2015) The impact of interest rates on electricity production costs. *Council on Economic Policy.* https://www.cepweb.org/wp-content/uploads/CEP_DN_Interest_Rates_Energy_Prices.pdf
NGFS (2021) Climate-related litigation: Raising awareness about a growing source of risk.
O'Connell, M. (2024) *Birth of a naturalist? Nature-related risks and biodiversity loss: Legal implications for the ECB.*
Oman, W., Salin, M., and Svartzman, R. (2024) Three tales of central banking and financial supervision for the ecological transition. *WIREs Clim. Change* 15, e876. https://doi.org/10.1002/wcc.876
People's Bank of China (2021) The People's Bank of China launches the carbon emission reduction facility [*WWW Document*]. http://www.pbc.gov.cn/en/3688110/3688172/4157443/4385345/index.html (accessed 13 September 2025).

Platform on Sustainable Finance (2025) Financing a clean and competitive transition – Monitoring capital flows to sustainable investments (No. final report).

Polzin, F., Sanders, M., Steffen, B., Egli, F., Schmidt, T. S., Karkatsoulis, P., Fragkos, P., and Paroussos, L. (2021) The effect of differentiating costs of capital by country and technology on the European energy transition. *Clim. Change*, 167, 26. https://doi.org/10.1007/s10584-021-03163-4

Razmi, S. F., Moghadam, M. H., and Behname, M. (2021) Time-varying effects of monetary policy on Iranian renewable energy generation. *Renew. Energy*, 177, 1161–1169. https://doi.org/10.1016/j.renene.2021.06.020

Schmidt, T. S., Steffen, B., Egli, F., Pahle, M., Tietjen, O., and Edenhofer, O. (2019) Adverse effects of rising interest rates on sustainable energy transitions. *Nat. Sustain.*, 2, 879–885. https://doi.org/10.1038/s41893-019-0375-2

Schnabel, I. (2021) *From market neutrality to market efficiency.*

Schnabel, I. (2022) *A new age of energy inflation: Climateflation, fossilflation and greenflation.*

Schnabel, I. (2023a) *Speech by Isabel Schnabel, Member of the Executive Board of the ECB, at the International Symposium on Central Bank Independence*. Sveriges Riksbank, Stockholm.

Schnabel, I. (2023b) *Monetary policy tightening and the green transition.*

Skyrman, V. (2024) *Industrial policy, progressive derisking, and the financing of Europe's green transition. ÖFSE Working Paper no. 78*, Vienna. https://doi.org/10.60637/2024-wp78

Smoleńska, A. (2025) European capitalisms in sustainability transition: The case of green bonds. *J. Eur. Public Policy*, 1–27. https://doi.org/10.1080/13501763.2025.2521395

Smoleńska, A., & Beukers, T. (2022). The ECB and financial stability. In T. Beukers, D. Fromage, & G. Monti (Eds.), *The New European Central Bank: Taking Stock and Looking Ahead* (1st edn, pp. 105–135). Oxford University Press: Oxford. https://doi.org/10.1093/oso/9780198871231.003.0005

Smoleńska, A., & Tokarski, P. (2022). The greening of the ECB Monetary Policy: A legal-economic analysis. In A. Herranz-Surrallés (Ed.), *Shining a light on energy*: 10 years of the Lisbon treaty, Natolin Nests Series No.1, College of Europe in Natolin, Warsaw.

Smoleńska, A., and van't Klooster, J. (2022) A risky bet: Climate change and the EU's microprudential framework for banks. *J. Financ. Regul.*, 8, 51–74. https://doi.org/10.1093/jfr/fjac002

van't Klooster, J. (2025) *Overcoming myopia in the ECB's 2025 monetary policy strategy review*. Dezernat Zukunft.

van't Klooster, J., and Weber, I. M. (2024) *Closing the EU's inflation governance gap – The limits of monetary policy and the case for a new policy framework for shockflation*. Study Requested ECON Comm. Eur. Parliam. https://doi.org/10.2139/ssrn.5069614

Waite, N. (2022) *Central banking and climate action – China steers credit to decarbonise.* Institute for Energy Economics and Financial Analysis.

Zhang, D., Wang, Y., and Peng, X. (2023) Carbon emissions and clean energy investment: Global evidence. *Emerg. Mark. Finance Trade*, 59, 312–323. https://doi.org/10.1080/1540496X.2022.2099270

Zilioli, C., and Ioannidis, M. (2022) Climate change and the mandate of the ECB: Potential and limits of monetary contribution to European green policies. *Common Mark. Law Rev.*, 59, 363–394. https://doi.org/10.54648/COLA2022029

PART V

Outlook

11

PROGRESSIVE INDUSTRIAL POLICY FOR THE GLOBAL SOUTH

A Latin American Structuralist Approach

José Miguel Ahumada and Fernando Sossdorf

11.1 The global economy in transition: from neoliberal globalisation to strategic rivalries

There is little doubt that the global economy is undergoing a profound transformation. Although the contours of the emerging international order remain blurred, it is increasingly clear that the neoliberal globalisation that governed international economic relations from the 1980s until the 2008 financial crisis is undergoing a fundamental mutation. This transformation is being driven by an intensifying trade war between the United States and China, unfolding within a broader context of technological, environmental, and social change shaped by the climate emergency and the ongoing digital revolution (Raza, 2024; UNCTAD, 2024).

The trade war has manifested itself across multiple international economic fronts. First, unilateral tariff threats and actions have initiated a growing structural trend towards economic fragmentation and a slowdown in global trade flows (WTO, 2025). In particular, U.S. tariff threats have compelled countries to renegotiate trade and investment rules to deepen ties with Washington, while simultaneously weakening their economic relations with China. Second, this conflict has prompted a resurgence of industrial policy in advanced economies. These policies have focused on three main objectives: reindustrialising domestic production (through measures such as the Inflation Reduction Act and the CHIPS Act under the Biden administration, centred on derisking via subsidies, grants, and financial support); import substitution (through barriers to foreign investment, such as the EU's Foreign Subsidies Regulation and the strengthening of FDI screening mechanisms); and the expansion of military production (via increased defence spending and loosening of public debt constraints, as in the cases of the EU, and France and Germany in particular).

DOI: 10.4324/9781003745563-17

Third, and more broadly, the trade war has catalysed a radical shift in the trade agendas of developed countries – moving away from the promotion of rule of law and multilateralism towards new priorities centred on strategic autonomy, sovereignty, and national security. These new criteria are, in practice, sidelining initiatives to tackle global challenges such as the climate crisis (Dosi *et al.*, 2024). Instead, the transition towards decarbonisation and electromobility has triggered a global race among developed economies to secure access to, provision of, and control over critical minerals such as lithium, copper, nickel, and rare earth elements located in various countries of the Global South. For example, the EU has been advancing trade agreements with countries such as Chile, Mexico, and MERCOSUR, in part to secure preferential access to the region's critical minerals (particularly lithium and copper) (Tröster *et al.*, 2025). China, for its part, has invested strategically in nickel production in Indonesia and lithium in Chile, while the United States has launched a public investment agenda to support domestic rare earth production and a package of industrial policies that subsidise firms that source mineral inputs either domestically or from allied countries (Ahumada *et al.*, 2025).

In this context, what role is Latin America playing within this international reconfiguration? What opportunities are emerging for the region to build new productive capabilities? This chapter offers both a diagnostic of the region and a set of progressive industrial and trade policy agendas aimed at fostering new development trajectories that can be productively dynamic, socially inclusive, and environmentally sustainable in the long term. The third section analyses the structural features of Latin America's productive and technological matrix, highlighting premature deindustrialisation, weak regional integration, and high vulnerability to the climate crisis. The fourth develops a progressive industrial policy framework grounded in four pillars: a pro-developmental and green FDI regime, a new model of productive regionalism, coordinated financial and tax strategies, and digital sovereignty. Finally, the conclusion emphasises the complementarities between a renewed Latin American development agenda and the progressive industrial policy initiatives currently unfolding within the European Union.

11.2 Contemporary Western industrial policies and implications for the Global South

The transitional juncture the global economy is currently undergoing is not one of stagnation but of reconfiguration. A set of emergent processes is shaping the global context in which countries of the Global South are embedded.

One key trend is the nature of industrial policy in advanced economies, which has been characterised by derisking strategies largely devoid of disciplinary mechanisms to ensure reinvestment aligned with global public objectives (such as addressing climate change). These strategies, that privileged "carrots without sticks" (Bulfone *et al.*, 2023; Gabor, 2023), are in part attributable to domestic political economy constraints that limit the capacity of these states to legislate conditionalities tied to public plans, thereby diminishing the regulatory potential of industrial policies and curbing their effectiveness in transforming productive structures (Gabor and Braun, 2025).

Beyond their character, the resurgence of industrial policy has been overwhelmingly concentrated in high-income countries. According to available data, the number of active industrial and trade policy interventions has surged from approximately 20,000 in 2014 to around 60,000 in 2025. Disaggregating these measures by income level reveals that, by 2024, 90% of active interventions were implemented by high-income (55%) and upper-middle-income (36%) countries. Moreover, an analysis of the type of interventions shows that high-income countries are uniquely capable of offering large-scale subsidies and financial incentives, while lower-income countries concentrate their interventions on tariffs and taxation (Alami *et al.*, 2025).

This asymmetry in policy instruments reflects structural disparities in fiscal, financial, and institutional capacities, positioning developed economies in a privileged stance within the unravelling multilateral trade system (Alami *et al.*, 2025). These economies can finance their industrial policies endogenously, and often bypass international trade rules that they themselves have previously promoted at multilateral, regional, and bilateral levels. In the meantime, such rules constrain the policy space of developing countries (Ahumada and Chang, 2025). In addition, advanced economies enjoy a regulatory advantage, derived from their control over key technological assets (protected by intellectual property rights) and the preferential treatment afforded to their overseas investments through an extensive network of bilateral investment treaties (BITs) and free trade agreements (FTAs).

In this context, countries of the Global South face a complex scenario. While developed economies possess the internal capacity to design and implement industrial policies, unilaterally erect trade barriers, and operate within an international legal framework that overprotects their tangible and intangible assets, developing economies lack these strategic tools. They tend to depend on external financing, are vulnerable to unilateral tariff actions, and face increasing pressures to constrain their policy space (Ahumada and Chang, 2025).

To illustrate this dynamic, it is instructive to examine the case of Latin America. Contemporary unilateral U.S. tariff threats against countries with which it maintains FTAs – such as Panama, Mexico, Colombia, and Chile – have made explicit how trade networks become instruments of arbitrary political leverage by dominant economies, a phenomenon described as "weaponized interdependence" (Farrell and Newman, 2019). These threats have compelled countries like Chile to enter renegotiations of FTA provisions, ranging from investment screening requirements to enhanced intellectual property protections. In other cases, such as Brazil, pressure has been exerted to modify domestic policies under threat of punitive tariffs. In this way, tariff threats have become selective and unilateral constraints on policy space – sticks that limit domestic autonomy. As Raúl Prebisch (1949) presciently observed, such tariffs function as de facto taxes imposed by developed economies on peripheral countries, undermining their development prospects.

Simultaneously, the EU has pursued the modernisation and negotiation of FTAs with MERCOSUR, Mexico, and Chile. These agreements aim not only to liberalise trade but also to reconfigure the region's policy space. For instance, the EU-MERCOSUR agreement restricts the use of key industrial policy tools, such as export taxes (used in Indonesia's nickel strategy). At the same time, in the case of Chile, contentious negotiations emerged over the regulation of critical minerals like lithium, leading to provisions that secure preferential access to such resources for the EU (Dünhaupt *et al.*, 2025).

Despite these ongoing negotiations, new trade agreements and unilateral pressures, the architecture of investment protection, e.g., Investor-State Dispute Settlements (ISDSs) mechanisms, remain firmly in place for developing countries, as do stringent intellectual property norms and restrictions on technology transfer enshrined in Latin America's trade agreements with developed economies. Thus, while policy space remains constrained by long-standing legal commitments, developed countries such as the United States can further limit that space through new unilateral threats.

This restrictive and geopolitically shaped regulatory framework coexists with a broader global techno-productive transition towards electromobility, in which Latin America risks becoming a contested zone among developed economies seeking access to and control over critical minerals. The region thus faces the risk of being relegated to a subordinate position in the emerging international division of labour associated with new green and digital technologies. The following section analyses how Latin America has arrived at this new global scenario, focusing on the region's key structural economic challenges and its position in the international economy.

11.3 Latin America, deindustrialisation and dependency

Latin America enters the new global industrial and technological reordering with severe structural constraints. These limitations, rooted in premature deindustrialisation, low productive complexity, limited intra-regional articulation, and multiple layers of dependence (monetary, financial, technological, and regulatory), have become even more visible in the current era of geoeconomic fragmentation.

11.3.1 Premature deindustrialisation and the erosion of technological capabilities

One of the most pressing challenges facing Latin America is the phenomenon of premature deindustrialisation. Unlike the historical trajectory of industrialised economies – which moved into the service sector after achieving high levels of industrial employment and technological sophistication – Latin American countries have seen a decline in their manufacturing share of GDP and employment at much earlier stages of development (Castillo and Martins, 2016; Palma, 2010).

This process has occurred without the parallel emergence of high-productivity service sectors, resulting in a structural decline in productivity and innovation.

Empirical evidence confirms that Latin America has experienced a long-term process of premature deindustrialisation, with the manufacturing sector shrinking both in its contribution to total value-added and in its share of employment. As shown in Figures 11.1 and 11.2, the share of manufacturing in total value-added peaked close to 20% in the late 1970s, but declined to under 15% by 2023. Similarly, manufacturing employment fell from nearly 18% in the 1980s to around 12% today. In countries like Brazil and Argentina, the manufacturing share of GDP dropped from over 23% in the 1970s to less than 13% in the 2020s. Meanwhile, economies such as Chile, Colombia, and Peru never developed significant manufacturing sectors, remaining heavily dependent on natural resource exports with little domestic value-added.

Deindustrialisation is not merely the loss of employment or value-added – it represents a deeper erosion of the structural conditions required for sustained development. From a structuralist perspective, the manufacturing sector has been – and will remain – the core driver of productivity growth, learning, and diversification. Its dense network of forward and backward linkages generates positive externalities across the economy, stimulates demand for skilled labour, and facilitates technological upgrading (Cimoli *et al.*, 2017).

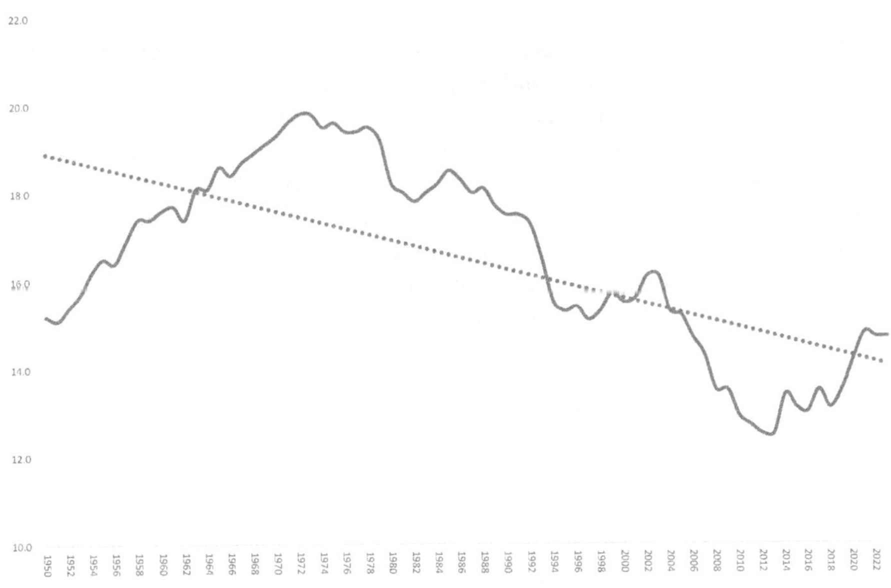

FIGURE 11.1 Share of manufacturing value added in total value-added (1950–2023), Latin America

Source: Author's elaboration based on UN Data.

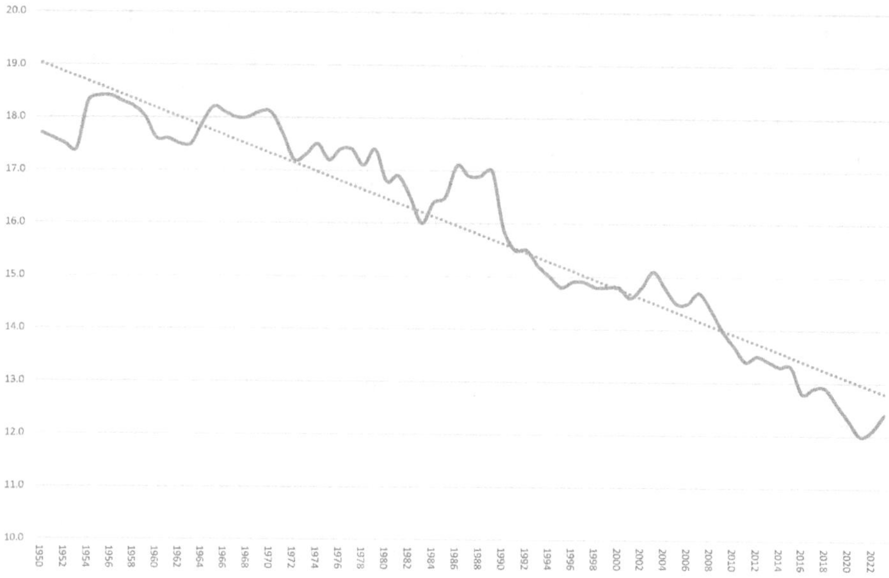

FIGURE 11.2 Share of manufacturing employment in total employment (1950–2023), Latin America

Source: Author's elaboration based on UN Data.

When manufacturing contracts, these virtuous dynamics are disrupted. The separation between production and innovation weakens cumulative learning processes, reduces the scope for technological spill-overs, and limits the emergence of complex and knowledge-intensive sectors. This concern has long been central to Latin American development thinking. Cimoli and Porcile (2011) have emphasised that transforming the productive structure – moving from low-productivity activities to sectors with greater technological intensity – is key to overcoming structural heterogeneity and the persistent dualism that defines the region's economies.

In this sense, the erosion of manufacturing in Latin America reflects more than just a sectoral adjustment. It consolidates a pattern of specialisation based on natural resource extraction and low-value services, thereby reinforcing external vulnerability, social inequality, and technological dependence. Revitalising manufacturing is thus not a nostalgic project, but a necessary condition for building productive sovereignty and inclusive development in the 21st century.

The loss of manufacturing capabilities becomes even more critical in today's global context. The current phase of geoeconomic fragmentation and technological competition requires states to possess strong productive and innovation systems. Without an industrial base capable of absorbing, adapting, and co-developing new technologies, countries risk being excluded from emerging value chains or relegated to their lowest segments. In this sense, Latin America's deindustrialisation

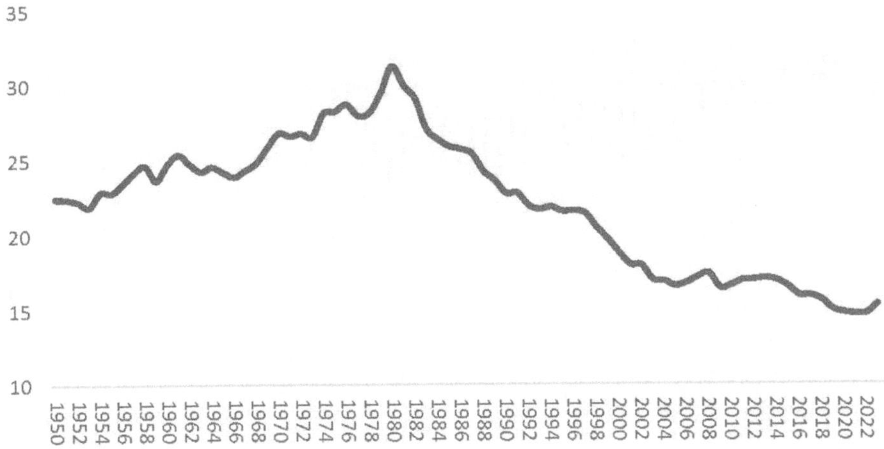

FIGURE 11.3 Latin America's labour productivity relative to the United States (1950–2023)

Source: Author's elaboration based on UN Data.

has not only weakened its current productive structure but has also left the region structurally unprepared to participate in the global race for technological sovereignty and strategic autonomy.

Technological asymmetries remain a key driver of structural divergence between Latin America and advanced economies. The persistent productivity gap with the United States, as shown in Figure 11.3, is not simply a matter of efficiency – it reflects deeper weaknesses in technological capabilities, innovation capacity, and the ability to absorb and adapt frontier technologies.

These technological asymmetries are directly reflected in Latin America's pattern of specialisation. Most countries in the region continue to rely on the export of commodities and low-complexity goods – primarily minerals, hydrocarbons, and basic agricultural products – whose competitive advantage stems from natural endowments rather than accumulated capabilities. As shown in Figure 11.4, with the exception of Mexico, the export structure of Latin American economies has become increasingly concentrated in either primary goods or low- and medium-technology manufactures, with limited presence in high-technology sectors. This pattern of "re-primarisation" not only limits value capture and learning opportunities, but also exposes countries to volatile terms of trade and external shocks. In periods of faster growth, imports of capital and intermediate goods tend to outpace export revenues, triggering recurrent balance-of-payments constraints that undermine the sustainability of development. In this sense, the region remains caught in a structural trap, where weak technological capabilities reinforce external vulnerability and limit the scope for productive upgrading.

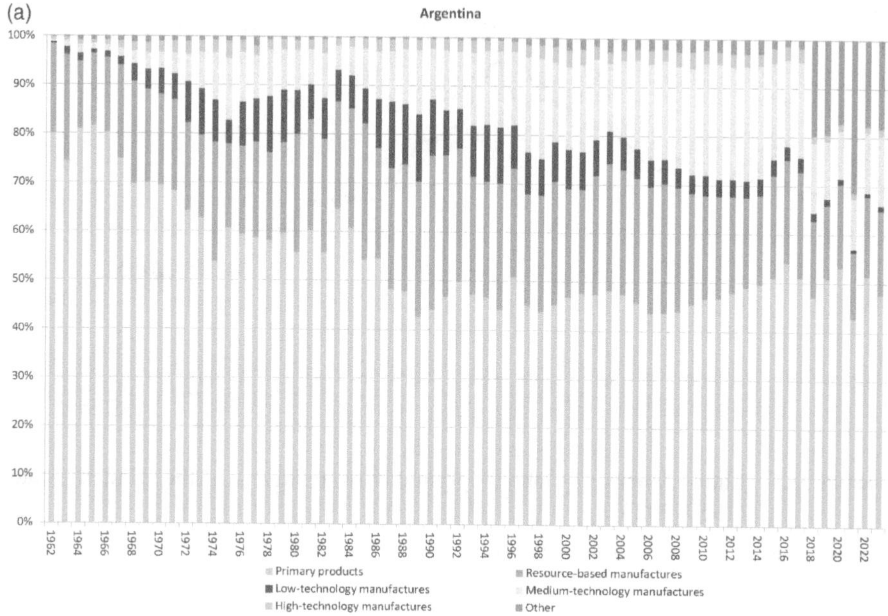

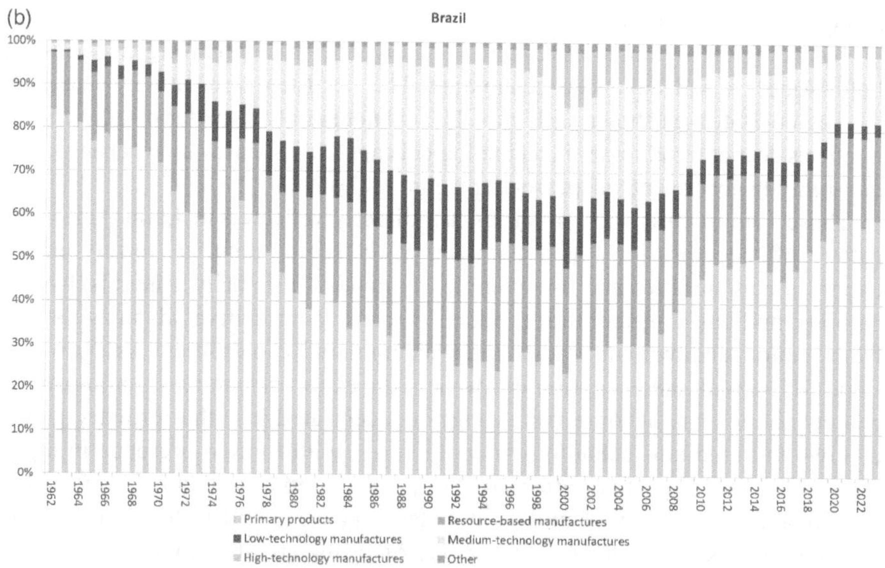

FIGURE 11.4 (a–c) Technological content of exports of Argentina, Brazil, and Mexico (1962–2023) (*Continued*)

Source: Authors' elaboration based on the United Nations, UN Comtrade database.

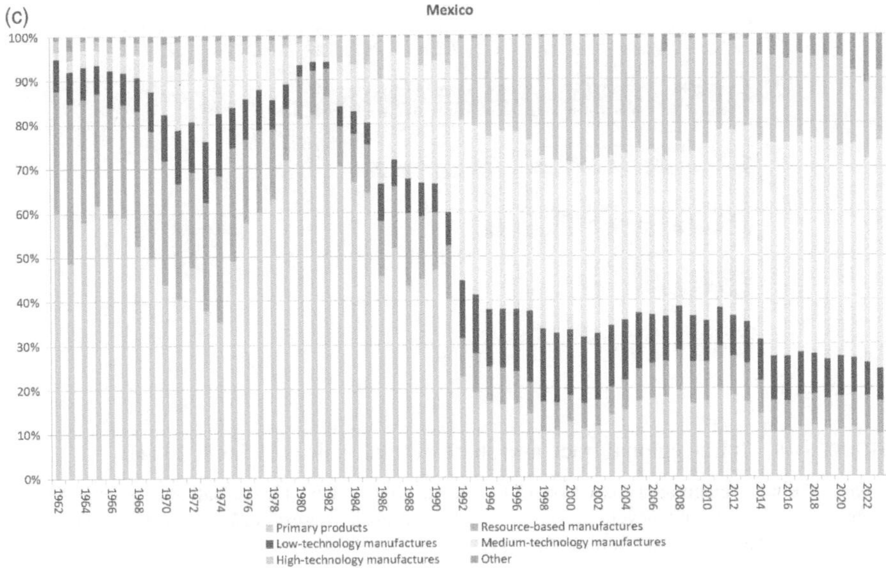

FIGURE 11.4 (Continued)

11.3.2 Low intra-regional trade and weak productive integration

A second structural vulnerability lies in the limited trade and production integration within the Latin American region. Unlike East Asia – which has built dense regional value chains through networks of subcontracting, investment, and technological learning – Latin America remains one of the least integrated regions in the world.

As illustrated in Figure 11.5, intra-regional trade represented only 13.9% of total trade in Latin America in 2024, placing it well below East Asia (48%) and the European Union (66%). Despite minor increases in the 1990s, the region has remained stagnant or even regressed in its integration efforts. This low level of intra-regional trade undermines economies of scale, limits technological spill-overs, and reduces the region's capacity to build autonomous value chains.

This problem is compounded by the nature of Latin America's most technology-intensive exports, which are disproportionately directed to regional markets – such as Brazil's pharmaceutical exports or Argentina's agro-industrial machinery. High-value sectors like these rarely reach global markets and instead depend on demand within the region. When regional demand contracts – due to crises or macroeconomic volatility – these sectors are among the first to decline.

The fragmentation of regional markets – a legacy of uncoordinated trade policies, lack of infrastructure, and overlapping integration schemes – has undermined efforts to build a productive regional space. While frameworks such as

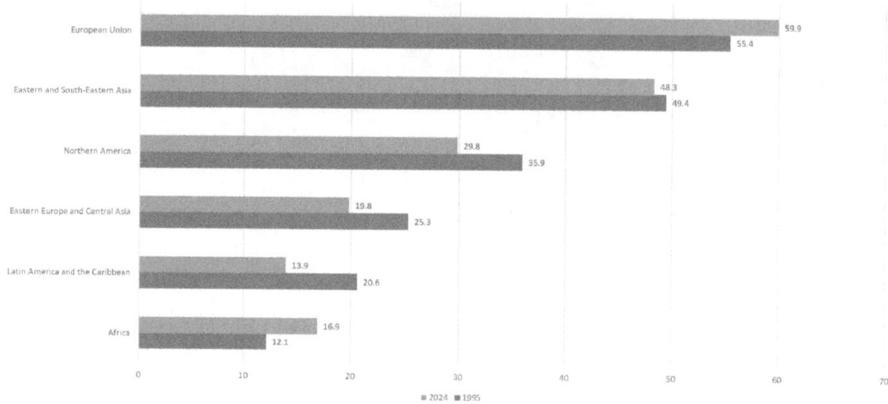

FIGURE 11.5 Intra-regional trade as a share of total trade (1995 and 2024)

Source: Author's elaboration based on UNCTADstat, Intra-regional trade database. United Nations Conference on Trade and Development (UNCTAD). Accessed August 2025. https://unctadstat.unctad.org/datacentre/dataviewer/US.IntraTrade

MERCOSUR, the Andean Community, or the Pacific Alliance have facilitated trade liberalisation, they have failed to create the institutional mechanisms needed for coordinated industrial development. The result has been the coexistence of multiple sub-regional blocs with weak articulation and divergent rules of origin, standards, and investment policies.

The low level of productive density and technological specialisation within Latin America also reflects the absence of a coordinated regional strategy to develop key sectors, especially those related to the green and digital transitions. Without such strategies, each country remains locked in a "race to the bottom" to attract foreign capital – often at the expense of regional cooperation and long-term development goals. Reversing this dynamic will require a new generation of regional institutions and policies that prioritise productive integration, knowledge exchange, and joint development of strategic sectors.

11.3.3 Monetary and financial dependence

Latin America's development has long been constrained by a persistent monetary dependence on the U.S. dollar. The dollar remains the dominant currency in trade invoicing, cross-border financing, and foreign exchange reserves throughout the region. According to ECLAC (2025b), 79.7% of the region's international bond issuances in 2024 were denominated in U.S. dollars, continuing a long-standing pattern of dollar dominance in Latin American financial markets. Despite a slight increase in currency diversification, the region's structural reliance on the U.S. dollar remains a source of financial vulnerability.

This structural currency mismatch creates major vulnerabilities. Because countries do not issue the currency in which they borrow, they are exposed to sudden shifts in global liquidity and exchange rates. This condition limits the ability of central banks to conduct countercyclical monetary policy, and subjects economies to external financial cycles beyond their control. In periods of U.S. monetary tightening – such as the post-2022 interest rate hikes by the Federal Reserve – capital flows tend to reverse, currency depreciation accelerates, and countries face inflationary pressures and rising debt burdens. These dynamics force central banks to adopt pro-cyclical responses, such as raising interest rates to defend exchange rates or contain inflation, which in turn depresses domestic investment and employment.

Moreover, access to international finance is highly stratified. Most countries in the region face credit constraints, high sovereign risk premiums, and dependence on credit rating agencies, whose assessments often amplify market volatility and reflect developed-country biases (Bustillo *et al.*, 2018). Only a few countries – such as Chile or Mexico – have achieved sustained access to capital markets under relatively favourable terms, while others – like Argentina or Ecuador – remain chronically excluded or subject to volatile financing conditions. This stratification reinforces financial asymmetries within the region and perpetuates a core-periphery dynamic in the global financial architecture.

Domestic financial systems, meanwhile, have failed to mobilise long-term capital for productive transformation given the absence of strong development banks. Credit in Latin America is both shallow and skewed towards consumption or real estate, with limited support for innovation, green infrastructure, or industrial upgrading. Most countries in the region lack dedicated financial institutions capable of channelling patient capital towards strategic sectors. With the partial exception of Brazil – where institutions such as BNDES have historically played a significant role in industrial and technological development – Latin American banks tend to operate with short-term horizons, high collateral requirements, and limited risk appetite. This constrains investment in sectors that require long gestation periods, coordination, and high uncertainty, such as clean energy, digital infrastructure, and advanced manufacturing.

These long-standing structural constraints coexist today with emerging signs of global de-dollarisation, as highlighted in recent research by J.P. Morgan (2025). Although the dollar continues to dominate global foreign exchange (FX) transactions (88%), foreign currency debt issuance (70%), and cross-border liabilities (48%), its share in central bank reserves has declined to under 60%, the lowest point in 2 decades. The most visible signs of de-dollarisation appear in commodity markets, where a growing share of energy transactions – particularly involving Russia, China, and India – are being settled in non-dollar currencies such as the yuan or rupee.

In parallel, Latin America remains the most dollarised region in the world in terms of bank deposits, with a deposit dollarisation rate of 19.1%, far exceeding Europe, the Middle East and Africa (15.2%) and Asia (9.7%). According to J.P.

Morgan, this deep financial dollarisation reflects a continued dependence on the dollar not only for external transactions but also for internal financial stability, especially during times of stress.

At a structural level, this financial dependence is not merely a result of recent monetary cycles, but the consequence of decades of deregulated financial liberalisation. As Botta *et al.* (2023) show, successive waves of capital inflows since the 1980s have reinforced premature de-industrialisation across Latin America, weakening the productive base of the region. Unlike East Asian economies – which combined industrial policy with capital controls – Latin American countries embraced financial openness without complementary productive strategies, leading to a reallocation of resources away from manufacturing and into low-productivity services or consumption-driven sectors. This legacy of financial openness has increased exposure to external shocks while constraining domestic capacity for structural transformation.

These vulnerabilities demand not only macroeconomic stabilisation tools, but a broader rethinking of development finance. As Botta *et al.* (2023) argue, macroprudential policies that curb excessive capital mobility can support not only short-term financial stability but also long-term structural change. However, Latin America currently lacks a coherent regional financial strategy. Unlike emerging powers such as China or Turkey – who have pursued deliberate efforts to reduce dollar dependence through bilateral trade arrangements, gold accumulation, and regional payment mechanisms – Latin American regional institutions remain fragmented, undercapitalised, or politically fragile.

In this context, financial dependence acts as a binding constraint on industrial policy and strategic autonomy. The region cannot determine the direction or scale of its development financing on its own terms. Instead, it remains subordinated to external markets, international financial institutions with limited countercyclical capacity, and foreign direct investment (FDI) conditioned by short-term profitability.

Reversing this dynamic will require a new generation of regional financial architectures: from cross-border payment systems and development banks with countercyclical firepower to financial instruments that mobilise long-term capital for productive, green, and digital transformations. In a world of growing geopolitical fragmentation and financial multipolarity, building monetary resilience is not only a technical imperative – it is a matter of sovereignty and development strategy.

11.3.4 Technological dependence and regulatory traps

Another core dimension of Latin America's structural dependency is its technological subordination to advanced economies and transnational corporations. The region has consistently lagged in investment in research and development (R&D), adoption of advanced technologies, and development of domestic innovation ecosystems.

According to ECLAC (2022), Latin America and the Caribbean spent only 0.56% of GDP on R&D (adding private and public expenditure) in 2019 – nearly 4 times less than advanced economies and far behind emerging leaders like China. Not only has the region failed to close the innovation gap, but the gap has widened in recent years. In contrast to OECD countries, where R&D investment has surpassed 2.7% of GDP, and countries like Korea or the United States spending more than 3% and 4%, respectively, Latin America has experienced a decline in R&D intensity since 2013.

This gap is compounded by a regressive structure of financing and execution. While in developed economies and China, business enterprises account for over 60–80% of R&D spending, in Latin America, the public sector remains the primary source of funding, with universities as the main executing agents. This limits the translation of R&D into applied technologies and commercial innovation. Most R&D in the region is directed towards basic research, in contrast to the experimental development focus seen in innovation-driven economies.

Patent activity reveals a similarly stark asymmetry. Between 2010 and 2020, global patent filings rose by 64%, but Latin America's share of global patents fell from 2.8% to 1.6%. Moreover, the vast majority of patents filed in the region come from non-resident applicants – over 90% in countries like Mexico and over 78% in Brazil. In both cases, U.S. sources account for a significant share of these filings, reinforcing the region's role as a peripheral node in global technology flows.

In countries like Brazil and Argentina, public research institutions have historically played an important role, but chronic underfunding, institutional instability, and political volatility have undermined their long-term impact. In the rest of the region, national innovation systems remain fragmented, under-resourced, and disconnected from industrial strategies.

This deficit has locked the region into a role as a passive adopter of foreign technologies, often through imported capital goods, licensing agreements, or embedded knowledge in FDI. The lack of technological autonomy reduces the capacity to adapt and reconfigure technologies according to local needs – especially in strategic sectors like health, biotech, electromobility, agriculture, or renewable energy.

The problem is compounded by intellectual property regimes embedded in FTAs and BITs, which disproportionately favour the interests of large firms based in the Global North. Clauses such as TRIPS-plus provisions and data exclusivity periods raise barriers to entry in knowledge-intensive industries and restrict the potential for reverse engineering, generic production, and localised innovation.

In addition, the ISDS mechanisms embedded in many Latin American investment treaties significantly reduce policy space. These mechanisms allow foreign investors to sue states for policies that affect expected profits, even when those policies pursue legitimate public goals like environmental regulation, public health, or industrial development. Several countries in the region – like Argentina, Chile, Ecuador, and Mexico – have faced costly ISDS cases linked to industrial or regulatory reforms.

These regulatory traps prevent countries from conditioning foreign investment on performance requirements (such as local content rules, technology transfer, or R&D commitments), limiting their ability to use FDI as a tool for upgrading. They also deter countries from implementing ambitious public policies for fear of litigation or retaliation under international arbitration.

Thus, while the Global North engages in active industrial policy – including subsidies, localisation, and export controls – Latin American countries remain bound by a regulatory framework designed to discipline them, not their counterparts. This asymmetry reinforces the periphery's structural role in the global economy: a supplier of raw materials and a passive market for high-tech goods and digital services.

11.3.5 Exposure to the climate crisis

Finally, Latin America faces substantial exposure to the impacts of climate change, both physically and economically. The region is home to a high concentration of climate-sensitive sectors, including agriculture, fishing, and water-intensive industries. At the same time, it contains key ecosystems – such as the Amazon, the Andes, and the Pacific and Atlantic coasts – that are especially vulnerable to rising temperatures, biodiversity loss, and extreme weather events.

Despite contributing less than 10% of global greenhouse gas emissions, the region is projected to suffer disproportionately from climate impacts. Climate risks in Latin America include a higher incidence of droughts, floods, tropical storms, glacial retreat, and sea-level rise – all of which threaten livelihoods, food security, and infrastructure.

This vulnerability is exacerbated by the region's economic dependence on fossil fuel exports (notably in Mexico, Venezuela, and Argentina) and carbon-intensive sectors such as mining, transportation, and monoculture agriculture. Without a coordinated strategy for climate adaptation and decarbonisation, the region risks facing both physical and transitional climate risks – that is, losses due to climate-related damages and economic exclusion due to new environmental standards imposed by trade partners or investors (e.g., the EU's Carbon Border Adjustment Mechanism, CBAM).

According to ECLAC (2024), Latin America has not accelerated its decarbonisation efforts at the pace required to meet global climate goals. While the global economy has doubled its decarbonisation rate since the 2015 Paris Agreement, the region has actually decelerated. In 2022, Latin America emitted approximately 0.6 metric tons of CO_2 per $1,000 of GDP (in 2015 dollars) – similar to the global average – but unlike other regions, it has not improved this indicator in recent years. If the global economy grows at an annual rate of 3%, the region would need to increase its decarbonisation speed by a factor of seven to meet the 1.5°C target. Failing to do so may lead not only to rising climate damage, but also to marginalisation from emerging low-carbon value chains.

At the same time, the green transition opens opportunities in strategic sectors such as renewable energy, critical minerals (lithium, copper), green hydrogen, and electromobility. Latin America already has the highest share of renewable energy in electricity generation in the world, 63.4% as of 2024, and enjoys significant potential in solar, wind, hydro, and bioenergy. However, the region currently exploits only a fraction of this potential, and faces major bottlenecks, including ageing transmission infrastructure and overreliance on climate-sensitive hydropower.

Furthermore, the necessary investments are substantial. ECLAC (2024) estimates that achieving the region's climate commitments would require annual investments equivalent to 3.7–4.9% of GDP through 2030. These figures underscore the scale of the structural transformation needed and the importance of aligning climate goals with industrial and financial strategies.

Without such alignment, green investments risk replicating the same extractive, enclave-based logic of past commodity booms – centred on raw material exports without local value addition, institutional strengthening, or community engagement. Hence, the transition to a low-carbon economy must be framed not only as an environmental necessity but also as an opportunity for productive upgrading, regional integration, and structural transformation.

In sum, Latin America's development is constrained by a multifaceted web of structural dependencies and vulnerabilities. The region remains locked in a subordinate position within the global economy, characterised by early deindustrialisation, weak productive integration, limited technological capabilities, and asymmetric exposure to global financial and climate dynamics.

The next section outlines a progressive industrial policy agenda that seeks to address these constraints not by retreating from globalisation, but by restructuring its terms. This agenda is grounded in four pillars: a new green FDI regime; productive regionalism; financial tax coordination; and digital sovereignty and regional development.

11.4 A progressive industrial policy agenda from the Global South

Latin America approaches this shifting global landscape carrying a set of structural constraints that have been analysed in the previous section. Together, these factors have eroded the region's growth capacity and put it at a disadvantaged position within global trade and investment flows. Addressing these challenges requires not just adaptation, but a strategic rethinking of the region's development model.

First, as already discussed, Latin America suffers from a low level of intra-regional trade and weak productive articulation. Unlike Asia – where platforms such as ASEAN have supported dense regional value chains and high-tech export dynamism – Latin America has failed to consolidate a robust regional market. As shown in Section 11.3.2, intra-regional trade accounts for only 13.9% of the region's total trade, one of the lowest figures globally. This is particularly concerning because the most sophisticated and value-added exports from the region are primarily destined to neighbouring countries (Sossdorf, 2024), which underscores the importance of revitalising a productive regionalism agenda, as will be discussed in the following subsections.

Second, while the region has a long tradition of industrial policy – particularly between the post-war era and the 1980s – these policies have significantly declined since the implementation of neoliberal reforms. Over the past two decades, industrial policy in Latin America has been inconsistent, susceptible to political cycles, underfunded, and limited in its ability to foster technological learning and spill-overs (Peres and Primi, 2024). Even during favourable conditions such as the 2003–2013 commodity boom, windfall revenues were largely allocated to redistributive programmes decoupled from structural transformation (Cimoli, 2023). This underscores the need for a new generation of industrial policies that are both politically resilient and strategically aligned with green and digital transitions.

Third, as previously noted, the region remains embedded in a multidimensional framework of dependence – monetary, financial, technological, and regulatory – that severely constrains national policy space. These forms of dependence not only limit the capacity of states to design autonomous development strategies but also expose them to external shocks and legal frameworks that restrict the use of key policy instruments. As shown in the previous section, Latin American countries often operate under currency mismatches, rely on external financing, adopt foreign technologies under restrictive IP regimes, and remain subject to investment treaties that curtail their sovereignty.

A progressive industrial policy agenda must not only address these structural limitations, but also (and considering the impact on the region), contribute to the protection of global commons – particularly the climate – and ensure the inclusion of diverse societal voices in policymaking. In this sense, Latin America's challenges imply an agenda of industrial policy that works at different scales, from national, regional to multilateral (Perrone, 2025). Today, industrial policy in the Global North is being reoriented towards national security, with limited emphasis on deep decarbonisation or regional employment upgrading (Dosi *et al.*, 2024). Latin America can offer an alternative: a participatory, sustainability-focused industrial strategy committed to safeguarding global commons.

11.4.1 A pro-developmental and green framework for FDI

FDI remains a key source of capital for Latin America. However, it has primarily targeted extractive industries, renewable energy, and domestic oligopolistic markets. Between 2020 and 2024, processed natural resources, mining, oil, and gas accounted for one-third of all investment announcements, while renewable energy comprised nearly 20% (ECLAC, 2025a). Yet, the region's role in electromobility-related value chains is limited to initial stages such as extraction and minimal processing of lithium or copper.

Several countries in the region have adopted national industrial derisking policies aimed at encouraging private investment in the production and processing of these critical minerals. Chile, Brazil, and Mexico, for example, have implemented clean investment incentives, long-term power purchase agreements (PPAs), joint ventures to diversify costs and risks, and state-guaranteed investment agreements.

However, these mechanisms operate within a private investment framework driven by short-term profitability, which limits both the scale and the pace of the green investment needed to confront climate change (Christophers, 2024; Gabor and Braun, 2025). To move beyond the derisking paradigm, the region should pursue a new pro-green developmental compact with FDI. By leveraging its market power in critical minerals such as lithium, copper, and rare earths, Latin America could introduce performance-based requirements that steer FDI towards more dynamic and sustainable productive activities. Such entry conditions could include technology transfer obligations – such as local content rules, reinvestment of profits in R&D, open-patent frameworks for domestic suppliers, and mandatory joint ventures with local firms (Ahumada and Chang, 2025).

Such regulatory frameworks have been crucial in the industrial policies of developmental states like Norway, South Korea, and China. For Latin America, a regional – not solely national – regulatory agenda for technology transfer is vital. This would avoid a normative "race to the bottom" among countries, reinforce regional bargaining power, and enhance each nation's negotiation leverage. Regional coordination should prioritise the creation of local productive capabilities in sectors where Latin America holds market power. These efforts should stimulate export diversification (towards more technologically complex stages in copper and lithium value chains), foster industrial and technical service linkages, and accelerate the shift towards green technologies.

Nonetheless, this agenda faces significant political economy constraints. These include collective action problems and diverging national interests, as well as legal barriers stemming from FTA and BIT clauses, particularly those involving investment protection and ISDS mechanisms, which de jure limit countries' options for implementing technology transfer measures (Chang, 2002; Thrasher, 2021).

Support from international partners, such as the EU, for a green investment regime would be decisive. In particular, the EU's social movements advocating for ISDS reform and less asymmetric investment frameworks create opportunities for advancing a new international agenda for collaboration.

11.4.2 Towards a new productive regionalism

The previous proposal gains real traction only when complemented by broader industrial policy agendas. A second fundamental priority is the consolidation of regional productive and trade networks. In a context of growing global fragmentation and uncertainty, Latin America must deepen intra-regional trade and investment to foster productive autonomy and reduce carbon footprints. Today, stability is grounded in proximity. Strategic sectors like electromobility – which depend on critical minerals like copper and lithium – offer a platform for regional productive diversification and value chain upgrading (Lebdiou, 2024).

Historically, successful development experiences have been tied to the consolidation of large domestic or regional markets. The U.S. exemplified such development via a dynamic domestic manufacturing market and dense investment networks. Similarly, East Asian industrialisation revolved around a regional trade and productive ecosystem led initially by Japan, which incorporated neighbouring countries into value chains. As Japan moved up the complexity ladder, it transferred mature industries to its neighbours (Kojima, 2000). Likewise, the European Coal and Steel Community (ECSC) began as a regional industrial planning initiative aimed at diffusing technological progress across the region.

Despite various attempts throughout the 20th century, Latin America has remained a fragmented "continental archipelago", both productively and commercially. Regional integration has often meant regional disintegration, especially as countries inserted themselves into global markets as natural resource exporters, weakening intra-regional manufacturing markets. Yet, today the region is well positioned in strategic sectors for the green transition, including wind, solar, and hydroelectric energy, green hydrogen, and critical minerals like lithium and copper. These resources may offer a shift from the "commodity lottery" to a "critical mineral and green energy lottery". The question is how to ensure this potential boom builds long-term productive capacities rather than another cycle of short-lived growth followed by stagnation. A key pillar is the creation of a regional industrial ecosystem around these strategic sectors. Regional value chains can offer greater stability, less external dependence, and a platform for regional mineral processing and industrialisation. Given the importance of lithium for electromobility and the Southern Cone's market dominance, a priority should be to establish a regional system whereby, for instance, lithium is extracted in Bolivia using Chilean and Argentine technology, incorporated into Brazilian batteries, and assembled into electric vehicles in Mexico or Brazil, or exported via Chile (UNCTAD, 2025).

This vision does not necessarily require a regional trade agreement – which remains difficult in Latin America – but rather a form of a new "productive regionalism". This includes: (1) strengthening bilateral and trilateral agreements for industrial and technological complementarity among regional firms; (2) sustained investment in bi-oceanic corridors and productive infrastructure; and (3) creation of intergovernmental public enterprises to act as innovation catalysts and develop dense, high-tech networks, as exemplified by Airbus or Eurostar in Europe.

Although Latin American regionalism has historically yielded limited results, current conditions of economic fragmentation, tighter environmental standards (favouring shorter value chains), and strong leverage in critical minerals create a unique opportunity to reorient policies towards coordinated regional industrialisation.

11.4.3 *Aligning productive regionalism with financial and tax cooperation*

The financial challenge facing Latin America's energy transition is twofold: scaling up investment and redirecting financial flows towards new green sectors (Galindo *et al.*, 2022). According to recent estimates, the region received an average of $52 billion per year in climate finance between 2021 and 2022, accounting for just 4% of the global total. This represents only 20–25% of the financing required to place the region on a low-carbon, resilient development path. The situation is even more dire in climate adaptation: of the $6.1 billion currently allocated, less than 10% of the estimated need of between $65 and 87 billion annually – is being met. This gap is particularly concerning given that the region harbours strategic ecosystems, is highly exposed to extreme climate events, and relies on climate-sensitive productive structures (Climate Finance Lab, 2024; Zero Carbon Analytics, 2023).

In capitalist economies, the availability of credit determines the scale and direction of investment. Governments, through central banks and financial systems, have the capacity to influence the pace and direction of economic growth. A core objective for Latin America should be to increase and steer investment towards strategic sectors aligned with green development. Three key measures are necessary. First, recapitalising existing regional development institutions, particularly the Development Bank of Latin America and the Caribbean (CAF), would allow them to expand their financing capacity and play a greater role in the energy transition. Second, strengthening institutional networks between regional development banks and national and interregional ones. For example, coordination between CAF, the European Investment Bank (EIB), the BRICS+ New Development Bank, and national development banks like Brazil's BNDES could support the articulation of a strategic regional development finance agenda (Ocampo, 2025). Ultimately, aligning national and multilateral development banks would enable joint investments in key sectors, improve access to favourable financing, and strengthen autonomy from global financial centres.

Third, to ensure influence over the direction of financial flows, credit should be tied to strict conditionalities and clearly defined selectivity criteria. These might include support for energy transition investments that incorporate local suppliers, partnerships with public firms, R&D spending, and reinvestment of a share of profits into the local economy (Gabor and Braun, 2025).

Taxation is also fundamental. Beyond their fiscal and redistributive functions, taxes can redirect capital from unproductive or rent-seeking sectors to productive ones. In 2022, tax evasion in Latin America reached 6.1% of regional GDP, while financial assets held in tax havens amounted to nearly 16% of its GDP. During Brazil's G20 presidency, a global minimum tax on the super-rich was proposed, with the potential to generate some $250 billion annually. While multilateral coordination is crucial, its implementation is slow and complex. As an interim measure, Latin America could push for a minimum regional corporate tax through platforms such as the Union of South American Nations (UNASUR) or the Community of Latin American and Caribbean States (CELAC), redirecting revenues towards regional productive transformation – particularly infrastructure for the energy transition. This would require that part of the revenue be administered by a regional institution (such as CAF or another representative body), which would define investment priorities in line with the regional productive agenda.

11.4.4 Digital sovereignty and regional development

The current transition is both ecological and digital. In the digital dimension, a profound structural gap persists between the Global North and the rest of the world. The digital economy exhibits strong network and scale effects that create inherent monopolistic tendencies. Large digital platforms, primarily headquartered in developed countries, benefit from first-mover advantages, controlling massive data flows and processing infrastructure that translate into growing competitive superiority. This advantage stems from, among other things, the free extraction of digital data that – once appropriated, processed, and transformed – becomes lucrative private digital assets (UNCTAD, 2021). The Global South often serves as an unpaid provider of this "raw material", with limited internal processing capacity, and thus depends heavily on foreign platforms, undermining both sovereignty and geopolitical autonomy.

In this context, Latin America must reclaim control over its digital resources. Just as the region once advocated for "permanent sovereignty over natural resources" in multilateral forums – a foundational principle of the Third World's campaign for a New International Economic Order – it can now champion "Permanent Data Sovereignty" in its own digital governance proposals and in broader efforts to reform the multilateral order (Ahumada and Chang, 2025). This principle can be operationalised through institutional mechanisms already adopted by some national digital sovereignty initiatives, such as public data repositories or strong data localisation measures (Chander and Sun, 2023).

However, reclaiming ownership of digital raw materials is not enough. Due to the digital economy's inherent scale economies and network effects, the ability to process this data efficiently requires access to them at a big scale. This calls for regional coordination in common investments in infrastructure – such as data centres and public broadband cable networks – to foster the emergence of national and regional digital processing hubs.

Finally, the region must ensure sufficient policy space in bilateral and multilateral trade agreements to implement and harmonise digital localisation requirements for foreign platforms and to levy taxes on digital services. These measures are currently restricted by provisions embedded in numerous trade agreements and are actively contested within the WTO. Advancing this agenda will thus require sustained international dialogue and legal reform (Ahumada and Chang, 2025).

11.5 Conclusions: towards global progressive alliances for transformation

Latin America enters this new international scenario with deep structural constraints – trade, financial, technological, and regulatory – alongside the severe and mounting impacts of climate change. In this context, industrial policy agendas must not only differ from and surpass those of advanced economies in ambition, but also move beyond the region's own past approaches to productive transformation. Yet, such ambition collides with Latin America's limited political and institutional capacity to implement coherent strategies. Long-standing problems of collective action and coordination persist, while technological and financial dependencies on developed economies continue to restrict policy autonomy.

To overcome these barriers, support from international partners such as the European Union will be decisive, particularly in fostering a pro-green investment regime and strengthening regional environmental governance. The EU's Green Deal and its policies on sustainable finance and carbon border adjustment mechanisms, alongside Latin America's Escazú Agreement and emerging frameworks for biodiversity and ecosystem protection, offer complementary bases for a bi-regional environmental and industrial partnership. The EU's progressive social movements – advocating for reforms to ISDS mechanisms and for more symmetrical investment frameworks – further open avenues for advancing a new international agenda of cooperation. For instance, coordination between CAF, the EIB, the BRICS+ New Development Bank, and national development banks such as Brazil's BNDES could underpin a strategic regional development finance agenda (Ocampo, 2025).

Such collaboration would not only expand the region's policy space and strengthen green financing capacities, but also help ensure a just global transition – one of the major challenges currently facing the international community.

References

Ahumada, J. M., and Chang, H-.J. (2025) A New International Economic Order for the XXI century: an agenda for industrial and trade policies from the Global South. *Review of Keynesian Economics*, 13(4), 562–580.

Ahumada, J. M., Kracht, W., and López, D. (2025) *New Thinking Around Critical Minerals in Latin America*. LAPEG, Georgetown: Georgetown University.

Alami, I., Taggart, J., and Chodor, T. (2025) Rebuilding the ladder? Contemporary contests over industrial policy. *Global Policy*, 0–1, 14.

Botta, A., Yajima, G., and Porcile, G. (2023) Finance-led premature de-industrialization and the role of external macroprudential policy for post-COVID-19 transformative development: Latin America in a comparative perspective. In E. Pérez Caldentey (Ed.), *Financial Openness, Financial Fragility and Policies for Economic Stability: A Comparative Analysis Across Regions of the Developing World* (pp. 381–397). Santiago, Chile: Economic Commission for Latin America and the Caribbean (ECLAC).

Bulfone, F., Ergen, T., and Kalaitzake, M. (2023) No strings attached: Corporate welfare, state intervention, and the issue of conditionality. *Competition & Change*, 27(2), 253–276.

Bustillo, I., Perrotti, D. E., and Velloso, H. (2018) *Sovereign credit ratings in Latin America and the Caribbean: trends and impact on debt spreads. Studies and Perspectives – ECLAC Office in Washington*

Castillo, M. and Martins, A. (2016) *Premature Deindustrialization in Latin America.* Serie Desarrollo Productivo, United Nations Commission for Latin America and the Caribbean, Santiago de Chile. https://hdl.handle.net/11362/40241

Chander, A., and Sun, H. (2023) *Data Sovereignty*. Oxford, UK: Oxford University Press.

Chang, H-.J. (2002) *Kicking Away the Ladder*. London, UK: Anthem Press.

Cimoli, M. (2023) Posglobalización y reindustrialización en América Latina. La condicionalidad de la política industrial y el "Keynesianismo-Igualitario". *Ensayos Económicos No. 82*, Banco Central de Argentina.

Cimoli, M. and Porcile, G. (2011) Learning, technological capabilities, and structural dynamics. In J. A. Ocampo and J. Ros (Eds.), *The Oxford Handbook of Latin American Economics*. Oxford, UK: Oxford University Press.

Cimoli, M., Porcile, G., Martins, A., and Sossdorf, F. (2017) Productivity, social expenditure and income distribution in Latin America. *Brazilian Journal of Political Economy*, 37(4), 660–679. https://doi.org/10.1590/0101-31572017v37n04a01

Christophers, B. (2024) *The Price is Wrong*. New York, NY: Verso.

Climate Finance Lab. (2024) *Latin America and the Caribbean: a region lagging behind on climate finance*. https://www.climatefinancelab.org/news/lac-region-lags-climate-finance/ (accessed 17 October 2025).

Dosi, G., Cristi, L., Riccio, F., and Virgillito, M. (2024) Industrial policies for global commons: why it is time to think of the ghetto rather than of the moon. *LEM Working Paper Series*, 2024/32.

Dünhaupt, P., Gräf, H., Jimenez, V., and Jungmann, B. (2025) Industrial policy space in emerging economies: the case of Chile and the energy raw materials chapter in the EU-Chile Free Trade Agreement. *IPE Working Paper*, No. 251/2025.

Economic Commission for Latin America and the Caribbean (ECLAC) (2022) *Innovation for Development: The Key to a Transformative Recovery in Latin America and the Caribbean (LC/CCITIC.3/3)*. Santiago, Chile: United Nations.

Economic Commission for Latin America and the Caribbean (ECLAC) (2024) *Development Traps in Latin America and the Caribbean: Vital Transformations and How to Manage Them*. Santiago, Chile: ECLAC.

Economic Commission for Latin America and the Caribbean (ECLAC) (2025a) *Foreign Direct Investment in Latin America and the Caribbean, 2025*. Santiago, Chile: ECLAC.

Economic Commission for Latin America and the Caribbean (ECLAC) (2025b) *Capital Flows to Latin America and the Caribbean: 2024 Year-in-review and Early 2025 Developments (LC/WAS/TS.2025/2)*. Santiago, Chile: ECLAC.

Farrell, H. and Newman, A. (2019) Weaponized interdependence: how global economic networks shape state coercion. *International Security*, 44(1), 42–79

Gabor, D. (2023) The (European) Derisking State. *Stato e Mercato*, 1/2023, 53–84.

Gabor, D. and Braun, B. (2025) Green macrofinancial regimes. *Review of International Political Economy*, 32(3), 542–568.

Galindo, L., Hoffman, B., and Vogt-Schilb, A. (2022) ¿Cuánto costará lograr los objetivos del cambio climático en América Latina y el Caribe? BID, *Working Paper, WP-1310*.

Kojima, K. (2000) The 'flying geese' model of Asian economic development: origin, theoretical extensions, and regional policy implications. *Journal of Asian Economics*, 11(4), 375–401.

Lebdiou, A. (2024). *Survival of the greenest*. Cambridge: Cambridge University Press.

J.P. Morgan. (2025) *De-dollarization: is the US dollar losing its dominance?* https://www.jpmorgan.com/insights/global-research/currencies/de-dollarization

Ocampo, J.A. (2025) *Financing for Development*. Cambridge, UK: Cambridge University Press.

Palma, J. G. (2010) Why has productivity growth stagnated in most Latin American countries since the neoliberal reforms? In J. A. Ocampo and J. Ros (Eds.), *The Oxford Handbook of Latin American Economics*. Oxford, UK: Oxford University Press.

Peres, W. and Primi, A. (2024) Industrial policy in Latin America. In M. Vernengo, E. Perez-Caldentey, and J. Ghosh (Eds.), *The New Palgrave Dictionary of Economics*. London, UK: Palgrave Macmillan.

Perrone, N. (2025) Mission impossible? Promoting global sustainable development in times of national industrial policies. *Global Policy*, 0, 1–8.

Prebisch, R. (1949) El desarrollo económico de la América Latina y algunos de sus principales problemas. *El Trimestre Económico*, 16(63), 347–431.

Raza, W. (2024) Towards a progressive industrial policy for the twin transformation in the European Union. *Synthesis Report (21/2025)*. Vienna: ÖFSE Research Report no. 21. https://doi.org/10.60637/2025-rr21

Sossdorf, F. (2024) The rise and stagnation of Chile's export cycle. *Latin American Journal of Trade Policy*, 7(18). https://doi.org/10.5354/0719-9368.2024.74309

Thrasher, D. (2021) *Constraining Development*. London, UK: Anthem Press.

Tröster, B., Papatheophilou, S., and Küblböck, K. (2025) *Strategic Autonomy Meets Global Dependency*. Vienna: *ÖFSE Briefing Paper* 36. https://doi.org/10.60637/2025-bp36

UNCTAD (2021) *Digital Economy Report 2021*. Geneva: United Nations.

UNCTAD (2025) Harnessing regional integration and green industrial policy for enhancing sustainable development in Latin America. *Policy Brief*, PB/2025/1 (No. 118).

UNCTAD (2024) *Trade and Development Report*. Geneva: United Nations.

WTO (2025) *Global Trade Outlook and Statistics*. Geneva: WTO Secretariat.

Zero Carbon Analytics (2023) *Promises and Reality of Climate Finance Flows in Latin America and the Caribbean*. Briefing, November 2024.

12

TOWARDS PROGRESSIVE INDUSTRIAL POLICY FOR THE TWIN TRANSFORMATION

A Proposal

Werner Raza, Christa Schlager, Viktor Skyrman, and Michael Soder

12.1 Introduction

The chapters in this volume demonstrate that the Twin Transformation first and foremost is a political process. As mature technological solutions already exist in many areas, e.g. solar PV, wind turbines, batteries, heat pumps, and electric vehicles, the major threats to the green and digital transformation have to do with social and political factors. While some of these factors emanate from increased geopolitical conflict or from global pandemics and thus are beyond the EU's direct sphere of influence, others, such as political and social resistance or lack of resources, can be overcome by determined political action within the EU. Indeed, recent modelling exercises have shown, for instance, that managing the distributional issues from carbon pricing will be pivotal to maintain social support for the Twin Transformation in the medium-term future until 2040 (Heussaff et al., 2024). Successful transformatory change is thus first and foremost a question of combined political commitment of the state, the corporate sector and civil society.

Given the profoundness of the required changes and their long-term nature, a successful green and digital transformation process will depend on promoting its legitimacy and maintaining it over the next 25 years. Evidently, this is easier said than done. Against the current background of multiple crises exacerbating societal anxieties, the challenge of the coming five years consists precisely in reinserting confidence both to citizens, workers and the business sector that the strategic agenda initiated with the European Green Deal needs not only to be maintained, but accelerated. This will place heavy demands on EU institutions and national governments. Both will have to balance the exigencies of the long-term strategic Twin Transformation agenda with those of managing more frequent short-term crisis situations. To perform this, governments will need enlarged capacities and

DOI: 10.4324/9781003745563-18

capabilities. Nonetheless, even the most capable government will not be able to do all of that alone. The cooperation of social actors supporting the strategic trajectory of the Twin Transformation will be pivotal.

As legitimacy forms the basis of the social bond between governments and the members of society, a reinvigoration of a progressive Twin Transformation agenda will depend on mobilising new sources of both input and output legitimacy. Input legitimacy will depend on providing a compelling vision for the transformation of society based on solidarity. Such a vision cannot be definitive, but should provide the basis for further discussion and development amongst a broad spectrum of stakeholders. The vision should lay down not only the overall objectives and principles but also give guidelines on specific policy areas. In our view, this should encompass six thematic axes, or pillars, as graphically represented by (Figure 12.1). These are (1) enhancing spaces for public participation, and (2) ensuring a fair distribution of benefits and costs. Output legitimacy will require (3) a strategic transformation agenda accelerating the transformation in key areas, (4) a governance framework with strong capacities and capabilities to implement reform policies, (5) a set of funding mechanisms and instruments proportionate to the required investments, and (6) an EU global cooperation agenda that mobilises international

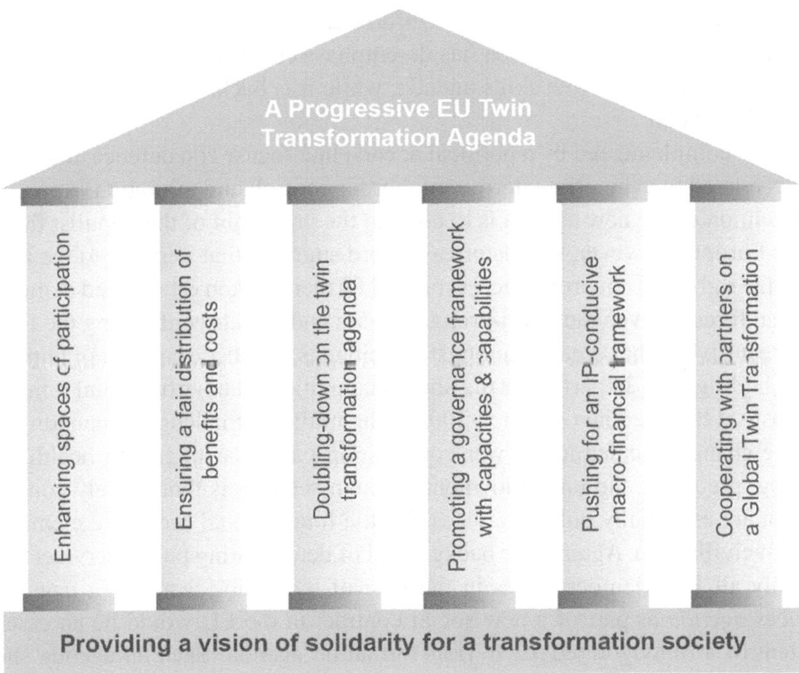

FIGURE 12.1 A progressive EU twin transformation agenda

Source: Authors' own elaboration.

support for the Twin Transformation. While none of this is new, and is to some extent reflected in the current framework of the Twin Transformation, amble room for improvement does exist. In the following, against the background of the policy agenda of the Commission as presented in particular in the new Competitiveness Compass (European Commission, 2025), we will briefly outline each of these elements in turn.

12.2 An agenda for a progressive industrial policy for the twin transformation

12.2.1 The basis: providing a vision of solidarity for a transformation society

In times of crisis, security becomes the overarching demand of both citizens and the business sector. To the sequence of shocks befalling Europe during the last five years, European policy-makers have responded by increasingly securitising every policy domain. While understandably defence has become a priority, the other priority has been economic security under the slogans of resilience, strategic autonomy, and technological sovereignty. Indeed, in tandem with competitiveness, the strategic guidelines of the new Commission have put economic security centre-stage (von der Leyen, 2024). Unfortunately, the ongoing political realignment under the new Commission has de-emphasised both the social dimension by essentially confining it to a skills agenda, while it is backtracking on the environmental dimension

This is complemented by a political agenda that focuses on defence and security threats related to cybercrime, terrorism, border control, and migration. Apparently, the intention of the new agenda is to contain the onslaught of the populist far-right across Europe. However, the historical record suggests that aligning to the agenda of the far-right will not prove successful and further weaken established democratic political forces. Given the multi-pronged crises and threats confronting the EU and the insecurity this has created amongst EU citizens, a holistic concept of human security highlighting in particular the socio-economic and environmental dimension will instead be essential (Altvater, 2003). The multiple challenges emanating from climate change, pandemics or war comprise in particular threats to health, food, housing, precarity, and unemployment. Human security is thus closely connected to what are essentially public services, i.e. the foundational economic elements of modern civilisation. Against the background of deteriorating public services across virtually all EU Member States in the face of increasing demand, a *new public services agenda* as part of a new social contract in the EU would be an essential element of a reinvigorated Twin Transformation agenda. Such an agenda should be based on the recognition that satisfying basic human needs stabilises society and thus forms the foundation for the capitalist market economy (see also Bärnthaler *et al.*, 2025). For all its merits, current Commission proposals, including investments in skills, lower energy prices, or to invest into the resilience of medical and drug supplies, address the foundational economy only in a partial and selective way. Amidst a higher frequency of natural hazards and extreme weather events, in conjunction with the likelihood of pandemics as well as of geopolitical crises, safeguarding social reproduction will arguably present one of the biggest challenges of the transformation period until 2050. Given the heterogeneity of public services across the EU and the deteriorating quality of provision, a renewed agenda to tighten the social safety net and to put a strong emphasis on the foundational economy would be a strong signal that the challenges of the Twin Transformation are tackled upon the basis of a strong sense of community and solidarity. Thus, confidence amongst EU citizens towards their political leaders could be re-established.

12.2.2 *Pillar 1: enhancing spaces of participation*

Under the title "Putting citizens at the heart of our democracy", the political guidelines of the new Commission proclaim the intention to strengthen deliberative democracy beyond elections and institutionalised politics (von der Leyen, 2024: 24). To this end, cooperation with civil society organisations shall be strengthened, and European Citizen's Panels shall put forward recommendations on specific issues. However, the document does not provide any further information about which topics shall be deliberated by these panels, or how many of them are foreseen during the next five years.

While the guidelines thus pay lip service to the need for more deliberative democracy, the specific agenda remains vague. Given the popular mistrust towards institutionalised politics, and the EU in particular, expanding on deliberative democracy by promoting alternative and experimental forms of participatory democracy represents a chance to reinvigorate trust in liberal democracy. As a matter of fact, the ability of established liberal democratic institutions, in particular parties, governments and parliaments, to articulate the interests of citizens and transform them into concrete political action, has suffered during the last decades. Instead, they are increasingly captured by powerful vested interests, scandalised by populist politics, and/or blocked by political infighting (Crouch, 2020; Lessenich, 2024). Re-injecting legitimacy into democratic governance by giving voice to citizens as well as civil society more generally, and provide them with spaces to co-design political agendas alongside established democratic institutions presents an opportunity also in the context of the Twin Transformation.

Institutional strengthening of participatory democracy could include for instance the establishment of a **Twin Transformation Council**, composed of high-ranking members from EU institutions, national governments, and civil society, including the corporate sector, trade unions, NGOs and academia. Such a council (i) should strengthen horizontal and vertical coordination, (ii) assess progress, identify and remediate problems, (iii) make strategy adjustments and identify high-priority issues for implementation. The Council would represent a significant enlargement of representation by including civil society organisations active in Brussels. It would, however, not directly involve ordinary EU citizens, nor would it be representative of all Member States.

Thus, two complementing structures could be envisioned. Firstly, **national Twin Transformation Councils**. These would also be composed of high-ranking members from the national and regional governments, parliaments, civil society, business and academia. Their tasks would be similar to the EU-level Council, but transposed to the national scale. Secondly, citizens could become involved via **Citizen's Assemblies/Panels**, both as transnational panels at the EU level, and as national (or regional) assemblies in Member States. Building on the experiences of previous panels at EU level (e.g. on food waste, virtual worlds and energy efficiency) as well as at national level (e.g. the Citizen's Climate Assemblies in Austria and the UK) or regional level (e.g. in the context of the Just Transition Plans), such assemblies could be tasked with elaborating proposals on specific issues relevant for the Twin Transformation at the respective level. By way of setting up a funding facility (e.g. within the framework of an expanded Just Transition Mechanism), the necessary financial resources could be provided for such a programme. Given previous experiences, two issues merit particular attention: (i) the lack of policy uptake; and (ii) the lack of public awareness (Jones et al., 2022). With the final result of an assembly being a set of policy recommendations, a lack of policy uptake and thus of policy impact represents a potential source of frustration for participants. A more formalised process that would oblige official institutions (e.g. the EC, the EU parliament, national governments, national parliaments) to respond to the recommendations, e.g. by holding a public debate, offer written opinions, why specific recommendations could not be accepted, provide regular implementation reports, etc., would be important in this respect. A series of public dissemination events and regular media communication are important to raise public awareness (Bozzini and Dapena, 2025).

Given its tradition of cooperative industrial relations, democracy in the EU also extends to the economic domain. This is explicitly recognised by the European Pillar of Social Rights. Pillar 8 highlights the need to promote social dialogue and the involvement of workers in social, economic and employment policies, and encourages collective bargaining. Facing the historic challenges of the Twin Transformation, the knowledge and experience of the social partners is indispensable for establishing transformation strategies that are both just in process and in outcome. A **closer cooperation with social partners and in particular trade unions** is thus important. Such cooperation could strive to, *amongst others*, (i) develop a legal framework at European level that guarantees the essential role of collective bargaining to anticipate and manage change and to maximise the transformative potential, while ensuring just transition and quality jobs; (ii) take initiatives to facilitate labour market transitions, not least by ensuring the right to training without cost to workers and during working time, mitigate the detrimental distributional effects of climate policies for vulnerable groups and make low-carbon and innovative technologies affordable and accessible to all; (iii) ensure full respect for the right to collective bargaining based on the prerogatives of trade unions as the bargaining agents for workers, as recognised by the Directive on Adequate Minimum Wages in the EU; and (iv) take specific initiatives to support collective bargaining and social dialogue in Member States that do not yet have a strong framework (Galgóczi, 2024).

12.2.3 Pillar 2: ensuring a fair distribution of benefits and costs

Structural transformation processes as profound as the Twin Transformation will inevitably result in producing a significant number of winners and losers. This includes both natural persons and companies, but also extends to regions, some of which will become important hubs for new sectors, while others will suffer from the closing down of old industries. To its credit, the Commission has recognised the latter problem and reacted to it with the JTM, through which support programmes for regions negatively affected by the green transition have been set up. Mostly due to capacity constraints, programme implementation has, however, been slow in many regions (see the contribution of Cirillo *et al.*, in this volume). The planned phase-out of the programme by the end of 2026 thus not only poses a risk to the sustainable impact of the programmes, but will arguably deepen the already widespread scepticism of rural populations with respect to the Twin Transformation. Given the long-term nature of the structural change processes affecting regions, stronger support mechanisms on a long-term basis are thus required. This could either be achieved by **putting the JTM on a permanent basis** or by using the structural and cohesion funds for this purpose. In any case, a follow-up programme must **address the capacity problems many regions have faced** in implementing regional just transition plans (RJTPs). Member States should also use the Social Climate Fund (SCF) (which starts operations in 2026) to complement the measures under their RJTPs, and thus coordinate their Social Climate Plans with their regional adjustment plans.

The **SCF** should also be used for national-level programmes to support affected workers through (i) early retirement plans, (ii) re-training and skills acquisition, and (iii) through public employment programmes, particularly in public services and the care economy. While it is expected that via the SCF (including national co-financing) up to €85 billion will be mobilised in the period 2026–2032, the programme thus being larger than the JTM, again the **issue of state capacities and capabilities** will have to be addressed, particularly in the more peripheral EU economies with weak public administrations. Any effective use of funds will critically depend on both the capacities of public administrations to effectively manage programme implementation and their capabilities for strategic planning in determining developmental pathways for their regional and national economies. A **more strategic approach to regional and national planning** will be critical for the successful steering of the Twin Transformation (Rodríguez-Pose and Bartalucci, 2023).

A third critical element to assure fairness has to do with **managing the benefits and costs at the level of companies**. Significant public funds are employed to support companies in transforming their business models. So far, the EU has focused on making sure that certain formal conditionalities mostly related to state aid and competition regulations are met by companies. The economic rationale for conditionalities is however mainly motivated by the desire to make sure companies reach certain performance targets with respect to e.g. production, innovation or skills acquisition. Also, given that any change promoted by public support will invariably affect the company's workforce, **co-participation of workers' representatives** (works councils, trade unions) is paramount not only for cushioning any adverse social effects, but also for retaining the support, and indeed, for mustering the motivation necessary throughout the workforce to join forces to successfully implement the required changes. **Public support for companies** must thus be **complemented by strong performance as well as social conditionalities.** This includes expanded participation and consultation rights for trade unions and works councils, which analogous to US practice under the Biden administration should form an integral element of public funding contracts (see the contribution of Raza in this volume).

12.2.4 Pillar 3: accelerating the transformation agenda

The strategic outlook of Twin Transformation policies in the EU has undergone several changes since 2019. While strongly focused on the green transformation initially, with the pandemic and the war in Ukraine, security of supply with critical goods, supply chain resilience and strategic autonomy have become more important. Based upon the Draghi Report, this economic security agenda has been coupled with a new competitiveness approach. As outlined in the new EU Competitiveness Compass, the Commission has started a process of implementing this new agenda. The document defines three "transformational imperatives": (i) closing the innovation gap, (ii) a joint roadmap for decarbonisation and competitiveness, and (iii) reducing dependencies and increasing security. With respect to implementation, the Commission emphasises regulatory simplification and better coordination as basic requirements, as well as (i) exploiting economies of scale offered by the Single Market by removing barriers, (ii) financing through an Investment and Savings Union and a refocused EU budget, and (iii) promoting skills for competitiveness and quality jobs while ensuring social fairness, as horizontal enablers.

While virtually all of these elements have already been contained in previous EU documents, what is new is the change in priorities. The Compass consolidates the shift from pursuing a broader socio-ecological agenda to one that puts competitiveness front and centre-stage. Accordingly, specific regulations introduced under the broader EGD agenda of the last few years, including in the fields of corporate sustainability reporting, corporate sustainability due diligence and the EU taxonomy, are under the threat of being watered down by forthcoming Simplification Omnibus proposals. A new company category of small mid-caps, comprising some 30,000 firms, will profit from regulatory simplification, that is, be exempted from most obligations under the above-mentioned regulations (and others). With respect to closing the EU's innovation gap, the Commission is similarly focusing on regulatory simplification as the panacea. It has, notably, proposed to establish a "28th legal regime" for innovative firms, which is intended to simplify applicable rules and reduce the cost of failure, including aspects of insolvency, labour law, and tax law. Instead of simplification, such a new regime might lead to regulatory uncertainty for companies – e.g. with respect to which purposes the respective national regime is applicable versus the new 28th regime. A straightforward effect of this new regime will be increased regulatory competition between Member States, arguably facilitating social dumping (Corporate Europe Observatory, 2025).

With respect to decarbonisation, the Compass announced a Clean Industrial Deal initiative with the aim (i) to make energy more affordable, though without envisioning major reforms to the EU energy markets, (ii) to strengthen the business case for clean production through new measures to encourage demand for low-carbon products, including through benchmarking/labelling, preference in public procurement and financial incentives. In terms of new funding mobilised for implementing the Competitiveness Compass agenda, apart from repurposing resources from the regular EU budget and simplifying the multiplicity of EU funding instruments, the Compass refers to the European Investment Bank's new TechEU investment programme and a new framework for transition-related state aid. A new Competitiveness Fund is announced under the next Multiannual Financial Framework (MFF), though no details on the latter are provided.

To summarise, the new competitiveness agenda is closely aligned with the demands of the EU corporate sector. Competitive pressures from global markets have been on the rise, and the implementation of the Twin Transformation agenda weighs on companies' capacities. Meanwhile, the new EC approach throws the baby out with the bathwater, as it almost exclusively relies on deregulation and liberalisation, including for tackling the EU's innovation gap. The green agenda is relegated to second place and is only considered when compatible with the overarching goal of competitiveness. Under these circumstances, it is highly questionable whether it will be able to deliver on the EU's decarbonisation and other goals until 2030 and 2050, respectively, as outlined under the EGD. What is more, the Commission's approach will not be able to remedy the EU's innovation gap, the latter being not caused primarily by too much regulation, but by structural factors related to the EU's innovation system (see discussion of Pillar 4).

By way of contrast, doubling down on the Twin Transformation agenda from a progressive point of view would, in particular, require a focus on the following elements during the next five years:

i A **stronger focus on reducing energy and material consumption** by (a) promoting energy efficiency measures (including through enhanced support for R&D), and by (b) accelerating the roll-out of the circular economy and the recycling of critical materials. This should be a key strategy of the European Union, because establishing a circular economy means greater added value for the European single market and less dependence on critical and strategic raw materials. In the short to medium-term, diversification of raw materials supply based on a comprehensive cooperation agenda with resource-rich countries of the Global South should be promoted (see also Pillar 6).

ii A **massively scaled-up EU investment programme for renewable energy**, with a focus on solar, wind, geothermal, and green hydrogen. At the same time, the electricity grids must be expanded quickly, and the gas grids must be dismantled or converted. Battery and pumped storage, flexibilities, and digitalisation must be systematically integrated in the energy system. Energy storage, smart grids, e-mobility with the integration of charging infrastructure and vehicles as flexible storage, as well as flexibly controllable power plants and digital platforms for intelligent networking and control must be enforced. Households and enterprises should have the opportunity to become prosumers or join a renewable energy community. Given the higher prices for renewable energy in Europe and because of declining interest of private capital for investing into the transformation of the energy system, a public funding preference should be given to not-for-profit companies, e.g. public companies or energy cooperatives at local, regional, or national levels, while preferential guarantees and loans should be provided widely through the EIB. The next EU financial framework should provide greater support for trans-European energy grids.

iii An **EU mobility strategy** that prioritises massive investments in railway infrastructure, supports electrified public transport at all territorial levels, and reduces private vehicle use via the promotion of car sharing and similar measures. Via public procurement and public support programmes, the transformation of the car industry should be directed towards a mobility system that increases public transport and reduces private car use. While accepting the reduction of European car manufacturing capacity as inevitable, public resources should be focused on retraining programmes for workers, and for supporting investment programmes into train production, buses, electric trucks and small passenger e-vehicles and other forms of e-mobility, thus providing directionality for the transformation of the automobile sector.

iv An **EU strategic industries strategy** that defines which productive activities deserve special treatment under (a) security of supply considerations including disaster preparedness (upon the basis of a human security lens), and for (b) accelerating the Twin Transformation. It should prioritise sectors, technologies, and mission areas with the highest potential to enhance productivity, competitiveness, prosperity, and societal resilience, building on existing national and European strategies. Special attention must be given to the decarbonisation of energy-intensive manufacturing and the transformation of foundational industries that provide essential materials, components and infrastructures such as steel, semiconductors, and electricity grids. Upon the basis of first but incomplete efforts during the last years, a systematic list of strategic industries should be elaborated and the public requirements put upon these industries in exchange for support should be specified, including the safeguarding of domestic "production capabilities & capacities" in strategic industries. At the same time, disruptive innovation must be promoted and key technologies must be rapidly scaled and implemented in Europe (see Pillar 4). Therefore, the strategy should also focus on key technologies and sectors with the largest growth and innovation potential, while addressing critical dependencies to ensure technological sovereignty and the protection of critical infrastructures. Implementation tools include local content and public procurement rules, lead market creation, skills development, and energy infrastructure investment to support the Net-Zero transition.

v An **EU digital sovereignty strategy** that (i) safeguards democratic and market control of the digital sphere via stringent regulation of Big Tech companies and social media; (ii) promotes forms of public digital infrastructures and storage, including public substacks and universal platforms, such as search engines and foundation AI models, all organised as a common governed by new public institutions with state and civil society representation.

vi **An EU skills agenda**. Building skills and expanding education and training are essential for creating good jobs and improving lives. A good education and training system forms the foundation for highly skilled workers. It is also the basis of new ideas and innovation. A priority should be to improve skills in science, technology, engineering, and maths (STEM), as well as to promote STEM careers, attract more women, and prepare people at all qualification levels for the digital and green transitions. This must be accompanied by a strong pillar of social rights that gives people the social security needed to cope with imminent changes and support them via retraining and transition phases (see also Pillar 2).

vii A **transformation agenda for the European food industry**. With the farm-to-fork strategy only half-finished and de facto blocked by farmers' protests in 2023/24, the transformation of the European food system needs a restart. The agricultural sector must also be subject to climate targets. This will require the following priorities: (i) Subsidies should no longer be granted to maintain the status quo, but only for improvements in the areas of animal welfare, biodiversity, environmental protection, and climate protection. Similarly, agricultural subsidies must be conditional on compliance with wage and social standards for agricultural workers; (ii) the promotion of organic farming including through producer subsidies should be stepped up, while subsidies to large-scale farming need to be progressively scaled-down; (iii) unfair competitive practices by large agri-food corporations and retailers should be strictly regulated, including pricing and contractual conditions; and (iv) where necessary, the transformation of the EU agriculture system should be flanked by trade protection measures.

12.2.5 Pillar 4: promoting a governance framework based upon strong capacities and capabilities as well as agile stability

Doubling down on the twin transformation agenda requires more than a set of clear political priorities. EU institutions and members states must also have the capacities and capabilities to steer and accelerate innovation and spur benefits broadly. Industrial strategies must focus on high-tech and key enabling technologies (KETs), as these serve as innovation drivers and provide the foundation for sustained competitiveness, prosperity, and productivity gains across sectors. By investing in KETs, such as advanced manufacturing, nanomaterials, life sciences, microelectronics, photonics, and quantum technologies, Europe not only fosters the emergence of future general-purpose technologies (GPTs) but also strengthens technological sovereignty and resilience in the face of global competition. It is also crucial that policies ensure broad and socially balanced access to high-tech benefits, addressing risks of inequality, digital divides, and social exclusion through education, infrastructure, and inclusive frameworks. Robust state capacity and state capabilities are indispensable to this effort. It provides the strategic foresight, policy coherence, and implementation power needed to properly plan, fund, regulate, monitor, and adjust the many interdependent initiatives that KETs and GPTs require.

The discussion of industrial policy and innovation governance (see in particular the contribution by Kattel and Raza in this volume) has highlighted the importance of promoting state capacities and capabilities. However, the new Commission intends to take an alternative route to closing the EU's innovation gap. In the Competitiveness Compass, it outlines an agenda focusing on start-ups and on improved market-led innovation cycles. Via a series of new sector-specific strategies, the Commission wants to address bottlenecks to market entry and scale-up, including relations between universities and business, cross-border mobility of talent and skilled workers, access to risk finance, barriers within the Single market, infrastructure constraints, as well as insufficiently targeted innovation support. Specific acts on AI, quantum computing, digital networks, clouds, biotech, advanced materials, space technologies, etc., shall facilitate innovation entrepreneurship, primarily via regulatory facilitation. With respect to innovation diffusion throughout the whole economy, an Apply AI Strategy will aim to boost new industrial uses of AI in sectors, including manufacturing, automotive, energy, robotics, pharmaceutical and aeronautics, as well as to improve public services, for example, in healthcare. Better EU-wide coordination and support of these AI vertical use cases shall be ensured via a "CERN for AI". With respect to changes to the institutional structure at the EU level, the European Research Council (ERC) and the European Innovation Council (EIC) shall be aligned along the same strategic interests and cooperate more closely. Currently in charge of promoting high-quality basic research, this might de facto undermine the ERC's independence. The EIC, currently in charge of promoting breakthrough innovation, shall be succeeded by an ARPA-like agency tasked to promote disruptive innovation. Whether this presents an opportunity will mainly depend on the mission, capacities and operational independence of the new agency. Apparently, the Compass does not follow up on the mission concept as developed for the Horizon Europe cycle 2021–2027. If true, this would likely reduce the space for orienting innovation programmes to socially desirable ends.

Although the proposals at this stage are rather general and often lack specificity, the overall trajectory points to a conventional conceptual understanding of innovation focused on the commercialisation of technology. This is in marked contrast to the research literature on innovation for the Twin Transformation. Particularly with respect to the green transformation, the literature on transformative innovation policy has emphasised the need for a broader and transdisciplinary understanding of innovation policies in the context of the required deep transformation of our current production and consumption models, including key features for policy such as anticipation, experimentation, participation and directionality (Edler et al., 2025; Schot and Steinmueller, 2018). As in particular the contribution by Kattel in this volume has shown, there is a need to foster **agile stability** in innovation agencies, and to allow for more experimentation and risk-taking while also helping to cultivate a higher tolerance for failure. For this purpose, innovation agencies need to **enhance their dynamic capabilities**, i.e. their ability to learn and adapt to changing circumstances. This can be fostered by introducing institutional learning processes, but also via promoting diversity more generally, in particular with respect to the recruiting of staff, or with respect to the staffing of programme and project evaluation committees. A **more diverse set of stakeholder representation in governance bodies** (e.g. boards, advisory committees) will also contribute to bringing in new visions and ideas. This is true both for the EU and the member state-level. Also, a **stronger coordination of the innovation agency ecosystem** across the EU is needed to exploit complementarities and promote inter-institutional learning. Though the EU cannot directly influence the mandates and modes of operation of innovation agencies across the EU, via its cooperation with national agencies in the course of implementing EU-funded programmes, the **Commission could leverage its role** by in particular (i) promote a discussion with Member States on the role of innovation agencies for the Twin Transformation with a view **to revise mandates to allow for more diverse forms of innovation policy** while accepting a higher risk of failure, (ii) by **reducing administrative requirements** for both national implementing agencies and applicants, thus freeing up resources to promote learning and thematic interchange, and (iii) by **scaling-up learning platforms for national agencies** to promote inter-institutional exchange and peer learning.

Besides the governance structure for promoting innovation, state capacities to implement industrial policy programmes will have to be strengthened more broadly, in particular at the national and local levels. The straightforward way to achieve this is through systematically **integrating and expanding, respectively, a funding component to promote the institutional capacities and capabilities of implementing agencies** within the overall programme design. These are also strategic entry points that include targeted public procurement, lead-market creation, tax- and subsidy-based incentives, and supported pathways for skills development and reskilling. Collectively, state capacities and state capabilities empower industrial policy by ensuring that investments in KETs and GPTs translate into productive, inclusive growth, national resilience, and climate-neutral transformation. Given that in many Member States, the absorptive capacities of existing institutional structures to implement programmes are limited, they create a bottleneck for swift and effective implementation that needs to be addressed.

12.2.6 *Pillar 5: closing the investment gap*

As underlined by the analyses of in particular Skyrman and Heimberger in this volume, the investment gap for the Twin Transformation might be estimated at between 2% and 4.5% of EU GDP, of which at least 50% should be supplied by the public sector. That would be equal to an amount between €360 and €800 billion per annum in the form of subsidies, guarantees, and loans.

The Commission wants to tackle this challenge by doubling-down on its de-risking approach. While lamenting the lack of risk appetite amongst private investors, it intends to incentivise private capital markets to channel the relatively high level of European household savings into productive investment and innovation. With its proposal for a European Savings and Investment Union, the Commission thus follows suit on the recommendations of the Letta and Draghi reports, respectively, on establishing a full EU capital markets union. Given that the securitisation of loan portfolios was a major reason for the Global Financial Crisis in 2007/08, the Draghi Report proposal to leverage securitisation for raising investment capital would however set a dangerous precedent.

If it is the case, as the Commission contends, that private capital markets and European banks have not provided the finances necessary for investment into the Twin Transformation, the obvious question is why sovereign borrowers should not go to capital markets and tap into the pool of savings themselves via public borrowing. Clearly, funding costs for sovereign borrowers would be lower than for private debtors. The obvious answer has to do with the fiscal constraints imposed by the reformed Stability and Growth Pact upon Member States and the political blockade spearheaded by Germany and some other fiscally conservative Member States to put common EU funding on a permanent basis. Given both the dire fiscal situation in many EU Member States and the clouded economic outlook for the coming years, it is entirely unclear how the required amounts to close the investment gap for the Twin Transformation are to be raised on private capital markets. Investors and their appetite for risk will only come back once the economic outlook has improved substantially. Thus, in the current circumstances, there exists a strong economic case for frontloading public investment to raise economic prospects and thus to stimulate the "animal spirits" of private investors. Also, for the sake of preventing a further widening of internal economic imbalances and structural heterogeneities, it is of paramount importance that most public funding should come from the central European level, and spent with a view to safeguard territorial cohesion.

Putting the temporal EU joint borrowing facility on a permanent basis would also be justified from a legal perspective, given that the Twin Transformation is an EU public good requiring a one-off fiscal effort (Poiares Maduro et al., 2021). Thus, instead of establishing a new Competitiveness Fund, as announced by the Commission, with the very limited resources available under the regular EU budget, a **Twin Transformation Fund** should be funded with money raised by the EU on capital markets. As an absolute minimum, the Fund should be capitalised to the tune of 1% of EU GDP over a 10-year time period (see also Heimberger and Lichtenberger, 2023).

As this represents the lower-bound estimate of the total EU public investment gap for the Twin Transformation, two complementary mechanisms should be contemplated. Firstly, the **EU's own resources could be raised**: this could include to direct more ETS revenues to the EU level (Pisany-Fery *et al.*, 2023), but could also mean to allow the EU to raise its own taxes, including via e.g. a financial transaction tax or a net wealth tax (Schratzenstaller and Krenek, 2019; see also Skyrman in this volume).

Secondly, as following up on the contribution by Bronstering *et al.*, in this volume, the **mandate of the ECB could be amended to allow for monetary financing of the Twin Transformation.** Notwithstanding the prohibition of monetary financing under the EU Treaty (Article 123 TFEU), the scope of this prohibition was de facto broken already in 2015, when the ECB embarked on direct asset purchases. With the ECB strategy review of 2020, outright purchases have been made part of the "normal" toolbox. In addition, the ECB could use a much wider array of policy instruments to promote the Twin Transformation, including through collateral frameworks, asset purchases (e.g. of green bonds), refinancing operations, and regulatory tools such as capital requirements, credit controls and mandatory disclosures (see also Dafermos *et al.*, 2023; Skyrman, 2024).

The expansion of guarantees and credit financing, e.g. by the EIB, should also be strongly promoted. After all, China has demonstrated the powerful leverage that public banks can generate. To be sure, any combination of these options is possible, and would indeed be desirable. The upcoming years, and in particular the next EU MFF 2028–2034, will give a clear indication whether the investment gap for the Twin Transformation will be closed or not.

12.2.7 Pillar 6: cooperating with partners on a global twin transformation

As expounded by the contributions of Guarascio *et al.*, Tröster *et. al.*, and Reiner and Stöllinger in this volume, the EU suffers from pronounced external dependencies with respect to energy, raw materials, clean tech products, as well as intermediate inputs (e.g. active pharmaceutical ingredients). The response of the Commission has consisted in a variety of measures, including to diversify supply chains to increase resilience. With respect to energy, the Commission has for instance supported the development of green hydrogen production in African countries. With respect to clean tech products (e.g. Solar PVs, batteries), the EU and Member States have promoted domestic production (e.g. via subsidies for onshoring of third-country companies). As far as raw materials are concerned, under the Critical Raw Materials Act, the EU has negotiated a series of Raw Material Partnerships (13 as of end 2024) with producer countries. These are basically Memoranda of Understanding (MoU), outlining future cooperation areas and establishing an institutional process including a roadmap with concrete projects, annual high-level meetings and a permanent Working Group. The MoUs routinely include a reference committing the parties to EU ESG standards and sustainable mining practices. The EU's Global Gateway Initiative is referred to as a financing mechanism (Küblböck et al., 2025).

Building on the ongoing implementation of the Critical Raw Materials Act, the Competitiveness Compass outlines both additional domestic and external policies. With respect to the former, the promotion of domestic production, stockpiling and diversification shall be pursued. The Commission will create a platform for the joint purchase of critical raw materials to identify the needs of EU industries, aggregate demand, and coordinate joint purchases. Also, the Commission announced to promote new Clean Trade and Investment Partnerships bringing together targeted trade and investment rules, financing and regulatory cooperation, into a single whole-of-government partnership. It is, however, unclear how these new partnerships will complement the existing raw materials diplomacy, including the Raw Material Partnerships that the EU has pursued under the Critical Raw Materials Strategy since 2021.

While it will be necessary for the EU to secure additional external supplies of renewable energy, critical raw materials and other necessary products for the Twin Transformation, any bilateral cooperation with producer countries needs to be based on (i) strict adherence to and **comprehensive application of the highest ESG standards for mining and production activities**, (ii) **EU support for technology transfer and the build-up of a processing industry** and value chain in producer countries, including through skills development for the domestic workforce and scientific and technological cooperation programmes with the EU, and (iii) **fair-benefit sharing with respect to mining/exploration contracts and pricing mechanisms**. While the EU corporate sector has traditionally emphasised the need to access abundant supplies of energy and raw materials at affordable prices, which with recent energy and raw materials price hikes has only become more pronounced, an **EU strategy offering partner countries technological and financial support** in building up their green and digital sectors is in the **enlightened self-interest of the EU**. This is equally valid for relations with the EU neighbourhood and the Global South. To this end, funding under the Global Gateway will have to be expanded, and cooperation with partner countries will have to be put onto an institutionally strengthened basis. As the contribution by Ahumada and Sossdorf in this volume underlines, industrial policy for the green transformation is not only a challenge for the EU, but should be pursued on a global scale, including in the countries of the Global South (see also Alami *et al.*, 2025). Spearheading international cooperation to this end with **a focus on real and honest partnership should be considered an opportunity for the EU** amidst a challenging geopolitical environment, which has dramatically exacerbated the EU's strategic vulnerabilities.

12.3 Conclusion

Democratic politics in the EU stands at a crossroads. Using public money and industrial policy for military rearmament while cutting social spending and deprioritising the green transformation will not deliver on sustainable economic growth and social well-being. Instead, this path will deepen both the ecological crisis and social inequities while likely exacerbating geopolitical conflicts. Such an approach ultimately plays into the hands of authoritarian populists. A change of course is urgently needed. Industrial policy offers a means to enhance a new economic model that is oriented towards economic well-being, promoting social cohesion whilst respecting ecological limits. In contrast to the prevailing policy discourse, the fundamental issue is not a lack of financial resources or competitiveness – Europe possesses both. Rather, what is missing is the political courage to address the Twin Transformation decisively through a proactive entrepreneurial state (Mazzucato, 2015) closely cooperating with all societal stakeholders. Progressive political forces, including trade unions, civil society, and academia, must advocate forcefully for such an approach. For the choice confronting European and indeed global society is stark: either change by design or change by disaster.

Our hope is that the analyses, ideas and proposals in this collected volume will offer some useful conceptual inputs for this vital project.

References

Alami, I., Taggart, J., and Chodor, T. (2025) 'Rebuilding the Ladder? Contemporary Contests over Industrial Policy'. *Global Policy*, 1–14. https://doi.org/10.1111/1758-5899.70064

Altvater, E. (2003) *"Menschliche Sicherheit" – Entwicklungsgeschichte Und Politische Forderungen. Thesen Zu Einem Umfassenden Friedenspolitischen Konzept.* AG Friedensforschung. http://www.ag-friedensforschung.de/themen/Theorie/altvater.html (accessed 24 October 2025).

Bärnthaler, R., Mang, S., and Hickel, J. (2025) 'Toward a Post-Growth Industrial Policy for Europe: Navigating Emerging Tensions and Long-Term Goals'. *Globalizations*, 1–25. https://doi.org/10.1080/14747731.2025.2501821

Bozzini, A. and Dapena, M. P. (2025*) Towards Meaningful Civil Society Participation at the International Level: Success Factors, Opportunities and Challenges* (81st edn.) OECD Working Papers on Public Governance. https://doi.org/10.1787/8ed04dc2-en

Corporate Europe Observatory (2025) 'A Social Dumping Disaster? EU's "28th Regime" Plans Could Help Corporations Bypass Member State Rules'. https://www.corporateeurope.org/en/2025/09/social-dumping-disaster-eus-28th-regime (accessed 24 October 2025).

Crouch, C. (2020) *Post-Democracy after the Crises*. Cambridge, Medford, MA: Polity.

Edler, J., Matt, M., Polt, W., and Weber, K. M. (eds.) (2025) *Transformative Mission-Oriented Innovation Policies: Revisiting the Role of Science, Technology and Innovation in Society*. Cheltenham, UK; Northampton, MA: Edward Elgar Publishing. https://doi.org/10.4337/9781803929521

European Commission (2025) 'A Competitiveness Compass for the EU, COM (2025) 30 Final'. https://commission.europa.eu/document/download/10017eb1-4722-4333-add2-e0ed18105a34_en (accessed 24 October 2025).

Galgóczi, B. (2024) *Industrial Policy for Quality Jobs and a Just Transition | Etui. Brus: European Trade Union Institute*. https://www.etui.org/publications/industrial-policy-quality-jobs-and-just-transition (accessed 24 October 2025).

Heimberger, P. and Lichtenberger, A. (2023) *RRF 2.0: A permanent EU investment fund in the context of the energy crisis, climate change and EU fiscal rules*. Vienna: Vienna Institute for International Economic Studies. Policy Notes and Reports. https://wiiw.ac.at/p-6425.html (accessed 24 October 2025).

Heussaff, C., Emmerling, J., Luderer, G., Pietzcker, R., Reissl, S., Rodrigues, R., and Way, R. (2024) *Europe's 2040 climate target: Four critical risks and how to manage them*. Brussels: Bruegel. Policy Brief Issue no. 23/24. https://www.bruegel.org/policy-brief/europes-2040-climate-target-four-critical-risks-and-how-manage-them (accessed 24 October 2025).

Jones, H. et. al. (2022). *Study on the Citizens' Panels as Part of the Conference on the Future of Europe. Finan Report. Version 2.0*. Technopolis group, Democratic Society, Henningsen Consulting. https://citizens.ec.europa.eu/document/download/cf17f39b-2967-401a-9a82-3794f5d780f8_en?filename=FINAL_DG%20COMM_Citizens%20Panels_Final_Report_REVISED_clean_DG%20COMM_FINAL_.pdf (accessed 24 October 2025).

Küblböck, K., Papatheophilou, S., Tröster, B., and Ulrici, L. (2025). *EU Raw Materials Partnerships: Mutual Benefits or Green Extractivism?* Vienna: ÖFSE Research Report no. 25. https://doi.org/10.60637/2025-RR25

Lessenich, St. (2024) *Grenzen der Demokratie: Teilhabe als Verteilungsproblem*. 5. Auflage. Ditzingen: Reclam.

Mazzucato, M. (2015) *The Entrepreneurial State: Debunking Public vs. Private Sector Myths*. New York, NY: PublicAffairs.

Pisany-Fery, S., Tagliapietra, S., and Zachmann, G. (2023) *A New Governance Framework to Safeguard the European Green Deal*. Brussels: Bruegel, Policy Brief. www.bruegel.org/sites/default/files/private/2023-09/PB%2018%202023_0.pdf (accessed 24 October 2025).

Poiares Maduro, M., Martin, P., Pisany-Fery, J., Weber di Mauro, B., Reichlin, L., and Steinbach, A. (2021) *Revisiting the EU Framework: Economic Necessities and Legal Options*. Paris and London: Centre for Economic Policy Research.

Rodríguez-Pose, A. and Bartalucci, F. (2023) 'The Green Transition and Its Potential Territorial Discontents'. *Cambridge Journal of Regions, Economy and Society*, 17(2), 339–358. https://doi.org/10.1093/cjres/rsad039

Schot, J. and Steinmueller, W. E. (2018) 'Three Frames for Innovation Policy: R&D, Systems of Innovation and Transformative Change'. *Research Policy*, 47(9), 1554–1567. https://doi.org/10.1016/j.respol.2018.08.011

Schratzenstaller, M. and Krenek, A. (2019) 'Tax-Based Own Resources to Finance the EU Budget'. *Intereconomics*, 54(3), 171–177. https://doi.org/10.1007/s10272-019-0817-0

Skyrman, V. (2024) *Industrial Policy, Progressive Derisking, and the Financing of Europe's Green Transition*. Vienna: *ÖFSE Working Paper no. 78*. https://doi.org/10.60637/2024-wp78

von der Leyen, U. (2024) '*Europe's Choice Political Guidelines for the Next European Commission 2024–2029*'. https://commission.europa.eu/document/download/e6cd4328-673c-4e7a-8683-f63ffb2cf648_en (accessed 24 October 2025).

INDEX

Note: *Italicized* and **bold** pages refer to figures and tables respectively, and page numbers followed by "n" refer to notes.

For Product Safety Concerns and Information please contact our
EU representative GPSR@taylorandfrancis.com Taylor & Francis
Verlag GmbH, Kaufingerstraße 24, 80331 München, Germany